MARXISM AND NATIONAL IDENTITY

SUNY series in National Identities
Thomas M. Wilson, editor

MARXISM AND NATIONAL IDENTITY

Socialism, Nationalism, and National Socialism during the French Fin de Siècle

Robert Stuart

State University of New York Press

Published by
State University of New York Press, Albany

Printed in the United States of America

Cover cartoon entitled Vive l'Armee! by Jules Hérault.

For information, address State University of New York Press,
194 Washington Avenue, Suite 305, Albany, NY 12210-2384

Production by Diane Ganeles
Marketing by Anne M. Valentine

Library of Congress Cataloging-in-Publication Data

Stuart, Robert, 1947–
Marxism and national identity : socialism, nationalism, and national socialism during the French fin de siècle / Robert Stuart.
p. cm. — (SUNY series in national identities)
Includes bibliographical references and index.
ISBN-13: 978-0-7914-6669-8 (hardcopy : alk. paper)
ISBN-10: 0-7914-6669-8 (hardcopy : alk. paper)
ISBN-13: 978-0-7914-6670-4 (pbk. : alk. paper)
ISBN-10: 0-7914-6670-1 (pbk. : alk. paper)
1. Socialism—France—History. 2. Nationalism—France—History. 3. National socialism—France—History. I. Title. II. Series.
HX263.S775 2005
320.53'15'0944—dc22

2005005677

10 9 8 7 6 5 4 3 2 1

For Max,
and in memory of Alice
(1917–1998)

Contents

Preface

This study was begun some years ago when I decided to explore "French Marxism and the National Question." Within weeks of commencing the project I discovered the richness of the relevant conceptual debates, and soon after that I began to understand the mammoth dimensions of the literature on French nationalism. Even more dauntingly, once I reengaged with the Marxists of the fin de siècle, I realized that nationhood suffused their textual legacy—even where I had least suspected it. Their angry dialogue with French nationalism suddenly loomed as an important, even decisive, determinant in the "meaning of Marxism." At the same time, the convoluted heritage that I was beginning to unravel amplified and sometimes challenged the insights of today's scholarship. My experience powerfully confirmed E. P. Thompson's belief that conceptual analysis and empirical history live healthily only when in harmony.

Suffice it to say that a project planned for a semester's writing has extended over a decade—as I have read and reread the Parti Ouvrier's corpus, battled to master the literature on nationhood, and studied work on French nationalism. In the process, my present, no less than the Marxist past, has acquired new meaning. Fin de siècle socialists, after all, struggled to make sense of a world governed both by parochial nationalism and global capitalism—a world, in fact, very like our own. Their insights (and their errors!) have proven uncannily apropos while reading my weekly *Economist* or watching Fox News.

Here I must make known my sympathies, since true objectivity, as contemporary historiography teaches, lies only in being critically aware of one's biases, and making others aware of them. So (deep breath) . . . The militants of the Parti Ouvrier are, at a century's distance, "my people." Despite Marxism's failures since their "time of hope," I still sympathize with the dream that capital's world-spanning imperium might someday, somehow, empower working people to construct something better. That dream has faded. Nonetheless, despite the "End of History" (aka "the end of Marxism"), I continue to reject postmodern legerity and neoliberal triumphalism. Sometimes dreams, however spectral, are better than reality, however crushing. As for nationalism, I am proud to confess myself a "rootless cosmopolitan," while sometimes yearning for the roots that ground others so comfortably. Having been born into a Canada that I now hardly know, having been raised in a

United States that was not mine, having resided in France, Britain, and Australia—whatever roots I have sunk are shallow indeed. Spectral dreams, shallow roots. . . . Hardly grounds for ideological arrogance! Nonetheless, my marginality, both political and national, has awarded me a liminal perspective of considerable use for this study.

I have accumulated obligations—both institutional and personal. In particular, I owe a debt to Corpus Christi College, Cambridge, where a visiting fellowship gave me tranquility and ideal working conditions. Without Corpus, this project would never have been initiated. The University of Western Australia, for its part, supported two extended research leaves that allowed me to revisit my European sources. Many individuals have also aided me in one way or another, and I thank them all. Richard Bosworth and Chips Sowerwine read the entire project in draft, however, and deserve particular gratitude, while being absolved of all responsibility for the errors, omissions, and infelicities that have survived their generous ministrations. Finally, my thanks and love to Viv, without whose support this book would never have been completed.

Introduction

At the end of summer during 1891, Europe witnessed two world-historical events. The socialist parties of the Second International assembled in Brussels, celebrating labor's mobilization against capital. Shortly thereafter, the French fleet visited Kronstadt, consolidating France's rapprochement with imperial Russia. Contemporaries noted this conjunction. The liberal publicist Jules Simon, for one, complained that the Brussels assembly had "substituted the class patriotism" of labor for the Baltic naval demonstration's "patriotism of peoples." If socialism prevailed, he warned, "the French" would disappear, displaced by "the proletariat."[1]

Simon's forebodings have not been realized. The workers of the world have not united into the universal "genre humain" promised by the *Internationale.* The nineteenth century gave way, not to the radiant socialist world order anticipated by Marx, but to a "world of nations"[2] imperiously commanded by nationalists, and sometimes brutally ruled by national socialists. How have Marxism's class warriors understood their struggle against nationhood, and their defeat? Badly, according to most accounts. Historians have identified Marxism's interpellation of nationalism as its "great historical failure," social scientists have condemned Marxist theorizations of national identity as mere evasion, and a particularly scathing account has even contemptuously suggested that there has been no such a thing as a genuine "Marxist theory of nationalism."[3] Marxists, their critics affirm, have championed a cosmopolitan humanism that has blinded them to the inevitability, and certainly to the desirability, of nationalist particularism. No wonder, then, that Marxism's militants have self-confessedly misunderstood and mishandled national identity.[4]

Much of this critical scholarship has fixed repetitively on Marx himself. Studies comment caustically on the master's indifference to nationality. Marx may have planned to write a book on the national question, but no more than 2 or 3 percent of his actual work, allegedly, even touches on the issue.[5] His critics suggest that Marx's overwhelming preoccupation with "world history" undermined his every engagement with that potent particularism, the nation. This charge, however, has been challenged. Marx's defenders contend that his vast corpus manifests profound, if ambiguous, insight into nationhood and nationalism.[6] But whatever the master's own success or failure, Marxism should not be judged primarily against Marx's work, but against the practice of *Marxists*, as the doctrine has lived and died only as incarnate in its militants. Their commitment and striving accorded Marxism its vast historical vitality, while their defeats and retreats have led inexorably toward today's "death of Marxism." Certainly the best analyses of Marxism's entanglement with nationalism situate the doctrine in milieus of militancy. The Soviet experience has undergone particularly intense study, if only because of the USSR's final nationalist implosion. The sanguinary war between Communism and fascism left one of the great sites of scholarly exhumation: a mass grave in which lie entombed some the past century's most inspiring visionaries and most ghastly despots. And Marxism's starring role in the drama of twentieth-century anti-imperialism has received due attention, despite Marx's own Eurocentric indifference toward peripheral "nations without history."[7]

But the doctrine's "golden age" during the Second International, Marxist socialism's own belle epoque, remains the locus classicus of Marxism's engagement with nationhood. Lenin and Stalin's opportunistic construction of a "nationalities policy" for newborn Bolshevism, Rosa Luxemburg's quixotic forays against Polish "socialist nationalism," Otto Bauer's inspired disassociation of statehood from nationhood—all have undergone skillful scholarly dissection.[8] Yet scholars' assessments of the Second International echo their critiques of Marx. Fin de siècle Marxists stand accused of promoting a "utopian cosmopolitanism"[9] that disabled their socialism. After all, the International never once placed the "national question" on its agenda. Ignorant obliviousness? Irresponsible neglect? Embarrassed avoidance? Perhaps nationalism during the belle epoque indeed constituted Marxism's "Achilles heel,"[10] its self-engulfing "black hole."[11] "Post-Marxists" have certainly highlighted this supposed lacuna in their former devotions. According to Régis Debray, a cosmopolitan revolutionary turned Gaullist ideologue:

> The "national question" is the critical gap in Marxist theory. In this small gap, everything not said in Marxism is concentrated and crystallized. And when the unsaid is said, it explodes all the rest. In this sense . . . the nation is like the atomic nucleus in a general conflagration of Marxism as theory and socialism as practice.[12]

"Black holes," "nuclear explosions," "general conflagrations"—confronted by the collision between Marxism and nationalism, critique waxes apocalyptic.

This rhetoric is overblown. Marx's work on nationality bequeathed a rich legacy, and Marxists of the "golden age"—the Bauers, Luxemburgs, and Lenins—richly embroidered it. Such enrichment might have been expected. The fin de siècle witnessed Marxism's transformation from a *cosmopolitan* congeries of militants into an *international* association of national parties.[13] How could these emergent "socialist-nationalist" organizations ignore the national question? In fact, they didn't. At the same time, a grisly protofascism clawed its way into Europe's political culture, menacing the ascendant socialists no less than the regnant liberals. How could Marxism slight this demonic manifestation? In fact, it couldn't. Despite critics' aspersions, fin de siècle Marxists thought long and hard about national identity, and thought well. Their "entanglement in perplexities that continue to entangle us" should ensure that "we would be wrong to call [their answers] to the national question passé."[14]

Bauer, Luxemburg, Lenin—these personae recur in studies of Marxism and nationalism. Mapping their names points to Austria, Poland, and Russia, to the marchlands of Eastern Europe. Studies of Marxism's encounter with nationalism move without exception from the founding fathers to theorists from the eastern multinational empires. According to these studies, Marxists in Western Europe largely ignored the national question, and in turn can be safely ignored.[15] Neglect of the French case, in particular, has been a troubling feature of this scholarship. Even French studies of Marxism and nationalism ignore France—despite the French having pioneered modern nationalism, despite the fascination of Marx and Engels with France, despite the Parisian ultra-Right's spearheading of nascent national socialism.[16]

Instead of suffering neglect, France should take center stage in any historical assessment of Marxism's long engagement with nationalism. France of the prewar Third Republic traced Europe's trajectory toward today's hegemonic synthesis of capitalist economics, liberal democracy, and the centralized nation-state far more clearly than did imperial Germany (still struggling to reconcile its Prussian legacy with its capitalist dynamism), more obviously than Victorian and Edwardian Britain (hardly democratic, and an imperial metropolis rather than a nation-state), and certainly more starkly than the ramshackle eastern empires of Austria and Russia (still mired in the legacy of early-modern state-building). The French Republic, in effect, prefigured today's neoliberal "end of history." At the fin de siècle, however, history dragged on. The near-mortal crises of the Republic—Boulanger's Caesarean uprising of the late 1880s, the anti-Semitic insurgency during the Dreyfus affair—foreshadowed the impending "era of fascism."[17] France, more than anywhere else on earth at the time, embodied both the force and the frailty of liberal nationalism.[18]

France of the belle epoque not only exemplified national liberalism and originated protofascist "integral nationalism," but gave birth in 1882 to a potent Marxist movement, the Parti Ouvrier Français.[19] Although little more than a militant sect during the 1880s, the POF transformed France's political culture during the 1890s, molding the Left to its Marxism before melding into the unified French socialist party of 1905. Led by Jules Guesde, one of

France's most charismatic orators and a vulgarizer of genius, inspired by Paul Lafargue, son-in-law of Marx and a brilliant, if erratic, ideologue, and reinforced by thousands of devoted militants, the Parti Ouvrier self-consciously represented Marxist socialism in France. There the POF pioneered the modern mass social-democratic party, invented much of the ceremony and symbolism of twentieth-century socialism (including the flying of the red flag, the singing of the *Internationale*, and the celebration of May Day), and organized the Parisian founding of the Second International. Across France, from the humblest mining village to the arrogant capital, the Guesdists (as they were known) indicted bourgeois rule, promoted proletarian mobilization, and augured the socialist revolution.

But what of the Parti Ouvrier Français and the "national question"? Like Marxists in Vienna or Warsaw, Guesdists had to respond to that interrogative. France, after all, prided itself on being the model nation-state, and its rulers ruled as "national liberals," even if (unlike their German counterparts) they never designated themselves as such. As a revolutionary party, as the French embodiment of international socialism, the POF needed to discredit a "certain idea of France" in order to undermine bourgeois hegemony. At the same time, Guesdists fought ferociously against rival claimants to the liberal succession. Paul Déroulède's paramilitary Ligue des Patriotes constituted an "anti-POF" that mobilized the French not only against the Germans, but against the Marxist "internal enemy." The virulent anti-Semitic movement patronized by Edouard Drumont, harbinger of the Holocaust, battled against the "Jewish socialism" of the Parti Ouvrier no less than against the Jewish bankers of the rue Lafitte. And Maurice Barrès's "national socialism" defined its "socialism" against Guesde's Marxism as well as against Ferry's national liberalism. How could French Marxists ignore the nationalist challenge, challenged as they were by both national liberals and national socialists? They couldn't, of course. During decades of ideological contention, the Parti Ouvrier formulated many answers to Marxism's "national question," from cosmopolitan repudiation of the nation to near-Barrèsian appropriation of nationalism. Yet this long, arduous, and ambiguous engagement between French Marxism and French nationalism has remained virtually unstudied.[20] As scholarship struggles to make sense of Marxism's epochal failure, the emblematic case of the Parti Ouvrier Français deserves scrutiny.

This study scrutinizes the Guesdists' experience analytically rather than through "narrative."[21] Guesdist discourse certainly responded to salient events, and makes sense only in terms of those events. The Parti Ouvrier's electoral successes of the 1890s, for instance, undoubtedly inflected the movement toward socialist nationalism, if only because its enemies discovered nationalism's utility in maligning the Guesdists' cosmopolitan convictions.[22] Nonetheless, the intricate dialectic between Marxism and nationhood during the French fin de siècle is best elucidated not by "telling a story" but by systematic analysis. The Parti Ouvrier certainly oscillated between alternative understandings of national identity, but little overall "development" occurred in its confused answer to the national question. Even during the POF's most "nationalist" phase during the mid-1890s, it remained permeated by cosmopolitanism, while socialist nationalism recurred in its record even during the sectarian 1880s. Indeed, a reading of Marx's own work or perusal of today's Trotskyist pamphlets reveals conflicted responses to national identity strikingly similar to the Parti Ouvrier's own equivocations. Marxism's unchanging imperatives defined the Guesdists' equivocal interpretation of national identity, while the Guesdists' oscillating viewpoint in turn tells us much about the unstable essence of Marxism. Analysis, not storytelling, best illuminates this fluid yet closely channeled discourse. Although attentive to the shifting setting of the French fin de siècle, this study dissects an invariant, if complex and at times even self-contradictory, "meaning of Marxism." It is an "anatomy," not a narrative.[23]

Chapter 1 anatomizes Marxism's "default mode," the conviction that "the workingmen have no country."[24] When obedient to this conviction, Guesdists repudiated all identities founded on "various human fragments disseminated across the planet" in favor of a "final human communion, a planetary internationalism."[25] This chapter elucidates the French Marxists' brilliant insights into a capitalist world market that transgressed every boundary, and their utopian expectation that bourgeois globalization would necessarily engender a working class without ethnic allegiance, a proletariat loyal to "only one homeland: the social revolution."[26]

Chapter 2 begins an examination, to be completed in chapter 3, of the French Marxists' forced recognition that "workingmen" did, indeed, "have a country." During the fin de siècle, national welfare systems, national mass media, and national primary education universalized national identity. At the same time, "social imperialism" and universal conscription generalized chauvinism. When Guesdists puzzled over the survival of a nationhood that "no longer has any rationale,"[27] they most often faulted bourgeois brainwashing in schoolrooms and barracks.

Chapter 3 dissects the Parti Ouvrier's encounter with "national economics." At their most disillusioned, Guesdists sometimes acknowledged that capitalist cosmopolitanism paradoxically engendered a "national proletariat." Ever-higher tariff barriers, the "Chinese Walls of patriotism,"[28] united protectionist French workers and employers against foreign labor and capital, while "native" and immigrant workers clashed bloodily throughout France's "national" labor market. Often, during the belle epoque, the Marxists' exhortation "Workers of the world, unite!" echoed frustration rather than hope. Indeed, the POF itself sometimes championed "socialism in one country," its advocacy of "socialization" segueing easily into enthusiasm for "nationalizations."

Chapter 4 analyzes Marxism's resultant Mr. Hyde persona, socialist nationalism, as opposed to its Dr. Jekyll, global cosmopolitanism. Capitalism's "international of financiers and thieves,"[29] Guesdists raged, speculated with the national interest, thereby poisoning the nation's very fecundity while betraying France to her enemies. Far from abolishing nationhood, the Parti Ouvrier promised that socialism would restore France "to her first place among nations."[30] In their socialist-nationalist persona, Guesdists vaunted themselves as France's only true patriots.

In sum, chapters 1 to 4 explicate Marxism's "erratic unity of opposites"[31] in the Guesdists' oscillation between cosmopolitanism and socialist nationalism. Chapter 5 moves to the POF's encounter with race. The French Marxists occasionally succumbed to their time's endemic racism, most frequently when terrified by a supposedly impending invasion of coolie laborers—"Chinese sodomites,"[32] as *Le Socialiste* coarsely characterized them. Most often, however, Guesdists derided "the theory of race" as "absurd, ridiculous, unrealizable."[33] The instance of anti-Semitism, so virulent in the France of the Dreyfus affair, best illuminates these Marxist ambiguities. Scholars have condemned Guesdists for their supposed anti-Semitism, highlighting the Parti Ouvrier's refusal to rally behind "that traitor Dreyfus,"[34] instancing the Guesdists' denunciations of Rothschild, "that villainous Jew from Frankfurt."[35] Yet the French Marxists also lauded Jewish creativity, and bemoaned their own inability to recruit Jewish militants.[36] Chapter 5 scrutinizes both the Guesdists' occasional racist failings and their fundamental antiracism, with particular reference to the POF's answers to the "Jewish question."

The belle epoque's nascent "national socialism" violently challenged the Parti Ouvrier's command of the proletariat, not least by mobilizing anti-Semitism against the French Marxists. This challenge supplies the rich subject matter for chapter 6, validating Tom Nairn's contention that fascism tells us much about the ultimate logic of nationalist politics.[37] Did Guesdists ever connive with France's protofascists, as has sometimes been alleged, thereby prefiguring the supposedly intermeshed "totalitarianisms" of the twentieth century? Did irresponsible French Marxists hope to seduce the nationalist ultras on the assumption that "nationalism is one of the harbingers of socialist triumph"?[38] Alternatively, did the two militant movements duel to the death, despite their shared hatred of the hegemonic liberals? Did infuriated Guesdists aspire to put the ultranationalists "up against the wall"?[39] And how did the Parti Ouvrier understand the origins, class identity, and destiny of the time's embryonic national socialism? Answers to these questions, until now virtually unasked, explicate a vital episode in the chaotic collision of class ideology with ethnic fanaticism.

Finally, to foreshadow a conclusion. The Guesdists inherited rich insights from Marx, and elaborated them richly. They engaged with aspects of nationalized modernity that Marx had hardly imagined, and foreshadowed many of twentieth-century Marxism's most brilliant theoretical engagements with ethnicity. Yet the brilliance of these illuminations often blinded the Parti Ouvrier to the benighted world of "blood and belonging." Blindness and brilliance. These antinomies of Guesdism tell us much about Marxism's travails in a war-riven "world of nations"—the unfortunate Guesdists' world, and unfortunately our own.

CHAPTER 1

"For Us the World!": The Guesdists against the Nation

In one of its incarnations, the POF validated the accusation that Marxists are alien to nationhood, strangers to patriotism, mere "rootless cosmopolitans."[1] Certainly Parti Ouvrier texts offer few hints of that "enracinement"[2] in landscape, kinship, and heritage so vital to national identity. The rhetoric of "blood and belonging" played virtually no role in the Guesdists' discursive self-construction, in sharp contrast to the instinctive nationalism characteristic of their ideological interlocutors—all of whom, from socialist-nationalist competitors like Jaurès, through National Liberal opponents like Ferry, to national-socialist enemies like Barrès, rejoiced in their national "roots." In the Parti Ouvrier's most cosmopolitan persona, the movement derided the *patrie* as a false god invoked by charlatans like Jaurès, Ferry, and Barrès to mislead the masses. Rather than mindlessly worshipping that fake "homeland," Guesdist obeyed *The Communist Manifesto*'s mandate, often underscored in Parti Ouvrier discourse, that "Communists . . . point out and bring to the front the common interests of the entire proletariat, independently of all nationality."[3] This injunction could be interpreted as repudiating nationhood, both as authentic historical experience and as valid political project, and *was* so interpreted when the Parti Ouvrier self-consciously embodied Marxism's "universal, placeless, and especially nation-less"[4] proletariat. Lafargue exemplified this ultracosmopolitanism when he quoted Renan's sour observation that "where socialism appears, there patriotism vanishes"—an observation that the Guesdist leader gleefully accepted, not as the intended criticism, but as unintended praise.[5]

This anational, even antinational, sensibility recurred sporadically throughout the POF's history, and was deeply grounded in the Guesdists' passions and preoccupations. Prosopographically, their openness to the world mirrored that of their German-Jewish-English master.[6] Long years of exile typified the life histories of the POF's leadership—the catastrophic Communard experience having ensured that, like Marx himself, Guesde, Lafargue and many of their lieutenants had joined European socialism's multitude of "uprooted." Guesde himself retained strong Italian connections from his exile years, during which Milan had witnessed his abandonment of youthful anarchism for proto-Marxist socialism, and his marriage to a beautiful and polyglot Milanese.[7] For his part, Lafargue exemplified nineteenth-century "multiculturalism" and "hybridity." Of Cuban extraction, flaunting Negro, Jewish, and American Indian blood, living an exile's life abroad in Spain and England, and married to a London-raised Jew (née Laura Marx), the Guesdist leader was often vilified as a foreigner . . . and rejoiced in the characterization.[8] On one occasion, having been viciously attacked as alien, Lafargue, described in *Le Socialiste*'s account (almost certainly in his own words) as "priding himself on being international," simply shrugged with indifference.[9] French, Cuban, Spanish, Carib, Jewish, Negro—none of these ethnic identities mattered. As far as he himself was concerned, Paul Lafargue was simply a socialist and, as such, a citizen of the world. Other militants proudly emphasized their own years of exile, asserting that the salutary experience had immunized them against nationalist contamination.[10] Yet other Guesdists—like the multilingual Charles Bonnier, who had taught French in Oxford—even if spared Communard banishment, exploited their ramified international networks to enfold themselves in a supposedly seamless fabric of cosmopolitan communion.

Nor were these instances of self-asserted cosmopolitanism individual eccentricities. The Parti Ouvrier as a whole was, in some ways, as cosmopolitan as its cadres. Its membership manifested the Party's relaxed openness to ethnic "others"—most obviously in the Nord, the heartland of Guesdism, where Belgians played a starring role first in founding and then in sustaining the POF.[11] Guesde's enemies, indeed, indicted the deputy from Roubaix as representing only the city's teeming naturalized immigrants![12] At the other end of the country, the Parti Ouvrier strove to recruit the Midi's many Italian workers, if necessary by appealing to them in their own language. Commenting on the formation of a "section italienne du POF" in the Savoy, *Le Socialiste* happily concluded that this commingling of French and Italians conclusively demonstrated that "for socialism and for the Parti Ouvrier Français, there are no frontiers."[13]

L'Egalité and *Le Socialiste* filled their columns with articles culled from the world's Marxist press—not least with articles against nationalism—even, or even particularly, when drawn from *German* socialist journals. Clara Zetkin, for one, might well have been on *Le Socialiste*'s staff, given her prominence in its pages. Financial reports emphasized foreign donations to the POF's coffers, almost as if to confirm nationalist slanders that the Parti Ouvrier was treasonously funded from abroad.[14] French Marxists, in turn, made demonstrative contributions to socialist movements elsewhere.[15] Guesdists confirmed their cosmopolitanism in noticing how, "each time there is an outburst of labor unrest in a particular country, it finds a sympathetic echo in all other countries."[16] Guesdists amplified those echoes. Their press publicized foreign support for French strikes, while urging French workers to support labor militancy abroad, on the clear and often explicit assumption that labor should recognize no ethnic boundary separating worker from worker.

As an instance of cosmopolitanism, *Le Socialiste*'s commemoration of the Commune's twentieth anniversary emphasized messages from friends outside France—missives from Liebknecht and Engels leading the edition, followed by best wishes from socialists in Spain, Holland, England, Austria, Denmark, Romania, and Italy, giving pride of place to Zetkin, and only then presenting French contributions.[17] The Parti Ouvrier's inclusive language politics reflected this openness to the world. On one fraught occasion, for instance, *Le Socialiste* elatedly reported the anti-Semitic *Libre Parole*'s fury over a workers' meeting in Paris, where foreign socialists had been invited to address the throng in their own languages, allegedly evoking enthusiastic cheers. Unlike the splenetic ultranationalists of the *Libre Parole*, the Guesdists' newspaper welcomed this multilingual concord.[18] German, French, Italian, English—all had *really* spoken the language of socialism; all had ignored the *Libre Parole*'s urging of "La France aux Français." At the same time, the Parti Ouvrier's press extensively covered the activities of foreign socialists exiled to Paris, and depicted them, not as resident foreigners, but as comrades with a non-French linguistic background—as, for instance, "German-language socialists resident in Paris."[19] Militants from across Europe embarked on speaking tours through France at the behest of the Parti Ouvrier, and socialist luminaries from many countries attended the POF's congresses, provoking well-publicized clashes with inflamed nationalist demonstrators.[20] Commenting on a violence-ridden tour of southeastern France by Rinaldo Rigola, a former Lyonnais member of the POF and recently elected socialist deputy in the Italian parliament, *Le Socialiste* summed up the experience by affirming that "Italian socialist party or French socialist party, we are citizens of the same nation, the nation of labor."[21]

"That Absurdity: A Preference for a Special Place": The Guesdists and Parochialism

In this universalist mode, Guesdists reviled all territorially embedded identities, and mocked not only nationality, but attachment to any *pays*—that untranslatable term for a native place, whether a dialect domain, a historically distinct province, a much-loved village, or a venerable Parisian quartier.[22] Most obviously, the Parti Ouvrier evinced no sympathy whatsoever for the nascent regional identities of the Bretons, Catalans, and Basques. Guesdists totally ignored these emerging "ethnies," although the POF had constructed powerful party organizations in Nantes, the Pyrénées-Orientales, and the Southwest. Even more indicatively, despite the Parti Ouvrier's deep implantation in the humid plains of the Nord, it never recognized a distinct Flemish identity among its adherents—whether in French Flanders itself, or among the thousands of

Belgian immigrants who sustained the POF in its strongholds of Lille and Roubaix. Flemish, Catalan, Basque, Breton—languages spoken by hundreds of thousands on the French periphery—might as well not have existed, for all the attention they received from the Parti Ouvrier. If the POF could thus simply ignore the still timid ethnic reassertion of the Basques or Catalans, it could hardly overlook the militant Languedocian and Provençal regionalist movements—blossoming as they were during the fin de siècle, sung into rebirth by the poetry of Mistral. Nevertheless, no editions of *Le Socialiste du Gard* appeared in the recently reinvented phrases of the langue d'oc. Instead, Guesdists cruelly mocked the Midi's regionalists, deriding their resurrection of a moribund linguistic tradition as pathetic and "grotesque."[23] Unwittingly, ironically, and in common with most of the French Left, the supposedly cosmopolitan French Marxists thus reinforced the jealous hegemony of the "national" language.

The Guesdists' obliviousness to France's own "nations without history" raises a disturbing question: did the Parti Ouvrier's absolute indifference to Basques, Catalans, Flemings, and Bretons and its hostility toward the renascent Midi express a veiled chauvinism, adherence to an all-conquering *French* identity thinly disguised as universalism?[24] So long as the Parti Ouvrier maintained its scathing hostility toward French nationhood itself, the answer to this question must be no. Within a genuinely cosmopolitan POF, the much-mocked "national" identity of France enjoyed no more legitimacy than the "regional" identity of an equally derided Languedoc. But on those other occasions (to be considered in subsequent chapters) when the Party shifted its identity politics from cosmopolitanism toward socialist nationalism, Guesdist indifference to France's multiple ethnic identities lends itself to more critical readings. At best, a "socialist-nationalist" POF has to be indicted for culpable neglect of long-standing historical injustices; at worst, for Francophone cultural imperialism.

Nor did Guesdists sympathize with the provincial localism that was cautiously reemerging from beneath France's Jacobin carapace. This reticence surprises. Despite much militancy in Paris's working-class quartiers, Guesdists had failed to make inroads into the capital's socialist subculture, so that the largely provincial POF might well have championed a provincial socialism against the overweening metropolis. Why not meld Marxism with the "regionalism" resurgent throughout provincial France—an inchoate identity as yet without fixed ideological orientation? The French, after all, genuinely experienced their many *pays*, felt them in their hearts as they felt for their families. Why not bind that heartfelt experience of home to the "imagined community" of global socialism, as nationalists would so effectively bind it to the imagined community of the nation?[25]

Yet the Parti Ouvrier utterly failed this opportunity. As true heirs of the First Republic's revolutionary centralism, Guesdists self-consciously rejected the dialectic between the organic local and the locally transcendent so impressively mastered by the ultranationalist Right.[26] Guesde paraded none of the intense Parisian "patriotism" characteristic of Edouard Drumont, although the Parti Ouvrier's leader was as much the son of *vieux Paris* as the chauvinist agitator. As for Barrès's flamboyantly publicized *enracinement* in his beloved Lorraine, the national socialist's affectation struck Guesdists as absurd, while the kindred particularism of the Action Française's Charles Maurras, both Provençal poet and integral nationalist, found no echo whatsoever in either the Parti Ouvrier's antinational or socialist-nationalist self-identities. The nation, for French Marxists, was either repudiated, along with its provinces, or construed, in the grand Republican tradition, as "one and indivisible." Ironically, the largely provincial Guesdists were thus de facto as centralist as the largely Parisian Blanquists. In practice, in the practicalities of headquarters, meeting places, and editorial rooms, the French Marxists' world turned on Paris—however cosmopolitan that world may have been as ideal, however local and provincial as embedded political culture. Not for French Marxists, then, their period's "reveil des provinces."[27]

The POF, indeed, campaigned ferociously *against* local identities, if only because such identities had planted deep roots in France's proletarian subsoil, and thereby impeded the Guesdists' cultivation of a nationwide, even worldwide, "working-class interest."[28] Manifesting these impediments, workers' diatribes against "foreigners" who invaded local labor markets sometimes referred to "immigrants" from other parts of France—an indication that, for the "popular classes," "French" nationality hardly became an instituted reality until the later nineteenth century, with the citizenship code of 1889 and the administrative identification of "resident aliens" in 1888.[29] Parisian building workers thus barely distinguished between Breton and Italian laborers who trespassed upon their terrain.[30] Acutely aware of this threat to proletarian unity, French Marxists fiercely criticized socialists like Paul Brousse and Jules Joffrin—Possibilists, Parisian notables, and leaders of the anti-Guesdist "municipal" tendency on the French Left—who shamelessly advanced the interests of their local constituents against "outsiders." The Parti Ouvrier's Possibilist enemies on the Paris municipal council had thus sought to solve the unemployment crisis of the 1880s, at least for Parisians, by denying employment to workers with less than six months' residency in the capital—a strategy that utterly outraged the Guesdists. Confronted by such exclusionary manoeuvers, the POF angrily contended that socialists represented a universal proletariat, not the arrogant exclusivity of the great metropolis, and certainly not the parochial selfishness of a Parisian quartier.[31]

In their critiques of parochialism, French Marxists at their most cosmopolitan simply denied that proletarians *had* local identities. "As to workers, where are their neighborhood interests [intérêts de quartier]?" asked Paul

Grados, one of the few Parisian leaders of the POF. "Everywhere," he continued, "they endure—at Batignolles no less than at Montrouge, at Grenelle just as at Ménilmontant—the same starvation wages and the same slums, the same exploiters and the same landlords." According to his reasoning, workers had the same class-interest and hence the same identity everywhere, "not only in the various quarters of Paris, but in every city and region throughout the land."[32] Once proletarianized, Guesdists like Grados argued, workers had been effectively uprooted—their identities thus everywhere identical, whether they loaded barges on the quays of the Seine or ships on the docks of Marseille, whether they excavated mine shafts in the Nord or tunnels for the Parisian metro. In their less absolutist reflections, however, Guesdists admitted, if only to deplore the fact, that some workers still manifested ingrained local identities. "All too many otherwise sensible people," *Le Socialiste* grumbled, "still have difficulty in ridding themselves of that absurdity: a preference for a special place, for the people they find there, and [have], as a consequence, a singular animosity toward those who live elsewhere."[33] Guesdists, in such moments of cosmopolitan extremism, evidently found themselves at home everywhere, or perhaps nowhere, but never somewhere in particular.

This absolutism has, for Marxists, repeatedly obscured the persistence of particularism, and has hindered socialism's mobilization of those—virtually everyone, in fact—who love their home or their homeland. Marxism's utopian universalism has, in particular, all too often forestalled creative engagement with the "national question," and thereby made Marxists more vulnerable to nationalism—whether as enemy or as seducer.[34] Marxism's resultant defeats and seductions have convincingly demonstrated that "it is only by 'going through' nationality, rather than around it, that we can get to the other side, to universality."[35] Why, then, have Marxists, when confronted by particularism, so often adopted "avoidance strategies"? Most fundamentally, they have refused to answer "the national question" (or the "question de quartier," for that matter) because they have failed to see its pertinence. They have founded their philosophical anthropology on the universal human capacity for creativity, rather than on individuals' particularizing hunger for self-identity. Manifesting creative capacities—or "labor," as Marxists have conceived creativity—has no particularistic implications, only implications for the individual or for humanity as a whole. Becoming a fine parent, being a good friend, conceiving a novel idea, crafting a beautiful pot—none of these necessarily divides "man from man" (or even man from woman!). They are groundings from which can grow cosmopolitan universality. Establishing self-identity, however, implies particularity defined against an "other" (initially, of course, against the parent). "I am a man, not a woman." "I am normal, not a pervert." "I am Catholic, not a Jew." "I am French, not German." All such identities are particularistic; all are potentially divisive. Combine their terms, represent the man, the heterosexual, the gentile, the Frenchman, and there emerges a "National Front"—patriarchal, homophobic, anti-Semitic, chauvinist. Marx was able to reject, even ignore, this divisive dialectic of identity formation because his own self-identity was so all-inclusive. "I am a human," he was wont to claim. "Nihil humani a me alienum puto" (Nothing human is alien to me).[36] He, like his followers, failed to realize that "real" individuals (even Marx himself, in his unthinking moments as Victorian patriarch or imperial European) humanize themselves through identification with "particular wholes" defined against others, as well as through laboring for *the* "greater whole" of universal humanity.[37]

At the same time, Guesdists were misled by their political theory, or by their lack of one. They shared Marx's bitter hostility to politics as "representation"—whether in the "general interest's" representation by Hegel's rationalistic bureaucrats, in Caesarist embodiment, or through "bourgeois parliamentarianism."[38] Guesdists thus remained trapped in a noble but vacuous commitment to direct democracy. Without bureaucracy, Caesar, or parliament, they had no way of embodying a people in a polity, while still expecting such embodiment on a world scale! Their political theory might, just conceivably, have legitimized the participatory democracy of a works council or a community forum, and Guesdists dreamt vaguely of a global commonwealth. But no intermediate entity between comradeship and cosmopolis made much sense within their (non)political paradigm.[39] No wonder Guesdists found it so difficult, if not impossible, to appropriate the nation, or even the *pays* or the province, for their political purposes!

Their universalistic political theory generated a further fallacy: the assumption that any polity short of cosmopolis meant war—an assumption remarkably similar to the brutal "realism" of the modern Machiavellians, albeit used to justify cosmopolitanism rather than an endless war-of-all-against-all. Guesdists here failed to distinguish between power-political *nationalism* and universalistic *patriotism.* The Parti Ouvrier might have adopted and adapted the "French" ideal of the "patriot-citizen," while rejecting the particularistic "Central European" mystique of "blood and soil."[40] Such patriotism could, at least in theory, have been blended with the Guesdists' treasured cosmopolitanism, and might then have articulated a range of nonexclusive Marxist identities—from the beloved locality, through nations as civic communities, to an all-inclusive world-state. Guesdists, unfortunately, conflated "patriotism," the legacy of antique Stoic republicanism, with "nationalism," defined as ethnic exclusion. This indiscriminate commingling of universalistic Republican patriotism with "blood and soil" chauvinism, and the Guesdists' repudiation of the two together, played into the hands of their enemies. France's liberal Republicans were given a "free goal," monopolizing civic patriotism, while the antiliberal national socialists appropriated ethnic "France" for their mythic cause—with Guesdists relegated to a universalism without concrete embodiment.[41]

"That Final Communion: A Planetary Internationalism": Guesdist Cosmopolitanism

The Marxists of the POF thus rejoiced in a cosmopolitanism at least as all-inclusive as Marx's own. In their universalistic mode, Guesdists pledged allegiance to "the grand homeland that is humanity"[42] and sharply distinguished the "homeland of which we dream" from "that of our chauvinists." The French Marxists' dreamworld encompassed "humanity as a whole," and promised "the liberation of every human being, without distinction of sex, of race, or of nationality."[43] As true heirs of the Enlightenment, Guesdists systematically incorporated the philosophes' humanistic universalism into fin de siècle socialism, loyal to Marx's maxim that "nothing human is alien to me." Loyalty to a particular place, to a particular people, as Guesdists understood such particularism, betrayed Marxism's all-embracing allegiance to global humanity. "For us the world!" cried Guesde: "A world become the great homeland for all in which we will all be equal citizens!"[44]

French Marxists inflected this Enlightenment trope with their own class-focused ideology. Just as integral nationalists arraigned "internal enemies" (including Marxists) before the court of national interest, so Guesdists indicted class traitors before the tribunal of worldwide humanity. In the Parti Ouvrier's rogues' gallery, "bourgeois nationalists" were the worst culprits. They had literally "alienated" themselves from the human race. As so often with the humanist dictum that "nothing human is alien to me," there lurked the latent suggestion that "all that is alien to me is inhuman." In keeping with the "othering" inherent in identity politics (even in the identity politics of cosmopolitanism), dehumanizing metaphor peppered Guesdist polemic. Nationalism was a noxious "weed" to be uprooted by the socialist plough;[45] it was "bestial," and transformed men into ravening brutes;[46] it was a "plague" against which socialism alone conferred immunity.[47] Weeds, beasts, bacilli—bourgeois nationalists were the "alien other" to socialist humanity.

On the other hand, Guesdists found compatriots wherever workers mobilized, whether they came "from Prussia or from Lorraine, whether they are Semites or Latins."[48] In the Guesdists' cosmopolitan code, the "homeland" to which Marxism pledged allegiance was "the workers' revolution" fought "without distinctions of nationalism or race."[49] This proletarian *patrie* was worldwide, fulfilling the promise of that radiant dawn of 1789 when "the homeland had not been . . . a bit of territory limited by geological determinism or the accidents of history"; when, instead, "the homeland was the revolution."[50] The POF thus claimed the "sublime internationalism of the revolutionary bourgeoisie" originally manifest in the Jacobins' First Republic, before that internationalism had "degenerated" into the Third Republic's "disgusting cosmopolitanism of thieves."[51] Once the workers' revolution had destroyed this repulsive "bourgeois republic," once socialism had triumphed across the globe, Guesdists expected the resultant socialist world order to dismantle the last barriers dividing man from man, whether they were the barriers of class or of nationality. Entranced by this messianic vision, the Parti Ouvrier eagerly anticipated the millenarian moment when "various human fragments, disseminated across the planet, will attain that final communion: a planetary internationalism."[52]

What, then, of that other "communion," the one in which French nationalists worshiped: the *patrie*—that "homeland" consecrated by the blood of ancestors, binding the ancestors' heritage to the aspirations of today's *enfants de la patrie*, incarnate in the numinous landscape of *la belle France*? Not for Guesdists such mysticism. Enraged by nationalism's "savage passions,"[53] Guesdists let fly an astonishing repertoire of vituperative rhetoric. "Savagery," indeed, was a favorite Guesdist characterization of nationalism, which was portrayed, for instance, as a "bloodthirsty and savage incitement to massacre."[54] According to the French Marxists, in a time commanded by the capitalist world-market and promised by history to the socialist International, nationalism had become as obsolete, ridiculous, and ultimately malignant as tribalism. Affronted by nationalist demonstrations against performances of Wagner's *Lohengrin* at the Paris Opéra, Guesdists contemptuously pointed out (ignoring Wagner's own Teutonic racism) that "Wagner, along with socialism, has history on his side. Patriotism can do nothing against either of them, or with either of them. It's too petty, and won't last."[55] Not for the Parti Ouvrier that absurd toast: "Wright [*sic*] or wrong, my country!"[56]

France, instead of emanating from her people's blood, instead of flowering from her fecund landscape, was for Guesdists a mere historical construct built "solely by force," the force that "alone has constituted the transient unity that carries the name French Nation."[57] Following the logic of this "constructivism," the Parti Ouvrier derided "natural frontiers" as geopolitical fantasy. Asking himself why a randomly winding river like the Rhine was treasured as a "national" boundary, Lafargue could find only one answer: "force!"[58] Strasbourg and Colmar may have become German in 1871 by force majeure, he admitted, but they had earlier been rendered "French" in exactly the same manner. Languedoc, for its part, had been incorporated into France during a thirteenth-century "crusade of extermination."[59] Simon de Montfort's genocidal campaign against Cathari Languedoc, according to the Guesdist, was only one of many royal instances of bloodletting that had eventually coagulated into "France." Paradoxically, the cosmopolitan Lafargue thus agreed with the ultranationalist Maurras: France had been constructed by monarchical aggression. The two ideologues, however, reached opposite conclusions from this historical insight. For Maurras, it legitimated monarchy; for Lafargue, it delegitimized the nation.

Following the logic of these antinationalist precepts, the Parti Ouvrier shunned France's national symbols. Guesdists chanted the *Internationale* rather than the *Marseillaise*, celebrated the Commune's anniversary rather than Bastille Day, and flaunted the red flag rather than the *tricolore*. The colors of the national flag, after all, supposedly symbolized the nation's tripartite division into classes: white for the aristocracy, blue for the bourgeoisie, red for the proletariat. The *tricolore* would soon be superseded—once class had been abolished.[60] Purged of bourgeois and aristocrats, the classless France of the future would fly the workers' red flag, as would the entire world—the *drapeau rouge* thus proclaiming both the end of class and the extinction of nationality. As for Bastille Day, it had supposedly degenerated into a bacchanalian orgy even as it had, to the Guesdists' chagrin, seized the popular imagination. "It must be admitted," Guesdists sneered after a particularly exuberant celebration, "that, as with most things national, the national holiday degenerates further with every year."[61] For the Parti Ouvrier, the *fête nationale* would "always be the celebration of others."[62] One POF section actually expelled militants caught celebrating the holiday![63] Summing up the POF's antinationalism, Lafargue quoted Renan's Stoic words during the siege of Paris: "Let France perish . . . there is above her the realm of duty and reason"—a realm that, for Lafargue (although certainly not for Renan!), included all the world where socialists strove "to construct the greater homeland of humanity" on "the ruins of [today's] lesser homelands."[64]

For Guesdists in this ultracosmopolitan mood, national identity was capitalist fraud. Bourgeois vendors of false consciousness peddled nationhood as another "opium of the people," but themselves abstained from their stupefying drug. Capitalists abjured nationhood. According to one of Lafargue's mordant satirical pamphlets, which "revealed" the invention by the global ruling elite of a "religion of capital," this all-conquering cult avowed that "capital knows neither homeland, nor frontiers, nor color, nor race, nor age, nor sex; it is an international deity, a universal deity; its law will rule over all the children of man."[65] As avatars of this universal divinity, the capitalists themselves had "only one homeland: the love of gold";[66] their "true nation" was "such and such a percentage of interest."[67] Developing this theme, the Congress of Montluçon, in formulating the POF's definitive edict on the "national question," thus indicted the cosmopolitan bourgeoisie's pushing of national identity as "the last word in confidence tricks."[68] The credulous might be conned, but bourgeois con men themselves never credited their own nationalist trickery.

The Parti Ouvrier's journalists and speakers regularly evoked the news of the day to illustrate nationalist fraud. Did the French fleet attend ceremonies inaugurating Germany's Kiel Canal? "So much the better for us!" exclaimed a delighted *Le Socialiste*. "Not only won't we have war, but [this incident] is so funny and so instructive [of nationalist hypocrisy]."[69] Did the mill owners of

Roanne protest that striking workers were betraying France by appealing for support to British textile unions? The Guesdist newspaper *L'Egalité* acerbically disclosed that these self-same "nationalist" employers imported textile machinery from Britain.[70] Did Paul Leroy-Beaulieu—editor of French capitalism's house organ *L'Economiste Français*, scourge of socialism, and proud patriot—propose an entente for the duration of the Boer War between French and German holders of Transvaal mining stock? Guesdists roared with laugher, since the resultant organization would intermingle "patriots [in France and Germany] who are thrown into fury by the very word 'internationalism.'"[71] Did the same Leroy-Beaulieu advise his plutocratic readers to liquidate their holdings in the underperforming French bourse . . . and invest their wealth in booming turn-of-the-century Germany? "So much for patriotism!" crowed *Le Socialiste*.[72] Did Leroy-Beaulieu attend a meeting in London of the "Liberty and Property Defense League" at the very moment when his political mentors were expelling the German socialist August Bebel from France? The conjunction, *Le Socialiste* pointed out, demonstrated "a logically implied contradiction": "[I]nternationalist, or at least antipatriotic, in its own interest, the bourgeoisie is only patriotic for—and against!—the proletariat."[73]

"Our Instructors in Internationalism": Globalization, Metahistory, and the Capitalist World Order

Why were Guesdists so convinced that "bourgeois exploitation is today international," that "it knows neither races nor frontiers"?[74] There was one obvious answer: the Parti Ouvrier's political economy. Like Marxists before and since, Guesdists repeatedly demonstrated that capitalism's commodification of the world and its logic of accumulation undermined every particularism, including nationhood.[75] The French Marxists faithfully followed the *Manifesto*'s portrayal of how

> the need of a constantly expanding market for its products chases the bourgeoisie over the whole surface of the globe. It must nestle everywhere, settle everywhere, establish connections everywhere. The bourgeoisie has through its exploitation of the world market given a cosmopolitan character to production and consumption in every country. To the great chagrin of Reactionists, it has drawn from under the feet of industry the national ground on which it stood. All old-established national industries have been destroyed or are daily being destroyed. They are dislodged by new industries, whose introduction becomes a life and death question for all civilized nations, by industries that no longer work up indigenous raw material, but raw material drawn from the remotest zones; industries whose products are consumed,

> not only at home, but in every quarter of the globe. In place of the old wants, satisfied by the productions of the country, we find new wants, requiring for their satisfaction the products of distant lands and climes. In place of the old local and national seclusion and self-sufficiency, we have intercourse in every direction, universal inter-dependence of nations. And as in material, so also in intellectual production. The intellectual creations of individual nations become common property. National one-sidedness and narrow-mindedness become more and more impossible, and from the numerous national and local literatures, there arises a world literature.[76]

Cosmopolitanism, Guesdists affirmed, was not some quixotic Marxist fancy. It was "already everywhere, in the clothes we wear and which owe their wool to Australia and their cotton to America; in the letters that we write and which international conventions transport to the four corners of the world; in the bread that we eat, baked from the wheat of Russia or India."[77] French Marxists of the belle epoque—like all Marxists, or at least all those of the Second International—ruthlessly discarded the "depreciated currency of supposed eternal principles" in favor of that "most vulgar yet most indispensable of realities, economic reality."[78] By this accountancy, nationhood was one of the most worthless of the fin de siècle's badly "depreciated currencies."

In pursuing this thesis, Guesdists highlighted the cosmopolitanism of France's supposedly nationalist industrialists—a cosmopolitanism described with scathing irony as "the patriotic procedures of employers for the promotion of national industrial prosperity."[79] If the Guesdists were internationalists, then how much more so were capitalists! Socialists like Guesde, after all, had never, unlike Eugène Motte—Roubaissian mill owner, ultrapatriot, and victor over Guesde during the 1898 parliamentary elections—invested their earnings in foreign factories, investments that then returned to France as cheap imports to dispossess the Roubaissian workers who had succumbed to Motte's nationalist blandishments. Having revealed a massive textile works under construction in Russian Poland, *Le Socialiste* drove home the fact that

> the headquarters of this enterprise are not in Russia, but in France. . . . Its owners are not Russians, but the industrialists of Roubaix, Tourcoing, and Lille. . . . They are the famous "patriots" of the "Union Sociale" who have hurled the epithet "internationalist" against Guesde.[80]

Thus the Parti Ouvrier understood supposedly "French" industrialists: corporate headquarters in France; class interest invested anywhere and everywhere.

In the POF's historical dramaturgy, "multinational corporations" strode forth as lead actors in the epic creation of the modern globalizing world. Utterly indifferent to nationality, these vast enterprises bought wherever products were cheapest, invested wherever returns were highest, and sold into the most lucrative markets, wherever they might be. Their shareholders' portfolios carried no passports as they toured the world, searching for the best coupon.[81] This insatiable accumulation process, according to the Guesdists,

> has increasingly substituted the world market for the national market. It has created new industries dependent on foreign sources for their raw materials and on foreign markets for their sales. . . . And, above all, its [internationalism] is in the exploitation of labor, which increasingly replaces a nation's workers . . . with Belgians, Spaniards, Italians, Swiss, Germans, not to mention Chinese, all turned against their brothers as low-price competition.[82]

Raw materials, markets, even labor—all were global, not national, despite the bourgeoisie's lying rhetoric.

However sincere the capitalists' nationalism (and the Parti Ouvrier rarely granted them sincerity), they had no alternative but to pursue an international and even antinational investment strategy. The POF's astute political economy demonstrated conclusively that, if "enclosed within 'national' frontiers, . . . capitalism could no longer function normally, and would soon collapse."[83] This accumulation imperative governed the world: it knew no limit, and certainly no national limitations. The foundation of Guesdist social and economic theory thus rested solidly on a "capitalist world system" that relentlessly "remakes the world in its image."[84] That image shone bright in the Guesdists' social imaginary:

> [N]o nation can any longer enjoy an independent existence. . . . Just as industrialization creates a division of labor within the workplace and within the nation, so it unites workers and nations. It works toward the abolition of class and the unification of the human race.[85]

In this classically Marxist analysis, capitalism moved with majestic inevitability toward its supersession—toward its own transcendence in the classless society of the future, and toward the abolition of nations, which would meld into cosmopolis.

Antinationalism was thus not a pernicious socialist plot, but a dynamic inherent in capitalism's commodification of the world. Cosmopolitanism was not the utopian dream indicted by realist statesmen, but the gathering reality of capital's global dominion. Just as eighteenth-century merchant capital had smashed provincial impediments to trade, constructing a cohesive national market and enabling the French Revolution's abolition of the ancient provinces, so twentieth-century finance capital would demolish nationally bounded economies, constituting an all-encompassing world market and dooming the nation-state. No longer economically necessary, France would follow Aquitaine into the wastebasket of history. In explicating the antinational logic of global capitalism, the Parti Ouvrier deemed capitalists, ironically, to be the Guesdists' own "instructors in internationalism."[86]

The Parti Ouvrier founded its cosmopolitan conception not only on political economy but on metahistory. The Guesdists' historicization of national identity, linked to their historicization of modes of production and "modes of reproduction,"[87] rendered the nineteenth-century bourgeois order of capital, patriarchy, and nationhood transient rather than eternal. How so? Each stage of world-historical development, French Marxists contended, had evoked contingent forms of "patriotism" appropriate to its primary mode of production—an insight that generated a surprisingly complex typology, depending on whether patriotism "was embodied in an individual phenomenon (the king, the chief, the family); a corporative entity (a city, a municipality, a guild); or, finally, a much greater body, a being much more complex (a nation, a province, an empire with its colonies)."[88] All these forms had been or would be transient. The patriarchal clan, the God-King's domain, the city-state—each ancient particularism had believed itself eternal; each had nonetheless succumbed to history's relentless erasure. The same would hold true for modern nationhood. Guesdists concluded that "no matter how recent the birth of patriotism, how much nearer its death!"[89]

These variations in patriotic modes, according to Guesdist historical thought, had been determined by mutations in the property system. Rulers whose wealth derived from the exploitation of a particular form of historical community would articulate their identity through a commensurate form of "patriotism." When a nomadic clan's property was engrossed by its chief, he necessarily focused its patriotic identity. Let the city-state—classical Athens, medieval Florence, early-modern Geneva—become the locus of property ownership, and patriotism became communal. With the rise of modern "French," "German" and "Italian" bourgeoisies whose economic domains transcended mere cities or provinces, the French, German and Italian nation-states had been born. As burgeoning capitalism created a proletariat with global interests, so arose a novel universalist identity, a contemporary "patriotism" of humanity as a whole.[90]

The Guesdists' "useable past" served them well in mastering their present. If the Parti Ouvrier sought to prove that the allegedly "French" bourgeoisie (whose wealth was actually drawn from around the world) would soon betray France, then the POF could recall how the wealthy of Athens had betrayed their polis to protect their property, when the interest of polis and property had diverged.[91] If French Marxists needed to explain why bourgeois, who had created the modern nation, now betrayed it, then Guesdists could relate how seventeenth- and eighteenth-century capitalists had been mercantilist, dependent on the force and favor of strong "national" states, while showing how contemporary capitalists, by contrast, had become cosmopolitan, their interests "disseminated across the globe."[92] If Guesdists sought to explain why the modern proletariat would never heed nationalist exhortations, they could demonstrate how workers under capitalism, unlike the intensely patriotic and securely propertied artisans of medieval towns, had had their means of production expropriated, and thus lacked any stake in "their" nations.[93]

Nor did the Guesdists confine their history lessons to explication of the past and interpretation of the present. A vision of the future conditioned their readings of both past and present, as has been the case with all metahistories, from the chronicles of Ur to Lyotard's vision of the "postmodern condition." Here, in their historical imaginary, the Guesdists augured an imminent utopia: the socialist unification of mankind. According to Alexandre Zévaès, youthful second to an aging Guesde,

> [T]he nation presents itself to the eyes of scientific socialism as a stage, as a stage in human evolution in which the tribe, the city, and the province have been successive phases. The International of tomorrow will be the culmination of that long evolution. It is the product of contemporary civilization itself.[94]

Tribes, cities, provinces, nations—their march through the millennia led toward cosmopolis.

The workers of the world incarnated this utopian potential. Their "particular interests as a class," Guesde contended, "coincide with the general interest, thus transforming the proletariat . . . into the champion of all humanity."[95] Unlike every preceding ruling class, a triumphant proletariat would usher in a genuine "commonwealth." Workers' property in their socialist order would not exclude others from ownership, from participation, and hence from belonging. Community would deepen to include all those once propertyless, and expand to encompass the world. Just as universal property-ownership would eradicate class divisions, so the consequent universalist identity would erase national distinctions. In *Le Socialiste*'s tracing of this trajectory into the future,

> at one time limited to the clan, to the tribe, the idea of the homeland has grown, forming the bourgeois [national] society of all those who have the same interest. It has arrived at its final stage with the proletariat: the International of producers. This [International] will be a very negation of the homeland . . . and this word will no longer have a raison d'être, for there will henceforth be only one class, only one collectivity.[96]

History promised global communion.

Easier said than done. Guesdists occasionally admitted that transition from the nationalist present to the universalist future would be more convoluted than this unilinear scheme suggested. At their most sophisticated, French Marxists foreshadowed Lenin and Trotsky's concept of "uneven and combined development." On one occasion, for instance, the Bonnier brothers explained that capitalism had, as yet, left some industries small-scale and individually owned, and therefore unready for "nationalization"; others large-scale and collectively owned through national share markets, and thereby ripe for such nationalization; and yet others all-encompassing in scale and globally owned, and thus ready for the "internationalization" that would be the destiny of all enterprise.[97] At the fin de siècle, the Bonniers conceded, local, national, and international proprietorship coexisted and clashed, to the befuddlement of any unitary socialist strategy. Clearheaded Marxists such as themselves, however, understood the simplifying logic of history. No Guesdist doubted for a moment that capitalist modernity drove toward transcendence of the nations that capitalism had first erected but would soon demolish—in their place constructing a world order to be inherited by the proletariat.

"All the Sons of Toil of the Universe": The Guesdists and Proletarian Internationalism

Despite their doubts about the imminence of universal globalization, Guesdists imagined an imminent universal proletariat. Capitalists, the Parti Ouvrier suggested convincingly, bought labor power at its cheapest wherever it might be found, and the resultant transnational dynamic, Guesdists argued, not so convincingly, had standardized wages across the globe, thereby creating "common conditions and common interests for workers everywhere."[98] In an astonishing triumph of theory over observation, Guesdists sometimes seemed to believe that this process had *already* everywhere equalized wages and conditions, instituting "common conditions" constitutive of a united global proletariat. In the categorical formulation of "Jacques Vingtras" (J.-B. Lebas, the future Guesdist mayor of Roubaix), the capitalist world system had already ensured that "the interests of workers . . . are [throughout the world] identical."[99] For the Parti Ouvrier, these "common conditions" and "common interests" rendered working-class nationalism nonsensical in practice and inconceivable in theory. Wherever workers lived, whatever their labor, they should realize, *would* realize, that "any isolated campaign . . . has become impossible. Only international militancy possesses any value."[100] Bourgeois cosmopolitanism—the agency that had created the world market in capital, labor, and goods—thus created proletarian cosmopolitanism, the agent of worldwide socialist revolution. This dialectic ensured that

> the nation is today a word devoid of meaning. Most civilized nations are exploited by a band of cosmopolitan capitalists, to whom have been delivered the soil, commerce, industry, and the national finances. These capitalists have only one homeland: the exploitation of every nation's workers. Workers dispossessed of land and tools . . . now have only one homeland: the social revolution, which will free them from cosmopolitan capitalist exploitation. That homeland is not contained within the frontiers of one nation, but embraces all the sons of toil of the universe.[101]

"All the sons of toil of the universe"—Marxism's constituency, humanity's hope . . . and the nation's doom.

The colossal emigration from nineteenth-century Europe, often evoked in *L'Egalité* and *Le Socialiste*, classically manifested the bourgeoisie's internationalization of its workforce. Cornish miners on the Victorian gold fields, Piedmontese masons in the building sites of Buenos Aires, Polish ironworkers at the furnaces of Pennsylvania—these regiments mobilized into "the army of the *sans-patrie*"[102] had been recruited not by socialism, but by capitalism. In the Marxists' amazingly optimistic (and wildly unrealistic) understanding of American society, the United States, that New World called into existence by capital, classically illustrated proletarian cosmopolitanism.[103] Systematically misled by their correspondents in New York and Chicago, the editors of *Le Socialiste* retailed accounts of American workers who had already mingled indistinguishably with midcentury German and Irish immigrants, and now welcomed the tidal wave of Italian, Polish, and Jewish labor sweeping across the Atlantic.

This American melting pot, for Guesdists, exemplified a worldwide dynamic. Throughout capitalism's global domain, among workers from San Francisco to Siberia, from Norway to Argentina, "unity and the common interest that it embodies ends by becoming dearer than any official homeland, which represents in [workers'] eyes only employers' . . . interests." Thus, "for the industrial proletariat, an international union has been created which is its true homeland."[104] French Marxists at their most cosmopolitan thereby validated Michael Walzer's insightful comment that "solidarity is the patriotism of the left; often it replaces the sense of citizenship and even love of country."[105] Certainly Guesdists, in their cosmopolitan guise, had no doubt whatsoever that

> the coming revolution will be essentially proletarian, and, since the conditions of life, since the goals, since the interests of the proletariat are *everywhere* identical, that revolution can only be international. . . . If the bourgeois revolution of the eighteenth century abolished the provinces, the workers' revolution will abolish the nations.[106]

Transfixed by globalization, the Parti Ouvrier welcomed a fusion of nationalities like that which had supposedly occurred within the American proletariat, and heralded a consequent worldwide working-class revolution that would institute a United States of the Earth.

This vision served Guesdists well in their running battles against critics of cosmopolitanism, critics whose nationalism collapsed into absurdity if posed against the awe-inspiring world market. When Maurice Barrès advocated unity between French workers and French capitalists against foreigners, and particularly against German workers and German capitalists, Guesdists contemptuously referred him to the capitalist mode of production, which supposedly bonded proletarians on both sides of the Vosges into a single revolutionary mass. "In place of national working-class combinations . . . we will see international combinations," predicted Albert Delon, the Guesdist leader in Nîmes. "We are moving toward a sort of European union"[107]—a vision well calculated to outrage the Euro-skeptical Barrès and his protofascist followers. Against Barrèsian nationalism, the Parti Ouvrier anticipated a day "when a German candidate will be able to stand for election in France, and a French candidate in Germany, because the workers will be united by the same militancy and the same cause on both sides of the border."[108] Guesdists thus based their ultimate ideological identity on the principle that

> socialists have only one homeland: the social revolution. All socialists, whatever their nationality, race or color, are fraternally united. The fundamental sentiment uniting them is hatred of capitalism and its agents, whether they're named Ferry, Bismarck, Salisbury, or Katkoff.[109]

For the Parti Ouvrier, socialists could only overthrow their Ferrys and Bismarcks by working together internationally. Uncoordinated proletarian national revolutions during the twentieth century would be as futile as uncoordinated local peasant insurrections had been during the Middle Ages.[110]

At their most prescient, Guesdists fully realized that "socialism in one country" would prove fatally vulnerable to international capital, in the same way that an isolated revolutionary France had eventually been defeated by the united ancien régime.[111] What is more, Guesdists argued, if national revolutions were necessarily doomed to defeat, then socialist assumption of "national" responsibilities under capitalism suggested an even worse consequence: catastrophic self-betrayal, rather than mere catastrophe. Guesdists foresaw the disastrous socialist-nationalist dynamic of August 1914, when socialist "statesmen" would mobilize their followers against foreign socialists and foreign workers, and do so in collaboration with their nations' bourgeois and with bourgeois nationalists.[112] As uncompromising advocates of proletarian unity across borders and fanatical opponents of class collaboration anywhere, French Marxists feared and detested adventures in national "solidarity," exemplified for them by Millerand's "treason" in joining a "bourgeois" government that included General Gallifet, the "butcher of the Commune." As "His Excellency the Minister of Commerce," Guesdists snarled, Millerand betrayed not only French socialism, but also the international working class. Such betrayal could not be countenanced, as working-class cosmopolitanism was the form of the future, the destiny of mankind, "the furnace in which will be founded all the melded elements of past society and of future humanity."[113]

Thus was Guesdism at its most cosmopolitan—pledging its allegiance to a universal humanity, embodying that humanity in the global working class, renouncing nationhood as a rotting revenant from the savage past, denouncing nationalism as malignant bourgeois ideology. This obstinate universalism should command our respect. Cosmopolitan inclusion, however utopian, is surely preferable to nationalist exclusion, however pragmatic; proletarian globalism, however spectral, is surely better than working-class xenophobia, however authentic.[114] For that matter, the Guesdists' stringent Marxism illuminated the hard realities of their world, and of ours. Who today, living under the dominion of the IMF, would deny capitalism's globalizing force? Trillions of dollars sloshing through international capital markets must overwhelm the skeptic. Who today would question that working-class militancy, if confined to single nations, must prove easy prey to capital? The vulnerability of nationally organized labor movements to footloose hedge funds cruelly demonstrates the point. The Guesdists' cosmopolitan convictions were extreme, but not completely deluded.

CHAPTER 2

"Dupes of Patriotism": Nationalism as Bourgeois Hegemony

Despite the globalization limned in the *Communist Manifesto*, nationhood has survived modernity. The century following Marx's death may have witnessed Marxism's transient ascendancy as socialism's master discourse, but it also experienced the far more spectacular triumph of nationalism. Whether in Paris during the Dreyfus affair, in Vienna during August 1914, in Berlin during the Nazi ascendancy, or in Moscow during the "Great Patriotic War," the question confronting Marxists became "who [is] the 'we' in the dominant political discourse, and who [is] the 'other' which defined that 'we'"[1]—"we workers" against capitalism, or the "we of our nation" against other nations? In this contest, national identity repeatedly "trumped"[2] class consciousness. Workers fought workers, if separated by nationality; employees and employers united, if allied by nationalism. And, even before our recent "century of total war," Marx and Engels had sometimes despaired at nationalism's class-divisive and class-collaborationist force, not least as manifest in France.[3]

Guesdists certainly had to contend with nationalism's enduring vitality. And they, too, like Marx and Engels, lapsed into consequent confusion, and occasionally despaired. After all, floods of nationalist enthusiasm periodically swept away the rivulets of Marxist militancy that crept across the contours of the French political culture—Boulangism inundating proletarian constituencies during the 1880s, Henri Rochefort's "national-socialist" *Intransigeant* far outselling *Le Socialiste*, and Pierre Biétry's ultranationalist "Jaunes" overnight erecting a labor organization far grander than the Guesdists' withered Fédération Nationale des Syndicats. Fin de siècle nationalists summoned workers to their cause, and French proletarians responded.

"Our Brethren of Alsace-Lorraine": The Parti Ouvrier and "Revanche"

Lorraine, that mutilated member of the French body politic, illustrated this Guesdist agony in microcosm, and in extremity. Even the incendiary magic of

Guesde's oratory fizzled when discharged in the mining villages and textile towns of the northeast, with their "proletariat that's so numerous, so compact, so oppressed, yet so little imbued with the principles of modern scientific socialism."[4] Nationalist heckling repeatedly barred Guesdists from even being *heard* by the metalworkers of the Meurthe-et-Moselle, the textile operatives of the Vosges, or the miners of the Longwy Basin.[5] It was only in 1899, for instance, that French Marxists finally established a POF branch in Lorraine's capital, Nancy, expecting that this hard-won bridgehead would soon mobilize workers "until now diverted by nationalist and anti-Semitic tricksters."[6] Not so. Maurice Barrès' "national socialists" easily prevailed against newly introduced Guesdism among Nancy's metallurgists, mill workers, and glassblowers. From first to last, Lorraine's proletarians mobilized against Germans, Jews, and immigrants, but not against capitalists.[7]

Why this Marxist fiasco in one of France's most proletarian regions? Quite simply, it happened because Guesdists repudiated revanche—that dream of "revenge" for the annexations of 1871 that so empowered the belle epoque's virulent nationalism, and that so saturated Lorraine's heated political atmosphere.[8] The Guesdists' own understanding of "1871" produced a very different agenda, and one with little resonance in the borderland. "The only revenge that matters," claimed the Parti Ouvrier, was "revenge for the Commune, for the thousands of workers massacred by the bourgeoisie."[9] Even more tellingly, the Parti Ouvrier detested the Alsatian "Protestaires" who doggedly defied their province's annexation to the Reich.[10] The Protestaires, after all, had voted unanimously for Bismarck's antisocialist laws. From the Parti Ouvrier's jaundiced perspective, those most infuriated by Germany's annexations of 1871—Déroulède's Ligue des Patriotes, Barrès' national socialists, the pro-French recalcitrants within the lost provinces—were all "bourgeois nationalists," antisocialist reactionaries, counterrevolutionaries. They, not imperial Germany, threatened aggression against both French and German socialists.

All the same, Guesdists realized full well that their enemies' cacophonous calls for "revenge" could drown out the "social question," so that its answer would be deferred to the distant future when France was once again whole. "If," the Parti Ouvrier worried,

> in order to organize themselves into a class party and pursue their liberation . . . which is that of all humanity, the proletariats of different countries have to await the return to the national cradle of all the lambs violently detached from the national flock, then the capitalist Minotaur will have many hundreds of years before him during which to levy his tribute of misery, tears, and blood from labor. That, of course, is what rulers and the wealthy everywhere are hoping for and working for with all their force.[11]

Fixated on the capitalist Minotaur, indifferent to Alsatian lambs, French Marxists sometimes simply dismissed Alsace-Lorraine as a nonissue. As Lafargue put it, in an ultracosmopolitan moment:

> The Alsatians—before 1697, before the Republic of Strasbourg, defeated by Louis XIV, was united, by brutal force, to France; before 1798, before the Republic of Mulhouse, under the threat of seeing its industry ruined by the customs barrier with which the Republican government of France had surrounded it, had succumbed—the Alsatians were not French. Today, now that Alsace has been brutally ripped from France, the Alsatians are no longer French.[12]

According to *Le Socialiste*, all that *really* mattered in France, in Germany, and in Alsace-Lorraine was the revolution, which would finally resolve both the social question *and* the national question. "We . . . socialists," Guesdists proclaimed, "witness with joy the swelling flood of German socialism, crossing the Rhine, climbing the Vosges, and ending by effacing the frontier that separates France and Germany."[13] Guesdist publicists regularly reminded their readers that the German Social Democrats had opposed Bismarck's annexation of Metz and Strasbourg, had endured brutal repression for their pains, and still advocated "self-determination" for Alsace-Lorraine.[14] Reinforcing the point, French Marxists highlighted vicious attacks launched by German nationalists against the SPD, accused of working for French revanchists—in ironic symmetry with those same revanchists' accusations that the POF worked for German imperialism.[15]

At the same time, Guesdists sought to demonstrate that bourgeois nationalists disdained Alsace-Lorraine—in reality, if not in rhetoric. The Parti Ouvrier elaborated an idiosyncratic thesis that "proved" that the French bourgeoisie had no desire whatsoever to recover the lost provinces, and that the French ruling class had encouraged their annexation to Germany. Why so? Because France's industrialists had benefited mightily from placing Metz and Alsace beyond the tariff wall that ran invisibly along "the blue line of the Vosges." Ceding Lorraine's coal mines to Germany, for instance, had skyrocketed dividend income from the Anzin Mining Company, vastly enriching its plutocratic French owners.[16] Guesdists actually contended that regaining Alsace-Lorraine would ruin French capitalism.[17] According to Lafargue,

> [S]o long as the capitalist order continues, Alsace must remain German, in the economic interest of France and of Alsace itself. However, once the social revolution has nationalized the means of production and abolished industrial competition, Alsace can return to France without danger. But, by then,

> Europe will form a single vast republic, then frontiers will have disappeared, then the imbecilic and barbarous patriotic passions [of today] will have been extinguished.[18]

As Lafargue summed up this thesis, "[I]t is difficult in a bourgeois world to reconcile the interests of wealth and homeland."[19] After the revolution, triumphant socialists would suffer no such difficulties—if only because bourgeois wealth and national homelands would then have disappeared together.

Alternatively, however, when Guesdists donned their socialist-nationalist persona, when they abandoned their stringent cosmopolitanism, they sought to demonstrate that the POF, above all, and perhaps alone, cared for Alsace-Lorraine—in sharp contrast to self-seeking bourgeois and hypocritical nationalists, who were "content with speaking of it always and thinking of it never."[20] This polemic, while evident throughout the Parti Ouvrier's history, became particularly prominent during the mid-1890s, after the election campaign of 1893 had demonstrated that nationalist attacks could lose Guesdists support in the Nord no less than in remnant Lorraine. Although French Marxists always abjured revanche, they sometimes claimed that they, unlike cynical bourgeois nationalists, had "not forgotten the little France detached from the greater," that "the workers of Alsace-Lorraine" had "their place . . . in the heart and in the ranks of the Parti Ouvrier."[21] Illustrating this supposedly heartfelt commitment, Guesdists organized a rally of Alsatians in French Lorraine, where two Alsatian SPD Reichstag delegates, banned by the German government from speaking in their constituencies, would finally be able to address their border-crossing constituents. When the French government forbade the rally and expelled the assembled Alsatians back to the Reich, the Guesdists enjoyed a field day in the Chamber of Deputies, their account of this exercise in Franco-German repression replete with descriptions of "weeping Alsatian women" forced back over the frontier by *French* police.[22] What better proof of who *really* sided with the unfortunate Alsatians?

If the ugly frontier ripping through Lorraine was thus buttressed by bourgeois on both sides of the border, then the ascendancy of socialism in both France and Germany prefigured the end of 1871's baleful legacy. Journalists at *Le Socialiste*, addressing their German comrades, affirmed that

> Alsace-Lorraine, far from dividing us, can only unite us. The suppression of borders, which is in our program as well as in yours, will transform our brethren of Alsace-Lorraine into a token of unity between our two victorious proletariats. In the name of the Parti Ouvrier Français, *Le Socialiste* joins itself to the *Sozial-Demokrat* to proclaim with a single voice: Peace and unity between the workers of all countries! War—and war to the death—to our national and international exploiters![23]

According to Guesdists, those "national and international exploiters" exploited the unhappy people of Alsace-Lorraine for propaganda no less than for profit. Only socialism promised surcease.

The Parti Ouvrier thus oscillated between two utterly contradictory theses: that the lost provinces mattered not a jot, or that the victory of socialism alone could return them to grieving France. In one persona, Guesdists gloried in their indifference to Alsace-Lorraine; in the other, they postured as the only hope for France's reunification. In both personae, however, French Marxists indicted bourgeois nationalists as essentially indifferent to the revanchism they pretended to champion, or even as complicit in the national mutilation from which bourgeois profited both economically and politically. Anticapitalism was the sole constant in this otherwise vacillating discourse.

"Binding Workers to the Homeland": Bourgeois Hegemony and the Welfare State

Faced by demoralizing realities like their failure to evangelize Lorraine, Guesdism's certainties sometimes wavered. Nationhood survived, Guesdists sadly admitted, as a formidable "obstacle to our propaganda."[24] According to the Parisian Marxist Georges Crépin,

> [E]verything [in bourgeois society] is calculated to inculcate savage passions into the people which can be ignited whenever the bourgeoisie tosses in a bit of incendiary material. [The bourgeoisie] has enveloped [the people] in an atrocious propaganda. . . . They have been saturated with it since their childhood. Their spirit has been entirely poisoned by it. The streets down which they walk carry the name of victories. There are statues of generals at every crossroads; everything is draped in the national colors; everything reminds their exhausted minds of that idiotic idea of the homeland. Open any newspaper, whichever comes to hand, and read the leader or the feuilleton—you'll find it loaded with ringing phrases about Duty and Revenge. In the evening, exhausted by a heavy day, head off . . . to any performance, and the singer . . . will evoke "Marceau, Hoche, Kléber!—Victor Hugo, his glory!—the wine of France, which is blue, white and red!" . . . Without questioning their own stupid fanaticism, [people] become patriots. Why? They don't know. Everyone's like that.[25]

When Guesdists sought to make sense of this everyday world, they had to explain or explain away the evident discordance between their experience of rampant nationhood and their theory of cosmopolitan capitalism. "How," they asked themselves, "to account for the survival of a [nationalism] that no longer has any rationale?"[26]

Why then *did* nationalism survive, even thrive, in a world owned by cosmopolitan bourgeois and promised to a transnational proletariat? Marxists have proposed a multitude of answers to this vexed question.[27] These many answers may be subsumed into two alternative paradigms: one of which specifies the "real" aspects of modernity that justify national identity, the other of which indicts nationalism as pernicious "false consciousness."[28] The two are not mutually exclusive, but Marxists have tended to emphasize the latter. They have assumed that, since workers should "naturally" opt for international socialism, those who opt instead for antisocialist nationalism must be utterly "irrational."[29] Nationalism, then, resembles religion—with both the ethnic and the transcendent occluding the "real" world, and with both "faiths" serving to divert workers from their "real" interests. Guesdists, indeed, often used this analogy, arguing that, "just as [the bourgeoisie] has abandoned its atheism and Voltaireanism in order to base its economic and political domination on religion, so it has abandoned the fraternity of peoples characteristic of its revolutionary period and instead fans the flame of *chauvinism*, which has become an instrument of oppression as powerful as religious sentiment."[30] This indictment warrants review.

During their many explorations of "false consciousness," contemporary Marxists have devoted much thoughtful attention to modes of "national integration," focusing above all on the welfare state and the "mass media." Guesdists of the belle epoque, however, neglected these two nationalizing instrumentalities. The superstructural "disciplinary regimes" and "cultural hegemonies" that have preoccupied recent "Western Marxists," sometimes to the near exclusion of Marx and Engels's own emphasis on political economy, played only a minor role in the Parti Ouvrier's critiques of nationalism. In this respect, Guesde and Lafargue reprised Marx and Engels rather than foreshadowing Poulantzas or Althusser. Not for Guesdists the dissection of modernity's "ideological state apparatuses,"[31] although these apparatuses proliferated during the fin de siècle.

This surprising neglect is exemplified by the Parti Ouvrier's indifference toward the "welfare state"—that complex of nurturing (and disciplining) institutions that the nation-state was developing to succor its citizens, thereby gaining the motherland her children's love and allegiance. "Motherland" . . . ? Such "familial" metaphor already suffused nationalist rhetoric well before the communitarian twentieth century.[32] Nationalists have always melded the real blood ties between parents and children with the fictitious blood ties between compatriots.[33] Since the later nineteenth century, however, as the nation-state has assumed an ever-greater role in the provision of health, education, and welfare, parental metaphors have gained a more powerful resonance. To affirm that "the working men have no country"[34] may have made sense when Marx wrote the line in 1848. "Their country," then, for most workers, meant avaricious tax collectors, oppressive policemen, and brutal recruiting sergeants. Marx's dictum, however, had lost much of its credibility by the fin de siècle, as mention of "fatherland" or "motherland" (the nurturing maternal image now more plausible than the authoritarian paternal one)[35] evoked instruction by state-paid teachers, care from national health services, and "social security" through nationally mandated unemployment and pension funds.[36]

In this sense, Guesdists appear surprisingly old-fashioned. Their episodic but fierce hostility toward *la patrie* manifested an unthinking equation of the modern "homeland" with an antiquated regime of overt class privilege. French Marxists all too often elided "the nation" with the "bourgeois state," that "public coercive power created by class division"[37]—an elision more appropriate to the France of Guizot than to that of Clemenceau. Witness Lafargue, writing as late as 1891: "For the worker, the homeland is burdensome and repellent: he knows it only by the weight it places on his shoulders. . . . The homeland imposes taxes on everything he eats, drinks or wears."[38] This ancient bracketing of burdensome state with repellent nation retained some residual force at the fin de siècle. For the popular classes, after all, "France" had long been little more than "the agents of the state"—royal, republican, or imperial.[39] The French state, across the centuries, had extortionately taxed the poor to finance its panoply of judges, soldiers, and tax collectors—all of them dedicated to maintaining this self-sustaining cycle of exploitation and domination, all obedient to the wealthy and powerful who profited from that cycle. Lafargue thus spoke for a venerable tradition of well-justified popular hostility toward both the state and "its" nation, but a tradition already half-effaced by the nascent welfare-state.

At the fin de siècle, the age-old repulsion between the common people and "their" nation, repulsion driven by the nation's equation with an exploitative state, had actually gone into reverse. Melding homeland and state increasingly legitimated the state, rather than discrediting the nation. The reigning French Republicans battened on this legitimating dynamic.[40] The sleek men in frock coats who thronged the corridors of power supposedly were as one with sweat-stained peasants at their ploughs or grimy miners at the coal face. The state belonged equally to them all as Frenchmen, nurtured them all equally as *enfants de la patrie*. Little wonder, then, that, when encountering such rhetoric, revolutionary Guesdists sometimes clung desperately to past political mentalities. The Parti Ouvrier insisted that the *patrie* was, in fact, no more than the oppressive and exploitative "bourgeois state," and urged "the people" to repudiate both.

The POF, however, sometimes abandoned this ur-Marxist absolutism, since the debunking equation of illusory homeland with real but repellent state generated crippling problems for Guesdist polemicists. Above all, it precluded a fruitful alternative: a revolutionary disjuncture between the rulers' *pays légal* and the people's *pays réel*—that maneuver deployed by so many insurgent nationalists against so many oppressive states.[41] Why *not* separate state from nation? As Marxists with a class agenda, Guesdists could then contrast the alienating, even alien, "bourgeois state" to the "real" working-class nation. When Guesdists instead "tightened the hyphen" in "nation-state" to the point where it disappeared entirely, they played into the hands of the ruling bourgeois, who could then claim the nation as their own. "Lengthening the hyphen" in "nation-state" promised greater rewards—on the principle that "it makes political sense for an opposition . . . to claim to represent the nation against the . . . state."[42] This card, however, could be played only by Marxists willing to essay a "radical patriotism," and thus risk a nationalist trump that might subject socialism to nationalism.[43] Guesdists, as we shall see in chapter 4, were sometimes willing to take this risk.

Anti-Marxists, for their part, strove mightily to fuse state and nation. This program enthused the many "communitarian" (as opposed to "socialist") critics of the fin de siècle's individualist free-market polity—a regime that, communitarians argued, abetted Marxism's cosmopolitan class warriors by alienating workers. According to national socialists, for instance, the coming "national revolution" could be truly national only if it cherished *all* the French, incorporating (exactly the right word for these corporatists) both France's humble and disadvantaged and her powerful and wealthy into a cohesive national community.[44] Nascent Christian Democracy and the "Solidarism" recently invented by "social liberals" followed exactly the same communitarian, corporatist, and anti-Marxist logic.[45] To these critics of laissez-faire, "nationalism" meant "care for the interests of all members of the community." "Patriotism," they proclaimed, "involves a spirit of solidarity, mutual aid, and fraternal charity."[46] Why? Asking himself the question "what is the point of my campaign for the protection of the workers?" Barrès confidently replied: "To bind them to the idea of the homeland!"[47] National socialists, Christian Democrats, and Solidarists all urged the nation-state to intervene against impoverishment, unemployment, and extremes of exploitation—the grounds for working-class alienation from the motherland, the breeding ground for cosmopolitan Red revolution.

How did nationalist communitarians articulate this anti-Marxist program? First, workers, having been deprived by proletarianization of property-owning security, would gain "social security" through nationally provided unemployment insurance, sickness benefits, and retirement funds. Workers would thus prosper as "shareholders" in the nation-state. Second, their fragile families having been disrupted by the market's vagaries, proletarians could expect their child rearing to be sustained by the nation. The nation-state would thus stand godparent at every working-class baptism. Finally, their traditional patterns of apprenticeship and trade solidarity having been destroyed by liberal anticorporatism, workers would be trained and their careers promoted by the nation. The nation-state would thus serve as a vast guild incorporating every proletarian. "Over many centuries," Barrès opined, "the French nation has managed to give its members political security. It must now protect them against the economic insecurity from which they are suffering at all levels."[48] Communitarian nationalists like Barrès, seconded by Christian Democrats and social liberals, originated the modern welfare state, determined as they were to refute Marxism's revolutionary claim that "the workers have no fatherland."[49] Their solidaristic program would rule the West until today's neoliberal reaction.

Thus, at the fin de siècle, whether in Edwardian Britain or Wilhelmine Germany, and even in Waldeck-Rousseau's France, governments had begun to protect labor from the vagaries of the "free" market. Once workers had mobilized as *citizens* with their power invested in the ballot box and the lobby group, rather than as *proletarians* with their power manifest in the strike and the street, they came to rely on "their" national state to regulate working hours against capitalism's voracious appetite for their life force, arbitrate labor disputes where labor might otherwise be overwhelmed by capital, establish minimum wages and acceptable working conditions protecting workers against the inhuman consequences of an unregulated labor market, and institute the welfare state's "social wage" that supplemented the meager wages awarded through the labor market. Reformist labor leaders cooperated successfully with bourgeois reformers to thus "humanize" capitalism.[50] Against every Marxist expectation, working hours *were* regulated, strikes *were* arbitrated, the worst iniquities of the labor market *were* checked, and unemployment, illness, and old age *did* gradually shed some of their terrors. French workers at the fin de siècle really did have some reason to view France and its state as "theirs."

Yet Guesdists virtually ignored this burgeoning counterrevolutionary enterprise. Why? How could French Marxists continue to believe that the "bourgeois state" and its nation would always represent class exclusion, but never social integration? One answer might be that France had been slow to elaborate a welfare state, certainly by comparison with imperial Germany. Wedded as they were to laissez-faire, the Third Republic's rulers detested Barrèsian "national socialism," the Christian Democrats' Christian socialism, and even the social liberals' Solidarism. Yet liberal orthodoxy wavered at the fin de siècle. The haut-bourgeois Opportunists and the petit-bourgeois Radicals—often against their better judgment, and always with second thoughts—mobilized their state wherever and whenever the invisible hand of the market had let drop the "national interest." France *did* move toward state-supported social protection, and French workers *did* respond with hope and, sometimes, with nationalist enthusiasm.[51]

There is a more plausible explanation for the Guesdists' obtuseness: that they ignored the welfare state *because* of its apparition. In the Marxists' nightmares, if not in their waking calculations, they must have been terrified that a "bourgeois" nation-state that protected its workers might indeed gain their loyalty. Best to deny the very possibility! Such denial became particularly evident once the Parti Ouvrier's "reformist" enemies had gained power after the Dreyfus affair. With Alexandre Millerand as minister of commerce, with a flood of social legislation before the Chamber of Deputies, Guesdist denunciations of the "false consciousness" inherent in social amelioration reached a paroxysm.[52] Marxist political economy made this "head-in-the-sand" strategy theoretically possible, if not very credible. According to Guesdism's theorists, capitalism exerted "a mysterious force that laughs at all legislative measures seeking to limit its power."[53] More credibly, the Parti Ouvrier denied that bourgeois France would ever be willing, even if it were able, to integrate workers into the nation.[54] French Marxists refused to believe that the French nation-state of the belle epoque might represent anyone but the bosses. For the Parti Ouvrier, "so long as the bourgeoisie exists . . . the bourgeoisie will be the ruling class. The [national] government, whether a monarchy, an empire, or a republic, will serve the capitalists and oppress the workers."[55] The communitarian welfare-state—dependent on national solidarity, working to enhance that solidarity—presupposed concord between wealthy and poor, employers and employees, the ruling class and the masses. The Guesdists' entire conception of the capitalist order, by contrast, rested on class *conflict*. When French Marxists encountered the reformist ideal of "labor negotiating with capital, as equal to equal,"[56] the Parti Ouvrier denounced this emollient vision as "treason and delusion."[57] According to the Parti Ouvrier, "national solidarity" would always be frustrated by "the bestial egotism of the bosses."[58] When faced by reformists' plans for national arbitration authorities and national labor market regulation, outraged Guesdists responded with the war cry "Long live the liberation of the workers by the workers themselves!"[59]

If Guesdists grossly underestimated the welfare state's nationalizing force, they largely ignored the mass media. Yet the popular press had, by the fin de siècle, already assumed its paramount role in forging the modern political culture, not least by imposing nationalism on an increasingly all-encompassing "public sphere." Chauvinism, after all, has always fouled popular journalism, from the Crimean War's "jingoism" to the Falklands conflict's "Gotcha!" How, then, could Guesdists have so neglected the revanchist, militarist, and racist *Petit Journal*, when it outsold *Le Socialiste* twenty to one?[60] What might account for this astonishing failure to engage systematically with the "bourgeois press"—that ultimate instrument of false consciousness that has impelled today's "eclipse of class," with our society's endemic class conflict obscured by a swirling cloud of tabloids?[61]

The most obvious answer to this question is that the new mass-circulation dailies, with their virulent ultranationalism, had, at the fin de siècle, as yet made little impact on the working class, appealing instead to a largely petit-bourgeois readership. Before the eight-hour day and "affluence," most industrial workers had neither the time nor the resources for even the "penny press." Thus, in impoverished Roubaix, *Le Socialiste* could still compete with *Le Petit Journal.* Guesdism throve within a doomed milieu of pamphlets distributed through reading groups, of *journaux d'opinion* read collectively in cafés and workplaces, of public meetings attended as a major locus of popular entertainment. In the Marxists' own destitute domain, they had yet to confront the capitalist "culture industry" in all its monstrous might.

Mass education, by contrast, could not be ignored. By the end of the nineteenth century, primary schooling had been imposed on all France's children. Proletarian young people were now subjected to the disciplines and doctrines of the schoolmaster, and the Republican politicians who presided so proudly over this vast project of "public enlightenment" ensured that schools drilled students in nationalism as forcefully as in the "three Rs."[62] Well might the modern nation be described as "the dictatorship of the professoriat"![63] France's "secular" schools were, in fact, not only dictatorial, but deeply religious—teaching, in the words of the great Republican propagandist Paul Bert, the "religion of the motherland, that cult and conviction, at once passionate and reasoned, which we wish to inculcate into the heart and spirit of our children."[64] And malleable young hearts and spirits, by their millions, were indeed molded to the nationalist faith.

For the Guesdists, this "education" indoctrinated the working class with nationalist false consciousness. Confronted by the rise of ultranationalist politics during the early twentieth century, challenged by the "nationalist revival"[65] so tragically incarnate in the bellicose "generation of 1914," Guesdists angrily attributed the phenomenon to "the public instruction given to our children, to whom it is explained that all those born outside our frontiers are enemies, savages against whose attacks we must always be prepared."[66] As the nineteenth century ended, the Parti Ouvrier became uneasily aware how powerful this indoctrination could be. Commenting on the ultranationalist triumph in Paris during the 1900 municipal elections, when the great city shifted its allegiance from the radical Left to the chauvinist Right, *Le Socialiste* blamed the "fall of Paris" on "bourgeois politicians" who had "poisoned the population with . . . patriotism, the poisoning beginning at the youngest age, in the primary school."[67] During the mid-nineteenth century, revolutionaries had feared the policeman; at the fin de siècle, Guesdists dreaded the schoolmaster.

"That System of Blood and Filth": The Guesdists and Social Imperialism

According to recent Marxist theory, capitalism's "ideological state apparatuses" have been buttressed by "social imperialism"—that ever-popular strategy whereby ruling classes mobilize subalterns through imperialism, xenophobia, and war.[68] The belle epoque exemplified this project, as Europeans imbued their political cultures with the martial drama of parading soldiers, embodied their national identities in flags newly unfurled on exotic shores, and judged themselves against Darwinian measures of "national fitness" for combat. Transfixed by eye-catching uniforms and foreign adventure, many metropolitan proletarians succumbed to the time's ambient imperialism—abandoning class war for international competition, defining themselves against subjected colonial peoples rather than exploitative bourgeois, identifying themselves as a ruling race rather than as an oppressed class. Imperialist "othering," in turn, evoked the anti-imperialism of its "others." If English workers in Liverpool could be mobilized against the Irish, so Irish workers in Dublin (and Liverpool!) could be mobilized against the English. Marx and Engels themselves had realized, if only from their frustrating experience of "the Irish question," that both ruling nations and those they ruled, failing "national liberation," abjured social revolution.[69]

Fin de siècle France manifested "social imperialism" in both those counterrevolutionary dimensions. Like the Irish, the French viewed themselves as victims. The loss of Alsace-Lorraine to Germany, that unforgotten and unforgiven "mutilation of 1871," awarded French nationalists their most potent issue. At the same time, like the English, the French considered themselves an imperial people. French carpenters and French building contractors, French dockworkers and French shipping magnates, French peasants and French grain merchants—all were cohesively *French*, when challenged by rebellious Algerians who hated them all equally. Ethnic identity politics had originally, from Boulainviller in the eighteenth century until Gobineau in the nineteenth, separated classes *within* France, with Germanic aristocrats distinguished from Gallic commoners. By the fin de siècle, however, France's increasingly racialized identity effectively distinguished a unitary nation from alien neighbors and subjects—thereby extinguishing class war beneath race wars.[70]

The POF loathed this dialectic, hating the "hatreds that politicians and financiers use . . . to bring on international conflicts."[71] Guesdists depicted the fin de siècle's fevered chauvinism as mere bourgeois propaganda wielded by "ringleaders whose prime purpose is to provoke the working class to murder, to pillage, and to arson . . . against our neighbors across the frontier—our fellow citizens of tomorrow."[72] The Parti Ouvrier's consequent antimilitarism and anti-imperialism contrasted sharply with the tradition from which Guesdism had emerged: that of the bellicose Blanqui and the warlike Communards. Fin de siècle political culture witnessed a profound transformation, of which Guesdist pacifism was one striking manifestation. The Right, which had once feared war and imperialism as roads to revolution, instead recycled them as barricades against the Left. The Left, in turn, became increasingly pacifist, abandoning its century-old conflation of the "people armed against reaction" with the "people armed against the foreigner."[73]

Not that the Parti Ouvrier cared much for pacifism and anti-imperialism as such. According to French Marxists, warfare and empire were mere symptoms of a sickened and sickening capitalism. Guesdists intended to cure the disease. Socialism, they contended, was the only balm for war fever. According to the Parti Ouvrier's adherents, the POF was France's "party of peace," but only because it was also "the party of labor, of socialism and of revolution."[74] High-minded liberals who promoted capitalism while opposing war and imperialism were at best obtuse, at worst perfidious. Kant's vacuous dream of perpetual peace, Guesdists were sure, could only be realized through Marx's hardheaded program of socialist revolution.

Unfortunately for Marxist revolutionaries determined to extirpate capitalism's ills, imperialism has proven to be a particularly nightmarish challenge: a sort of metahistorical brain tumor—insidious, progressive, incurable, and eventually fatal. What Alvin Gouldner has described as "nightmare Marxism," Marxist theory that undermines faith in socialism's inevitability,[75] has focused acutely on the ways in which metropolitan workers can be corrupted by the "superprofits" of international "unequal exchange."[76] Workers, too, it transpires, may profit from exploitation, if they and their masters jointly exploit colonial "others." The Parti Ouvrier, however, resolutely resisted "nightmare Marxism." Guesdists never even hinted that French workers, as beneficiaries of empire, might benefit from being French.

Although French Marxists never developed Leninist insight into imperialist "labor aristocracies," they still reviled the French empire—denouncing it as a burden on metropolitan proletarians, as an atrocity committed against conquered peoples, and as a source of corrupt bourgeois profit. According to Guesdists, "theft, torture, and murder" were the real contents of imperialist "patriotism."[77] The POF mocked the imperialists' narcissistic argument that France embodied a "superior civilization destined to prevail"—an arrogant Eurocentrism characterized by Guesdists as "error, not only from a moral viewpoint, but from an ethnological perspective."[78] As empire, the Parti Ouvrier sneered, France's "superior civilization" manifested only "in Maxim guns, alcohol, opium, and venereal disease."[79] When confronted by anti-imperialist revolts, Guesdists foreshadowed the Third International's enthusiasm for "national liberation movements." Such revolts, the POF affirmed, were "a necessary phase through which all peoples must pass on the way to development."[80] When Egyptians or Malagasies revolted against imperialist marauders, Guesdists cheered.

The Parti Ouvrier remained absolutely true to its precept that

> internationalism is not, and cannot be, the subordination of one nation and the elevation of another, the sacrifice of one nationality to another, but rather

> the liberation, by the combined efforts of the workers and socialists of all lands, of all the fragments of a humanity finally united, thereby becoming a single united family.[81]

"Social imperialism" thus attained no purchase over the POF, in admirable contrast to, for instance, Hyndman's contemporary Social Democratic Federation. Convinced that workers would never be seduced by imperialist temptation, the Parti Ouvrier maintained the Second International's *pur et dur* faith in an "incorruptible working class and irreconcilable class struggle."[82] As a consequence of their own purity, however, Guesdists disregarded the many ways in which workers could indeed be corrupted by empire's wealth, pomp, and power. If French workers had been more immediately vulnerable to imperialist co-option, as British workers proved to be during the Boer War, the Parti Ouvrier's insouciance would have cost it dear.

The Parti Ouvrier's overly optimistic version of Marxism also generated systematic misreadings of the intersection between war and "bourgeois hegemony." Above all, the POF all too often assumed that bourgeois nationalism's trump card, patriotic solidarity during war, could never be played. According to Guesdists at their most naive, high explosives, rapid-fire small arms, and long-range rifled artillery had made warfare virtually unthinkable, even for the most ruthless of generals. In the Parti Ouvrier's prescient vision of future war, if the unthinkable were to actually happen, battlefields would be "slaughterhouses many kilometers square where hundreds of thousands of men will be massacred without glory and without heroism."[83] The Guesdists' error, having brilliantly foreseen the all-conquering mud and murder of the Somme, lay in believing that future Haigs would flinch from such horror.

Reinforcing their skepticism about the bogyman "war threat," Guesdists sometimes credited the old adage that war meant revolution. According to the Parti Ouvrier at its most optimistic, the social conservatives who ran the Third Republic would never dare to mobilize the "proletariat in uniform."[84] The mass conscript armies of the belle epoque, if mobilized, would march on capital. In a rather more complex, if equally optimistic, Guesdist understanding of the issue, warfare generated yet another "contradiction of capitalism." Going to war would indeed destroy capitalism, as armies mutinied against the social order. But *not* going to war would also ruin a bourgeoisie that depended on ever-escalating military expenditure, just as peace would fatally sap bourgeois regimes that relied on chauvinism.[85] In the authoritative formulation of the POF's National Council:

> We favor peace, peace to the limit, because it works to our advantage and against the capitalist domination that has to be destroyed and that is able to

> prolong its miserable and malignant existence only through divisions and antagonism between peoples. We favor peace because the bourgeois order is fated to die of it.[86]

Either way, through war or peace, socialism would win.

A darker vision shadowed this optimism, however. War would indeed lead to revolution, Guesdists were sure, but victorious socialists might inherit only ruins. "It's not just the bourgeoisie that will disappear in the catastrophe [of a modern war]," Charles Bonnier predicted gloomily, "but so too will all the still healthy elements that might serve us in the construction of a new society."[87] A nation traumatized by war, "its social edifice collapsed,"[88] would be the worst imaginable building site upon which socialists might raise their New Jerusalem. With such forebodings, as with their prefiguring of the Somme, the French Marxists prophesied impressively. What better representation could there be of the Bolsheviks' woeful legacy from the past, after Russia's devastating years of war and civil war, than that of a "collapsed society"?

Finally, at their most pessimistic, Guesdists very occasionally admitted that nationalist warmongering might actually work. Foreign wars, they conceded, offered capitalist regimes "their last chance to obviate the imminent social revolution."[89] If the gaunt specter of future war manifested as social imperialists hoped, "the social revolution might indeed be deferred to the Greek Calends."[90] Workers would fight workers, rather than combating capitalists; socialists would tear at socialists, rather than at bourgeois. Thirty years before Sarajevo, a prescient Guesde foresaw that "although the class war is the order of the day for proletarians everywhere, a European war would be fatal . . . as it would rupture [socialism's] necessary international unity."[91] August 1914 proved him right. Guesde himself, that doughty class warrior, joined France's all-party (and all-class) Government of National Defense, once he confronted German proletarians in *feldgrau* advancing on Guesdist Roubaix.

The nightmare of socialism-destroying warfare darkened further when the Parti Ouvrier decided that such conflicts inhered in the bourgeois order, that "war is to capitalism what cholera is to the Ganges Delta—a necessary effect."[92] In their bleakest analyses, French Marxists pointed out that

> the progress of capitalist production does not consist, as bourgeois idealists believe, in the pacification of conflict, nor in the establishment of harmony between interests. On the contrary, today each step forward leads us toward conflict.[93]

Why bourgeois bellicosity? In answering this question, Guesdists mobilized virtually every argument that Marxists have ever advanced to equate war with capitalism.[94] They regularly, of course, identified warfare as inherent in bourgeois nationalism, contending that "the idea of war" was linked "to that of patriotism, as cause and effect."[95] War justified nationalism, nationalism vindicated war—a self-reinforcing dialectic that the Parti Ouvrier indicted as a conspiracy to divert workers from class war toward war between nations. The "warfare state" thus apparently reinforced bourgeois hegemony far more effectively than the "welfare state" ever could. Guesdists could still dismiss the welfare state as utopian; they could hardly so dismiss the belle epoque's already fully realized militarism and imperialism.

In less conspiratorial analyses, Guesdists discerned a contradiction between the world's "forces of production" and "relations of production"—a contradiction that explained the dysfunctional international order. The disjuncture between hypertrophied modern production and antiquated private ownership, Guesdists argued, ensured interminable international crises. Great transnational companies trampled across the world market, but remained individually owned, as if they were still local firms. These behemoths stalked the earth, wreaking havoc wherever they trod, not least by collapsing the fragile edifice of international order.[96] Only their taming, their socialization, would restore harmony to the global economy, and thereby grant peace to a tormented world.

More often, however, the Parti Ouvrier obscured this globalizing perspective behind a critique of "national economics." Guesdists argued that war, or more specifically *preparation* for war, shored up national capitalisms otherwise doomed by the "falling rate of profit."[97] As local enterprises, industrial sectors, or entire economies exhausted their domestic investment opportunities, economic entropy doomed them to a lingering death. Armaments expenditure, however, promised a reprieve. According to this version of Marxist political economy, military spending opened final frontiers to locally confined capitalisms that had otherwise depleted their expansionary potential, but would wither without expansion. Governments poured wealth into armaments not so much to strengthen national defenses, but to resuscitate "national industry."[98] Governments risked war so that the their bourgeoisies did not risk bankruptcy.

The falling rate of profit also diverted domestic capital toward foreign opportunities, thereby launching "capital flight." Predatory investors hovered over the globe like vultures, driven from metropolitan markets by declining rates of return on capital, swooping upon every peripheral high-profit opportunity, only to quarrel furiously over the spoils, thereby provoking "financial wars"[99] between their sponsoring governments. At the same time, capitalists in mature economies engaged in an increasingly desperate search for external markets, as ruthless impoverishment of their own workers generated an unintended but inexorable decline in domestic demand and profitability.[100]

Responsive to their capitalist backers, "bourgeois states" thus sought to appropriate as much of the underdeveloped world as they could, with commercial wars the inevitable consequence. Challenged by the liberal contention that commerce meant peace, Guesdists riposted that "it's precisely commerce . . . that ignites war."[101] Only the triumph of socialism, the Parti Ouvrier contended, could short-circuit this diabolical dialectic between capitalist profit-seeking and international conflict, for "only then will disappear industrial and commercial competition between man and man and between nation and nation and thus war between peoples; . . . only then will peace and harmony reign between all the members of the great human family."[102] For French Marxists, international disorder manifested the "order" of capitalism

A severe critic would highlight the Guesdists' consequent unconditional adhesion to the *Primat der Innenpolitik*, indicting their reduction of international relations to socioeconomic relations.[103] French Marxists certainly repudiated the guiding premise of fin de siècle social imperialism: that the imperatives of international competition structured, and *should* structure, a nation's domestic politics. Unlike today's Marxists and post-Marxists, scarred as they have been by the "era of world wars," the Parti Ouvrier contemptuously dismissed this Clausewitzian conception. Not for Guesdists the *Primat der Aussenpolitik*. At the most, war lurked on the horizon of the Guesdists' worldview, at times profoundly menacing, sometimes implicitly autonomous of "class war," but never theorized in its own right, never understood as an independent historical variable.

Why this reductionism? Did the Guesdists' antinationalism determine their resistance to nationalist "realism" about war, or did their obliviousness to Clausewitzian insight command their antinationalism? The alternatives are not mutually exclusive: causality flowed smoothly in both directions, with the two causal currents greatly amplified by the relative tranquility of international relations during the Guesdists' heyday.[104] Nor were French Marxists altogether wrong in their philosophy of international relations. Who today denies that international order manifests social order? The "new history of international relations" conclusively demonstrates the overdetermination of diplomacy by the domestic realm.[105] Nonetheless, the brilliance with which the POF highlighted these realities blinded it to the many ways in which the international order in turn conditioned social order.[106]

In sum, Guesdist analyses of international affairs abounded with insight. Only the most shameless apologist for capitalism would dismiss linkage between disequilibria in the capitalist world-economy and the belle epoque's waxing diplomatic disorder. Armed and armored against each other by "national economics," the great powers of the fin de siècle *did* represent competing national capitalisms. Imperialism and the capitalist world-market *did* determine each other's fate through a potentially self-destructive dialectic.

The Parti Ouvrier's ideologists, however, never synthesized their many insights. Instead, their understanding was profoundly unstable, even self-contradictory—shifting from the conviction that capitalist modernity made large-scale warfare inconceivable, to arguments that capitalism necessarily marched off to war; oscillating between the assumption that war would bring the revolution, to apprehension that the burgeoning warfare-state had erected a near-impassable barrier against socialist advance.

"Militarism"—the mustering of young Frenchmen under a sword-bearing officer caste, the generalization of military values throughout the broader society—fascinated and frightened Guesdists quite independently of warfare itself.[107] French Marxists even suspected that France's soldiers were not intended to fight wars at all; that their real purpose was counterrevolution, not national defense; that the French army, "called the national army because it oppresses the nation,"[108] served only as a weapon against "the workers, who are the internal enemy."[109] Europe's armies armed themselves not against each other, *Le Socialiste* contended, but "against workers and socialists."[110] For Guesdists, the sight of parading soldiers did not evoke memories of the Army of the Loire heroically fending off Prussian invaders in 1870. Instead, tramping boots and ranks of fixed bayonets recalled the merciless Versaillais of 1871, advancing through the smoldering ruins of revolutionary Paris. The uniform—proudly donned by France's professional soldiers, and devoutly worshiped by France's professional nationalists—was worn, according to Guesdists, as a "livery of slavery and murder."[111]

The army's many imperial engagements during the belle epoque did nothing to reassure Guesdists. The vicious pacification of Tonkin, mass-murdering punitive expeditions in Madagascar, the periodic brutalization of restive Algerians—all were presented by Guesdists as training exercises for future metropolitan repression. The Parti Ouvrier opposed imperialism if only because "the generals of the ruling class, in our civil wars, will treat the French as they have treated the Arabs and the Mexicans."[112] This thesis stood uneasily against the Guesdists' alternative conviction that Europe's armies marched forth as "the proletariat in arms," that mobilization meant revolution. The POF, however, made a distinction between France's conscripted metropolitan forces and the largely professional colonial army, with the latter maligned as a saber in the hands of "the Cavaignacs, the Bréas, the Saint-Arnauds, the Espinasses, the Lamoricières, the Clinchants, and the Gallifets, those mass murderers of French republicans and revolutionaries."[113] France's ultranationalists unwittingly confirmed Marxist paranoia. After all, Maurice Barrès embodied his national-socialist ambitions for France in Marshal Gallieni—not despite but *because* of Gallieni's genocidal ferocity as Madagascar's military governor.[114] Guesdists had good reason for anxiety.

Their fears were intensified by the dire intuition that militarism—with its hierarchical, authoritarian, and ultranationalist values—modeled future capitalist regimes.[115] All France, Guesdists feared, might some day be marshaled onto a vast parade ground. Memories of the First and Second Empires amplified these fears. "Boulangers, like the Bonapartes," Guesde pointed out, were "born from the military."[116] The paramilitary leagues of the 1890s, and particularly the Ligue des Patriotes in its ultimate protofascist metamorphosis, reinforced the Guesdists' dread of militarized counterrevolution.[117] When confronted by Déroulède's martial project for France, by the LdP's program of disciplined internal unity and chauvinist mobilization against the alien, Guesdists warned that it augured reactionary regimes to come no less than harking back to nineteenth-century Bonapartist dictatorships. At their most prescient, Guesdists suggested that militarized autocracy might some day rescue the bourgeoisie from revolution, that "the supremacy of the army and the ferocious worship of the saber" would one day save "a social order [capitalism] that cannot exist without oppression and illusion."[118] These insights foreshadowed later Marxist critiques of fascism, some of the most trenchant of which were to link Mussolini and Hitler to Napoleon and Louis Napoleon.[119] Quaking before the prospect of neo-Bonapartism, Guesdists understandably detested the military and its repressive lineage. They dreaded the advent of a social order founded on militarism, "that system of blood and filth."[120]

Which is not to say that Guesdists themselves were completely immune to a certain "socialist militarism." After all, at the fin de siècle, genuinely "universal" conscription, shortening of the once punitive term of service, and more humane treatment of conscripts had transformed the once hated army into a genuine "school of the nation,"[121] and a school looked back on with nostalgia by some of its proletarian alumni. More specifically, the Nord—bastion of the industrial working class, and the Guesdists' own redoubt—had been horribly scarred by Prussian occupation during 1870–71. As community leaders, Guesdism's local luminaries had to conciliate their neighbors' militarized and sometimes militaristic traditions, as when Guesde himself spoke during a commemorative service at the war memorial of Croix, "saluting those who have died for the homeland."[122] The POF even sought to organize its own movement of socialist war-veterans![123] This attempt to appropriate the army for socialism featured strongly during the Guesdists' riposte during the mid-1890s against their electoral enemies, all of whom indicted the Parti Ouvrier as a cabal of traitors. Nonetheless, "militarism" remained a minor theme in the Parti Ouvrier's ideological repertoire, and one designed to recruit proletarian ex-soldiers more as proletarians than as soldiers.[124] The Parti Ouvrier's municipal "military manoeuvers" amounted to little more than support by Guesdist town councils for the families of serving reservists, families that otherwise suffered atrociously from the absence of breadwinners—"tricolor patriotism," according to *Le Socialiste*'s characteristic denigration of both the *tricolore* and patriotism, being "only interested in appropriating the head of the family, while installing misery and starvation in the home."[125] Even at their most militarized, French Marxists instinctively lapsed into antinationalism.

The Parti Ouvrier never experienced a Boer War, much less an equivalent of August 1914—episodes when militaristic ultranationalism prevailed triumphantly against Marxist cosmopolitanism. Nor did Guesdists dream that Barrèsian "national socialism" would mutate into a Europe-wide fascist movement that, for a brief bloodstained moment, would exterminate socialism across the continent. And they certainly never envisaged the wars between avowedly Marxist states that since the Soviet invasion of Hungary and the Sino-Vietnamese conflict have contributed so lethally to the "death of Marxism." Nonetheless, the Parti Ouvrier's uncertain engagement with its "age of empire" foreshadowed the agonized reassessment of Marxist certainties after 1914, suggested many of the contradictions between theory and practice that would first defeat and then destroy the Third International, and manifested confusions characteristic of recent "neo-Marxist" and "post-Marxist" encounters with capitalism's triumphant world-system. The POF's anti-imperialism and antimilitarism were admirable in principle, less so in performance.

Overall, then, the Guesdists' theorization of nationalism as bourgeois hegemony, for all its brilliance, suffered from systematic lacunae and instabilities. The POF failed to fully comprehend the many ways in which the modern nation-state, whether as welfare state or warfare state, integrated its citizens[126] into a undoubtedly "imaginary" but nonetheless cohesive community. Perhaps because the Guesdists believed that the "bourgeois state" would never serve anyone but bourgeois, perhaps because their understanding of politics still reflected the exclusive nineteenth century rather than the inclusive twentieth, they never correctly gauged the prevalence and potency of proletarian nationalism. More extensive exploration of social imperialism and better focused illumination of "ideological state apparatuses" awaited later generations of Marxist theorists. The resulting engagement has led away from Marx and toward Foucault, away from the Marxist critique of political economy, with its revelation of the "truth of regimes," and toward the Nietzschean deconstruction of disciplines that mold masses into (nationalist) "regimes of truth."[127] Marxists of the belle epoque, however, had not yet embarked on this theoretical adventure. Unlike today's post-Marxists, Guesdists still looked to Engels for guidance, not Nietzsche.

CHAPTER 3

"National Economics": Protection, Migrant Labor, and French Marxism

Marxists have reviled nationalism, and particularly working-class nationalism, as mere "false consciousness." But might it instead be an "authentic" aspect of modernity? Might even workers manifest "natural" nationalism? Some Marxist now agree with more eclectic theorists that both the "vertical affiliations" of nationhood and the "horizontal affiliations" of class are "normal" responses to modernity. According to this consensus, "imaginary" national communities are real enough—"materially" embodied as they are in the welfare state, the warfare state, and, not least, in "national economics."[1] Critics of the "false-consciousness" interpretation of nationalism thus portray nationhood as no less "natural" than class consciousness; nationalism as no less "authentic" than socialism—with the two ideologies everywhere conflicting, commingling, and even, at times, fusing into socialist nationalism.[2]

This dialectic has arisen within labor's own political economy. In workers' lived experience, the nation has been far more than a mere "imagined" community. Training and apprenticeship, employment and unemployment, workplace conditions and relations, occupational health and safety, invalidity and retirement—all have fallen into the protective embrace of the nation-state. This tightly regulated "nationalization" of the labor market has been far more evident in workers' day-to-day lives than the global mode of production that actually determines their class status. Bourgeois, *not* workers, have existentially "lived" globalization—buying and selling on global markets, globe-trotting themselves as they trace capital's international networks, constituted as individuals by a transnational class-culture of clothing, cuisine, leisure, friendship, and intermarriage. Few workers have experienced anything similar. For well over a century, the "workers of the world" have been far more "national" than the world's increasingly cosmopolitan bourgeois.[3]

Yet bourgeois too have sometimes been thoroughly "national." Marxists, of course, have usually argued that capitalism is preeminently, even exclusively, globalizing. But coexisting uneasily with this argument has been the alternative understanding that capital is *not* cosmopolitan, or at least that it is not consistently cosmopolitan. Marxists have even suggested that capitalism *necessarily* inhabits the nation-state—the provider of the "law and order" essential for contracts, the guarantor of the financial structures demanded by exchange, the builder of the infrastructure without which commerce would be impossible. Marx and Engels themselves viewed the nation-state as "a good thing," not because they were nationalists, but because nation-building empowered capitalist development, and thereby prefigured the transition to socialism. In the Marxist classics, bourgeoisies engendered modern nations, while the modern nation bolstered the bourgeoisie.[4]

Both the experience of proletarians and the needs of capitalists have thus empowered an all-embracing "national economics." Led to this conclusion, Marxists have nonetheless balked at its implications, if only because the very existence of a "national economy" militates against class conflict.[5] Employers and workers, capital and labor, bourgeoisie and proletariat—however the dyads are denominated, they manifestly share a common interest in "national development." A nation that prospers, nationalists have argued, offers prosperity to both capitalists and workers; an impoverished nation imposes poverty on both. Classes must collaborate for their nation's good! Outraged Marxists have refuted such class collaborationism by arguing that the supposed "national economic interest" is mere "bourgeois class interest." Dispossessed workers supposedly have no stake whatsoever in "their" national economy. Whether a capitalist nation be rich or poor, Marxists have insisted, its workers will suffer impoverishment.

This intransigence has rarely convinced. Today, all but the most dogmatic Marxists have conceded, however reluctantly, that workers indeed have a stake in their nation's prosperity. National affluence need not benefit the proletariat, as the proportion of a nation's wealth accruing to workers will always depend on labor's strength vis-à-vis capital. But national prosperity is a *necessary*, if not sufficient, condition of workers' well-being, as even the strongest working class will suffer from an impoverished economy.[6] Workers' resultant commitment to national prosperity, their complicity in "national economics," thereby integrates labor into both the capitalist social order and the nation-state.

Most Marxists thus no longer denigrate nationalism as mere "false consciousness," conceding instead that the nation is a "material" reality with its own grounding in the modern political economy.[7] Rather than surviving as a residue soon to be swept away by globalization, instead of persisting as an illusion soon to be obliterated by socialist enlightenment, nationhood, chastened Marxists acknowledge, will live on into the future. "Nationalism," they now admit, "has been as 'natural' a response to capitalism as socialism,"[8] and will endure as long as capital does—if not longer.

"The Chinese Walls of Patriotism": The Guesdists, Free Trade, and Protection

At the fin de siècle, Guesdists too could not ignore national economics. They would have liked to have done so, but their times were against them. The last decades of the nineteenth century witnessed France's transition from laissez-faire to protectionism—a transition paralleled throughout the capitalist world, apart from stubbornly free-trading Britain.[9] This mutation necessarily inflected Marxism's own development. The nascent Marxism of the mid-nineteenth century had been very much a product of Britain's "imperialism of free trade." Marx's cosmopolitanism, his devotion to an unmediated global perspective, and his repudiation of closed community all reflected the same mid-Victorian conditions and convictions that animated Cobden and Bright's free-trading liberalism. By contrast, the Marxism of the Second International had to accommodate itself to a novel (or resurrected) bourgeois political economy that had abandoned faith in the market's "invisible hand" for trust in the nation-state's highly visible iron fist—above all when the neomercantilist nation-state intervened against the free play of international exchange. Marxism's traditional cosmopolitanism hardly disappeared, but "inter-nationalism" increased its salience, and occasionally lapsed into full-fledged socialist nationalism.[10]

The mentalities imposed by "nationalizing" capitalism certainly suffused fin de siècle political culture. The French may have lagged behind imperial Germany in developing protectionist economic policies. They certainly lagged the Germans in formulating the solidaristic social programs associated with "Listian" national economics.[11] But France nonetheless followed the Reich, albeit some paces behind. Powerful interest groups had long resisted the free-trading policies initiated by the Second Empire's Cobden-Chevalier Treaty of 1860, and tariff policy had stalled during the 1870s and 1880s as protection stalemated laissez-faire. During the 1890s, however, protectionism triumphed—partly because the agricultural depression mobilized landowners behind protectionist industrialists, and partly because France's bourgeoisie discovered protection as a surety of social peace. By the 1890s, especially after the Méline tariffs of 1892, the well-being of "national industry" measured statesmen's status, France marshaled for trade wars as well as for war itself, while the French imagined their nation as a closed community of producers no less than as a collectivity of independent citizens.[12]

Fin de siècle protectionism, however, was as much about social defense as about economic policy. The alternative to protection, pundits opined, was "to lower the wages of workers, which is a serious and dangerous business."[13] The long deflation of the later nineteenth century indeed imposed reductions in nominal wages across Europe, with consequent labor unrest and working-class political mobilization. Free trade geared every economy into this global deflationary dynamic. Critics of laissez-faire, advocates of a protectionist political economy, nationalist economists—all tacitly accepted the Marxist assumption that unfettered world markets were thus everywhere reducing the price of labor power toward subsistence levels, and would thereby compel the world's workers toward world revolution. At the end of the nineteenth century, this apocalyptic vision darkened further. Commentators from across the political spectrum dreaded a future in which the newly industrializing Orient, with its vast labor reserves, would further impoverish European workers, eventually driving them to desperation.[14] According to the protectionists' zero-sum appraisal of the global market, employment for Osaka's textile workers meant sackings for Roubaisian operatives, Shanghai's prosperity implied Lille's impoverishment, unlimited labor supply in the Ganges Delta meant starvation wages across France. Neither French workers nor their employers were reassured by the laissez-faire litany that all was nonetheless for the best in the best of all possible (free-trading) worlds.

In contrast to the revolutionary risks of unconstrained globalization, protectionism supposedly guaranteed workers both secure jobs and a living wage. Capitalists who protected their markets (and their profits!) could protect their workforce against impoverishment, and thus protect themselves against proletarian revolution. Goodwill (at least toward conationals) fused with capitalist self-enrichment and bourgeois self-defense in an irresistible protectionist mélange.[15] The protofascist "national socialists" who flourished during the 1890s explicitly founded their class-collaborationist program upon this fusion of overt altruism with covert self-interest. The Ligue Antisémitique summed up national socialism's economics as the imperative "to protect 'national labor' without any distinction between social classes against . . . the competition of foreigners."[16] The ascendant Christian Democrats and even many among France's previously free-trading liberals and Radicals eagerly seconded this protectionist mandate.[17] France's "social problem," nationalists agreed, should be solved at the expense of foreigners, thereby restoring peace between France's classes. As the Méliniste journal *Le Travail National* emphasized, "protectionism is the best defense against socialism."[18]

French proletarians, at least in part, responded to protection as nationalists hoped they would.[19] Paradoxically, the breakneck expansion of the world economy during the belle epoque actually *accentuated* the proletariat's "nationalization." Roubaisian textile employees thrown out of work by cheap imports from Lodz felt little solidarity with Polish spinners and weavers; Lyonnais silk workers suffering from the burgeoning Italian export trade resented the Piedmontese proletarians who benefited from it. Many of France's unhappy workers thus backed their employers' pleas for protection against "unfair" foreign competition. Vosgian textile employees and Vosgian mill owners were equally

Méliniste; the ironmasters and the metalworkers of the Massif Central collaborated to protect their antiquated industry; sugar beet magnates and sugar-mill employees campaigned together against imported cane-sugar. "Material interest"—the hard realities of comparative prices and competing products, the even harder realities of bankruptcy and unemployment—drove the juggernaut of nationalist class-collaboration.

This juggernaut sometimes overran Marxist socialism. French workers readily blamed their ills on foreign competition—evident in everyday life, and comprehensible in everyday terms—rather than on the labyrinthine capitalist malignancies revealed by Marxism's abstruse value theory.[20] And the protectionists' diagnosis of those ills offered a reassuring "second opinion" to Marxism's daunting prescription. For many workers, protective tariffs promised an immediate surcease to their suffering, compared to the uncertainty of socialism's revolutionary surgery. The workers of the world united less readily in 1900 than they had in 1848. They had their tariffs to lose.

How did Guesdists respond to this challenge to their cosmopolitan socialism? With consternation. They worked desperately to devalue the debate between protection and free trade, fully understanding its class-collaborationist potential. Once protection became the issue, French Marxists feared, both protectionist workers and their free-trading fellows would align themselves with their employers rather than with each other. Given the malign logic of economic nationalism, the cotton manufacturers and textile workers of the Nord would unite against low-price competition from Poland, while employers and employees in the Parisian luxury trades would combine to maintain an open world market for their incomparable products.[21] Class war would succumb to tariff wars and wars over tariffs.

Class collaboration, from the Guesdists' perspective, was not necessarily the worst part of the matter. Not only might workers and employers unite, but France's protectionist workers could be set at daggers drawn with their free-trading "comrades." In the Guesdists' worst nightmares, they imagined a civil war between workers in France's protectionist industrial cities and workers in free-trading "commercial and maritime towns, such as Le Havre, Bordeaux, Marseille."[22] For a Marxist movement that was above all else dedicated to working-class solidarity, international tariff wars (dividing French from foreign workers) and domestic wars over tariffs (dividing the French proletariat) were utter anathema.

The Parti Ouvrier's most common reaction to these twin nightmares—the nightmare of class collaboration between "nationalized" capitalists and workers, the nightmare of conflict between protectionist and free-trading proletarians—was to ridicule trade policy as corrupt bourgeois business. "When [bourgeois] need protection, one speaks of national labor, when it's really just a matter of a couple of industrialists who fear foreign competition," Charles

Bonnier commented cynically. "But, when it's a matter of their exports, of their financial affairs, then free trade reigns supreme."[23] Socialists and workers, Guesdists sternly advised, should shun self-interested bourgeois debates over trade.

Advice that was easy to give, but difficult to take. French workers, if protectionists, cared too intensely about their firm's viability within a globalizing economy or, if free traders, worried too much about their industry's future when constrained by "national" economics for French Marxists to delete protection from the proletarian agenda. Driven by polemical imperatives, impelled by their constituents' immediate economic concerns, Guesdists themselves reluctantly entered into the bitter debates that swirled about protectionism. When thus engaged, they usually replicated Marx's bias in favor of free trade.[24] They indicted protection as profoundly regressive, as a "return to the barbaric epoch when each nation, each locality, had to limit its needs to what it could produce itself."[25] French Marxists drew dispiriting pictures of life without global exchange. Diets would be boring and unhealthy, clothing rudimentary and inadequate, industry little more than the local blacksmith and the village potter. In their free-trading persona, Guesdists contended that protectionists "wounded the just interests of other peoples, oppressed and robbed our own, and impeded the overall development of humanity."[26]

"The overall development of humanity" . . . French Marxists knew very well that the modernity they cherished, the modernity of worldwide progress and universal humanism, depended on ever-expanding globalization, and they fully accepted Marx's enthusiastic portrayal of capitalism's world-spanning civilizing mission.[27] According to *Le Socialiste*,

> [I]f we revolutionary communists regard with indifference the oratorical jousts between protectionists and free traders, we nonetheless hope for the triumph of the latter. We know that free trade generalizes and intensifies working-class misery, [but it also] . . . unifies nations once barricaded behind the Chinese walls of patriotism, . . . and creates in every country a proletariat having the same needs and the same aspirations to liberation.[28]

Free trade universalized bourgeois exploitation, but also cosmopolitan solidarity. Capitalist globalization, Guesdists were sure, augured global socialism.

The Parti Ouvrier's most common critiques of protectionism, however, cited not its metahistorical malignancy but its malign effect on France's consumers. For the POF, protection, as "a tax on bread,"[29] simply increased the cost of food for working-class shoppers. This opposition to *agricultural* protection came easily to Guesdists. Damning the protectionists' exclusion of cheap American grain, cheap Argentinean meat, and cheap Caribbean sugar diverted attention from the question of industrial tariffs, which genuinely divided the POF's working-class constituency—*every* member of which, however, yearned for cheap bread, low-price beef, and inexpensive confectionary. At the same time, the Parti Ouvrier, in campaigning against agricultural protection, ran no risk of alienating its rural constituency. Guesdism had few, if any, supporters among the protectionist wheat, cattle, and sugar-beet growers of the northern plains—most of them prosperous farmers, many of them agrarian capitalists. The Parti Ouvrier mustered its rural supporters among the small-scale mixed-crop farmers of the Midi, themselves vulnerable to escalating grain, beef, and sugar prices. To the POF's pleasure, its polemicists found that they could easily unite peasants and proletarians against what they called a Méliniste "famine pact."[30]

Some of the Parti Ouvrier's arguments, however, transcended such simple consumerism. On occasion, indeed, Guesdists echoed Ricardo's splendid free-trading polemics. In one such instance, Lafargue analyzed the costs of protecting the iron and steel industry, pointing out that exclusionary tariffs greatly increased metal prices for France's beleaguered engineering industry. Cosseted ironmasters, however, could win external markets through dumping their product abroad—a strategy that advantaged no one except a few predatory French metallurgical companies and, ironically, *foreign* engineering firms.[31] France as a whole suffered terribly by thus violating the laws of comparative advantage. Reflecting Marxism's origin in classical political economy, Guesdists here seconded France's dwindling coterie of Manchesterian liberals.

Nonetheless, the Guesdists' free-trading principles sometimes wavered. At times willing to sacrifice theory to polemic, the Parti Ouvrier appropriated protectionist rhetoric for its own socialist purposes. The POF could be found berating capitalists for jeopardizing the "national interest," with Guesdists mocking "patriotic bosses who don't show the slightest repugnance when profiting from foreign goods at the expense of the products of their own country."[32] At their most innocuous, such polemics simply demonstrated that bourgeois nationalists were hypocrites; at their most insidious, they implied socialist protectionism. This implication very occasionally became explicit, particularly when evoked by "capital flight." In Lafargue's plaintive words, for instance: "[I]f the billions invested elsewhere had remained in France and served to develop our industrial and agricultural technology, French workers would have at least some chance of recovering their stolen wealth on the day when they seize power and expropriate the capitalists."[33] Lafargue's fantasy of financial autarchy paralleled the protectionist musings of French industrialists, who dreamed of replacing Paris's cosmopolitan merchant banks with nationally orientated "industrial investment banks."[34]

Guesdists even fell foul of that ultimate protectionist nightmare: Asian industrialization. Imagining Chinese economic development during the upcoming twentieth century, *Le Socialiste* shuddered. "No taxes, abundant manpower at low prices, lots of raw material, and steam engines! Tomorrow, China will inundate Europe with its inordinately cheap products."[35] In this version of the "yellow peril," French workers were not so much threatened by imported "coolie labor" as by that same coolie labor beavering away in the teeming slums of Shanghai.[36] Guesdists well understood how capitalists could exploit such international differentials to justify low and falling wages, thereby turning the workers of the world against each other. Such exploitation ensured that "in this universal divisiveness, proletarians everywhere become the only barrier to raising or even maintaining salaries. Workers end up impoverishing each other."[37] Might protection short-circuit this "universal divisiveness"? In the POF's most cosmopolitan persona, it refused such solutions in favor of a worldwide socialist commonwealth. But lying behind this cosmopolitanism lay the twisted shadow of proletarian protectionism.

"A Jealous and Hostile Mob": Immigrant Workers, Guesdists, and Xenophobia

To an even greater extent than protection, immigration powered the ascent of working-class national economics in fin de siècle France, as hundreds of thousands of foreign laborers "invaded" the country.[38] This invasion lacked the grandeur of 1870 or 1914, but nonetheless evoked its own chauvinist hysteria, provoked resistance movements, and wrote its casualty lists. Surveying the battlefields of the French labor market, xenophobes were sure that the invaders were winning. By the 1880s, in the depths of depression, foreign labor already furnished 7 or 8 percent of France's workforce. And, as the economic boom of the later 1890s coincided with France's demographic stagnation, the figure rapidly increased to 10 percent, the highest level in Europe. By the early twentieth century, an "invasion force" of 1,150,000 foreign workers had penetrated France[39]—with Spaniards bivouacking in the vineyards of Languedoc, Belgians consolidating their entrenchment throughout the northern textile industry, and Italians infiltrating the mines and steelworks of Lorraine. According to a racist like Gustave Le Bon, this silent invasion was more frightful than the worst defeats inflicted by marauding armies.[40] Other nationalists agreed. "The foreigner," Barrès trumpeted, "is poisoning us."[41]

This human wave from abroad overwhelmed Guesdist bastions across industrial France, and undoubtedly shifted the balance of class forces in favor of capital. Virtually unlimited Belgian labor in Roubaix, for instance, imposed a cutthroat local labor market "as close as anyone could come to an ideal Marxist scheme of capitalist exploitation."[42] Capital's "reserve army of labor" in Roubaix's region consisted of mercenaries, not conscripts, with Belgian immigrants composing fully a quarter of the Nord and Pas-de-Calais's workforce.[43] The flexibility of such imported labor stabilized French capitalism and increased employers' rate of return on capital. During booms, foreign workers reduced domestic wage pressure; during busts, immigrant workers were repatriated, loading the costs of crisis onto noncitizens.[44] And, whether boom or bust, immigrant laborers weakened trade unions (their transience, vulnerable legal status, and linguistic disabilities discouraged organization) and broke strikes (without community attachments, they were easily recruited as strikebreakers)—thereby earning them an unenviable sobriquet as "the providence of struck factories."[45] Witness the heroic ten-month glassworkers' strike at Rive-de-Gier during 1894, one of the great battles of fin de siècle labor militancy—smashed by the company's recruitment of *German* strikebreakers![46] Finally, on the rare occasions when immigrant workers mobilized against French employers, they often did so by forming their own associations. Yiddish-speaking clothing workers in Paris exemplified this separatism, organizing their own exclusive union and supporting the particularist Bundism of their Russian origin.[47] Even immigrants' *militancy* weakened working-class solidarity!

Given such circumstances, xenophobic invective suffused proletarian discourse. Enraged labor militants even vilified thoroughly *French* strikebreakers as "Italians"![48] Embittered by their subjection to an increasingly global labor market, France's "native" workers ferociously resisted "alien" threats to their precarious well-being, concentrating their fear and fury on vulnerable foreign laborers rather than on the well-protected French capitalists who imported them. Intercommunal conflict increased in proportion to the swelling influx of immigrants, sometimes culminating in mayhem and murder.[49] As the violence escalated, even the Parti Ouvrier could not completely discount bloody incidents like the massacre of Italian salt workers at Aigues-Mortes. Guesdists would have *preferred* to ignore such terrifying events, but, in the end, had to take them seriously indeed. Communities that mobilized against foreigners, disheartened Marxists recognized, defied socialist mobilization.[50]

The rampant national socialists of the belle epoque certainly battened on the "defense of national labor." Their ugly travesty of the national anthem turned ethnic cleansing into an employment program:

> Go home foreigners,
> That'll give us some work
> And put up our wages.
> Chase out of the country
> The whole gang of Yids.[51]

What a contrast between this protofascist *Marseillaise Antijuive* and the Guesdists' *Internationale*! At every turn, sour xenophobia empowered the national socialists' assault on Marxism. The Ligue des Patriotes' bitterly anti-Marxist "new nationalism" owed much of its ascendancy during the "Great Depression" to labor protectionism, as desperate French workers blamed immigrants for their suffering. Later, during the 1890s, Barrèsian national socialism and the political anti-Semitism patronized by Drumont ruthlessly exploited working-class xenophobia, not least to turn workers against the cosmopolitan Parti Ouvrier. And, at the beginning of the twentieth century, the violently anti-Marxist "Yellow" trade unions became synonymous with hostility to immigrants.[52] Proletarians bellowing "La France aux Français!" everywhere challenged others chanting "Workers of the World, Unite!" The protofascists' class collaborationism was founded on anti-immigrant sentiment. "French capital stands shoulder to shoulder with the French worker," trumpeted Maurice Barrès (against all the evidence), "not with [the foreign] worker."[53] From the Boulanger crisis to the Dreyfus affair and beyond, demagogic abuse of foreign workers served national socialists well—mobilizing the working class against the nation's enemies, rallying workers behind the "national" revolution against the liberal Republic, and marshaling the proletariat behind capitalism against Marxism. French Marxists understandably dreaded this ultranationalist "dupery and reaction."[54]

Worse yet, socialism and xenophobia sometimes met and merged, to the Parti Ouvrier's horror. Boulangist labor militants of the late 1880s had passionately demanded "French jobs for the French!"—the quasi-socialist Left Boulangists' variant of "La France aux Français!"[55] Their passion survived Boulanger. Mine workers' murderous attacks on Belgian immigrants in the Pas-de-Calais during 1892 were organized by the socialist (albeit anti-Guesdist) municipality of Liévin, and the French perpetrators of this "ethnic cleansing" actually denounced their victims as *l'armée de réserve du capital* (the reserve army of capitalism)—echoing Marxist terminology, if not Marxist cosmopolitanism. Worse yet, when an Italian anarchist assassinated the French president, workers in Voiron rioted against local Italians while flaunting the red flag![56] Class mobilization and xenophobic militancy were not as mutually exclusive as the Parti Ouvrier liked to think. Its own rhetoric and symbolism could be mobilized by others against "aliens."

Sadly, Guesdists themselves very occasionally succumbed to xenophobia. In one shameful instance the POF, for instance, presented immigrant workers as "a jealous and hostile mob which, . . . having lived off us and spied on us, will return arms-in-hand."[57] Succumbing to the dominant nationalist metaphor, *Le Socialiste* even described the influx of foreign workers as "an invasion" that might benefit individual employers, but which was enormously damaging not only to French workers, but to "French industry" (a nationalist category that rarely surfaced in Guesdist discourse). Immigrants, the newspaper charged, would eventually return home, revealing "the secrets of our technology to our foreign competitors."[58] Antoine Jourde—the Parti Ouvrier parliamentarian from the Gironde, and always the most nationalist of Guesdists—actually proposed a total ban on foreign labor, a ban that he hoped would be backed by the entire workers' movement, including his own POF.[59]

Jourde was to be disappointed. The Parti Ouvrier, and certainly Guesde himself, never dreamed of expelling foreign workers.[60] The movement's authorized spokesmen, in fact, violently opposed such exclusion, always rejecting it in their capacity "as internationalists not wishing to distinguish between proletarians, whatever their origins."[61] Indeed, at their most internationalist, French Marxists simply refused to recognize that there could be such beings as "foreign" workers, given that proletarians everywhere shared a common citizenship in the world of labor. This stubborn cosmopolitanism enjoyed some contemporaneous currency. The concept of an "immigrant" worker, at the fin de siècle, had, after all, only recently crystallized among proletarians and employers—mid-nineteenth-century social mentalities having made few distinctions between "French" and "foreign" within the *classe laborieuse*. National distinctions may have been clearly apparent to the "nationalized" elite, but these ethnic subtleties were applied largely within and between the midcentury's nationalized elites, not to the supposedly amorphous and nationally indistinguishable "masses." Working-class mentalities had reinforced such bourgeois prejudice. In Marx's Paris of the 1840s, for instance, trade solidarity had bonded German compositors to their French fellows, while originary identities had sundered Auvergnat laborers from equally "French" Bretons. "France" had meant little to both employers and employees during those years before the creation of a genuinely "national" labor market.[62] The Guesdists' presumption that the working class lacked national definition thus resonated with residual nineteenth-century reality.

The belle epoque had imposed new realities, however. On those occasions when the POF had to concede that, by the fin de siècle, immigrant workers *did* possess a distinctive identity, Guesdists almost always empathized with them, sympathetically pointing out that foreign workers had been recruited "into the most repugnant and dangerous of jobs."[63] How could French workers denigrate, much less exclude, laborers who labored at tasks the French themselves repudiated? Apart from thus recognizing foreign workers' sad condition, the POF sympathized with their political dilemma. If immigrants seconded French labor militancy, employers would have them expelled; if they refused to participate in strikes, their fellow workers would ostracize them.[64] An impossible choice!

For the POF, then, the immigrant worker was no less the innocent victim of capital than the native workers whose jobs he jeopardized. He was characterized as

> isolated, most often without his family, ignorant of even the language and customs of the country to which he is brought, and thus unable to defend himself. This factory-fodder from Belgium, Italy, Germany, Switzerland—and they haven't given up dreams of China—is perfect for French employers, who can exploit it at will without fearing resistance.[65]

Instead of advocating the exclusion of this "factory-fodder," Guesdists embraced it. As the Parti Ouvrier patiently explained to France's anxious workers, low wages and poor conditions were inflicted by capitalist malignancy, not by the foreigners' feeble competition. According to *Le Socialiste*, "[T]he expulsion of the 300,000 foreigners who work in France [an indicative underestimation] will have absolutely no effect on the precarious situation of our nationals."[66] Whatever France's labor force, whether it was ethnically homogenous or nationally diverse, capitalism would drive wages toward their subsistence minimum.[67]

Abandoning this gloomy Lassalleanism, Guesdists sometimes argued (not unlike their laissez-faire liberal enemies) that French workers actually *benefited* from immigration. How so? Immigrants, the POF contended, enhanced domestic production (French capitalists, if deprived of their labor, would certainly decamp to foreign shores) while expanding the domestic market (immigrants not only produced, but consumed). In a vivid illustration of this argument, *Le Socialiste* imagined "a city with a hundred thousand foreign workers out of its four hundred thousand people, like Marseille, which saw all the foreigners disappear overnight"—a catastrophe that "the inhabitants would find dreadful, as the resulting void, inflicting great harm on trade by the lack of both consumers and producers, would make them wish to flee the place as if it were a damned city."[68] French workers, the Parti Ouvrier insisted, should welcome immigration, if they knew what was good for them.

Not that Guesdist polemic relied on such immediate self-interest, if only because depicting immigrants as profitable producers and willing consumers replicated the sordid motives of the governments that presided over France's liberal (in both senses of the word) immigration policy. Instead, ready as always to ascribe the characteristics of the proletariat's militant minority to the entire working class, Guesdists attributed their own principled antinationalism to all French workers, who supposedly "disdained the barbarous prejudices of race and nationality,"[69] who "never asked for the passport of any worker before opening their ranks to him and making room for him at their side."[70] Confronted by the xenophobic labor league "La France aux Français," *Le Socialiste* rhapsodized that

> from one end of France to the other, French and foreign workers are tightening their bonds, sharing drinks together, every day. The hatred that suppos-

> edly divides them is a myth, for the workers are becoming increasingly conscious of their interests which only unity can lead to triumph, and all the Leagues in the world won't be able to divide them from each other: they are marching in greater and greater accord toward their common emancipation.[71]

Most Guesdists, most of the time, thus pretended that their own cosmopolitanism typified the French working class as a whole. In the very midst of the nationwide anti-Italian rioting attendant on Caserio's assassination of President Loubet, *Le Socialiste* brazenly asserted that "no socialist worker, no trade unionist, will perceive an Italian [worker] as an enemy, but rather as a brother in suffering."[72]

This assumption had some contemporary grounding. Skilled foreigners *did* assimilate easily into the French working class, and were in turn easily accepted by their French fellow workers. It was the immigrant subproletariat that repulsed, and in turn was repulsed.[73] German compositors in Paris and Belgian glassblowers in Carmaux were indeed soon exchanging drinks with their French comrades, even while Italian street-sweepers and Spanish grape-pickers were being harried from their hovels. Given that French socialism recruited its militants among craftsmen and skilled workers, the Guesdists' fantasy that French workers were generously inclusive made some sense—at least to such militants. Over a million naturalizations during the belle epoque undoubtedly manifested ready assimilation. Guesde himself, with his Italian wife, would have understood such *réenracinement* at its most intimate.[74]

Nonetheless, some immigrant laborers *did* break strikes, and some French workers *did* murder their foreign "comrades." Most immigrants, after all, were not skilled workers busily assimilating into their working-class communities, but transient unskilled laborers driven from pillar to post by uncaring employers and hostile fellow workers. These unfortunates were administered in a two-tier labor hierarchy carefully designed to privilege the French at the expense of the foreign, when not using the foreign to challenge the privileges of French workers.[75] The results of such privileging, and its challenging, were utterly predictable, and often sanguinary. How, then, did the Parti Ouvrier understand the bloody violence that so frequently sundered French from immigrant workers?

The French Marxists' favorite polemical strategy, apart from blissful ignorance, reduced intercommunal quarrels to trivial local exceptions proving the cosmopolitan rule. After all, Guesdist journalists assured their readers, "the foreigners who drive down wages are a tiny minority. And if the foreign colony provides its quota of traitors ready to submit to the capitalists, then there are . . . French who do the same."[76] But French Marxists could not really dismiss affrays like the Aigues-Mortes massacre as "regrettable conflicts that hardly have the importance attributed to them,"[77] although the Parti Ouvrier strove to diminish even that calamity. When unable to ignore or devalue such atrocities, Guesdists denied that workers committed them. According to the Parti Ouvrier, for instance, vagrant "lumpenproletarians" had murdered the Italians at Aigues-Mortes, not "real" workers—an evasion that maintained the long Marxist tradition of attributing proletarian sins to the polymorphous lumpenproletariat.[78]

In sum, apart from the Parti Ouvrier's very few and utterly aberrant outbursts of xenophobia, the movement interpreted France's "invasion" by immigrant labor with characteristic cosmopolitanism. Foreign workers, Guesdists maintained, posed absolutely no threat to French workers—first, because the proletariat's sad lot was inflicted by universal capitalism rather than by immigrant invaders, and, second, because French and "foreign" workers would soon bond as friends and comrades. These theses had enough credibility to sustain decades of Guesdist polemic. But, overall, on this issue, French Marxists spun fantasies founded on socialist hope, not analyses based on galling national experience.

"The Guilty Party": Global Capitalism and Parochial Workers

Guesdists, however, sometimes abandoned their comfortable fantasyland, conceding the repugnant prevalence of working-class xenophobia. On the occasions when French Marxists admitted that French workers *did* ostracize foreigners, how did the Parti Ouvrier construe this unhappy phenomenon, which so flatly contradicted the movement's cosmopolitan faith in worldwide working-class solidarity?

The POF usually responded to working-class xenophobia by pleading with anti-immigrant workers to come to their senses, to realize that they were acting "against their own class for the greater profit of the bosses."[79] Workers injured themselves when they injured immigrants; only bosses benefited, adding welcome working-class divisiveness to the superprofits extorted from immigrant labor. Lapsing into their paranoid mode, Guesdists ascribed working-class xenophobia to bourgeois manipulation. "Employers," contended the Party's *Programme*, "encourage the divisions and hatreds that . . . arise between workers of different nationality, as these conflicts prevent any combination for the defense of the workers' labor power."[80] If bourgeois benefited, Guesdists insisted, bourgeois must be responsible.

French Marxists deployed this argument in several directions. Above all, the POF alleged that the ruling elite manipulated conflict between French and foreign workers to antisocialist advantage.[81] *Le Socialiste* contended, for instance, that the "official" press encouraged French chauvinism as a response to incidents like the Aigues-Mortes massacre.[82] However dedicated that press may have been to liberal orthodoxy, including capital's right to import workers from the cheapest labor pool available, whether French or foreign, stuffy journals like *Le Temps* and *L'Economiste Français* still slyly inflamed the ethnic conflicts consequent on such importation. These establishment journals could then deride Marxism's picture of the "workers of the world uniting" as a vacuous myth conclusively disproved by "reality." The Guesdists' furious response to this anti-Marxist maneuver indicated their sensitivity to such derision.[83] If bourgeois ideologists were right, if the Marxists' supposedly monolithic proletariat indeed fractured easily along ethnic fault lines, then the Parti Ouvrier's perspective on the past, its politics of the present, and its faith in the future were all compromised, even exploded.

Guesdists convinced themselves that successive governments had encouraged, even created, just such fractiousness. The Parti Ouvrier bitterly pointed out that the "bourgeois state" banned foreign membership in French unions, thereby precluding interethnic labor solidarity, while exempting foreign workers from social security contributions, thereby pitting them against more expensive French workers.[84] And employers who imported German or Italian strikebreakers could count on the immigration authorities, Guesdists cynically noted. Residency permits would always be forthcoming. A frontier hermetically sealed against itinerant socialist speakers would be open to hungry job-seekers, while immigrant workers recruited into the French socialist movement would be unceremoniously expelled from France. From the Guesdists' jaundiced viewpoint, the frontier that defined the nation-state served the bourgeoisie by dividing workers from each other, both internationally *and* domestically. Labor laws, employment regulations, immigration rules—all had but one end: "to divide the proletariat, arming some against the others, in order to dominate and exploit them all more easily and more profoundly."[85]

Guesdists, however, reviled not so much capitalism's agents as capitalists themselves. Neither scheming ministers nor lying newspapers actually *created* interethnic conflict, according to the POF. Instead, employers themselves fomented the sanguinary episodes that punctuated relations between French and immigrant workers. Guesdists argued that capitalists, however nationalist in principle, necessarily practiced cosmopolitan labor recruitment. According to Guesde, "[L]owering the price of labor must be the supreme law . . . so that it is not only permitted but commanded, where the labor of Italians or Spaniards is offered more cheaply, to employ that labor at the expense of the stomachs of nationals."[86] Confronted, for instance, by the murderous conflict between French and Belgian miners at Liévin during 1892, the POF furiously concluded that

> the guilty party is not . . . the foreigners who, evicted by famine from their unnurturing homeland, go to where there's bread and, in order to eat, will

> work at any price, nor the locals who, thus challenged, defend as they can an already insufficient salary. Those who are responsible in the first place, the real and direct assassins, are the bosses who . . . in order to increase their profits, buy at cut-rate a labor force from beyond the Alps, beyond the Pyrenees, or beyond the Vosges; it's the capitalists who . . . make use of misery abroad . . . to create misery at home.[87]

The Parti Ouvrier had a point. In its redoubt of Roubaix, the movement confronted employers who thrived by importing Belgian *frontaliers* (daily commuters across the virtually nonexistent border) while at the same time basing their local political hegemony on exploitation of the resultant ultranationalism among impoverished French workers—an "irony" that, as one of these capitalists' celebrants has commented, they "probably enjoyed."[88] Capitalism's cosmopolitan dynamic, coupled with bourgeois manipulation, thus fractured the working class, with workers negotiating the intricacies of the French labor market as proletarian Frenchmen or proletarian foreigners, but *not* as proletarian "workers of the world."

In the Parti Ouvrier's laceratingly realist moments, it recognized these "objective" causes of intercommunal conflict. The global labor market, Guesdists reluctantly concluded, "naturally" pitted low-wage immigrants against the "native" workers they displaced. Marx, after all, had himself bemoaned the division between "aristocratic" English artisans and "lumpen" Irish laborers, and the Guesdists' own period witnessed the massive creation of ethnic "labor aristocracies"—not least as a continental elite in the workers' "utopia" of Australia (with its exclusionary "white Australia policy"), as race-war unionism in the United States (with its increasingly ethnicized working-class stratification), and as a privileged caste within the nascent racist polity of South Africa (with its separate and grossly unequal white and black working classes).[89] Lille and Lyons were not Liverpool or Melbourne, much less San Francisco or Cape Town, but the Guesdists, like English, Australian, American, or South African socialists, nonetheless themselves encountered intraclass conflict manifest as ethnic exclusion, and were well aware of the miserable British, Australian, and American experiences (although not, apparently, of the South African). In coming to terms with these sad realities, the French Marxists contrasted the mobility of capital with the vulnerability of labor, and demonstrated that, while the world market ensured bourgeois cosmopolitanism, it divided the world's working class. In France itself, "bosses make foreign workers starve French workers," thereby inciting "hatreds that politicians and financiers use . . . to bring on international conflicts."[90] Guesdists thus attributed working-class xenophobia to the very capitalist globalization that otherwise supposedly guaranteed proletarian cosmopolitanism.

When French Marxists acknowledged this dire dynamic, they sometimes shifted gears from revolutionary exhortation to reformist pragmatism.

In this mode, Guesdists proposed a minimum wage that would "put an end to the [ethnic] conflicts that so often bloody our construction sites. Peace will thus be restored within the great family of workers."[91] Building contractors would no longer preferentially hire cheap foreigners, since they would no longer be cheap, while French and foreign laborers could unite in concord. At the same time, Guesdists demanded a shorter working week. If work were more equitably shared, they hoped, competition between French and foreigners would cease.[92] As Lafargue put this recurrent theme, "[A]s soon as there is enough work, and wages that allow one to survive while working, no proletarian will think of demanding the expulsion of foreign workers."[93] French Marxists even imagined the universalization of this solidaristic regime. If France adopted it, would not other nations follow suit? "Once internationally implemented," the Parti Ouvrier hoped, equal pay for native and immigrant workers everywhere would "ensure that all workers, without distinction of race, will enjoy the full fruits of their labor."[94] Internationally agreed-upon labor laws "would put an end to today's hatreds," given that French workers attacked foreign laborers only because immigrant workers "despite themselves . . . depress wages."[95]

A standard wage for French and foreign workers and a reduction in working hours, however, would not entirely solve the problem of intercommunal labor conflict, as employers would still hire immigrants by preference, given that foreign workers had no right to labor organization, and incurred no social-security costs. The POF challenged these divisive distinctions, urging, for instance, the extension of employer liability to foreign victims of French industrial accidents. Such coverage would eliminate one of the major labor market "advantages" of immigrant workers. At the same time, Guesdists campaigned energetically against the law barring foreign workers from participating in strikes or organizing unions.[96] If foreigners entered the French labor market on fully equal terms, Guesdists predicted, conflict between immigrants and natives would soon cease.

Troubling ambiguities clouded these reformist plans. First, did the Parti Ouvrier hope that their achievement would exclude foreign workers from the French labor market? Probably not. *Le Socialiste* never suggested that protecting immigrants from poverty wages would also protect French workers from immigrants. The Parti Ouvrier's proletarian constituency, however, might well have read an exclusionary agenda into proposals to strip immigrant workers of the "advantages" that made them so employable. And, on one occasion, the exclusionary cat was let out of the cosmopolitan bag. Antoine Jourde, so often the limit case of Guesdist nationalism, happily noted that "the day when employers are obliged to pay foreign workers the same salary as they pay our nationals . . . our people ["our people," French employers!] will prefer to hire Frenchmen rather than foreigners."[97] In this startling instance, admittedly a wild aberration in the POF's record, Jourde lapsed unequivocally from revolutionary cosmopolitanism into class-collaborationist nationalism.

There was a second, and more significant, ambiguity: Guesdists (apart from the egregious Jourde) never really took their own "reformism" very seriously. When pressed, the POF always repudiated the very possibility of ameliorative reform. According to the Parti Ouvrier's rigorous conception of the bourgeois order, ameliorations that challenged capital's dominion would necessarily be frustrated by "industrial evolution—which has no heart."[98] Thus, even when Guesdists were advocating universally-applicable minimum wages and minimum conditions, they patently believed that the "bourgeois Republic" would rebuff these proposals—exactly *because* such reforms would protect French labor from the brutal competition of low-wage foreigners and ward immigrants against the exploitation that so enriched and empowered the bourgeoisie.[99] The Parti Ouvrier pressed reforms in the confident expectation that they *would* be rebuffed, thereby further discrediting bourgeois rule among workers.

In the end, then, when faced with intercommunal conflict, French Marxists—apart from a halfhearted, if not totally hypocritical, reformism—retreated to the pious hope that "foreigners working in France will link themselves with the French, which will eliminate the old hatreds."[100] When these hopes were dashed, French Marxists, as was so often the case, deferred the problem to the utopian future, when all such dilemmas would be resolved.[101] Once workers, French or foreign, had all rallied to socialism, they would no longer fall prey to nationalist demagoguery.[102] And, come the revolution, nationalism would disappear from the world of work. "Foreign" workers of the future, entering socialist France, would be met by comrades intoning

> The world is large, and all men are brothers. Come among us and earn your daily bread; we don't fear your competition. Support yourselves and support your families, as salaries will no longer, because of you, be reduced and restricted.[103]

The workers of a socialist world, no longer divided by capitalist labor markets, would finally unite.

"National Property": The Economic Foundations of Socialist Nationalism

And what of that impending socialist world? Marxism's utopia has always been predicated on the "socialization of the means of production." Social order and international order here conjoined. As the Bonniers put it, "[T]here's absolutely no . . . incompatibility between the nationalism that socializes individual interests and the internationalism that socializes national interests. The socialization that forms nations also unites them."[104] In other (less terse) words, socialist nationalism would eliminate class conflict *within* nations by socializing the means of production, while these "nationalizations" would eliminate capitalist clashes *between* nations and ready the world for a universal socialist commonwealth. "Nationalizations" thus led unproblematically toward "internationalization." Perhaps. But, in a more skeptical assessment, the nationalism of "nationalizations" sapped the cosmopolitanism of "internationalization."

The key expressions here are "socialization" and "nationalization"—with both terms signifying "collectivization of the means of production." Yet they are not synonymous. Theoretically, "socialization" need not mean "nationalization," as there are many societies apart from the nation, some subnational, others transnational. Nonetheless, in Marxist practice across a century, and implicitly in Marxist theory from Marx onward, the "socialization" of the means of production has meant their appropriation by a socialist nation-state. Guesdists certainly manifested this slippage of meaning. According to Guesde's authoritative words, "[A] party such as ours, which is based on a program of *nationalization* [Guesde's stress] . . . must inevitably take a national form."[105] How, Guesdists plaintively asked, could anyone possibly accuse the Parti Ouvrier of being antinational, when its entire program turned on "*nationalization*, the reappropriation [of national wealth] by the nation, state monopolies as the road to nationalized production, creation of national [social] services, etc."[106] How indeed!

At the fin de siècle, this "nationalism of nationalizations"[107] remained a dream of the future, and a dream not to be realized by the French. Unlike its sister movement, the Russian Social Democratic and Labor Party, the Parti Ouvrier would never dress its dreams in reality, never clothe its theory in practice. Yet the contours of a socialist-nationalist economy emerged dimly from the vagaries of Guesdist discourse—manifesting as a social order in which "the old nation having disappeared, workers busy themselves in reconstructing another." The Parti Ouvrier pledged that, "in place of antagonistic individual interests—which at present turn the national patrimony into a battlefield where some triumph by dividing the others and by appropriating the living force of the homeland—[we socialists] will establish coherence, the solidarity of individual interests nationally associated and organized."[108] How, Guesdists demanded, could France possibly be "sane and normal" when convulsed, as she was under capitalism, by perennial class war? Only victorious socialism could resuscitate France as "an organism that one can develop, and that can develop itself . . . through reforms embracing all the organs of the great social body."[109]

This construction, "organs of the great social body," is telling—and disturbing, as it instances an atypical conjunction between socialist nationalism and national socialism. Ultras of the Right also imagined France as an "organism," with classes working harmoniously together as the nation's vital "organs." Guesdists angrily repudiated this irenic conception of "actually existing" capitalism, but replicated its ideal of organic harmony in their vague vision of a collectivist France. For all the fundamental differences between these organicisms, the visions of the class-conflictual Guesdist Left and class-collaborationist nationalist Right shared a common crucial feature: their all-encompassing organism was to be *France*, the national "body politic."[110]

Once the socialization of the means of production had instituted a post-capitalist and harmonious France, how would this "nationalized" nation relate to the rest of the world? On rare occasions, Guesdists limned the nebulous outlines of a future collectivist "globalization." Charles Bonnier, for instance, prophesied a socialist Europe nurturing the "young and vital forces of the Orient" to the mutual advantage of both East and West—rescuing the former from capitalist exploitation, saving the latter from capitalism's coolie labor ("the new Mongols").[111] The mechanisms of such global "solidarity," however, remained obscure, even invisible. Neither Marx himself, nor any Marxist since, and certainly no Guesdist, has ever suggested "how the proletarians of the world were in practice to unite to appropriate human productive forces on a world scale."[112] French Marxists, indeed, sometimes forgot the "world scale" altogether, as their utopian vision contracted toward socialist-nationalist autarchy. "The proletariat's well-being," French Marxists earnestly urged, should be "founded on a corporative communism [communisme corporatif] that will allow the workers to produce for themselves, and that will substitute an ever-larger domestic market for the disruptive and malignant quest for external markets."[113] Here Marxist socialism degenerated into a Proudhonian parochialism infinitely remote from Guesdism's usual devotion to world-spanning modernity, but highly indicative of the nationalizing logic of "nationalizations."

The POF's "nationalism of nationalizations" aimed at restoring the proletariat to the nation by restoring the nation to the proletariat. The "nationalization of the means of production" was characterized by Lafargue as "the proletariat's possession of a patrimony in its homeland." Workers could "not possess [such a] patrimony until property, torn from the failing grasp of the capitalist class," had been "transformed into national property, which will then be common to all the children of the same homeland: then and only then will the proletarians cease to be *sans patrie*."[114] The Parti Ouvrier thus proclaimed itself a "national and patriotic party"—indeed, the *only* "national and patriotic party," because "its program is one of nationalization and its militancy is nationalizing and organizing, that is to say patriotic above all else in the sole meaningful sense of the word."[115] At such moments, particularly frequent during the 1890s as the POF (the newly denominated Parti Ouvrier *Français*) fought off the charge of treason, Guesdists recognized that the nation-state that they otherwise so often dismissed and derided actually underpinned their own project. No other political framework accorded with economic "collectivism."

Opposed in theory to both nationhood and state worship, Guesdists unwittingly promised unprecedented power to the socialist nation-state. Unaware of their own contradictions, Guesde and his followers never admitted that their "nationalism of nationalizations" implied a nationalism more radically nationalist and a state worship more firmly founded upon the state than even the protofascists' "national corporatism." Nonetheless, the ultranationalist political culture and the hypertrophied state institutions of "socialism in one country" already loomed on the Marxist horizon. The autarchic consequences of "nationalizations" were soon to become evident with the advent of "really existing socialism."[116]

The POF's disparate theses on national economics never congealed into a systematic "party line." Méliniste tariffs were denounced, but their challenge to Guesdist internationalism also evoked an occasional shamefaced "socialist protectionism." Nationalist attacks on immigrant labor met with Guesdist scorn, but with little beyond halfhearted "reformism" or cosmopolitan utopianism as an alternative. Guesdist utopianism, in turn, promised unproblematic internationalism, but only through "nationalizations." These aporias stemmed to some extent from the Parti Ouvrier's theoretical incoherence, but also from hard reality.[117] Apart from capitalism's epochal crisis between 1914 and 1945, that system has successfully harmonized its national embeddedness with its cosmopolitan world order, thereby synthesizing "the local and the global." Marxism, by contrast, has never managed to integrate its cosmopolitan principles into its national practices. The Parti Ouvrier's muddled response to nationalism's economic ascendancy during the belle epoque cruelly revealed this shortcoming.

Ironically, the "national economics" that the Guesdists so vehemently denounced would eventually, during capitalism's decades of crisis, give the heirs to Second International Marxism their opportunity—whether as Stalinist "socialism in one country" or as social-democratic "national Keynesianism." Then, for three generations of Marxists, socialism constituted itself as an ascendant reality. During our own recent fin de siècle, however, a resurgent capitalist world-system has unconditionally defeated "socialist nationalism," whether as Stalinism or as social democracy—leaving Marxists with their cosmopolitan ideal intact, but without a political economy in which to embody it.[118] A future socialist globalization now appears to be as inconceivable as past socialist nationalisms seem indefensible.

CHAPTER 4

"Proletarian Patriotism": The Guesdists and the Nationalist Temptation

Nationalism's multisecular ascendancy has cruelly tested cosmopolitans. Whether it has been eighteenth-century liberals or nineteenth-century socialists who have championed modernity, its universal promise has been repeatedly betrayed, with both liberals and socialists degenerating from their original cosmopolitanism toward exclusionary nationalism.[1] Why? Because modernity's foundational promise of "Liberty, Equality, and Fraternity" begged the questions of "Liberty *for* whom?" "Equality *between* whom?" and "Fraternity *among* whom?" According to cosmopolitans, of course, these questions require the same simple answer: for, between, and among "all human beings." All of them? A project easily affirmed, but in practice virtually impossible.[2]

The French Revolution, after all, began as the voice of free men everywhere, but then, during its terrible years of war and counterrevolution, sank into xenophobic nationalism. The Bolshevik revolution, too, degenerated from its universalist inception into murderous "anticosmopolitan" campaigns. And, during the French fin de siècle, the same nationalist involution characterized the period's "crisis of Marxism," during which the "birth of fascist ideology" emerged from the time's increasingly destructive "revision" (better: "repudiation") of Marxist cosmopolitanism.[3] Modernity's universalism, then, whether liberal or socialist, has occasioned, even required, a self-contradictory particularity.

Socialism, however, has suffered this self-contradiction with particular intensity.[4] By definition *social*, it has always relied upon "really existing societies" far more than has liberalism, with its socially attenuated project. Socialists' commitment to collective freedom as well as to individual liberty, their passion for social as well as for civic equality, their pledge of fraternity among comrades as well as among citizens—all have rendered them far more dependent on national encadrement than liberals have ever been.[5] The liberals' worldwide Kantian "civil society" and their impersonal "world market" have, after all, always seemed considerably more plausible as alternatives to nationhood than has the Marxist aspiration to an almost unimaginable socialist "global community."[6] Cosmopolitan socialism, then, because it has been so genuinely social, has also been particularly vulnerable to particularism.

Certainly Marxism's theorists have systematically encountered this vulnerability, and have systematically succumbed to it. Their embodiments of "modes of production" (feudalism or capitalism as analytical categories) in "social formations" (Phoenicia or Germany as particular societies) have manifested a persistent aporia—with modes of production exhaustively conceptualized (Marxism's great theoretical achievement), but with social formations always arbitrary in theory while firmly national by implication.[7] Indicatively, in characterizing "social formations," both Marx and Engels themselves consistently "used the term 'nation' as equally applicable to polities from the Phoenicians to the Germans both before and after unification."[8] From Marx and Engels onward, then, Marxism's powerful deconstruction of the capitalist mode of production has been applied to particular social formations, while the "primordial" ethnic identity of these formations has remained untheorized, even unnoticed.[9] Nationhood has thus lurked balefully behind the apparently universal categories of Marxist analysis, waiting to pounce upon its unsuspecting adepts.

And pounce it has—no less in practice than in theory. The nationalist hegemony infused by the welfare state, the chauvinist passions encouraged in the warfare state, the nationalizing "material interests" enforced through "national economics"—these armatures of the nation-state have repeatedly constrained and, in the end, suffocated Marxism's class cosmopolitanism. All anti-Marxists, most scholars, and even many Marxists have thus come to the conclusion that "allegiance to national communities will always trump all other forms of solidarity."[10] The iron determinism of geographical community, the vectors of heritage and history, the mind-forged manacles of language and culture—all have seemingly bound the world with far greater force than have the tenuous ties of class.

Marxism's tortured history testifies to this nationalist hegemony. The doctrine's many crises witnessed its repeated surrender to nationhood: initially during the nationalist paroxysm of August 1914, then throughout the interminable experience of "socialism in one country," and finally at the recent "End of History." Ironically, today, at the very moment when national welfare states are disintegrating under the impact of neoliberal individualism, when national warfare states are being dismantled in favor of mercenary military professionalism, when national economies are dissolving into the world market, "post-Marxists" everywhere are abandoning their erstwhile cosmopolitanism for an uncritical celebration of premodern or postmodern "difference," including ethnic difference.[11]

Some contemporary Marxists, however, stubbornly refuse to surrender cosmopolitan class politics to ethnic divisiveness. For these defenders of the faith, nationhood itself has always been inflected by class conflict—even if class identity, in turn, has always been conditioned by ethnic context. Far from abandoning themselves to nationalism, therefore, these intransigents have fought heroically to appropriate the nation for international socialism, and sometimes to appropriate it for a *cosmopolitan* socialism.[12] Even at today's "End of History," this dialectical understanding of class and ethnie, of cosmopolitanism and nationhood, offers theoretical potency and political purchase. How much more so, then, at the fin de siècle, with Marxism still in the ascendancy.

The very amorphousness of nationhood reinforces this syncretic logic. The nation has been so polyvalent as to meld with *any* ideology—even ostensibly cosmopolitan Marxism.[13] Nationhood, indeed, has provided the ultimate "matrix of meanings"[14] within which modern ideologies have competed for dominance. Liberalism, Conservatism, socialism, even (under very peculiar circumstances) anarchism—all have "naturalized" themselves by appropriating the "national interest," all have equated themselves with "their" nation's "national character" (Americans as "inherently" individualistic and freedom-loving—i.e., liberal; Germans as "naturally" community-minded and disciplined—i.e., Conservative). Once an ideology has thus legitimated itself as "national," it can delegitimate its enemies as "alien": a death blow in any ideological combat. French nationhood at the fin de siècle thus stood vacant as an "empty signifier" waiting to be "articulated"[15] with a hegemonic ideology. French liberals triumphed during the early Third Republic with just such a strategy—identifying "their" Republic with a "true France" of Liberty, Equality, and Fraternity. National socialists such as Barrès strove mightily at the fin de siècle to recover "France" for the Right.

And the French Marxists? Like so many cosmopolitans before their time, and since, Guesdists discovered that "you have to position yourself *somewhere* in order to say anything at all"[16]—even to say cosmopolitan things. For the Parti Ouvrier, that *somewhere* had to be France. Whether because of the hidden logic of the POF's Marxism, because of the social and cultural imperatives of the movement's time and place, or because of the nature of modern politics in general, the Party's experience proved the dictum that nationalism must be "the idiom of all contemporary political feeling"[17]—even the feelings of Marxist cosmopolitans. Whenever the Guesdists moved from the general to the particular, from universal principles to everyday pragmatics, they moved from "humanity" to "France." The Parti Ouvrier thus learned that "the socialization of the nation has as its natural corollary the nationalization of socialism."[18] Even the movement's most fervently antinational militants, even the ultracosmopolitan Lafargue, sometimes surrendered to the ardent nationalism of many French workers, of comrades such as Jourde, and of virtually all their enemies.[19] Cowering before the tsunami of nationalist passion that washed across the "age of empire," the POF sometimes resolved to ride the wave, rather than to withstand it.

But there was more to the matter than force of circumstance. Marx and Engels, too, had sometimes lurched from cosmopolitanism into what looked suspiciously like nationalism. At mid-century, they regularly seconded what they regarded as "progressive" nationhood. Witness their devotion to Polish freedom, or Engels's enthusiasm for Irish independence. Why did these self-avowed cosmopolitans back some of the most fanatical nationalist movements of their time? The answer? Pure opportunism. Marx and Engels measured how the national self-assertion of the Poles and Irish might empower socialism, and made their decisions accordingly. In such calculations, particular nationalist movements (even, perhaps, particular nations!) could be either "good" or "bad," depending on their class orientation and revolutionary potential. Thus, when "the nation" was mobilized by Bismarck against the SPD, nationalism was renounced and denounced. But, when mustered against the hated czarist empire by insurrectionary Warsaw, nationhood was zealously supported. As with Marx and Engels, so with their followers. From Marxists' engagement with the Fenians until their recent involvement in "national liberation movements," they have everywhere maintained this tradition of opportunism—with Lenin and Stalin's manipulative "nationalities policy" its ultimate expression, and Rosa Luxemburg's pristine (and failed) absolute cosmopolitanism the exception that proves the rule. So long as Marxists, even Stalinist Marxists, maintained their ultimately universalist principles, they were not "nationalists" in the exorbitant sense of making *the* nation or *a* nation their *ultimate* value. But, as Marx and Engels themselves demonstrated, they could still be *instrumentally* nationalist in particular cases, so long as their favored nations worked toward socialism.[20]

Needless to say, it is easiest to celebrate one's own homeland as embodying the hopes of humanity, as destined for greatness, as a "good thing." And, needless to say, as children of Europe's longest-established and most successful "nation-state," French Marxists sometimes succumbed to such self-indulgent logic. They had august precedent for this episodic Francophilia. As an offspring of the gallicized Rhineland, Marx himself had been politically "socialized" by French socialism—whether by Trier's own Saint-Simonians during his youth, or through his brief but intense experience of revolutionary Paris during the 1840s. The French socialists whom Marx had read as a young man, and with whom he had fraternized as a youthful émigré, never doubted for a moment that socialism's future lay with France. And, for the rest of his life, Marx, too, half expected that Paris would initiate the workers' revolution. French socialists of the belle epoque, including those of the Parti Ouvrier, were sure of it. After all, Guesdists proudly proclaimed, France had already given birth to two of the three great pre-Marxist socialists (Saint-Simon, Fourier, and Owen), while hosting all three of the first engagements in the modern class war (Lyon 1832, Paris

1848, and Paris 1871).[21] Like revolutionaries everywhere from 1789 until 1968, Guesdists might well cry "Vive la France!"

Guesdists had, indeed, been profoundly marked by their nation's legacy of revolutionary nationalism. When in socialist-nationalist attire, French Marxists donned the heritage of the First Republic, that militant moment when France supposedly represented not only her own interests, but the entire world's aspiration to liberty, equality, and fraternity. "We are," Guesde proudly proclaimed, "very much in the tradition of our country when we assume, as our cause, the internationalism of the great revolutionaries of 1793."[22] Such "Jacobin" socialism, eventually to have a great future in the hands of Communist historians, became particularly prevalent during the 1890s, as Guesdists struggled against a multitude of Republican enemies—all claiming that the newly ascendant POF was "alien" to France," all mobilizing the mystique of revolutionary nationalism against Marxist cosmopolitanism. The role of "real patriots," claimed the Guesdists, defensively identifying themselves as such, "is to take up the revolutionary tradition of the last century [the eighteenth] and announce the fraternity of peoples."[23] Given this heritage, a French identity affirmed universality, rather than betrayed it.

That identity, according to French Marxists, had been sadly betrayed by the bourgeoisie's degenerate chauvinism. It was no accident, according to the Parti Ouvrier, that so many of the fin de siècle's ultranationalists repudiated 1793.[24] "Integral nationalists" like Charles Maurras indeed anathematized the Revolution—no doubt because of the Jacobins' hostility to provincial and corporative particularity *within* France, but above all because of the revolutionaries' transnational universalism *beyond* France. In that epochal transition discerned by the wise Russian theologian Vladimir Soloviev—from the nation as embodying universal values, to the nation as the denial of universality—socialist nationalists like the Guesdists represented the former moment, ultras like Maurras the latter.[25]

In the Marxists' metahistorical narrative, French nationhood had thus dwindled from the country's grand cosmopolitan role during the Great Revolution into Maurras's posturing patriotism. Guesdists would thus have agreed with Soloviev's damning diagnosis of nationhood's teleology . . . to a point. But the degenerative logic of nationalism, Guesdists were sure, could be reversed—and *would* be reversed. "International socialism," Guesde confidently predicted, "far from threatening France, is destined to restore her to the first place among nations."[26] In Lafargue's figuring of this paradoxical revelation,

> France has been and still is one of those nations that initiates and guides human development: she cannot herself develop and change without exercising an international influence. . . . The socialists will once again place France at the head of the European peoples. She will once again become the nation that awakens the world with her ideas and her social struggles. . . .

> Socialist France has become the universal homeland: socialist internationalists everywhere have two nations, the one where chance has had them born, and France, their homeland by adoption.[27]

Le Socialiste rejoiced when it learned Bismarck feared that the next invasion of Germany would resemble the ideological War of the First Coalition, with the red flag replacing the *tricolore* at the head of resurgent French armies marching on Berlin.[28] An insurrectionary France, Guesdists promised, would indeed someday disseminate revolutionary socialism beyond the Rhine, just as Jacobin France had once spread revolutionary liberalism. German socialists would soon embrace liberating French invaders, just as German Jacobins had once welcomed the armies of the First Republic. "June 1848 and May 1871 have drowned [European] socialists' love for capitalist France in blood," the Parti Ouvrier sadly admitted. "But there is a France that socialists of all nations adore with an ardent devotion: revolutionary France, the France which . . . will plant the Red Flag of the social republic throughout Europe."[29]

At their most nationalist, Guesdists sometimes dropped that red flag for the *tricolore*. "It belongs to us as well as to you, the *tricolore* flag," Guesde cried out to France's rulers, "and I defy you and forbid you to monopolize it!"[30] At that moment, the Guesdist leader shamelessly disavowed his Party's innumerable denunciations of the national emblem. Even more astoundingly, the red flag itself, usually presented as the transnational, even antinational, insignia of the universal proletariat, was instead sometimes deployed as "the old national flag, under which our forefathers fought against the Romans, and Jeanne d'Arc against the English."[31] Here, the *drapeau rouge* ceased to be the standard of the global proletariat, and flew instead as the oriflamme, the scarlet banner of Saint Denis and medieval "true France." Joan of Arc herself, soon to become the patron saint of French ultranationalism, rode forth under the oriflamme as "proletarian patriotism"[32] incarnate. For the Guesdists, in their socialist-nationalist guise, the peasant girl of Domremy represented the plebe no less than *la belle France*. Indeed, La Pucelle represented France *because* she represented plebeians. Marxists, too, could mobilize the romantic medievalism so beloved of nationalists.

This socialist nationalism could take troubling forms. In making France the marker of socialism, Guesdists all too easily and all too often measured their foreign friends by their "Frenchness," as in the case of a certain Crivelli, who, "although of Italian origin," nonetheless "had a virtually French temperament and spirit: intelligent, ardent, passionate in all noble causes."[33] What would Crivelli's "temperament and spirit" have been had he, instead, reflected his "Italian origin"? Would he have been, as seems to be suggested, "stupid, pusillanimous, petty in his preoccupations"? And did Guesdists *really* believe that their French compatriots shared a "temperament" of intelligence, passion, and nobility? French financial speculators? French colonial policemen? French journalists of the reptile press? In their socialist-nationalist persona, Guesdists were patently not immune to nationalism's trivial stupidities.

Worse yet, the Guesdists' episodic affection for "their" France foreshadowed the self-destructive nationalist paroxysm of August 1914. French Marxists insisted that they would defend even a bourgeois-led France, if that France were unjustly attacked. Had not "French internationalists . . . accepted the crushing burden that France had assumed [after 1871] in order to repair her forces and reconquer her rank as the prime military power?"[34] The Parti Ouvrier's 1893 congress thus resolved "that France, if attacked, will have no more ardent defenders than the socialists of the Parti Ouvrier, convinced of the great role reserved for her in the coming social revolution."[35] Unfortunately, German socialists, too, believed in their nation's revolutionary mission, and assumed that Germany, as the hope of the socialist world, would have to be defended, if attacked. In August 1914, French and German socialists—convinced that their nations were indeed under attack, persuaded that their countries prefigured the socialist future—would mindlessly slaughter each other at the behest of their despised rulers.[36] And, when French soldiers finally did march into the Rhineland in 1919, they did so behind the *tricolore* of bourgeois France, not the red flag of revolution, and sometimes they marched behind the *tricolore against* the red flag.[37]

These contradictions in the Guesdists' ideology are best revealed in the POF's ferocious hostility toward anarchist cosmopolitanism. As Guesdists themselves had so often done, Jean Grave, Elisée Reclus and the journalists of *Le Père Peinard* denounced national identity as a malignant false consciousness imposed by bourgeois brainwashing.[38] Surely Guesdists and anarchists were thus brothers in cosmopolitanism? Not for a moment. French Marxists relentlessly condemned anarchist antinationalism as ignorant, nonsensical, and counterproductive—even indicting anarchists who shouted "A bas la France!" as police provocateurs![39] This double standard vis-à-vis antinationalism typified the Parti Ouvrier's broader relationship to anarchism. When resiling from their own most radical beliefs, Guesdists habitually ascribed them to the anarchists, thereby abjecting an unwanted part of themselves onto the *frères-ennemis* they had previously excluded from the socialist movement. The extreme violence of Guesdist antianarchism, in this instance, manifested the savage strain imposed on the French Marxists by the schizophrenic disjuncture between their cosmopolitan and socialist-nationalist personae.

"Guesde Candidat des Prussiens": The Parti Ouvrier on the Defensive

The Guesdists' periodic capitulations to nationalism must be situated in their polemical context. From the POF's foundation until its subsumption into the

SFIO, its many adversaries monotonously charged Marxists with being "alien" to France and indicted Marxism as an "imported" German doctrine.[40] A Parisian parliamentary candidate, for instance, having denounced his socialist opponent as advocating "the abolition of all property, of the family home, of the army, and [above all] of the nation," then terminated his tirade with the rhetorical question: "Surely you will not allow this disciple of the German Jew Karl Marx to attempt the realization in Paris of those toxic schemes hatched on the other side of the Rhine?"[41] Such assaults on Marxism came from every point on the ideological compass. Ultranationalists, however, specialized in the genre. According to his own account, Paul Déroulède had become a ferocious antisocialist when "alien" red flags were flaunted at a military commemorative service, and the nationalist demagogue then strove unrelentingly for the rest of his life to have that emblem of proletarian internationalism banned from France. Maurice Barrès, for his part, anathematized Marxism, a supposed compilation of rabbinical dogmas from Trier, as manifesting both the soulless materialism of the Germans and the arid logic of the Jews. According to Barrès, the collectivism of the POF was no more than "a fantasy evoked by the imagination of a few messianic Semites."[42] Charles Maurras reinforced the theme, despising the Parti Ouvrier as yet another German invasion. He spoke for all France's ideologues of *la terre et les morts* ("the land and the dead," the French equivalent of the Germanic "blood and soil") in proclaiming that "[Marxist] socialism was rejected by the very soil of France."[43]

The extreme Right, however, had no monopoly on such invective. Even the POF's socialist competitors joined the clamor. Xenophobia was to be expected from the Blanquists—always ultranationalist, and with their dominant faction sliding toward protofascism. But others, like Benoît Malon and Gustave Rouanet, precursors of Jaurès's irenic socialism, also denounced Marxism as

> the ultimate stage in the evolution of the German historico-fatalist school that was a reaction against eighteenth-century [French] philosophy. Marx's thought was essentially anti-French. Hence the complete rupture with our traditions, with our old socialist parties, effected by [Marx's Guesdist] translators.[44]

From extreme Right to extreme Left, via the flaccid liberal center, every French faction (apart from the anarchists) berated the Parti Ouvrier for its cosmopolitanism.[45]

The POF's enemies most often denounced the movement as more Teutonic than French, as a treasonous offshoot of the German Social Democratic Party, itself supposedly German nationalist and anti-French.[46] Nationalists of every stripe regularly charged that the *real* purpose behind the Parti Ouvrier's cosmopolitanism was subversion of national identity, thus rendering France more vulnerable to German aggression—a subversion allegedly underwritten by

Hohenzollern secret-service funds. During the decisive election campaign of 1893, for instance, Guesde's enemies in Roubaix placarded a poster entitled "Guesde Candidat des Prussiens" that accused him of "betraying his country and accepting money, as the price of his betrayal, from the hands of those who . . . butchered our women and children."[47] According to the Guesdists' innumerable enemies, the POF came not from the French Left, but from the German East.

To nationalist delight and Guesdist dismay, many French workers fell for this aspersion. The POF's endemic weakness in Paris manifested the capital's patriotic political culture—with the city sealed against Marxism by the Blanquists' chauvinist insurrectionism and the Possibilists' Republican nationalism. Over the centuries, after all, Paris had *made* France, and the city's plebeians, in their modest way, fed from the same trough as its nationalist intellectuals, bourgeois, and bureaucrats. Workers elsewhere, however, even workers in half-Belgian Roubaix, exhibited a national passion similar in kind, although lesser in degree. Guesde, campaigning to represent Roubaix, survived the nationalist onslaught of 1893, but succumbed in 1898. Nor was Guesde the only prominent Marxist savaged during that poll. Gustave Delory, the mayor of Lille and the POF's leader in the all-important Nord, lost his bid for election to the Chamber of Deputies because he had welcomed a delegation of German socialists to his *mairie*. And, on one utterly humiliating occasion (the Ninth Congress of the POF), the Party's leadership was forced to request police protection for German comrades threatened by an enraged nationalist mob—and this in Lille itself, the heartland of French Marxism![48] The terrified German delegates could retreat to Berlin; Lillois Guesdists had to go on living with their furious neighbors. Whether as frustrated national leaders in ultranationalist Paris or as traumatized provincial militants in Lille, French Marxists paid a high price for their internationalist notoriety.

How did they calculate that price, and how did they weigh it against their cosmopolitan principles? They certainly recognized a cost. According to the Party's National Council,

> [I]n their impotent rage at the Parti Ouvrier's ascendancy, our class enemies are using the last weapon in their armory: slander. They're attempting to travesty our internationalism, as they've tried to travesty our socialism. Those who are trying to present us as *sans-patrie* are the same people who, throughout a century, have permitted the invasion and dismemberment of our homeland . . . we'll not allow them to parody our glorious cry *Long live the International!* as the pathetic belch *Down with France!*[49]

In response to such "slander," if slander it was, the Parti Ouvrier, it must be reiterated, often pleaded "guilty" to the charge of being *sans-patrie*. When adversaries alleged that the Parti Ouvrier was a "German import," for instance, the POF sometimes recklessly agreed.

> Yes indeed! We're a product of the Marx factory. We've emerged from *The Communist Manifesto*, and, as this demonstrates, we're a German import. . . . The indigenous products of the Constans-and-Clemenceau factory are begging for a tariff wall against the foreign ideas that encumber and paralyze them.[50]

Brave, no doubt, but hardly prudent, and certainly false. As subsidiaries of a global enterprise, "Marx factories" were scattered across the globe, albeit being most productive in Germany, and Guesdists were foolish to concede their enemies' point. Such self-immolation was rare, however. More often, more wisely, and more accurately, the Parti Ouvrier insisted that theories like Marxism had no national provenance whatsoever. They were "neither French nor German, but true or false."[51] By this more sensible criterion, Marxism was *true*, not Germanic; the Parti Ouvrier was in the right, not from the East.

The Parti Ouvrier, nonetheless, refused to disown its German friends, however intense the pressure to do so. Quite the contrary. Guesdists prided themselves on their trans-Rhenian connections, and assiduously cultivated the SPD's support during their ongoing war against other French socialisms. Guesde and Lafargue had triumphed over Brousse's Possibilists during the 1880s with the aid of Engels and the German Social Democrats, and, at the turn of the century, Kautsky and the SPD reinforced a beleaguered Guesde against Jaurès's Independent Socialists. During the great orators' famous debates during 1904, in responding to Jaurès's attempt to oppose "French socialism" to "German Marxism," Guesde retorted that this maneuver, if successful, would create "as many socialisms as there are different nationalities. It would be nothing less than the negation of proletarian internationalism."[52] For the POF, in this cosmopolitan mode, there was but a single socialism: its Marxism—one with the SPD's identical ideology, because worldwide and universally valid.

Nevertheless, despite their proud internationalism, French Marxists were *French*, and they often enough affirmed the dignity and distinctiveness of that national identity within the global socialist community. When angered by the SPD's attacks on the Parti Ouvrier's "reformist" agrarian policy, for instance, or antagonized by Bebel and Liebknecht's own tolerance of "reformists," Guesdists were quite capable of flaying the German socialism they otherwise exalted, and occasionally they identified the Germans' flaws as *German*.[53] But, whether praising the SPD or denouncing it, the POF always demanded full equality in the worldwide community of collectivists initiated by "Karl Marx, Bebel, and Liebknecht for Germany, England, and America, [and] Guesde and Lafargue for France and Belgium."[54] Indeed, even when arguing sensibly that ideas had no nationality, Guesdists could slip badly. Marx's thought might be universal, and therefore certainly not "anti-French," but even in making this powerful point a Guesdist could then demonstrate that Marx had been "pro-France" in his adherence to the "French intellectual tradition"![55] Cosmopolitan universalism, even for Marxists, was obviously far easier in theory than in practice. Guesdists discovered that they could participate in the worldwide socialist movement only by periodically affirming their French particularity—both with their foreign friends, and against their domestic foes.

Above all, against their domestic foes. At its worst, the Parti Ouvrier's defensive appropriations of French national identity could lapse into xenophobia. When the POF was criticized as internationalist by a certain "M. Edwards" of the Parisian "bourgeois press," for instance, *Le Socialiste*'s riposte moved unthinkingly from cosmopolitanism to socialist nationalism and on toward national socialism. The Guesdist journal suggested that Edwards was himself "of Jewish origin and, we believe, English—others say Levantine," so that his profession of French patriotism "bewilders our simple understanding as good Gauls."[56] Good Gauls! How far from the French Marxists' alternative characterization of themselves as "foreign imports." The contradiction was characteristic. Guesdists systematically oscillated between denial and exploitation of their national identity—with both tactics responding to nationalist attacks on Marxist "rootlessness," but the one never successfully reconciled with the other, and neither free of disturbing excess and unhappy consequences.[57]

"Making Money while Ruining the Homeland": The Parti Ouvrier on the Offensive

On the battlefields of French ideological discourse, as the Parti Ouvrier's enemies bombarded the movement with charges of treason, the POF returned fire. French Marxists scourged capitalists as irredeemably "antinational," lambasted bourgeois as venal traitors, and assailed antisocialist nationalists as the real *sans-patries*. Guesdists here prolonged a long socialist tradition.[58] Ever since the early nineteenth century, first Fourierists, then Proudhonians, and finally Blanquists (but never Saint-Simonians!) had demonized the haute bourgeoisie as foreign to France. The merchant bankers of Paris, French socialists had alleged, were parasitic, predatory . . . and *alien*. This rhetoric tapped a deeply ingrained popular antipathy toward hauts bourgeois—traditionally viewed as remote from *la France profonde*, as more at home in London and Vienna than in Paris itself, and as altogether foreign to grimy but productive Roubaix and Roanne. At the turn of the century, the more sincere "national socialists" such as Rochefort and Drumont best represented this tradition. These ideologues of the populist ultra-Right explicitly claimed the antibourgeois (and anti-Semitic) legacies of Fourier, Proudhon, and Blanqui.

But similar "socialist-nationalist" critiques of cosmopolitan capital suffused the Left, including, at times, the Marxist Left. On that Left, in a weird inversion of the *Manifesto*, globalizing capitalists, rather than sweeping away barbarous barriers to worldwide communion, instead became traitors to the nation, while socialist workers, instead of "having no homeland," became repositories of the national interest *against* capitalist globalization. Such critique, when offered by French Marxists, sat strangely with their more common enthusiasm for capitalism's worldwide civilizing mission.

Why were capitalists traitors to France? Guesde answered this question definitively at the very birth of the POF. "Capital," he contended, "does not have, and cannot have, a homeland, or rather, to make much the same point, there where the rate of return is highest, even if it's among enemies, there is capital's homeland."[59] ("Enemies" abroad? What a peculiar trope for the assiduously cosmopolitan Guesde!) From the Parti Ouvrier's perspective, bourgeois were, "above all, businessmen. They know what's what: a penny's a penny; the homeland's nothing."[60] ("Homeland"? So much for the Marxists' rootless cosmopolitanism!) It therefore hardly surprised Guesdists when they caught Paul Leroy-Beaulieu, the doyen of French national liberalism, recommending to his bourgeois readers that they place their investments anywhere but in low-interest France, even if such placements were German. Whether French or German, whether Jewish or gentile, the bourgeoisie, according to Marxists, represented an abstract capital that recognized no national community, no ethnic solidarity, and no linguistic belonging in its blind fixated search for the maximum rate of return.

Despite capital's abstract lack of embodiment, Guesdists sometimes personalized it in France's "dynasties bourgeoises"[61]—those inbred families of notables who had long ruled the nation without, according to POF, ever becoming truly French. When Jean-Paul-Pierre Casimir-Perier became president of France, for instance, the Guesdists compiled a xenophobic charge sheet against him that began with his grandfather's frustration of union between Belgium and France (thus protecting the Casimir-Periers' lucrative Anzin coal mines against Belgian competition), continued by pointing out that the Casimir-Periers were "half Russian" and (worse yet!) descended from the Russian general who had burned Moscow and thus defeated France in 1812, and concluded by asserting that the president's relatives were "French foreigners" who had all invested their vast fortunes outside France.[62] Such accusations were well calculated to outrage French "commoners"—long distrustful of the great notables' overweening power, envious of their enormous wealth, and suspicious of their cosmopolitan connections.

On most occasions, however, Guesdists indicted capitalism's market-driven (ir)rationality for betraying France, rather than indicting individual capitalists. In one such indictment, *Le Socialiste* analyzed the decline of the Massif Central's charcoal-fueled forges, and their replacement by more profitable Atlantic-coast mills dependent on British coking coal and Spanish iron ore. According to anxious Guesdists, this metallurgical transition from the interior to the sea rendered France pathetically vulnerable to a superior naval power. "But what does that [vulnerability] matter to capitalist France," *Le Socialiste* asked rhetorically, "so long as it's profitable?"[63] Why was the pacifist Parti Ouvrier worried about France's strategic vulnerability? Quite simply because bourgeois could be blamed. The usually antimilitarist POF repeatedly criticized the French bourgeoisie *exactly* for neglecting the country's defenses.[64] By implication, in these polemics, a socialist France would shelter behind stronger fortifications, sail forth in mightier battleships, and marshal more army corps than the militarily impotent France of the bourgeoisie. In this peculiar argument (admittedly rare), bourgeois were not at fault for their militarism (the usual Guesdist charge), but for their *lack* of martial spirit. France's "Parti de l'Etranger" (the "party of the foreigners," an insult commonly launched against the POF) was really, *Le Socialiste* claimed, "composed of those who denounce us as *sans patrie*."[65] In "the trial before patriotism," the POF affirmed, Marxism was "not the accused, but the prosecutor."[66]

Guesdists pressed their case in several jurisdictions. The world market, in particular, offered a happy hunting-ground for Parti Ouvrier prosecutors. Despite the POF's principled commitment to free trade, Guesdists lapsed easily from their principles, savagely denouncing capitalism's international commerce, whether manifest in imports or exports. On such occasions, the POF sadly observed that the world market compelled the nation to export its proletariat's product, with supposedly noxious consequences—particularly for proletarians. As usual, capitalists were at fault. "As men of our land," wrote Edouard Fortin, translator of Marx's works (who should thus have known better),

> [industrialists] think only of producing for other lands. As guardians of the homeland, they work only for elsewhere. It's thus that these French patriots each year eject beyond our borders one billion seven hundred million [francs worth] of French production.[67]

Fortin here forgot that exports, and the resultant imports, benefited both "other lands" and "our land"—the Ricardian essence of his movement's predominant free-trading convictions.

Capitalists, Guesdists charged, were no less nation-killers when they imported. Nationally produced goods were no good, the Parti Ouvrier sneered, if importers could buy abroad more cheaply. Commenting on an industrialist who excused his imported German machinery by its incomparably low price, *Le Socialiste* scathingly summed up his purchasing policy as "making money while ruining the homeland."[68] Again, not for socialist nationalists the Ricardian free-trading faith—the faith that, when nations produced on the basis of their comparative advantages, they all benefited from mutual exchange. Instead, according to the Parti Ouvrier in its socialist-nationalist mode, "comparative advantage" meant only the comparative advantage of bourgeois class interest over the French national interest.

Guesdists also denounced foreign investment, both as French investment among foreigners and as foreigners' investment in France. The nation's capitalists, according to the POF, gained their wealth at home, but placed it abroad—to their profit, but at France's expense. In an exposé of French industrialists who invested in Russian Poland's burgeoning textile industry (a reiterated Guesdist grievance), *Le Socialiste* denounced this "stealing of French jobs" as "un crime de lèse-patrie."[69] "High treason against the nation"! What right did cosmopolitan Guesdists have to lay such a charge? Perhaps the right of reply. The "treason" of capital flight, after all, had been committed by the same ultranationalist capitalists who denounced Guesdists as *sans-patrie*. At the least, the northern textile magnates, with their ultranationalist rhetoric in politics and their ultraprofitable factories in Lodz, were guilty of gross hypocrisy.

Even more than foreign direct investment, Guesdists reviled portfolio investment abroad—that vast and accelerating outflow of French savings into foreign stocks and bonds that, at the fin de siècle, had turned France, or at least the French bourgeoisie, into the world's rentier. This outflow, too, was supposedly high treason against the nation. Indeed, it was far worse than the "real" treason perpetrated by spies. Spies, *Le Socialiste* cynically remarked, reduced the risk of war by alerting governments to their enemies' clandestine military preparations. By contrast, bourgeois rentiers betrayed their country in a far more fundamental way—by exporting their wealth to France's detriment, reinforcing competitors' economic advantages, and enhancing the military power of France's enemies.[70] When French nationalists "proved" that Dreyfus was a traitor because his fortune was invested in Germany, the Parti Ouvrier riposted that *all* rich bourgeois placed their capital where it would earn the most—whether at home or abroad, whether among friends or enemies. *Le Socialiste* ruled that "because such treason is everywhere, it can basically be concluded that it's nowhere . . . unless it's resolved that the great traitor is capital itself."[71] Guesdists so resolved. Having detailed the ways in which the "wealth created . . . by the nation that works" (that is, by the working-class "nation") had been exported by greedy bankers "in order to militarily and industrially equip rival nations," Lafargue fumed that capital "knows neither homeland, nor humanity, but only the percentage of interest."[72] A few thousand extra securities, or a secure France? Bourgeois would always favor their portfolios.

As for foreign investment in France, Guesdists abominated exploitation of the nation's workers by "alien" capitalists. Having investigated frightful working conditions at an English-owned textile mill outside Reims, *Le Socialiste* raged that

> bourgeois rule, whether monarchist or republican . . . never defends the interests of French workers, even against foreign capitalists: it delivers . . . the workers without defense to exploiters from all over the world. It's thus that bourgeois governments understand patriotism.[73]

Apparently, there was something particularly outrageous about *foreign* exploitation of French textile workers, and something particularly intolerable about the French state's complicity with *British* capitalists. The Parti Ouvrier, in this instance, seemed to be suggesting that Rémois workers would be better off if exploited by French mill owners. As a protectionist and nationalist, Barrès would have wholeheartedly agreed. But, as Marxists, Guesdists had no business distinguishing, even implicitly, between iniquitous "alien" and benign "national" employers. Nonetheless, when overwhelmed by spasms of socialist nationalism, Guesdists very occasionally wobbled down the slope toward just such Barrèsian "national economics."

Enervating outflows of exported wealth, a suffocating influx of foreign goods—this socialist-nationalist depiction of a grinding clash between the capitalist world market and the "national interest" hardly exhausted the Parti Ouvrier's armory of invective. The POF's arraignment of nation-killing capitalism also tapped the time's terror of demographic decadence. At the fin de siècle, the French worried incessantly about their country's low natality and consequent slow population growth. France was moribund, even dying! It was all the fault of capital, claimed Guesdists, who accused the bourgeoisie of "nationalicide."[74] Why? Because the bourgeois preference for accumulation over procreation, combined with capital's exhaustion of its workers' life force, had tipped the demographic balance from birth toward death. Capitalism, mourned French Marxists, "valued the wealth of employers over the existence of France, whose declining natality condemns her to disappear through infiltration or engulfment."[75] *Le Socialiste* worried that

> the French nationality is on its way to being suffocated under the pressure of ultraprolific Italians and Germans. And in order to save ourselves from tomorrow's inevitable invasion, all that our ultrapatriotic economists can imagine is to have us invaded today by introducing into our factories, into our shops, even into our public service, the largest possible number of trans-Vosgiens and trans-Alpins. *Prussianize ourselves!* Such is the apex of their science. Thanks, idiots! Please permit us to prefer a socialist . . . France to an Italian or a German one created by suffocation or infiltration. Once all the means of production have been nationalized, we'll no longer fear to make children, and we'll make lots of them, by God! as many as necessary, without having to leave the pleasure of making them to others, to our neighbors.[76]

So much for the Parti Ouvrier's cosmopolitanism, renounced for an international baby-making contest! Still, polemical efficacy compensated for theoretical incoherence. Guesdists reveled in their "discovery" that France's demographic decadence stemmed from capitalist exploitation. Only socialism, they were sure, could rejuvenate the motherland. Come the revolution, France would once again be fecund.

If France's impending "suffocation" by prolific neighbors could be portrayed as capitalist "nationalicide," then working-class emigration was equally to be condemned, although it remained less of an issue than demographic stagnation. The French, after all, had largely abstained from the nineteenth century's trans-Atlantic mass migration. Nonetheless, the Parti Ouvrier emphasized its hostility toward workers abandoning France for abroad. Guesdists explained that "French capitalists have not yet succeeded in expelling French proletarians" in any great number "because [French workers] have an absolute revulsion against emigration."[77] But, if workers *did* begin to flee capitalist France, the POF promised that Marxists would categorically oppose the exodus. Flatly contradicting the Parti Ouvrier's usual enthusiasm for international labor mobility as a surety of socialist cosmopolitanism, Guesdists affirmed that "as internationalist socialists, [we] are the enemies of emigration; we have no desire for workers to quit their natal land; we wish them to find their well-being at home."[78] According to a socialist-nationalist POF, proletarian emigration from bourgeois France would betray both proletariat and nation.

Antisocialists commonly slandered the French Marxists as being really Germans—portraying individual Guesdists as abject disciples of their German Jewish prophet, denouncing the POF as a subservient offshoot of the Teutonic SPD. During the 1880s, Guesdists reversed the slander, arraigning the Third Republic's supposedly nationalist rulers as servile German agents. With lethal repetitiveness, the POF recalled 1871, when "the bourgeoisie, out of fear of Parisian revolution, opened the city's gates to the Prussians."[79] This bourgeois treason, according to the Parti Ouvrier, endured across the decades. The Parti Ouvrier bitterly marked the ways in which Paris collaborated with Berlin against labor. During industrial insurgencies, *Le Socialiste* snarled, "Freycinet puts his bayonets at the service of German exploiters [established in France], while Bismarck returns the favor for French exploiters established in Germany."[80] As with the labor movement, so with socialism. Year after year, exiled militants resident in Paris were summarily expelled by the police prefecture at the behest of foreign secret services, including the German political police, and, year after year, the Parti Ouvrier caustically demonstrated how "the patriotism of our ruling bourgeois is of a very special nature. It receives its orders from Humbert of Italy, from William of Prussia, and Alexander of Russia."[81] In a weird Marxist replication of the belle epoque's chauvinist paranoia, French appeasement of Berlin met with Guesdist outrage. Just as French socialists of the 1930s would charge that the bourgeoisie preferred German conquest to leftist government ("Better Hitler than Blum!"), so Guesdists charged French capitalists with following an abject policy of "Better Wilhelm than Guesde!" The bourgeoisie, Lafargue suggested bitterly, "would prefer to see France under the boots of Bismarck rather than . . . in the hands of the proletariat."[82]

During the 1890s, as the Quai d'Orsay's policy shifted from conciliation of Germany to cultivation of Russia, so Guesdist polemic switched from highlighting Franco-German cooperation to denouncing the Russian alliance. When French police harassed Russian dissidents who had sought asylum in Paris, these refugees attained iconic status in the Guesdist press. Why, Guesdists asked, this shameful abandonment of France's glorious tradition of political asylum? When French diplomats subordinated their country's "national interest" (not least French interest in the recovery of Alsace-Lorraine) to Russian foreign policy (which had no desire whatsoever to reverse the settlement of 1871), *Le Socialiste*'s international reporting emphasized the shame of the Russian connection. Why, the POF asked, this self-destructive diplomacy? Guesdists easily answered their own rhetorical questions. According to the POF, France's Russian entanglement arose from St. Petersburg's voracious appetite for foreign capital and from French capitalists' equally voracious appetite for easy profit. What did it matter to the bourgeoisie if France's wealth was squandered in corrupt and insecure, but nonetheless lucrative, loans to the bankrupt Russian treasury? "What patriots these ruling bourgeois are!" *Le Socialiste* remarked sarcastically.[83] In the French Marxists' persona as the *real* French patriots, they angrily insisted that "the French bourgeoisie doesn't have the right to even speak the word *patrie*—this bourgeoisie that, having inherited a great nation . . . has reduced her in less than a century to her present sad state, territorially despoiled and lying dishonored at the feet of the emperor of all the Siberias."[84]

For Guesdists, the arms trade disclosed bourgeois treason at its most baleful. The industrialists who produced armaments, the merchants who exported them, and the bankers who financed their purchase had no care but for profit. Commenting, for instance, on a couple of Berlin financiers who had organized a vast loan to the Russian state, a loan that would be used to underwrite Russia's rearmament, *Le Socialiste* concluded that "these German bankers are no exception [to the rule that capital has no national allegiance]: Jews, they have underwritten the oppressor of their race; Germans, they have helped raise an army against their nation."[85] French armorers were no better. The Parti Ouvrier revealed with feigned shock that the Chinese and Vietnamese soldiers resisting France's invasion of Indochina had been armed with *French* weapons. "Ah!" *Le Socialiste* exclaimed. "What a lovely thing is bourgeois patriotism!"[86]

Once European war broke out, Guesdists predicted, workers would be astounded to discover that all the combatants had been armed by their enemies. The armaments industry would have achieved a nationally catastrophic but vastly profitable business-exchange: "the ultimate in patriotism, as it's understood by capitalists."[87]

Thus advanced the Guesdists' counterattack against France's "bourgeois nationalists." The Parti Ouvrier damned capitalist commerce as corrosion of the nation, capital flight as vampiric predation on France's substance, bourgeois demographics as "nationalicide," and Republican diplomacy as treason. Charitably interpreted, this invective merely countered attacks on Guesdists as *sans-patrie*. "You're one too!" Yet these counterattacks elicited troubling ambiguities. In the Parti Ouvrier's socialist-nationalist critiques of capitalist globalization, the world market no longer spread as a civilizing force eventually to be appropriated by the proletariat, but instead raged across the globe as a nation-killing menace. When posturing as patriots, Guesdists thus abandoned international revolution in favor of national revolution against the cosmopolitan bourgeoisie.

"We Complete Nationalists": The Guesdists as French Patriots

In their guise as socialist nationalists, Guesdists reviled "bourgeois patriotism" while championing the "real thing": proletarian patriotism. They had doctrinal warrant. Closely studied, Marx's texts sanctioned both working-class cosmopolitanism *and* socialist nationalism. The *Manifesto*'s famous assertion that "working men have no country" was closely followed by the affirmation that "since the proletariat must first of all acquire political supremacy, must rise to be the leading class of the nation, must constitute itself *the* nation, it is, so far, itself national, though not in the bourgeois sense of the word."[88] Which argument to emphasize? That the proletariat had been stripped of national particularity? Or that revolutionary workers must come to embody their nation? By the fin de siècle, within the Second International, the latter increasingly prevailed. The affirmation that "the working men have no country" had, for many Marxists, mutated from cosmopolitan boast into nationalist lament.[89] From Dublin to St. Petersburg, from Oslo to Athens, socialism increasingly meant giving "working men" a country by seizing a country for them.

In their socialist-nationalist persona, Guesdists exemplified this transition to affirmation of the "national, though not in the bourgeois sense of the word." They crafted an alternative theory of nationalism that identified the proletariat as France's "national class." This concept of a "national class" is one of the most intriguing ideas in the Marxist repertoire, and a concept that has clearly distinguished Marxism's episodic nationalism from that of its enemies.

Rather than classes uniting around a socially transcendent national interest (the ideal of both national socialists and national liberals), Marxists have argued that one class alone embodies the nation "when [that class] serves the general interest in serving its particular interest."[90] For "patriotic" Marxists, then, the proletariat can embody the nation only by fighting the class war, by "serving its particular interests." At the same time, Marxist theorists have argued, modern class hegemonies prosper *only* when and where they have thus donned national clothing.[91] For socialist-nationalist Marxists, then, the workers will win the social war because they really *are* the nation.

"Bourgeois hegemony" was the exemplar for this theory. According to Marxism's metanarrative, the bourgeoisie had triumphed as "les bourgeois conquérants,"[92] as modernity's ascendant "national class"—forcing the unification of Germany upon recalcitrant Junkers, molding the intractable peasants of Piedmont and Puglia into "Italians," and, above all, commanding France as "La Grande Nation." Guesdist historians elaborated this exemplary tale. According to the POF, the "Patriot" faction that initiated the French Revolution in 1789 and then carried it to triumph under the Jacobins had been a selfish class-party of "bourgeois revolutionaries." But these self-regarding bourgeois had also heroically defended France against cosmopolitan counterrevolution, both domestic and foreign. Quiberon and Valmy had been triumphs for the bourgeoisie *and* for France. The class that had given the eighteenth-century French their gallant Patriots had woefully degenerated, however, represented as it was during the belle epoque by the despicable Opportunists. Having exhausted its historical mission, the bourgeoisie had abandoned France, devoting itself instead to cosmopolitan parasitism—thereby replicating the role of the historically transcended aristocracy.

As the bourgeoisie faltered in the historical relay-race of progressive "national classes," the proletariat seized the baton. When the Parti Ouvrier contrasted France's proletarians with bourgeois, it represented workers as "fulfilling their [national] duty"[93] to France. Revolutionary against capitalist exploitation, patriotic against cosmopolitan capital, France's workers had constituted themselves as the new Patriot Party: the Parti Ouvrier. It would lead the nation into a radiant future, toward the final realization of the ideals of 1789 that had been so travestied and then so completely abandoned by the degenerate bourgeoisie. Ironically, by sowing this hegemonic aspiration among workers, the POF powerfully contributed to the "nationalization of the masses." France's proletarians, after all, were far more likely to be seduced by the Guesdists' socialist nationalism than by the Barrèsians' national socialism or the Oppportunists' civic nationalism.[94] The Hegelian "cunning of reason" thus ensured that nationalism's demiurge found a powerful historical agent in cosmopolitan Marxism.

When fully assimilated by its Marxist proponents, this theory of the "national class" resulted in sociological "double vision." For the POF, France doubled into a nation of bourgeois nationalists (essentially fraudulent, really representing capitalist cosmopolitanism) and a nation of socialist patriots (the true France, representing working people's national authenticity). There were "two Frances," Guesdists argued, because "all nations . . . are divided into classes with antagonistic interests that are, as a consequence, enemies."[95] Lafargue enlisted classical philosophy and the English novel behind this insight. "Every nation," he wrote, "when founded upon private property, is divided into two enemy nations. Socrates, more than two thousand years before Disraeli, proclaimed this truth."[96] "Two enemy nations" in "every nation." . . . According to Guesdists, an "international" war raged *within* France.

These "intranational" enemy nations generated their own distinctive nationalisms. "There is not *one* patriotism," Charles Bonnier insisted. "Each [class] possesses its own."[97] One patriotism, the proletariat's socialist nationalism, authentically represented the nation; the other, degenerate "bourgeois patriotism," violated the "true interests of France."[98] As self-avowed representatives of a working class that represented the real nation, Guesdists abandoned their antinational cosmopolitanism for socialist nationalism, vaunting themselves as personifying the "true interests" of the "true France." French Marxists felt that they could, in this socialist-nationalist personification, "declare ourselves patriots" with a clear conscience, for "it is we, the international socialists, who alone have taken up the defense of the interests of the great mass of our compatriots."[99] French Marxists pledged to defend the "the idea of the homeland, . . . the living remnant of France, transmitted to [us socialists] across the centuries." They would, in turn, "transmit it to the generations that will follow us."[100] Barrès himself could not have put it better—had he been a mystical socialist nationalist rather than a mystical national socialist.

While socialist nationalism obviously contradicted the Guesdists' otherwise stringent cosmopolitanism, it nonetheless empowered a robust "internationalism." According to the Parti Ouvrier, the proletariat's hegemony *within* nations would ensure amity *between* nations. Guesdists portrayed the hegemonic workers of the future as "extending the hand of friendship across borders while working to give their own nations the highest degree of development."[101] Not for working people the chauvinism, racism, and militarism of the degenerate bourgeoisie. The revolutionary working class in each country embodied both their nation's national interest *and* the entire world's Kantian aspiration to "perpetual peace." As representatives of such workers, Guesdists could thus represent themselves both as France's only true patriots *and* as the nation's only real internationalists. "French socialists are French just as German socialists are German," Guesde affirmed. "What we've signed with them is not a mutual pact of treason against our respective homelands, but rather a solidarity pact aimed at the liberation of all homelands into a humanity regenerated and free."[102]

In this formulation, "internationalism" was not "the denigration and sacrifice of nations, but their recognition, even their consecration" (contrast with the Parti Ouvrier's interpretations of internationalism as a cosmopolitan campaign against nationhood!).[103] According to *Le Socialiste*,

> [T]he role of a patriotic internationalist will be . . . to struggle against everything that isolates his own nation, everything that particularizes it. His patriotism will consist in developing everything that might adapt it [to the common good], everything that might contribute to the common interest of the International, and thus gradually lead to union between the nations.[104]

The triumph of the International depended upon this free development of free nations, and would in turn empower that free development. As usual, the Guesdists historicized this insight into a teleology that led toward utopia—just as they did with their antinational cosmopolitanism. "The *international or human* homeland toward which we are moving," Guesde promised, "is the highest stage of that long evolution of which the family, the tribe, the province, and the nation have been successive phases. It operates, not by the death, but for the life of nations, to whom it will bring peace and well-being."[105] Guesde explained (misleadingly) that "just as in 1789, when the French nation was being constituted, the cry of 'Vive la France!' did not mean 'Down with Normandy!' [Normandy was actually to be abolished by revolutionary departmentalization] . . . so no more does the cry 'Vive l'Internationale!' mean 'Down with France!'"[106] This socialist-nationalist dialectic was why, Guesdists affirmed, "we internationalists are . . . the complete nationalists, while M. Maurice Barrès and his [chauvinist] friends are simply limited nationalists."[107] Barrèsian ultranationalism betrayed both France and humanity; Marxist socialist nationalism, by contrast, affirmed both. In their socialist-nationalist persona, Guesdists would have fervently seconded that great twentieth-century theorist of national identity, Frantz Fanon, when he argued that "national consciousness . . . is the only thing that will give us an international dimension."[108]

Understandably, the Guesdists' "bourgeois nationalist" adversaries derided the POF's chiliastic expectation that socialist nationalism would usher in a utopian "perpetual peace." Even if such dreams were desirable (and many nationalists instead viewed war as the "hygiene of nations"), they were impossible. Nations, these "realists" argued, *defined* themselves through conflict—a definitional truth that would be just as applicable to future socialist nations as it was to the current capitalist ones. Even the socialist "nations" emergent within the states of the fin de siècle supposedly warred against each other. The nationalists' most telling critique of socialist internationalism asserted that the parties to the "International" quarreled just as fiercely as did the belle epoque's bellicose "bourgeois" states. In particular, the Guesdists' enemies sought to demonstrate that French socialists and German socialists replicated the conflicts between the Third Republic and the Reich.[109] These demonstrations had considerable force. Bebel and Guesde could hardly shoot each other, as socialists would do in the future—the future that would see Russian tanks clanking into the People's Republic of Hungary, skirmishes between the Soviet Union and Communist China, and socialist Vietnam's invasion of (putatively) socialist Cambodia. But the acrimony that marred the International's "fraternal" congresses foreshadowed the worse to come, and thus legitimated the "realist" critique of Marxism's internationalist idealism.[110]

Guesdists responded to such critique with little more than dogmatic denial. According to French Marxists, workers' interests were by definition compatible, whether those interests manifested within nations or between nations. Confronted by conflict within the International, Guesdists retreated toward utopia:

> The day will come, and it's not far off, when [bourgeois chauvinism] will finally disappear to make way for the only reasonable patriotism, which will exclude all chauvinism and will encompass all nations in a global fraternity and solidarity, nations retaining their own characters and their own particular qualities, but combining them and adding to them, rather than separating them. And then will be realized, under the flag of socialism, Schiller's prophesy, hymned by Beethoven: "Embrace each other, you millions!"[111]

The extraordinary repetitiveness of such florid rhetoric measured the anxiety that it repressed. In their cosmopolitan persona, after all, French Marxists fully agreed with nationalist "realism": nationhood meant war.

Close reading of the Guesdist corpus reveals an oscillation between contradictory paradigms: the repudiation of nationhood, on the one hand, and the appropriation of national identity, on the other. Both rhetorics—that of antinational cosmopolitanism and that of socialist nationalism—served the POF well in its long war against "bourgeois" nationhood, but the Party's two personae were never reconciled, much less synthesized. French Marxists, of course, denied self-contradiction, and the denial sometimes rang true—but only so long as Guesdists aligned socialist nationalism with internationalism, rather than with cosmopolitanism. As Guesde made the point, "[I]n being internationalist, and in rejoicing in the title, socialists don't cease to be French."[112] Perhaps. . . . Unfortunately, a century of disillusioning experience—including the experience of the Parti Ouvrier—has discredited any such easy harmonization of the socialist universal with the national particular. Irresolvable conflict between cosmopolitan telos and nationalist reflex better represents Marxism's enduring reality—as it represents the abiding truth of our modern world.

CHAPTER 5

"Savage, Brutal, and Bestial Mentalities": The Guesdists and Racism

Of all the ideologies besetting Marxism, racism has been the most rabid. Certainly the Parti Ouvrier could not ignore its challenge. Racists ravened across fin de siècle Europe. Racist historians read the past as a Darwinian contest; racist sociologists legitimated social hierarchy as biological variation; racist ideologues assailed Marxists as traitors to the race. Traumatized by the debacle of 1870–71, some of the French succumbed to this bacchanalia, forsaking their ancestral ideals of equality and fraternity for a hierarchical and exclusionary racism previously more characteristic of Central Europe.[1] France, indeed, exemplified the time's racist onslaught on Marxism. Georges Vacher de Lapouge and Jules Soury's metahistory of decadent and virile races thwarted Marxism's teleology of transcended and ascendant classes; Gustave Le Bon's racial sociology subordinated the working-class "masses" to "natural aristocracies" of (literally) breeding; Maurice Barrès concocted his potent anti-Marxist brew from racial ingredients.[2] The Parti Ouvrier's reaction to this aggression classically illustrates Marxism's fraught encounter with ideological ethnicity. It warrants scholarly recovery.[3]

"Barbarous Sentiments": The Guesdists and Racism

Once domiciled in Paris, "race" came to mean many things. At its most formidable, as pseudoscientific dogma, it became a biological "essentialism." The racist French of the belle epoque could be found angrily disputing their identities as "Nordics" or "Mediterraneans," sagely measuring each others' skulls, and debating the relative merits of the dolichocephalic and brachycephalic, while smugly founding their intercontinental superiority upon "whiteness," with superficial skin color supposedly manifesting their transcendent "racial soul." In the stuffy academy no less than in the bohemian cafe, a "narcissism of minor differences" reigned supreme. Less noxiously, "race," in popular parlance, could mean little more than "nation," with publicists writing of the French or British "races"—a casual usage that reinforced an anything but casual ultranationalism. Between these vacuous extremes, between the fake precision of "racial science" and the flaccid rhetoric of journalistic convenience, dwelled a vast array of empty signifiers parading as ethnic absolutes, from which void marched forth bizarre entities such as the "Latin race."[4] How, then, did the Parti Ouvrier engage this dire discourse?

With humanistic honor. One of the Guesdists' most distinctive, most surprising, and most admirable traits was their bitter hostility toward racial prejudice, and this at a time when racism fouled every other ideological discourse. Such impermeability to racist infiltration, of course, might have been expected of French Marxists. Their German Jewish master had despised "race theory," and certainly detested the racists' "master thinker," Marx's contemporary Arthur de Gobineau.[5] Even Marx's own racist remarks, including sporadic calumnies against his natal ethnicity, manifested only the ire of a cosmopolitan confronted by particularism. Marx may have hated the Jews (as anti-Marxist Jews have alleged), but only when Jews expressed a separate, and separatist, identity. In the same way, he hated (he was a great hater) the French, the English, and the Germans, or, for that matter, the Bretons, the Welsh, and the Sorbs—so long as they identified themselves as particularistic "races." For Marx, ethnic militants—whether Jewish or anti-Semitic, French or German, black or white—betrayed universal humanity by asserting racial particularity.[6]

Guesdists thus remained almost entirely unsullied by their time's otherwise all-pervasive racism. Unlike so many of their compatriots, they never attributed "national" differences to biology. Not for Guesdists the "mythology of the blood" propagated by Volkish gurus. According to the POF, the racist rulings of Lapouge or Soury were utterly nonsensical, and certainly unscientific. "Scientific" socialists should ignore them. Rather than entrapping themselves in the dim dead-ends of racial mythology, the Parti Ouvrier urged socialists and workers "to struggle against the system [capitalism], for which the individual is nothing, and race still less."[7] French Marxists summarily dismissed the notion that racial identity bonded the French to each other. What bonds linked ebullient Languedocians to dour Normands, asked the POF, apart from manacles locked into place by bloodstained Crusaders or ruses woven by conniving royal intendants? Certainly not some racial destiny manifest in "la terre et les morts"! Guesdists had nothing but contempt for the "obsolete idea of 'the union of peoples of the same race,'" declaring it "false, reactionary and ridiculously impractical."[8]

If race failed to bond the French one to another, it could hardly separate them from others. In the POF's first of many edicts on the subject, *L'Egalité* insisted that

> the theory of race is absurd, ridiculous, unrealizable. . . . There are no longer races: there are only interests and classes; it is easier and more logical to unite

> the Latin bourgeoisie to the German and Anglo-Saxon bourgeoisie than to unite the bourgeoisie and the workers . . . of the same race. That union between the bourgeoisie of all nations and all races has been an accomplished fact for a long time. Let's now create the union of the workers of the world, without any distinctions, in order to challenge the bourgeoisie of all races and all nations. The Parti Ouvrier recognizes no races, only classes![9]

Guesdists relentlessly reiterated these propositions: the dominance of a panracial bourgeoisie, the coming-to-be of a transracial proletariat, and the irrelevance of race as compared to class. According to the Parti Ouvrier, those who "confounded . . . race with social system"[10] thereby misunderstood the past, misjudged the present, and falsified the future.

The POF's antiracism reprised the "globalization theory" of the movement's nationalism critique. According to the Parti Ouvrier, capitalists ignored race in their ravenous quest for surplus value, just as they ignored nationality. Black or white, Asian or Occidental, Aryan or Semite—all were exploited with fine impartiality. "Only class interest, that grand leveler, indicates the truth," proclaimed Charles Bonnier, one of the most cosmopolitan of the Parti Ouvrier's theorists. "There's no longer a racial question under capitalism; the factory accepts all men, black, yellow, or white, and they're all equal before the machine."[11] At its most extreme, this class reductionism woefully misconstrued worldwide proletarianization. A few fin de siècle capitalists may have dreamt of indiscriminately marshaling the global masses into their factories, but cultural and political barriers blocked such multiracial labor recruitment, even if it could have been genuinely imagined by the racist bourgeois of the belle epoque. At the same time, Guesdists were wrong to think that, for workers, "servitude is neither white, nor yellow, nor black; it's [solely] proletarian."[12] For many of the world's workers—in the mines of the Rand, on construction sites throughout America's Mexican borderland, among the rubber plantations of Southeast Asia—servitude issued as much from ethnicity as from class. In Algiers or Nouméa, as in San Antonio or Singapore, and to some extent even in Marseille or Paris, capitalist globalization elicited both class war *and* race war.

Despite these disheartening realities, or perhaps because of them, the Parti Ouvrier urged socialists everywhere to preach the antiracist catechism to the workers of the world, to lead a crusade "of proletarians of all races against the capitalists of all races."[13] According to the POF, a black socialist from Martinique should address white workers in France as a socialist, not as a black; a white socialist from Roubaix should greet black workers in Fort-de-France not as a white, but as a socialist. Marxists everywhere, the French Marxists were convinced, could rest assured that "racial differences did not exist within a socialist proletariat."[14] In the Parti Ouvrier's transcendent vision of the future, and even in its perspective on the present, the whites of Roubaix and the blacks of Fort-de-France melded into the red of the International, and thus became the Interracial. In the categorical words of the Parti Ouvrier's *Programme*, "[T]he emancipation of the productive class is that of all human beings without distinction . . . of race."[15]

This feckless dismissal of the proletariat's racialized reality will today seem utterly bizarre to most Marxists and to all post-Marxists—obsessed as they are by the ignominious collapse of class politics before resurgent racial identity in Rotterdam or Dreux, by recurrent explosions of racist violence from Tower Hamlets to Rwanda, by the renaissance of "scientific" racism in bell curves and ethology. Nonetheless, the Parti Ouvrier's insouciance accorded well with some aspects of France's nineteenth-century experience.[16] Unlike American or South African Marxists, militants of the POF were spared the daunting labor of constructing a united socialist movement for a racially divided society. Regardless of France's much-mooted rupture between "Nordic racial types" in the north and "Mediterranean types" in the south, in spite of frantic craniometry, despite the best efforts of the racist Right, the French suffered few racial conflicts during the belle epoque, apart from a sui generis anti-Semitism overlapping the country's national, religious, and "racial" cleavages.[17] And, even during the anti-Semitic convulsion of the Dreyfus affair, Guesdists did not endure the ethnic predicament confronting their comrades of the Russian Social Democratic and Labor Party. Unlike its sister party to the East, the POF never encountered any equivalent of the Bund, defiantly recruiting Jewish workers into an exclusively Jewish socialist party.[18] The Parti Ouvrier, then, if it so wished, could usually dismiss the "race question." In Roubaix or Roanne, even in Paris or Marseille, the Guesdist "making of the French working class" contended against fractures of gender, nationality, and religion, but rarely of race.

This relative immunity to racial conflict, of course, hardly pertained in Algeria or the colonies, where every aspect of politics turned on "white supremacy." But race war in Constantine or New Caledonia rarely impinged on the Parti Ouvrier's ideological awareness. After all, the racialized *outre-mer* hardly impacted on the metropolitan working class whose travails so obsessed the Guesdists. At the fin de siècle, Roubaisian employers imported cheap Belgians to work their mills, not the even cheaper but as yet inaccessible Algerians—and Roubaix interested the Parti Ouvrier far more than Algeria, Black Africa, Indochina, and the Antilles combined. When Guesdists scanned the historical outlook, seeking to anticipate storms that might check the proletariat's headway toward socialism, it was nationalism that clouded the horizon. No wonder the Parti Ouvrier gave so much attention to nationhood, and so little to race—often failing, or refusing, to acknowledge the latter's existence.

Very occasionally, however, the Parti Ouvrier uneasily recognized a "biological" sociology separate from the economic order. Guesdists then identified a "milieu cosmique," which established "les races humaines," as distinct from "le milieu économique," which generated the classes of capitalist society.[19] As if subliminally guided by this insight, French Marxists unthinkingly accepted "racial" distinctions between Europeans and non-Europeans, although without granting such identities as "white," "Negro," or "Asian" analytical force or ideological weight. Nonetheless, the Parti Ouvrier tacitly distinguished between these "races" and European "nationalities," and accorded them very different polemical handling.[20] The POF determinedly minimized "national" distinctions between, for instance, the French and Germans, but laxly accepted racial "difference" between Europeans, Asians, and blacks. No doubt the Parti Ouvrier's desperate desire to consolidate its "International" explains these alternative discursive strategies. The Second International, of course, remained almost entirely European, with little participation by Asians, blacks, or even South African, antipodean, and American whites.

The Parti Ouvrier thus casually assumed that some "natural" difference did indeed distinguish "whites," "Asians," and "blacks" from each other, although the POF manifested little interest in the "milieu cosmique" that supposedly differentiated them. Certainly the Guesdists exhibited none of "scientific" racism's obsession with race hierarchy and racial purity. Quite the contrary. Confronted with "race mixing," Guesdists foreshadowed today's postcolonial celebration of "hybridity." On one occasion, for instance, the POF commented acerbically on Britons' reluctance to interbreed with "natives," a squeamishness supposedly in sharp contrast to the behavior of the French, who had engendered a multitude of fertile *métis*: the proliferating hybrids "to whom," Guesdists confidently predicted, "the future will belong."[21] *Métis*, the Parti Ouvrier argued with a peculiar inverse racism, were especially vital and creative, and thus apt for historical leadership. French Marxists practiced what they preached, elevating the ostentatiously hybridized (and undoubtedly creative and vital) French-Jewish-Cuban-Negro-Carib Paul Lafargue to coleadership of the POF.[22] As for racial hierarchy, Guesdists eagerly anticipated an impending socialist revolution in Africa and the Caribbean that would there inaugurate "the dictatorship of the proletariat of the black race"[23]—an anticipation illustrating the Parti Ouvrier's characteristic vulnerability to racial categorization, but also the movement's almost complete immunity to racial prejudice.

Despite the Guesdists' carefully cultivated indifference to race war, the fin de siècle's many racial conflicts did sporadically impinge on their ideological awareness—most frequently with European anti-Semitism, sometimes during colonial *razzias*, and occasionally with American lynchings. At the same time, bewildered Guesdists found themselves beset, even at home, by racist doctrines that undermined their "scientific socialism." Enemies such as Edouard Drumont, who accepted Gobineau's dictum that "the ethnic question dominates all problems of history," ostentatiously disputed Marx's belief that "all history is the history of class struggle"; Barrèsian ancestral determinism flatly contradicted the Marxists' historical materialism; and the anti-Semites' pursuit of race war disrupted the proletariat's mobilization behind Marxist class warriors.[24] How, French Marxists uneasily asked themselves, could meaningless "racial" differences so divisively intersect with the battlefronts of the class war—if not often in metropolitan France, then often enough abroad?

On the rare occasions when Guesdists sought to answer this vexing question, they discerned a cunning plot to substitute race for class. Financial speculators, according to the POF, diverted the rage of the petits bourgeois they despoiled onto innocent Jews; cosmopolitan capitalists set Algerian colons and indigenous Moslems to fighting each other, while exploiting both; the American plantocracy ruled vulnerable poor whites by deflecting their anger onto even more vulnerable poor blacks. Capitalist accumulation, Guesdists demonstrated, negated race, but bourgeois hegemony throve on it. Outraged by the barbarous survival of racial prejudice, Guesdists furiously denounced the "grotesque theory of race invented by fraudulent bourgeois scholars to enable despots to turn men against each other."[25]

Very occasionally, however, Guesdists themselves succumbed to their epoque's ambient racism. Sadly, at the fin de siècle, it was not always true that Marxist socialists suffered "neither from race hatreds nor from nationalist hatreds" and that they "left these barbarous sentiments to the bourgeoisie."[26] The Parti Ouvrier's most egregious lapses into racism always responded to the era's proletarian version of "the yellow peril"—that scenario in which cosmopolitan capitalists would flood the "white" labor market with Asian "coolies." "It will be the Western proletarian, who has a wife and children, who'll be replaced by these Chinese sodomites," raged *Le Socialiste* in one such highly unrepresentative paroxysm of racial terror and racist terrorism. "It will take years of vicious war, as in the United States, to drive these born thieves of the workers' bread into the sea or force them to return home."[27] Such tirades against coolies (Chinese "pédérastes,"[28] as Guesde once uncouthly libeled them) were rare and aberrant in the Parti Ouvrier's otherwise monolithically antiracist legacy. But they nonetheless exemplified the historical vulnerability of socialism, even Marxist socialism, to racist contamination (not to mention homophobia!).

Hostility to Asians failed to penetrate deeply into the POF, certainly by comparison with the Left's racist corruption in the United States or Australia—if only because French employers, unlike their American and Australian counterparts, never materialized the free-trade fantasy of infiltrating low-cost East Asian workers into high-cost "white" labor markets. But the Parti Ouvrier nonetheless terrorized its working-class constituency by "revealing" how French capitalists still schemed to replace their "lazy, self-indulgent, and drunken workers"[29] with hardworking, self-denying, abstemious Chinese. Employers supposedly intended to import Asian labor simply because "wherever there are semibarbarians, like the Chinese, who can live . . . on a handful of rice, [capitalists] not only *can* but *must* recruit yellow laborers in order to starve white workers."[30] In a fantastical exaggeration of this racist paranoia, *Le Socialiste* even informed its readers that experiments were underway in the United State to replace human workers with trained monkeys—a project whose success would be met with universal joy among capitalists, as they could then "starve the entire human race in order to pocket yet a few more pennies."[31] Only socialism, the Parti Ouvrier augured, would safeguard white workers against impending Asian (and simian!) invasion.

Guesdists on rare occasions escalated this ugly polemic into a virtual "battle of civilizations," projecting a nightmare vision of Europe overwhelmed by an Orient resurgent on waves of capital investment. This "renaissance of [the Asiatic] people," which, Guesdists suggested, "should be cause for rejoicing," instead threatened "the ruin of Europe." Who was to blame? It was "the bourgeoisie, [which] has launched itself blindly into unlimited production, and which has thus put civilization at risk."[32] Inundated by low-cost East Asian products, Europe's stay-at-home capitalists would only be able to survive, the Parti Ouvrier warned, by replacing their high-cost local labor with low-cost Asian immigrants, so that all the world's workforce, from Peking to Paris, would soon be yellow.[33] Only a triumphant socialism could prevent Europe's resultant "Asianization." According to a panic-mongering *Le Socialiste*, Asians were

> on the march in order to invade Europe, which [Asia] will ruin if it finds {Europe] on its arrival still in a state of capitalist civilization. We have no time to lose, and there is no other barrier that can stop the Chinese or Japanese coolie except the communist and collectivist civilization that will not accept [the Asian's] low-cost labor, and will repel him back to . . . Asia.[34]

So much for proletarian internationalism! According to this preposterous prediction, France would have to choose between "the conquest of Europe by the yellow race and the conquest of political power . . . by the proletariat."[35]

Such psychotic excesses rarely soiled the Parti Ouvrier's cosmopolitan persona, although they have received disproportionate attention from critics of socialist racism.[36] Actually, sympathetic reference to "coolies" vastly outnumbered instances of anti-Asian paranoia in Guesdist discourse. Even when foretelling "Asiatic invasion," the POF usually empathized with the "so-called inferior races, who wish to take their revenge [by migrating into Europe] for the conquests and insults loaded upon them by European civilization."[37] In these more representative Guesdist accounts of the world's racial dynamics, capitalists and imperialists, not coolies, embodied the "yellow peril." According to the Parti Ouvrier, the itinerant Asian workers scattered across the world suffered exploitation in its most extreme form, alienated as they were from both their labor power and their people. They deserved socialist sympathy, not racist denigration.

In this more empathic mode, Guesdists depicted "coolies" as exemplary workers, rather than as sodomitical invaders. Chinese laborers, according to the POF, were "hardworking by piety, sober by nature."[38] These admirable qualities constituted the real "racial" threat to Europe, as "capitalists naturally wished to employ such workers, whose sobriety and patience are increasingly necessary [to support] the luxury and greed of the bourgeoisie."[39] European and Asian workers, Guesdists urged, thus shared a common cause: proletarians both East and West should strive as one to rid their world of bourgeois parasites. When considering transcontinental relations among workers, Guesdists almost always proposed a revolutionary alliance between "yellow" and "white" proletarians, an "alliance that would embrace all the exploited, whatever race they belong to—the whites of Europe and of America, just as much as the blacks on Martinique, or as the yellow coolies of the United States or of Australia."[40] This cosmopolitan alliance-strategy—overwhelmingly dominant in Guesdist discourse, profoundly in keeping with Marx's humanism, and catastrophically blind to the time's global realities—counseled a proletarian union of all the world's races, rather than a fortress Europe armored by socialism against Asiatic invasion.

Given the Parti Ouvrier's absence from French Indochina, Asian workers remained abstractions in Guesdist polemic, whether portrayed as threatening invaders or as potential comrades. Not so with blacks. On Guadeloupe and Martinique, Guesdists strove mightily to mobilize black workers against the islands' white planter elite. In the course of this mobilization, the charismatic (and black) leader of the Parti Ouvrier in Guadeloupe, Jean-Hégésippe Légitimus, became both the founder of Antillean socialism and one of the first and greatest champions of the islands' long-oppressed blacks. His two-front war against class exploitation and racial domination should have evoked Guesdist acceptance that black workers suffered both as exploited proletarians and as dominated blacks—a requirement very occasionally met, as when the Parti Ouvrier dispatched its best wishes to workers in the colony of Guadeloupe, who had "a double battle to sustain"[41] against class oppression and racial discrimination. Most often, however, Guesdists, even black Guesdists, simply ignored the racial dimension of the Antilles's ugly society.

Today, this neglect must seem highly culpable. Yet the Guesdists remained admirably free of their time's antiblack racism. After all, in the fin de siècle's conventional racial hierarchy, blacks crouched submissively at the bottom, barely above the great apes. Yet not a single instance of contempt for the "Negroid" or hostility toward blacks sullied the Parti Ouvrier's record. The worst that might be attributed to the POF would be one or two implicit devaluations of the blacks' grievances by comparison with those of whites. The POF, for instance, seemed to be more outraged by the "Massacre of Fourmies," with its white French victims, than by the even bloodier killings on Martinique during 1900, which the Parti Ouvrier nonetheless denounced as a "massacre recapitulating Fourmies."[42] Murdered black militants on Martinique, unfortunately, seemed to matter a bit less to their Party than did slaughtered white demonstrators in the Nord. And Légitimus, while always lionized, was also occasionally patronized, his speeches being described, on one unfortunate occasion, as having been delivered "with a slightly exotic accent, [but] in good French and in excellent form."[43] Nonetheless, the Parti Ouvrier explicitly included the workers of the islands ("our black friends")[44] as part of its proletarian constituency, and never denigrated them for their color, when noticing it at all. Remarking that "Negroes . . . are entering, at this end of the century, into the proletariat and consequently into the socialist movement," the Parti Ouvrier discovered to its joy that "as soon as they are proletarianized, blacks comprehend the class war and . . . by their energy and their organization, have shown themselves to be admirable soldiers of the workers' cause."[45] For proof, Guesdists could point to the apex of their own party. As coleader of the POF, Lafargue ostentatiously prided himself on his mélange of Caribbean ancestries, identifying himself without qualm as "a product of my Negro extraction."[46]

Guesdists not only welcomed blacks into their comradeship, but explicitly repudiated "white supremacy." This noxious racist formula, French Marxists alleged, had been concocted by the world's ruling class to set superordinate whites against subaltern blacks, thereby subordinating both to global capital. At the same time, white racism supposedly reflected bourgeois revulsion against nascent black labor militancy. Commenting on the fin de siècle revival of antiblack racism in the United States, *Le Socialiste* explained that while once the Negro had been "a brother [to bourgeois American whites] when it had been a question of turning him into a free laborer," now, "having become suspect of wanting to appropriate the fruit of his labor," the Negro had once again become "the enemy, the inferior over whom the 'white' will have the right of life and death."[47] Lynchings, race riots, white privilege and black exclusion—all manifested capital's malignancy. Black and white workers, Guesdists urged, should unite to fight against both the capitalism that exploited them equally and the bourgeois hegemony that so divided them.

For all their hatred of white American racists, and despite their enthusiasm for black Antillean socialists, Guesdists would still have preferred to ignore the "race question." The Parti Ouvrier's studied indifference toward the racial dimension of its own implantation in the Caribbean, where newborn Antillean socialism undoubtedly assailed white planters not only as planters but as whites, itself indicated the extent to which French Marxists discounted racial conflict. When describing Caribbean workers' abominable suffering, Guesde, Lafargue, and even Légitimus usually ignored the fact that they were black. For Marxist militants, the anguish of the black plantation worker was proletarian, not racial.[48] This elision of race may, to some extent, have reflected a "taken-for-granted" equation of class with ethnicity. In the Antilles, everyone knew, black equaled worker, and worker equaled black.[49] Nonetheless, the Guesdists' conviction that black workers in the Caribbean differed not at all from white workers in the *metropole* also manifested the Parti Ouvrier's humanistic universalism. Studiously avoiding racial "difference," French Marxists enfolded blacks into socialism's "great human family, without distinctions of race."[50] According to Alexandre Zévaès, "[F]or us socialists, the Negro workers of Martinique, who are so odiously exploited, are our brothers in a common humanity, workers having the same rights and the same aspirations, proletarians having their place in the ranks and in the heart of the great French socialist family."[51]

The Parti Ouvrier thus characteristically preferred to ignore its era's festering racial conflicts—conflicts that, in Point-à-Pitre or Fort-de-France, strained the color-blind Marxist vision of class politics, but which were as yet comfortably remote from fin de siècle Lille or Lyon. The very infrequency of Parti Ouvrier commentary on racism indicated a disabling blind spot in the movement's understanding of the modern political culture, with consequent failures of vision that would have cost the POF dearly in less favorable (metropolitan French) circumstances.

"A Socialism of Fools": Guesdists and the Anti-Semites

During January 1899, as France convulsed into the nationwide anti-Semitic frenzy occasioned by the Dreyfus affair, a Jewish girl of Nantes was grossly insulted by an anti-Semite. Her furious brother accosted the culprit and forced him to apologize, and the next day their father's watchmaker shop was in turn assailed by an anti-Semitic gang. Passersby rushed to the aid of the beleaguered Jews, a battle ensued, the police intervened . . . and arrested the public-spirited passersby! In itself, this little story merely recapitulates that sad moment in French history—a time of racist outrages, civil war in the street, and a culpably incompetent state. But this minor incident must intrigue students of Marxism, as one of those arrested was a local leader of the POF.[52] What motivated him? Sympathy for his beset Jewish neighbors? Identification with a persecuted people? Hatred of the rampaging national socialists who menaced his own movement even while assaulting Jews? We will never know. But we *can* discern the ideological motifs that governed *Le Socialiste*'s reporting of the fracas, and of so many like it during those fraught years.

Scholarship demands such discernment, if only because the French Marxists have been so neglected in studies of "Marxism and the Jewish question." At the same time, in the voluminous literature on the "Jewish question in France," the Guesdists are frequently, even usually, indicted as anti-Semitic. In some recent work, this indictment has been so tendentious as to barely warrant refutation. But serious scholarship has echoed the charge.[53] According to scholarly consensus, Fourier and Proudhon's toxic legacy (the two ideologues hated "Jewry" with an almost insane ferocity) has percolated down the generations, periodically poisoning French socialism, from the belle epoque's left antiDreyfusards until today's left anti-Zionists.[54] But the Guesdists? Were they infected?

It is tempting to answer this question with an a priori yes. At the fin de siècle, even the most rigorously cosmopolitan socialist could hardly evade the time's all-pervasive anti-Semitism. Nonetheless, before the Holocaust, there was anti-Semitism and anti-Semitism. Some of it was superficial and episodic, and hardly inhibited determined opposition to political racism, or even, on occasion, adoption of militant philo-Semitism. Jaurès's valiant campaign against the anti-Dreyfusard anti-Semites is deservedly well remembered, his careless anti-Semitic asides deservedly less so. Zola is rightly famed for the great Dreyfusard manifesto *J'Accuse*, but also wrote the rightly forgotten anti-Semitic *L'Argent*. Clemenceau led the Dreyfusards with the same strategic genius he later gave to wartime France, but also flinched from the "greasy Jews" he encountered on holiday in Carlsbad. Even the Jewish hero of the epic struggle for Dreyfus's liberation, the wonderful Marius Bernard ("Bernard Lazare"), tarnished a noble life with occasional casual denigration of his own beleaguered people.[55] If socialist "anti-Semitism" was of this sort, it should carry little historical weight.

Yet socialist anti-Semitism of the fin de siècle sometimes *was* racist in a systematic ideological sense, rather than being superficial, incidental, and of little consequence. Socialists, after all, contributed their francs to the Monument Henry, that roll call of anti-Semitic fanaticism—and contributed as socialists. The aggressive protofascism of the 1890s, in one of its most virulently anti-Semitic metamorphoses, erupted out of the decaying corpse of Blanquist socialism. And Jules Guérin, leader of Paris's anti-Semitic mobs, had been spawned from the capital's Rochefortite socialist milieu.[56] There is cause indeed to suspect fin de siècle French socialists of genuine racial anti-Semitism.

But the Guesdists? Cosmopolitan anti-anti-Semitism? Occasional careless prejudice? Or ingrained anti-Semitism? One answer given to this question is that the Parti Ouvrier's Marxism, far from immunizing the movement against racist pestilence, actually inculcated the plague. Was not Marx himself a notorious "self-hating Jew"?[57] The belle epoque offered some support for this diagnosis. French anti-Semites, after all, gleefully appropriated Marx's supposedly anti-Semitic essay on the "Jewish question," thereby enlisting the great theorist under their bloodstained banner. Here we have "guilt by association," at least. More seriously, an American scholar has argued that Marxism's overvaluation of production, and the doctrine's consequent denigration of commercial "circulation," alienated Guesdists from the Jews, a people who were believed to inhabit only the circuits of commerce and finance.[58] But whatever the specific argument, liberal ideologues and scholars, detesting both anti-Semitic national socialism and Marxist anticapitalism, have regularly fused their two great enemies into a single poisonous amalgam, no less (if less effortlessly) during the belle epoque than at today's "End of History." Thus traduced, Marxism's long history of anti-anti-Semitism disappears from the historical record.

Marxist historians without liberal parti-pris have inadvertently reinforced this tendentious conflation of Marxism and Nazism. Claude Willard, the Communist intellectual and premier historian of the POF, has revealed moments of Guesdist anti-Semitism, notably an ugly outburst in one of the Party's most heterodox provincial papers (*La République Sociale* of Narbonne), and his incidental mention of this unfortunate occasion has been deafeningly amplified in subsequent appropriations of his research. That the Marxists' authoritative Parisian press remained effectively unsullied by anti-Semitism has, as a result, been virtually overlooked.[59] This blindness to the evidence is absurd. The POF imposed no equivalent of the "democratic centralism" later championed by Communists like Willard, so that the Parti Ouvrier's local newspapers sometimes diverged wildly from the national "party line." That the eccentric and literally peripheral *République Sociale* has come to represent French Marxism during the fin de siècle is therefore an astounding and utterly unjustified substitution of Narbonne for the nation.[60]

Worse yet, Willard identified the Parti Ouvrier as aligned with anti-Semitism because the movement's militants appeared *against* anti-Semitic speakers in "conférences contradictoires," thereby supposedly lending the anti-Semites socialist credibility—a charge that would make the Guesdists equally guilty of abetting political Catholicism (they spoke against the Christian Democrats), procapitalist liberalism (they debated the Opportunists), and Conservative monarchism (they contested the traditional Right). Should Guesdist orators have dodged debate, flinching from duels with their anti-Semitic enemies, during a period when "conférences contradictoires" were the prime fora of popular political culture? Surely not! Again, this minor absurdity in an otherwise magnificent study has become canonical—representative, astoundingly, of Guesdist connivance with anti-Semitism.[61]

Even when the Parti Ouvrier denounced its anti-Semitic enemies, historians have complained that the Party's willingness to quote their rhetoric made the movement complicit with them. Guesde himself—a great hater, but a hater of capitalism rather than of Jews—has been accused of anti-Semitism, albeit without serious evidence.[62] And, at its most ridiculous, in the hands of Bernard-Henri Lévy, the charge of anti-Semitism has been leveled against the POF because both the Marxist Lafargue and the anti-Semitic Drumont denounced the army's massacre of workers at Fourmies, and because Guesde, like Drumont, attacked the Rothschilds. Apparently the POF should have applauded the butchery of its Fourmisien supporters, because the responsible subprefect was Jewish (a racial identity totally ignored in the Guesdists' invective, however central it may have been in Drumont's). As for Rothschild, Lévy seems to suggest that the violently anticapitalist Parti Ouvrier should have spared him socialist critique, because France's premier plutocrat was a Jew.[63]

Such "scholarship" barely warrants critique. Yet a close reading of the Guesdists' textual legacy does reveal troubling material. When confronted, for instance, by the fin de siècle's illicit intimacies between finance and politics, *Le Socialiste*, in the aftermath of the Boulanger crisis and the Panama affair, recalled Balzac's *La Maison Nucingen*, with its vivid portrayal of the imaginary Frédéric de Nucingen: embodiment of the Jewish financial elite, manipulator of the apparently powerful, and caricature of the real-life Rothschilds. Driving home the point, the Guesdist paper then cited the avowedly anti-Semitic Second Empire socialist Alphonse Toussenel as having further illuminated Balzac's lurid portrayal of plutocratic wealth, occult power, and public corruption—but in reality, rather than in fiction.[64] Anti-Semitism? Perhaps. Yet perhaps not. Recalling that the royalist money financing the Boulangist campaign had been raised from the Jewish banking community, *Le Socialiste* concluded its exposé with the observation that "the [liberal] Opportunists are implicated in Panama; the [Boulangist] Orleanists dig deep into Jewish strongboxes. Money obviously has no religion."[65] On which aspect of these texts should we focus? On the invidious attention to "Jewish strongboxes"? Or on the cosmopolitan contention that the ruling establishment was incarnate in the cash nexus, not in race or religion? Anecdote might enforce either emphasis.

Most "discoveries" of Guesdist anti-Semitism have resulted from just such anecdotal foraging in the POF's voluminous textual legacy. Trolling through a random selection of texts without research rigor, choosing instances without attention to context, and "interpreting" them without hermeneutical empathy—these "methods" allow easy condemnation of the Parti Ouvrier. Researchers with the opposite parti-pris, using the same casual methodology, could easily reach exactly the opposite conclusion, praising the Guesdists for their supposed philo-Semitism. A single speech might be subjected to these conflicting interpretive strategies, as with Lafargue's address to his party's congress at Montluçon during 1898. Here he could be quoted as denouncing Drumont as "a dirty Jew," and as suggesting that "the megarich of modern Jewry stand shoulder-to-shoulder with the capitalist class, of which they are destined to become, at the moment of revolutionary peril, the most intelligent, the most cynical, and the most ferocious leaders."[66] Stop there, and Lafargue seems to be flirting with anti-Semitism. Go on, however, and he points out that "if in the past and in the present the Jews have allied themselves with the oppressors of humanity, they have also rendered humanity inestimable services"—moving in his account from Jewish heroes of the Marxist intelligentsia such as Spinoza to the conclusion that it was "a Jew, Karl Marx, who founded and inspired the International and who forged the theoretical arms which will give socialism its victory."[67] Anti-Semitism? Hardly! What to make of such textual ambiguity? For the scrupulous historian of ideas, this particular polemic, as any other, yields its meaning only through rigorous explication. As a text, it must be situated in its discursive domain—with its place established in relation to the Guesdists' massive textual legacy and, more challengingly, in dialogical relation with the Guesdists' interlocutors. Anachronism and anecdote will not do. Instead, Guesdist texts must be rigorously read for their "pragmatics," for their intent and consequence in time and place.[68]

A first observation from such an examination: however forcefully the "Jewish question" may have been posed, Guesdists would have preferred to ignore it. For the POF, spats between "Jewish financiers" and Christian anti-Semites were bourgeois business, and thus no concern of Marxists. These meaningless affrays, Guesdists argued, deflected socialists from class conflict—whether to war against the Jews, or to dispute with anti-Semites. Such deflections had to be avoided. Thus, despite Drumont's best-sellers, despite inflammatory oratory from the Ligue Antisémitique Française, despite the Dreyfus affair, the Parti Ouvrier self-consciously endeavored to disregard class-disruptive anti-Jewish racism (and, for that matter, class-disruptive philo-Semitism). When Drumont, for instance, peevishly suggested that the French Marxists had failed to fathom "la question juive," *Le Socialiste* ironically riposted that "Monsieur Drumont is right, for once: we have no desire to have anything to do with the Jewish question."[69] This refusal to rush to "the defense of the Jews, who aren't any better than the Christians," and the Parti Ouvrier's consequent injunction to "leave to the Radicals [France's left-liberal party] the monopoly on declarations in favor of the Jews,"[70] must appear—in hindsight, after the Shoah—to have been dreadfully misjudged.

What was the basis for this misjudgment? Essentially, the Parti Ouvrier had convinced itself that the anti-Semites were a negligible nuisance. Thus convinced, Guesdists dismissed anti-Semitism as "a purely artificial movement, launched by a few fourth-rate scholars and mandarins, intended to feed the need for excitement that occasionally grips the masses."[71] Even when confronted by Karl Lueger's Vienna, French Marxists discounted the Viennese anti-Semites' terrifying triumphs, confidently predicting that "this coalition of reactionary interests and ideas, this poorly articulated mixture, will soon evaporate without leaving a trace"[72]—an utterly awry assessment of the mayor, the movement, and the city that would so odiously tutor the young Hitler. As for France's own anti-Semites, the POF despised them for believing that their country's ills had been caused by "a few thousand individuals belonging to a race other than our own."[73] "All that is required," Guesdists were sure, was "to expose this thesis for it to collapse of itself."[74] French Marxists dedicated themselves to such exposure, and confidently awaited anti-Semitism's collapse.

In the Guesdists' exposés, capitalism alone caused France's ills, and the "socialization of the means of production" alone could cure them, not "the [anti-Semites'] murder of a race."[75] Guesdists thus dimly imagined genocide, but dismissed its possibility along with its rationality. On one occasion, for instance, the Guesdists mocked Drumont by comparing him to his inquisitorial forebears, who had genuinely believed that Jews murdered Christian babies. By contrast, the best that the contemporary anti-Semite could manage, according to a contemptuous Parti Ouvrier, was the lame assertion that "the Jews, *it is said*, tortured young Christians," with *Le Socialiste* sardonically suggesting that the italicized (in the original) qualifier "would extinguish the flames of any auto-da-fé."[76] The fanatics of the Inquisition had been burningly sincere, Guesdists sneered, but anti-Semites like Drumont merely played at mass murder. "We won't," the Guesdist newspaper smugly concluded, "take Monsieur Drumont seriously until his first auto-da-fé."[77] Given their inveterate optimism, Guesdists anticipated no such horror. They believed that the anti-Semites' efforts to reinstate the medieval ghetto, along with the massacres that had enforced its boundaries, would inevitably misfire. Anti-Semitism, the Parti Ouvrier confidently predicted, "will never be able to construct an impenetrable barrier between the Jews and the peoples of other races."[78]

Indeed, the Parti Ouvrier sometimes suggested that anti-Semites did not believe their own incendiary propaganda. Guesdists alleged that France's ultranationalist and ultramontane militants surreptitiously cultivated the Jewish financiers they otherwise claimed to hate. As *Le Socialiste* mordantly reminded its readers, "Baron" Rothschild held his title not from France, but from the pope![79] The Guesdist newspaper often reported Catholic aristocrats' attendance at social occasions hosted by Jewish financiers. When the chips were down, Guesdists jeered, when it was the case of a good party chez Rothschild, "class always trumps . . . race."[80] Social reality, the social reality of Saint-Germain soirées and country-house weekends, validated Guesdist cynicism. Society anti-Semites like Boni de Castellane indeed frequented the Jewish elite.[81] In the world of anti-Semitic aristocrats and Jewish financiers, wealth called to wealth, and met a warm reply. Where Guesdists went wrong, of course, was in their assumption that elite solidarity would always master wild-men among the more plebeian anti-Semites.

The Guesdists' dismissal of anti-Semitism, however misjudged it may have been, was not anti-Semitic. But the Parti Ouvrier *can* be accused of refusing to take sides in clashes between anti-Semites and their enemies. When Drumont, for instance, demanded that the POF protest against the liberal government's dismissal of the democratically elected but violently anti-Semitic mayor of Algiers, Max Régis, *Le Socialiste* disdainfully retorted that

> if, in order to fulfill the wishes of M. Drumont, we were to protest against the arbitrary actions of the prefect [of Algiers] . . . we would also have to protest with equal indignation against the measures taken by Régis that will exclude the Jewish workers of Algiers from their jobs. It's only by such a double condemnation of the abuse of power . . . that the Parti Ouvrier Français will be able to deploy its class propaganda in the Algerian departments, where there are already militants who aren't taking their orders from either the prefecture or from the mayor.[82]

This blind indifference to the ideological (not to mention ethical) contrast between the pogrom-promoting Régis and the antiracist prefect must appear profoundly obtuse, even deeply immoral, to our Holocaust-sensitized twenty-first-century eyes.

In any case, the Guesdists could not *really* ignore Drumont and Régis. By the late-1890s, the Ligue Antisémitique Française had recruited between five and ten thousand devoted militants, placing the LAF on a par with the POF itself.[83] On the street, in public halls, even on the factory floor, Guesdists encountered agitators against the Jews—agitating furiously against Jewish finance, against the "Jewish Republic" . . . and against "Jewish" Marxism. Could the Parti Ouvrier really disregard these anti-Semitic ultras? Of course not. By 1899, anti-Semitic and Guesdist street fighters would be battling each other in streets across France. At the same time, could the Parti Ouvrier really ignore Drumont's journalism, when everyone else read it, either in horror or with relish? Obviously not. The editors of *Le Socialiste* followed the *Libre Parole* with fascination, refuting Drumont's scurrilous commentary at every opportunity. Guesdists thus systematically belied their pretense of indifference. Beyond that shallow pretense, how *did* the Parti Ouvrier engage with the anti-Semitic ascendancy?

Perhaps by gearing anti-Semitism's surging energies into the drive toward socialism—not least by manipulating the fratricidal feud between bourgeois anti-Semites and bourgeois Jews. This coolly detached strategy was, again, not in itself anti-Semitic. But supping with the devil risked a poisoning, however pious the intent. Certainly, when we encounter a Guesdist leader in the Loire-Inférieure suggesting to a friend that it was tactically "wise to allow Jews and Jesuits to scratch each other's eyes out,"[84] the historian must flinch. And what of the following guidelines on steering between wealthy Opportunist Jews and rich Catholic anti-Semites?

> When the balance tips a little too far in the direction of the Semites, our duty is to rebalance it toward the anti-Semites, and vice versa. Our contempt being equal for Jewish and for Christian capitalists, the more revelations they bring us [against each other], the happier we'll be.[85]

In retrospect, after Auschwitz, *Le Socialiste*'s Machiavellianism appalls.

This amoral detachment, with its indiscriminate melding of liberal Jews with racist Catholics, in turn provoked liberals to indiscriminately meld anti-Semitism with Marxism. Guesdists thereby suffered that commonsense and commonplace, but always simpleminded, ideological gambit: "guilt by association." Angry Opportunists understandably, if foolishly, assimilated the anti-Semitism that assailed them from the national-socialist Right to the Marxism that assaulted them from the anticapitalist Left. Particularly in the aftermath of the Panama scandal, as the Opportunists' Republic tottered under the onslaughts of Right and Left, it proved easy enough to conflate the two antiliberal insurgencies. According to the oligarchy's jaundiced judgment, national socialists and Marxist socialists manifested as "spirits of the same lineage."[86] Anatole Leroy-Beaulieu, a vociferous spokesman for the bourgeois elite of the Third Republic, wrote an entire book "establishing" the complicity of anti-Semitism and socialism. And the political police, eager servants of the ruling Opportunists, continued to suspect covert collusion between the POF and the anti-Semites well into the period of the Dreyfus affair, during which, admittedly, the Guesdists rallied courageously against anti-Semitism. The Dreyfus affair's aftermath, however, revived liberal suspicion, as the Parti Ouvrier and the anti-Semitic Action Française ferociously assaulted the "Bloc" of bourgeois Republicans and reformist socialists that had claimed the Dreyfusard legacy. Guesde may have attacked the Waldeck-Rousseau and Combes ministries from the Left, and Charles Maurras from the Right, but, to the beleaguered Bloc, Left and Right attacked together.[87] The phantasmagoric concept of "totalitarianism," with its lumping of antiliberal fascists and antiliberal socialists into a single dread monstrosity, long predated its Cold War popularization.

The phantasms of liberal paranoia stalked abroad wrapped in broadsheets, as France's "public sphere," or at least its Grub Street, seemingly validated the Opportunists' horror stories. The louche journalistic milieu of the fin de siècle intermingled Marxists with anti-Semites, as in the enormously popular *Cri du Peuple* of the 1880s, or in Barrès's astonishing *La Cocarde* of the mid-1890s. Anti-Semites never contributed to the austere *Le Socialiste*, but a few of *Le Socialiste*'s stable of contributors wrote for some very questionable journals. Guesde himself signed editorials for Séverine's *Cri du Peuple*, apparently without worrying too much about the proprietress's hatred of Jews. And Clovis Hughes—one of the most prominent, if least orthodox, figures associated with the POF—threw himself into the adventure of Barrès's *Cocarde*, side by side with the anti-Semitic Charles Maurras. But it was the Guesdists' ambiguous relationship with Edouard Drumont that best supported the liberals' rhetoric of "guilt by association." Eclectic as always, the anti-Semitic propagandist happily appropriated Guesde's abuse of the ruling establishment to buttress his own diatribes. According to the racist ideologue, his Marxist counterpart was "not a political intriguer, but a man of faith and passion."[88] Drumont even praised Guesde's socialism, albeit with many qualifications. "The end pursued by [such] socialists of good faith," Drumont decided, "is very noble and their enterprise is very necessary"[89]—plaudits that socialists could well have done without, at least in retrospect.

And the Guesdists on Drumont? It has been alleged that they, like so many socialists of the time, were intimidated by his mounting popularity, or were at least overly impressed by his polemical triumphs. The Parti Ouvrier sometimes *did* laud Drumont's work, deciding on the occasion of the publication of *La France Juive*, for instance, that "one has at last found oneself in the presence of a writer who is sincere, passionate to the point of madness, striking out right and left, wounding both friends and enemies."[90] *Le Socialiste*'s gushing reviewer then suggested that "carried away by his hatred of the Semites, the Catholic pamphleteer—who has forgotten that his Christ was born of a Jewess, that his God had embodied Himself as a Jew—has ended up, without realizing it, by 'downing' finance in general, without distinction of race or religion."[91] In much the same way, the Guesdist newspaper praised Drumont's *Le Secret de Fourmies* for its bravura demolition of the hated Opportunists.[92] At such moments, to Guesdists reading their *Socialiste*, Drumont must almost have seemed "one of us."

Not yet, Guesde or Lafargue would have cautioned, but perhaps someday. Guesdists conjectured that the mazy paths of anti-Semitism led toward an anticapitalism purged of racism, and thus into genuine socialism. They evaluated even the Marquis de Morès—the most colorful, charismatic, and popular of France's many anti-Semitic adventurers—as a prospective recruit to their cause. Having been overwhelmed by Marxist logic during a bruising debate, the chastened marquis had supposedly conceded that the future indeed belonged to the Parti Ouvrier and its "collectivism." According to the POF, such (actually imaginary) concessions were to be expected. After all, the anti-Semites of the 1890s closely resembled the Boulangists of the 1880s, and

French Marxists fondly remembered how leftist Boulangists had succumbed to socialism during the early 1890s, as Boulangism's disillusioned militants abandoned the disintegrating "National Party" for the ascendant Parti Ouvrier. Why not once again, with anti-Semitism shedding its disenchanted supporters, even its disheartened leaders, into the lap of an expectant POF?[93]

For Guesdists, then, there were anti-Semites and anti-Semites, just as there had been Boulangists and Boulangists. The Parti Ouvrier, for instance, sharply distinguished some of Drumont's followers, supposedly "left" anti-Semites, from the "Stockers [*sic*] and other pontiffs of anti-Semitism, who generally incline toward the conservative party."[94] Commenting cheerfully on anti-Semitism in Stöcker's Germany, *Le Socialiste* rejoiced that

> where [anti-Semitism] is an expression of the capitalist order itself [in areas like Hesse, where local capitalists tended to be Jewish], anti-Semitism will be forced, sooner or later, to work for us, because, behind the Jew, it will eventually find the capitalist. That's not to say that we should help the anti-Semites: that would only compromise us without any benefit, but their transient successes shouldn't displease us. Once they are unable to keep their promises to the peasants and small businessmen, these will turn toward us. [Such anti-Semitism] is simply a preparatory school in which, in certain countries, the ignorant have to enroll, before entering into the advanced classes of socialism.[95]

The Guesdists predicted that France's own "left" anti-Semites would soon qualify for this educational promotion, smugly remarking that "enlightened by our knowledge of the class war that dominates the past and present of human history, we have predicted and prophesied this rising tide of [anti-Semitic] reaction. Today's reaction . . . will precipitate tomorrow's revolution."[96] If anti-Semitism was the "socialism of fools,"[97] then Guesdists eagerly anticipated the day when anti-Semites would grow wise.

The Parti Ouvrier's expectations were hardly groundless. Fin de siècle anti-Semites themselves sometimes recognized that popular anti-Semitism expressed a displaced anticapitalism. Considering his working-class electors, Barrès had mused: "Listen to the mob at public meetings crying 'Down with the Jews'; it is 'down with social inequalities' that should be understood."[98] "Jewish," Barrès concluded sagely, "is only an adjective used to designate usurers, hoarders, [and] speculators on the stock market—all those who abuse the omnipotence of money."[99] The Third Republic's usurers, hoarders, and speculators apprehensively agreed. Having encountered Drumont's vituperations, haut-bourgeois opinion ruled "that anti-Semitism is the most dangerous form of socialism; that it is, in reality and above all, a campaign against the moneyed classes."[100] Putting this ruling into practice, bosses in Lorraine sacked workers who had campaigned for Barrès. According to the infuriated bourgeois of Nancy, the anti-Semitic leader's "national socialism" was too socialist and insufficiently national, while his anti-Semitism was irrelevant. Given such testimony, Guesdists could legitimately hope for a socialist outcome to their time's jarring collision between class interest and racial prejudice. Their hopes, however, should not be construed as indicating some Guesdist affinity with anti-Semitism.[101] There was no such affinity. Instead, according to the Marxists, anti-Semitism was false consciousness—an annoying obstruction on the road to revolution that would somehow have to be avoided, negotiated, or leveled.

Fin de siècle anti-Semitism's locus classicus, of course, was the Dreyfus affair—that moment when the French chose sides in one of history's most spectacular ideological affrays, and chose sides for or against a Jew. In our historical memory, the Dreyfusards, those who fought for Alfred Dreyfus, exemplify liberalism's inclusive "civil society," while the anti-Dreyfusards, those who valued the army's honor above Dreyfus's rights, symbolize ultranationalism's ethnic exclusion. But what of the French socialists, during this time of choice? Scholarship has suggested that the Dreyfus affair marked a decisive moment in their history, as they veered abruptly from their traditional anti-Semitism toward principled antiracism.[102] True enough, perhaps—for Malon's "Integral Socialists," with their anti-Semitic Proudhonian traditions. But *not* for the Guesdists. From first to last, from the beginning of the affair until the triumph of the Dreyfusards, they clung to their own anti-Proudhonian and antiliberal traditions: affirming, as they had always done, class conflict against race war, and fighting single-mindedly to insulate workers from "bourgeois politics"—whether the politics of anti-Dreyfusard revolutionary racism, or the politics of Dreyfusard "Republican Defense."

The Guesdists' neutrality during the affair evoked at the time, and has evoked since, bitter accusations that the Marxists were anti-Semitic. Historians have charged that "the Guesdist movement, on the basis of its class logic, ranged itself in the anti-Dreyfusard camp."[103] This is historical travesty. Guesdists splashed the anti-Dreyfusards with at least as much ideological vitriol as they sloshed over the Dreyfusards. But the charge has stuck in the scholarly literature, much of which assumes that the Guesdists' strategy of "a plague on both your houses" indicated covert or even overt anti-Semitism. Anyone who plagued the Dreyfusards, it is illogically argued, must thereby have been an anti-Dreyfusard, and thus an anti-Semite. Since "Guesdists welcomed the anti-Semitic diatribes of Drumont," asks Pierre Birnbaum, "does not their hatred toward Rothschild explain their comparable hostility toward Captain Dreyfus?"[104] The answer to this "question" must be, quite simply, no. The Guesdists did *not* welcome Drumont's anti-Semitism, except as an idiocy that might mutate into something more sensible; they did *not* hate Rothschild as a Jew, but as one banker among many, some Jewish, others not; and they were hostile toward Dreyfus because he was an army officer and a bourgeois, *not* because of his race.

Like all the French except Dreyfus's immediate family, the Guesdists initially assumed that the captain was guilty as charged. Significantly, however, during this preliminary stage of the affair, the Parti Ouvrier's national press ignored Dreyfus's Jewish origins. He was abused as an officer, reviled as a bourgeois, and denounced as a traitor (with the POF again wrapping itself in the *tricolore*). But the French Marxists never identified "that traitor Dreyfus"[105] as a Jew. If the Guesdists' initial refusal to support revision had been motivated by anti-Semitism, they would certainly have highlighted the captain's ethnicity. After all, for *real* anti-Semites like Barrès, Dreyfus's race proclaimed his guilt, and his guilt indicted his race.[106] Guesdists, however, unlike the anti-Semites, detested Dreyfus because of his class, *not* because of his people.

During 1898, as the affair's bizarre personae swept the stage, Guesdists still cold-shouldered the Dreyfusards (and, a fortiori, the anti-Dreyfusards), even though Dreyfus's guilt had become problematic indeed. Further "proof" of Guesdist anti-Semitism? Not at all. With France's ruling elite fractured into warring factions, the Parti Ouvrier simply refused recruitment into either camp. Guesdists justified this refusal with the same argument that the POF had used against becoming involved in the Boulanger affair. Why, Guesdists asked in 1898, as they had asked in 1889, should socialists defend the "bourgeois Republic" against its bourgeois enemies, or, for that matter, why should they join its assailants? True socialists, Guesdists staunchly argued at the inceptions of the two crises, had to oppose *both* enemy factions. Urged to support the Dreyfusards, French Marxists remembered that their earlier abstention during the Boulanger years had worked wonderfully well. Then, once France had finally emerged from its bitter factional conflict, Brousse's reformist socialists, who had signed up with the ruling establishment to defend the Republic, had exited the crisis utterly discredited by their association with the corrupt and unpopular Opportunists. Those other socialists—like most of the Parisian Blanquists, who had enlisted with the Boulangists to overthrow the regime—staggered forth wholly confounded by the ignominious collapse of the general's cause. The Parti Ouvrier, by contrast, had benefited mightily from its neutrality, maneuvering unscathed across the no-man's-land between Boulangists and Republicans, recruiting the walking wounded from Boulangism's battlefields, and eventually mobilizing the survivors into a triumphant Marxist blitzkrieg across France's corpse-strewn ideological terrain.

The Guesdists' abstention from the Dreyfus affair can thus easily be explained by exactly the same calculation that had justified their disengagement from the Boulanger crisis, and that abstention was legitimated, at least within the POF, by Guesdist successes during that earlier episode.[107] Today's historians need seek no anti-Semitic motives for Marxist abstentionism—unless such motives can be textually demonstrated. The historian-critic of the Guesdists might credibly contend that humanitarian duty toward Dreyfus should have preempted Marxism's single-minded mustering of the working class—characterized as workers were either by indifference to the captain's fate or dispute over his guilt. The same critic could safely suggest that the immediate defense of the liberal-democratic Republic should have prevailed against the Marxists' long-term aspirations to a working-class revolution against it. But no critic can credibly argue that the Guesdists' abstentionism indicated sympathy for the anti-Dreyfusard cause, which the Parti Ouvrier detested, or that their stance implied support for the anti-Semites, whom the POF despised. Guesdists simply put (their) first things first, thereby spurning both racist ultras and antiracist Dreyfusards.[108]

Nor were the French Marxists alone in subordinating the "human rights" of others to their own political imperatives. For Guesdists, the *Realpolitik* underlying the affair was soon cruelly revealed, as the POF fought desperately during 1903 to raise France against the czarist empire's murderous Kichenev pogrom. The French Marxists discovered—to their dismay, but not to their surprise—that *none* of the prominent Dreyfusard "Ministerialists" would join them in attacking France's anti-Semitic ally.[109] No historian would seriously suggest that the Ministerialists' recalcitrance disclosed latent anti-Semitism. Quite simply, raison d'état prevailed . . . once the Dreyfusards were the state. Sauce for the Dreyfusard goose is, however, also sauce for the Guesdist gander. However reprehensible the French Marxists' abstention from the Dreyfus affair must seem today—since the Holocaust, after the re-establishment of liberal hegemony, at the "End of History"—the Guesdists of 1898 deserve the same historicist understanding one necessarily accords the erring Ministerialists of 1903. Both Dreyfusards who, confronted by the Jewish dead at Kichenev, flinched from antagonizing Nicholas II, and Guesdists who, encountering Dreyfus's tragedy, refused to intervene, pursued pragmatic agendas free of anti-Semitism.

So much for the Dreyfus affair. Are there other blemishes on the Guesdists' record that better validate the charge of Marxist anti-Semitism? What of the Parti Ouvrier's vociferous hostility to speculation and financial swindling—capitalist malignancies so often, at the fin de siècle, embodied in the baleful figure of "Rothschild"? What are we to make of Lafargue's rabble-rousing edict that "the real Republic will not exist until the day that Rothschild is . . . before the firing squad"—the edict that would earn the Guesdist leader both a term in the Saint-Pélagie Prison and lasting infamy among historians, who have adduced it to "prove" his anti-Semitism?[110] Had Lafargue urged the eminent banker's execution because Rothschild was a Jew, or because he was an eminent banker? And what of Lafargue's assertion that "it is not by starving part of the population for the sake of a handful of speculators that the agricultural crisis will be overcome"? Such comment, according to one of the most impressive studies of French anti-Semitism, attested "common ground" between the Guesdist leader and the anti-Semites—because of the "close similarity in [their] rhetoric."[111] Was Lafargue using code, with "speculator" really meaning "Jew"? Or was he simply denouncing the "free" market? Anti-Semitism or anticapitalism? Only a close, considered, and exhaustive interrogation of the Parti Ouvrier's textual record can resolve these questions.

Such interrogation reveals some troubling rhetoric. A fall in dividend payments at the Bank of France, for instance, was described as likely "to cleave the souls of the Jews of finance."[112] Why not the gentiles of finance, as well? What of *Le Socialiste*'s attack on one of its many journalistic enemies as having been employed by that "swindling Jew Reinach"?[113] Why not simply "the swindler Reinach"? Worse yet, Guesdists very occasionally seemed to link capitalism as a system with the Jews as a people, thereby apparently seconding the fundamental trope of left-wing anti-Semitism. Lafargue, for instance, once identified the Jews as the "leaders of capitalist society" because of "their financial genius."[114] As if gentile financiers never sparkled on the Paris Bourse, or bought their way through the Chamber of Deputies! And, most tellingly, during the aftermath of the scabrous Panama affair, the National Council of the Parti Ouvrier denounced the French bourgeoisie for "surrendering the labor and savings of the nation to the cosmopolitan exploitation of financiers like Hirsch and Cornélius Herz"[115]—a denunciation of the ruling elite that might well have come from any of France's left-wing anti-Semites, not least because of its (profoundly un-Marxist) distinction between a "French bourgeoisie" and "cosmopolitan exploitation" embodied in two Jews.

This apparent "anticapitalist anti-Semitism" was, however, vanishingly rare in Guesdist discourse, and, more significantly, was massively overbalanced by incessant affirmations that financial swindling owed absolutely nothing to the Jews *qua* Jews. Guesde exemplified the POF's "party line" by pointing out that

> neither the Barings, who have scoured the English market for a century, nor the Mackays, the Goulds, and the Vanderbilts who exercise, in the midst of the American republic, the imperial powers of the billionaire, have the least ancestor in common with our Rotschild [*sic*]. That hasn't stopped them and won't stop them from acting as highwaymen on the roads of commerce, industry, and savings in exactly the same way as the Semite of the rue Laffite.[116]

Guesdists inveighed against "the Rothschilds, the Erlangers, and the other Jews and Christians of the gold international"[117] as a globalized financial elite that ran the world totally without reference to race, not as Drumont's "international Jewish conspiracy."

Even the Parti Ouvrier's slips into apparent socialist anti-Semitism were far less anti-Semitic than they might appear to us today, if they were anti-Semitic at all. How so? In the nineteenth century's unsavory parlance, a "jew" (in this sense often uncapitalized) could be anyone devoted to moneygrubbing—whether Jewish or Christian, "Semite" or "Aryan," Shylock or Scrooge.[118] Toussenel, so often identified as the archetypical socialist anti-Semite, actually begins his *Juifs: Rois de l'Epoque* with this very point: "I call, like the people, by the despised name of Jew, every dealer in money, every unproductive parasite, living off the substance and the labor of others. Jew, usurer, dealer are for me synonyms."[119] Toussenel set out to savage "jews" as defined by usury (the book is at least as derogatory about the English as about ethnic Jews), although his hysterical essay dreadfully miscarried by presupposing that *all* ethnic "Jews" (and all the English!) were money-obsessed "jews." Such an indiscriminate conflation of the ethnic and the social, for us today, suffices to discredit the equation of "the despised name of jew" with financial predators. But this nineteenth-century usage did not, at the time, necessarily indicate anti-Semitism. Even French Jews of the belle epoque, some utterly committed to their own ethnic community, casually and unashamedly adopted the era's, to us, anti-Semitic terminology.[120]

Historians have played fast and loose with this semantic anachronism, unthinkingly translating our own wounded sensitivities to the fin de siècle. Michel Winock, for instance, begins his popular account of "the Left and the Jews" by depicting a Republican deputy of the 1890s denouncing "juiverie." Winock presents the terminology as anti-Semitic, although there is nothing in the quotation to suggest that the deputy might not, in fact, have been attacking financial swindling, whether by Jews or gentiles.[121] Other historians have been more aware of anachronism, but have still insisted that the use of "jew" as synonymous with "financier" implied anti-Semitism, even when the usage arraigned Christian bankers and spared nonexploitative "Israelites."[122] Such hypersensitivity is understandable, since Auschwitz. Who would today describe sharp practice as "jewing" somebody? But the words of a nineteenth-century ideologue should not be read as if they had been written in the aftermath of Hitler's hateful crimes—crimes that would have absolutely horrified Lafargue or Guesde, if only because (but not only because) the Nazis coddled the "jewish" Deutsche Bank while murdering millions of nonexploitative "Jews," many of them Marxists.

Close reading of the Guesdists' canon, in its contemporaneous context rather than in Hitlerized retrospect, makes it very clear that the Parti Ouvrier's occasional use of "Jew" in an apparently anti-Semitic sense almost always referred, not to ethnic Jews, but to financial speculators, of whatever race or religion. Guesdists thus denounced "the Jews, *circumcised or not*" who ruled as financial masters over all nations as "the kings of the epoch, according to Toussenel's apt expression,"[123] while at the same time repeatedly affirming that, among France's speculators, the nation had "lots of Jews and *Christians, who don't need to be circumcised to be Jews*."[124] The Parti Ouvrier was, indeed, quite explicit about this terminological ambiguity, on one occasion laboriously explaining that

> the Jew, in France, for peasants, gets mixed up with usurers and bourgeois capitalists. There are certainly some Jews among those who oppress our peasants, but how many more uncircumcised and Christians. The Jews, in France, have become mixed into the general population far more quickly than in Germany, and it's only in the upper echelons of finance that one finds pure examples of the race. Thus it is that during the struggles in the countryside anti-Semitic slogans aren't understood. When [anti-Semites] cry "Down with the Jews!" [peasants] take the word in the broad sense of usurer that it has in the language, and see nothing Semitic in the epithet.[125]

When confronted by this misunderstanding, Guesdists denounced the confusing usage that had occasioned it. The Parti Ouvrier thus angrily condemned anti-Semites for designating financiers with "the utterly incorrect denomination of 'Jews.'"[126] Historians must be at least as alert to lexical ambiguities as Guesdists were. We, too, when encountering the word "Jewry" in fin de siècle discourse, need to ask ourselves whether it referred to ethnicity, or to finance, or to both.

The decisive fact about this aspect of the Guesdists' ideological record, however, is the sheer *rarity* of such usage. Guesdists devoted millions of words to savaging capitalism, but few to assailing *"juiverie,"* and then in the term's nonracialized "economic" sense. France's real anti-Semites devoted millions of words to attacking the Jews, but attacked capitalism rarely, and then as ethnicized *"Juiverie."* The Marxists and anti-Semites of the belle epoque inhabited wildly divergent discursive universes—the one economistic, the other racialized. Their terms excluded each other, even on those rare occasions when they overlapped.

During their own period, Guesdists mounted exactly the same argument—but in defense of Marx against anti-Semites who had appropriated his otherwise long-forgotten writings on the "Jewish question." Marx, it will be remembered, had played with the multiple meanings of "Jew" and "jew" to demonstrate that Jewish emancipation inhered in "jewish" bourgeois civilization, since capitalism generalized *"juiverie."* He had then argued that *true* emancipation, both for Jews and gentiles, required liberation from *juiverie*/capitalism. Guesdists swore, rightly or wrongly,[127] that Marx had *not* been anti-Semitic in so arguing, since the capitalist *"juiverie"* he assailed was no more Jewish than it was German or Christian. The French Marxists fully accepted Marx's judgment that "the Jews have been emancipated because Christians have become jews,"[128] and they fully subscribed to Marx's dream of a panracial revolution against *"juiverie."* But the Guesdists' reading of Marx, with its careful distinction between "Jew" and "jew," "proved" that his texts were *not* anti-Semitic.

But what about the Rothschilds? Historians have highlighted the nineteenth century's penchant for first reducing capitalism to finance, and then reducing finance to the great Jewish banking family. French anti-Semites mercilessly exploited this reductive logic, tapping into petit-bourgeois and peasant dread of financial concentration to arraign even the most inoffensive Jew as being one with the much-hated Rothschilds. Mastered by ignorance or stupidity, fin de siècle socialists sometimes added links to this dishonest chain of "reasoning," condensing both capitalism and the Jews into the rue Lafitte's spectacular exemplar of both. But what about the Guesdists? Did they, too, personalize finance in a Jew, and the Jews in Rothschild?

French Marxists certainly perpetrated the former reduction, albeit very infrequently. On one unfortunate occasion, for instance, the Parti Ouvrier explicitly justified such reductive personification of finance capital, explaining limply that "socialists attack Rothschild because he personifies modern finance."[129] As if Marxists had not struggled for decades against exactly such simpleminded reduction of social evils to evil personalities! Charles Bonnier, in another unhappy instance, targeted a memorable polemic specifically against the Rothschilds, whom he colorfully described as "a family . . . protected by all the laws of all the European codes that would all have to be overthrown before you could get at them, yet at the same time perfectly free of all restrictions and all limits, obeying no code, no customs, sovereign master of the globe."[130] "Sovereign master of the globe"—silly imagery more characteristic of Drumont's Gothic imagination than of Marxism's rationalist political economy. The Guesdists' assaults on that "villainous Jew from Frankfurt"[131] thus all too often highlighted the Rothschilds' race, as with yet another scorching attack on "Rothschild, that Jew"—described as having "ripped off France whether as the grandfather, the father, or the son [a reference to the three generations since the emigration from Frankfurt]."[132] There was no reason, of course, why Guesdists, as anticapitalists, should have exempted the ultracapitalist Rothschild from socialist critique. Working-class Jews themselves denounced him as a predator, not least because of his predations upon other Jews.[133] Unfortunately, when the radically anticapitalist Guesdists highlighted Rothschild's ethnicity, they played into the hands of anti-Semites who were following a radically different, and sometimes radically procapitalist, agenda.

For this very reason, most of the Guesdists' many references to the Rothschilds were nonracist or even explicitly antiracist, with French Marxists hastening to affirm that their real enemies were all the "Rothschilds, whether circumcised or uncircumcised."[134] In other words, the Parti Ouvrier fought a class, not a race. As Guesdists never tired of pointing out, not all financiers were Jewish. The POF did agree with anti-Semites that a "plutocracy," a "financial banditry," ruthlessly plundered France, but the French Marxists always insisted that these malefactors of great wealth included "Catholics, Protestants, and free thinkers"[135] as well as Jews. Indeed, the Guesdists maliciously suggested that Christian financiers were far more predatory than even the most exploitative of Jewish moneylenders![136] The Parti Ouvrier, forgetting its occasional slips, then denied ever having conflated finance capital with the house of Rothschild. When that ideological jackdaw Drumont, for instance, tried to steal Guesde for his anti-Semitic cache of characters, alleging that the Guesdist leader had once demanded that Rothschild be put against a wall and shot, the Parti Ouvrier reacted with fury. Guesde, the POF pointed out angrily, had actually written that "when the Revolution comes, Rothschild and his like, whether Jews or Christians," would have to be imprisoned to protect them "from an enraged people." Marxists like Guesde, *Le Socialiste* remonstrated, "refuse to play the anti-Semites' game and know perfectly well that war against bourgeois society could not be reduced to a campaign against such and such an individual."[137] The French Marxists may have very occasionally wavered from this wise guideline, but it nonetheless governed their war against the anti-Semites, if not always their war against Rothschild. For the POF it was not the case, as philo-Semitic philofinanciers have argued, that "it is a short step from hatred of international bankers to hatred of Jews."[138]

In any case, the Guesdists, unlike almost all other French radicals, whether of Left or Right, accorded financiers only secondary significance in France's class structure, and dismissed finance as being unimportant, compared to industry. During their many dissections of French capitalism, they repeatedly argued that "finance is not . . . a cause, but an effect," as "financial centralization derives from industrial centralization."[139] When Guesdists indulged in the simpleminded but irresistible rhetorical convenience of personifying France's mode of production, capitalism was embodied not in bankers (some of them Jewish), but in France's industrialists (all of them gentile, and most of them Catholic). Capital was figured forth in the person of Eugène Motte (textile magnate of Roubaix, deadly political enemy of Guesde, and patron of Notre-Dame-de-l'Usine) or in the Schneiders of Creusot (steel lords, hardfisted adversaries of the labor movement, and devout Catholics). The Guesdists always sought to "prove," during their many debates with anti-Semitic enemies, that France's real exploiters were Christian Frenchmen, not "alien" Jews.[140] According to *Le Socialiste*,

> [O]nly finance—and that in part only—is in the hands of those Semites that one denounces as the workers' calamity. But far from preying upon workers,

> far too impoverished by their employers to have any savings . . . finance only menaces and wounds those who live on [the workers'] backs. As Guesde wrote in 1886 in relation to the Rothschilds, is there a single worker to be found on the highroads of the stock exchange and in the forests of speculation where finance carries out its robberies?[141]

Where workers "were really being robbed," the Parti Ouvrier affirmed, "there's not a single semite [*sic*] . . . not at the coal mines of Anzin, [not] among the blast furnaces of Creusot, [nor] in the black country of Montceau-les-Mines."[142] Those who exploited workers, according to the POF, were incorporated as "Christ et Cie," not as "Moïse et Cie."[143] Guesdist anti-Semitism? Hardly.

Whether lorded over by Jews or gentiles, the "feudalization" of the means of production by *les gros* advanced irresistibly, according to Marxist political economy. Unlike the anti-Semites, however, Guesdists *welcomed* this capital concentration. In the Marxists' historical imaginary, the logic of unintended consequences ensured that capital's endless self-aggrandizement led inexorably toward socialism. French Marxists thus *rejoiced* in finance-capital's ever-expanding domain; they *delighted* in capitalism's universalization of *"juiverie."* In Guesde's own words,

> It's for us, it's for the new [socialist] order, that the financiers of all races and all religions and irreligions are working. . . . Anti-Semitism, even in its indictment of a category of wealth owners, is thus essentially reactionary. It's struggling against an inevitable evolution that, while crossing the desert of financial panics and bankruptcies, is leading our species toward the promised land of socialized property.[144]

This Marxist faith that capitalism led toward a final entry into socialism's "promised land" completely severed the Guesdists, with their trust in progress, from the anti-Semites, with their dread of decadence.

The sanguine Guesdists loved to cite Engels's famous diagnosis that anti-Semitism was a pathology of backwardness. According to Marxist diagnosticians, the anti-Semites' putrescent presence always indicated a pathological "reaction [among] *medieval* social categories destined to disappear in modern society."[145] Future eruptions of the anti-Semitic plague, Guesdists trusted, would thus be confined to benighted nations "where production is still in the hands of peasants, of the landed classes, of artisans, and such groups not yet having emerged from the Middle Ages."[146] At the fin de siècle, in the Guesdists' political geography, anti-Semitism still throve in the backwoods of Eastern and Central Europe, had become virtually inconceivable in such hypermodern societies as Britain and the United States, and, as modernity advanced, would soon decline toward similar insignificance in France.[147] Modernity immunized against anti-Semitism.

This antithesis between arrogantly modernist Marxism and putatively reactionary anti-Semitism suffused the Parti Ouvrier's many attacks on Drumont. When the anti-Semitic ideologue, for instance, appropriated the Fourmies massacre for his anti-Semitic purposes, *Le Socialiste* caustically pointed out that Drumont's real constituency was among the ultrareactionary officers who had perpetrated the killing, not among the progressive workers who had been its victims.[148] "Drumont," the Guesdists angrily charged, "sums up everything that is radically antisocialist. He's an ultraconservative."[149] This charge rang true. Drumont had begun his spectacular career as an impassioned advocate of "heritage," lamenting the nineteenth century's demolition of *vieux Paris*. Not for Drumont the wonders of progress. He even detested new fangled electric lighting! Guesde, like Drumont, had been born in the heart of ancient Paris. Yet not a word of his voluminous writings betrays the slightest nostalgia for the antique alleys of his natal Isle Saint-Louis. Instead, in Guesde's vision of past and future, the march of progress, even its destructive parade through the wreckage of France's rich heritage, cleared a terrain for the erection of socialism. The electric lights blinking on across Paris, for Guesde, brilliantly illuminated that vast metahistorical construction site.[150]

In the same way, when surveying capitalism's fortifications, the Marxist leader and the anti-Semitic journalist measured them similarly, but drew up very different plans for their future. Their surveys? Guesde fully accepted Drumont's sketch of "the great banking house, the big factory . . . , the department store, all [casting] their shadow on the horizon like a feudal castle of the past, and small firms, like the small dwellings of old, afraid of their terrible neighbors."[151] But Guesde and Drumont's plans differed fundamentally. Like his petit-bourgeois constituents, Drumont cowered before capital, at the best raising a desperate jacquerie to raze its citadels. By contrast, Guesde marshaled the working class to seize the castles of capitalism, planning to renovate them into the airy edifices of utopia. Quoting Engels's characterization of the anti-Semites as concealing their conservatism "behind a socialist figleaf," *Le Socialiste* denounced "Drumontism" as "essentially reactionary." "It struggles," the Guesdist newspaper concluded contemptuously, "against the inevitable evolution that leads our species . . . toward the promised land of socialism."[152] That "promised land" again! Over the heavily fortified horizon of capitalism lay the Guesdists' Zion.

More prosaically, French Marxists mocked anti-Semitism's backward-looking political economy. The anti-Semites' only alternative to capitalism, a "return to corporatism,"[153] supposedly demonstrated both their economic illiteracy and their ultraconservatism. Guesdists, for instance, reproached Drumont for ignoring "the complete transformation that, by the substitution of collective mechanical apparatus for the individual tool of preceding centuries, has occurred in modern production," and faulted him for his pigheaded loyalty "to the small-scale production of yesteryear, with its craft work in which the boss 'was also a worker.'"[154] Anti-Semites, Guesdists charged, wished to retreat into Arcadia. History, however, was irreversible. One went forward, or one went nowhere. Violent reaction could not compensate for the anti-Semites' economic ignorance and social stupidity. "Fill the streets . . . with the corpses of Jews," *Le Socialiste* admonished, "and the great engines of modern production, the power of large capital, will remain just as burdensome, just as deadly."[155] As a prediction of anti-Semitism's twentieth-century betrayal of its petit-bourgeois constituency, the point was well taken. But *Le Socialiste*'s journalist could hardly have imagined that his macabre image of corpse-strewn streets would one day become grisly reality.

The most difficult, but also the most cogent, proof of Guesdist resistance to anti-Semitism requires reading their record for *absence*. A discourse's *not said*, after all, tells us at least as much about it as does its *said*.[156] When a historian, for instance, demonstrates that "most" socialists pandered to anti-Semitism during the Panama scandal,[157] his observation provides a criterion against which to judge the Parti Ouvrier. The judgment? Not guilty of pandering. Across the many articles that Guesdists wrote during the Panama affair, there was not a single instance of blaming Jews as such for that shaming episode. The French Marxists *did* harp upon the scandal, both during its course and subsequently. The very word "Panama" came to serve them as metonym for squalid politics. But they blamed capitalism for that squalor, not the "usual suspects" among Jewish financiers. If Guesdists—like professional anti-Semites such as Drumont and Guérin, or "Aryanist" socialists such as Auguste Chirac and Albert Regnard—had indeed hated the Jews as a "race of speculators and swindlers," then the Parti Ouvrier would undoubtedly have highlighted the misdeeds of Baron de Reinach and his disreputable Jewish associates. They did not, instead targeting capitalism as the occult force behind Panama's peculations.

And what of the positive "other" to the Semites: the "Aryans," that mythical master-race beloved of racist anthropologists? For the belle epoque's anti-Semites, Aryan soulfulness countered Jewish calculation and valiant Aryan warriors thwarted cowardly Semitic dealers, while the Aryan's cultural creativity nullified the Jew's aesthetic "aridity." Overwhelmed by this weird hallucination, some socialists, particularly Blanquists sliding toward fascism, fancied that their own "Aryan socialism" safeguarded France against both the "Jewish capitalism" emanating from the Rothschilds' rue Lafitte and the "Jewish socialism" radiating from Marx's London. Even the "Integral" socialist milieu that crystallized around Benoît Malon, otherwise a seedbed for socialist Dreyfusards, succumbed to Aryanist contamination. Racist ideologues like

Regnard and Chirac were welcome in Malon's circle, but, in sharp contrast, never once appeared within the Parti Ouvrier's jealously guarded domain[158]—if only because Chirac and Regnard's "spiritual" Aryan socialism had been carefully crafted to challenge Marx's supposedly "Jewish" historical materialism.[159] During a period when dramatic Aryan-versus-Semite dichotomies so often structured the play of politics, Guesdists ostentatiously spurned the "Aryan" saints, heroes, and geniuses who strutted the ideological stage, just as Marxists ignored the "Semitic" seducers, villains, and parasites so loudly booed by less discriminating political audiences. Racism's voguish cast of characters never featured in the Parti Ouvrier's dramaturgy—dominated as it was by class actors.

Just as Aryanism never sullied Guesdist discourse, so the POF abjured the virulent antireligion of some left anti-Semites, with their accusation that the Jews had begotten Christianity, and that their jealous God now reigned over Christian civilization's sickening synthesis of church, state, and cash box. During the Second Empire, radical young intellectuals—well versed in the classics and revolted by Louis Napoleon's ugly amalgamation of Catholicism, Caesarism, and plutocracy—had ascribed all three debilities to Jewish monotheism, to Jehovah's unconditional triumph over antiquity's wholesome (and Aryan!) polytheism. The Jewish poison seeping through the Christianized Roman Empire, quasi socialists like Gustave Tridon contended, had dribbled undiluted down the centuries, eventually infecting Europe's nineteenth-century body politic and throwing up a putrid mess of arid theocracy, authoritarian politics, and usurious exploitation. Did the POF agree with Tridon and his fin de siècle disciples? Not for a moment. Guesdists certainly despised Christianity, and many Marxist intellectuals had matured within the same atheistical Bohemian milieu that had spawned anti-Christian anti-Semitism. But French Marxists never once blamed their time's miseries on supposedly Jewish Christianity.[160] For Guesdists, both Judaism and Christianity manifested superficial false consciousness; they were symptoms to be explained, not pathogens to be blamed. When Guesdists sought an etiology for Europe's many maladies (including Judaism and Christianity, but also anti-Semitism and anticlericalism), they identified capitalism as the plague bearer.

Nor, in Guesdist polemic, was there the slightest hint of aesthetic anti-Semitism—that paranoid conviction, so typical of the times, that Jewish patrons, Jewish critics, Jewish publishers, and Jewish gallery-owners greedily commercialized culture, and thus degraded art and literature into tasteless merchandise. Guesdists believed that France's cultural life *had* been corrupted, that artists and writers served Mammon rather than the Muses. "Genius and erudition as much as shoes and cattle," the Parti Ouvrier grumbled, had been debased into mere commodities.[161] And French Marxists repeatedly denounced this commodification as having bred "mental degeneration and moral rot."[162] Yet, despite endless diatribes against fin de siècle "bourgeois culture," the Parti Ouvrier never once suggested that the Jews were to blame. Not for Guesdists the anti-Semites' fulminations against "Jewish art." Guesdists knew very well from whence came their time's cultural debility. It issued solely from the bourgeoisie's exploitation of art and artists.

Finally, Guesdists, despite their pretensions to high theory, worked to *popularize* the Marxist message. They lived as pamphleteers, as journalists, as soapbox orators. Were they ever tempted by the anti-Semitic sensationalism that awarded the Assumptionists' *La Croix* and Drumont's *Libre Parole* their hundreds of thousands of fascinated readers?[163] Never. Not one of anti-Semitism's melodramatic tropes surfaced in the Parti Ouvrier's ocean of polemic. If informed by *Le Socialiste* alone, a French worker of the fin de siècle would never, for instance, have "known" that a lurid Jewish underworld of pimps and brothel owners ran the "white slave trade"—enticing naive French women into prostitution and selling "Aryan" children to the brothels of Buenos Aires.[164] Nor did the Guesdist press ever retail the fin de siècle's horrific tales of Jewish ritual murder. A reader of *Le Socialiste* would never have "discovered" that Jews bled Christian children to death during their Passover rites—supposedly in Hungary and Ukraine, but perhaps also in France's own Châtellerault. The grotesqueries that ensured anti-Semitism's tabloid popularity found no echo in the Parti Ouvrier's rationalistic public discourse, for all that Guesdists occasionally embellished their journalism and oratory with vivid anti-capitalist (but never anti-Semitic) illustration and anecdote.

Having addressed supposed evidence of Guesdist anti-Semitism—the POF's equivocal role in the Dreyfus affair, the movement's critique of finance capital—and considered the anti-Semitic temptations offered to French Marxists but rejected by them, what does the Guesdist record actually tell us? The answer is straightforward: Guesdists despised the anti-Semites and repudiated anti-Semitism. Morès, Drumont, Barrès, Guérin, and even the enormously popular Henri Rochefort—all were insulted, ridiculed, and refuted.[165] Guesdists conceived their conflict with the anti-Semites as a war to the death, with victory for Marxist collectivism auguring a sticky end for national-socialist anti-Semitism. Reporting, for instance, on the POF's successful foiling of the Marquis de Morès's attempted seduction of Lille's workers, *Le Socialiste* crowed that, henceforth, there would no longer be "race war, but only a class war that will be pursued toward all and against all"[166]—and particularly against the anti-Semites. The Parti Ouvrier thus vaunted Marxism as the last best barrier against the rising tide of anti-Semitism, wherever it still advanced. Boasting of the Parti Ouvrier's success in facing down the anti-Semitic mobs of the Dreyfus affair, *Le Socialiste* launched the slogan "Anti-Semites of All Lands, Beware!"[167]

This Guesdist hatred of anti-Semitism was to be expected, given the anti-Semites' hatred of Marxism. Crusading to save France from the international Jewish conspiracy, a supposed amalgam of "Jewish quack socialists and bankers,"[168] French anti-Semites repeatedly denounced the POF's Marxism as wholly "Semitic in conception."[169] Wittingly or unwittingly, they charged, Guesde and Lafargue served the Jews. All the major anti-Semitic ideologues advanced this argument. Drumont may have located the headquarters of *La France Juive* on the rue Lafitte, but he also viciously attacked the "German socialism inaugurated by the Jews Lassalle and Marx," that "exploitative and lying socialism of the Jews, so different from real socialism."[170] "Real socialism," for Drumont, was his own "national socialism" of class collaboration and ethnic exclusion, while "German socialism," the "socialism of the Jews," was the POF's class-conflictual and cosmopolitan "collectivism." Barrès, for his part, subscribed to exactly the same anti-Semitic anti-Marxism. According to the great theorist of national socialism, the Parti Ouvrier had founded its alien ideology upon "unverifiable fictions that have issued from the imaginations of a few messianic Jews."[171] Catholic anti-Semites of the nascent Christian Democratic movement seconded the national socialists. Militant *abbés démocratiques* like the Abbé Garnier, fighting for France and their faith in the mill towns of the north, violently attacked the POF as their race's enemy, no less than their God's.[172] Finally, that greatest national-socialist threat to French Marxism, Biétry's "Yellow" trade-union movement, scourged Guesdism as a Semitic front organization. According to Biétry, "[W]here [Marxist] socialism passes, there the way has been cleared for the Jew."[173] For anti-Semitic crusaders like these, victory for anti-Semitism augured the death of Marxism.

The racism of Drumont, Barrès, the Abbé Garnier, and Biétry may have developed initially as a critique of capital, albeit in capital's fantastical form as racialized "Juiverie." But these anti-Semites soon abandoned their always equivocal war against "plutocracy" (waged in vague alliance with "other" socialists) to lead determined assaults on "Jewish Marxism" (in not-so-vague alliance with plutocrats). These self-proclaimed "national socialists" had discovered that an anti-Semitism that mobilized against plutocratic wealth, if only against Jewish wealth, lost bourgeois sponsorship. Why forfeit the favors of the rich, when workers continued to prove so recalcitrant to anti-Semitism, and their meager and episodic support so unrewarding? Selling racist anti-Marxism to peasants and shopkeepers proved far easier than peddling anti-Semitism to proletarians. And anti-Semitic anti-Marxism could be marketed as an infinitely more profitable commodity than anti-Semitic anticapitalism . . . when retailed to wealthy bourgeois.[174]

Guesdists cannot speak against their traducers of today, as they once attacked their own time's "straight-faced jokers who pretend that socialism and anti-Semitism are one and the same thing."[175] But imagine Guesde's ghost returned to confront Lévy and his fellow "jokers." As past master of the *conférence contradictoire*, a revenant Guesde would easily discredit the tendentious allegations made against his movement. As if scripting such an encounter, the Parti Ouvrier reprised its record at the beginning of the twentieth century, vaunting its decades of "anti-anti-Semitic" militancy.[176] The movement had every right to do so. Across the decades, amid the tempest of the Third Republic's politics, whatever the temptations to anti-Semitism, Guesdists rigidly obeyed the antiracist guidelines they had early established for themselves. Hear Lafargue at the inception of his movement: "The socialist party divides men solely into capitalists and socialists; all those who want to preserve the present social order are our enemies; all those who desire the expropriation of the capitalists . . . and the socialization of the means of production are our friends, whether they are from Prussia or Lorraine, whether they are Semitic or Latin."[177]

Trivial deviations from this antiracist imperative—occasional unthinking jibes, sporadic lexical ambiguities—cannot sully the Parti Ouvrier's cleaving to its Semitic friends or obscure the Guesdists' hatred of their anti-Semitic enemies. Scholars who have foregrounded supposedly anti-Semitic trivia in the Guesdists' record while ignoring that record's "anti-anti-Semitic" substance would emerge chastened from their encounter with Guesde's infuriated ghost.

"Brave and Wise Jews": Guesdists and the "Jewish Race"

So much for the Guesdists' embittered encounter with the French anti-Semites. But what of their encounter with France's Jews? Here, the Parti Ouvrier's rejection of racist identity politics sometimes overshot the mark, carrying far toward philo-Semitism. Listen again to Lafargue. "Personally," the Guesdist leader opined, "I have the most profound admiration for the Jewish people, who have been insulted and trampled upon across the centuries, but who have never been defeated, who have never submitted, who have finally rebounded from their long and abject oppression and overwhelmed Christian Europe with their billions."[178] The "facts" of the matter, the Jews' stubborn particularity and increasing power within "Christian Europe," resembled the scenario advanced by Drumont. But the same historical *facts* were given absolutely opposite *meanings* by Marxists and anti-Semites—evoking admiration from the former, abomination from the latter.

The Guesdists placed the Jews at the very heart of their Marxist metanarrative—which extended from the days of Christ, usually identified as a Jew and frequently lauded as a protosocialist, to the epoch of Marx, also identified as Jewish even while saluted as the patron saint of socialist modernity.[179] Why this surprising "racial" discrimination in the Parti Ouvrier's otherwise class-obsessed historiography? The anomaly arose to some extent because Guesdists enjoyed taunting anti-Semites—often maliciously pointing out that the Christian Drumont and the Marxist Guesde shared discipleship to Jews. More seriously, French Marxists evolved their "philo-Semitism" because they believed (as did anti-Semites!) that the Jews had been the entrepreneurs of modernity. The "economic role [of the Jews]," Guesdists asserted, "has been . . . eminently useful, and one should not forget them when considering societies' economic development. In effect, they encouraged the advance of feudal society toward bourgeois society."[180] For the Parti Ouvrier, of course, modern times were a profoundly positive experience—infinitely preferable to the benighted feudal past, and foreshadowing a radiant socialist future. Drumont, on the other hand, detested modernity, loathing the Jew's "progressive" historical role as much as Guesdists admired it.

The French Marxists, it must be emphasized, explained the Jewish aptitude for modernity with historical sociology, not biological racism. The Jews' medieval exclusion from most trades, according to the Parti Ouvrier's many history lessons, had limited them to lives of "speculation, scholarship, and calculation"[181]—thereby uniquely adapting them to impending modernity. As a consequence, "no race," according to the Parti Ouvrier, was "more meditative, indeed more expansive, and more given to discussion."[182] Clever Jews, Guesdists maliciously suggested, necessarily prevailed over muscle-bound Christians—once Jews and gentiles competed in a world of speculative, scholarly, calculating modernity. The Parti Ouvrier relished this ironic linkage between medieval persecution and modern mastery. Highlighting how Christianity had itself created the Jewish financial power so reviled by Christian anti-Semites, *Le Socialiste* wickedly suggested that "it's therefore our Christians who have created the wicked Jew."[183] For Guesdists, anti-Semites represented medievalism's futile reaction against the modern Semite's "intelligence and aptitudes, and the skills that place the Jews in the first rank of all the branches of knowledge that are open to them."[184] No wonder furious anti-Semites—subjected to this contemptuous denigration, confronted by this philo-Semitic historiography—indicted the Guesdists as "Jewish socialists"!

The Parti Ouvrier brazenly seconded the indictment. On one occasion, for instance, having enumerated the many prominent Jews who had animated nineteenth-century socialism (preeminently Marx, of course), *Le Socialiste* then quoted Engels, who had reportedly written that "as for myself, isn't there a certain [reactionary] press that has transformed me into a Jew? It's true that if I had to choose, I'd certainly prefer to be Jewish rather than a marquis."[185] Both of the POF's great mentors were thus presented as "Jewish"—Marx by birth, Engels by choice. It was within the POF's much-admired SPD, however, that Jews figured most prominently—a prominence frequently highlighted in the

Guesdist press, sometimes to the disadvantage of France's own Marxism. "The German socialist party," Lafargue commented sadly, "counts in its ranks numerous brave and wise Jews. We're sorry that there are so few Jews among us here in France; for Jews are clever, intelligent, untiring, and devoted."[186] The Guesdists' only qualm about characterizing Marxism as "Jewish" seemed to be their fear that they themselves were not Jewish enough!

Was this occasional philo-Semitism generally characteristic of Guesdism, or merely a response to particular circumstances? It has been suggested that the decisive moment in the French Left's abandonment of its residual anti-Semitism came with the discovery, during the 1890s, of a Jewish proletariat—if not in France itself, then in Russia or Britain.[187] Quite suddenly, in the Left's political imaginary, militant Jewish workers battling czarist reaction in Vilnius and organizing the impoverished in East London eclipsed rapacious Jewish financiers—bankers to tyrants, the embodiment of global capitalism. This transition may indeed explain some variation in the Guesdists' answer to the "Jewish question," as they moved from the 1880s' assumption that all Jews were bourgeois (even if some, like the eminently bourgeois Marx, had abandoned their class for socialist militancy) to the 1890s' recognition that many Jews were thoroughly proletarian.[188] Not that Guesdists, when identifying Jews as members of the enemy class, had thereby been anti-Semitic. Far from it. Even during the 1880s, when "Jew" did seem to mean "bourgeois," Guesdists knew very well that bourgeois did not mean Jew. The Parti Ouvrier detested anti-Semitism just as much during the 1880s as during the 1890s, simply because Drumont et Cie stupidly directed popular anticapitalism against Jews as a race, rather than against bourgeois as a class. But so long as the Parti Ouvrier believed that all Jews were bourgeois, it had little incentive to defend them from anti-Semitic attack, even while the POF itself attacked anti-Semitism. In 1886, for instance, when Lafargue derided anti-Semites as envious of Jewish wealth, and as planning to steal it for themselves, he still seemed to take it for granted that all Jews were wealthy.[189] He impugned the anti-Semites, but did not defend the Jews—whose role in the bourgeoisie's internecine battles left him indifferent. Anti-Semitism was anathema to the Marxists because it deluded workers, not because it attacked Jewish bourgeois.

Once Guesdists became aware that many Jews were proletarian, however, the Parti Ouvrier gained another compelling reason for attacking the anti-Semites: the Party's absolute devotion to proletarian unity. Anti-Semitism not only diverted workers from their true enemy, the POF suddenly realized, but turned them against one another. Anti-Semitic divisiveness therefore had to be utterly expunged from French working-class culture, and proletarian Jews incorporated wholesale into the socialist movement. As soon as the Parti Ouvrier noticed Jewish workers, it dutifully shepherded them toward the enfolding shelter of the socialist *genre humain*.

But when *did* Guesdists abandon the myth of universally bourgeois Jewry for recognition that many Jews were proletarians? Surprisingly, hints of this transition had already appeared during the early 1880s, at the very inception of the POF. In one of the first of many Guesdist critiques of racial politics, *L'Egalité* demonstrated that races would never behave as coherent historical actors, simply because they were so fissured by class conflict. Jews were adduced as an extreme case, given that "the Semitic race is the one that is least connected with the peoples among which it lives, the one that has remained the most compact and the most united."[190] Yet, according to *L'Egalité*, even this stereotypically exclusive "Semitic race" was far too class-divided to empower Jewish political solidarity.[191] By implication, a Jewish working class opposed Jewish bourgeois, although its location and dimensions remained frustratingly obscure. By the 1890s, however, Guesdists were making the point far more explicitly. "Classes exist within the Jewish race," Guesde characteristically argued before the Chamber of Deputies. Jews, too, according to the Parti Ouvrier's leader, possessed both "a wealthy class and a proletarian class."[192]

As one might have expected from the cosmopolitan POF, its first engagements with real Jewish proletarians occurred, not in encounters with France's (admittedly tiny) Jewish working class, but through the Guesdists' wide-ranging internationalism. During the 1890s, French Marxists developed a passionate concern for Russian Jewry—supposedly largely proletarian, and certainly subjected to systematic racial persecution. At the same time, the POF developed links with radical Jews in London's East End and New York's garment district—both immigrant milieus having become fertile seedbeds for fin de siècle Marxism.[193] By the mid-1890s, Guesdist texts were replete with references to a worldwide Jewish proletariat, including occasional mentions of France's own working-class Jews. As the Parti Ouvrier now pointed out, "[T]here are thousands upon thousands of Jewish proletarians, and these Jewish workers are the worst exploited and the most miserable of all." Guesdists drew the necessary political conclusion. "And it's in the face of this fact [Jewish proletarianization]," Guesde chided, "that we socialists are asked [by anti-Semites] to consider anti-Semitism to be a struggle against capital . . . ? What a joke!"[194] How, Guesdists demanded, could socialists possibly attack poverty-stricken artisans, just because they shared a "racial" identity with the plutocratic Rothschilds? French Marxists couldn't launch such attacks, of course. Guesdists had long ridiculed Drumont for coddling Christian bankers; now they reviled him for insulting Jewish workers.

France's own Jewish workers nonetheless remained a shadowy presence in Guesdist discourse, even during the 1890s—always there, but never compellingly personified in the tailors, cobblers, and seamstresses of the Marais. By contrast, the Parti Ouvrier focused obsessively on Russia's Jews during their tragic pogrom years.[195] This obsession arose, at least to some extent, from the Guesdists' hatred of France's recently concluded Russian alliance. How, a furious Parti Ouvrier demanded, could supposedly enlightened France ally itself with undoubtedly reactionary Russia, when the Russian empire was committing mass murder against its Semitic subjects? Guesdists, as always, easily answered their own rhetorical question. In the POF's account of East European ethnic politics, Russia's Jews had massively mobilized behind socialism. The persecution of Jews by imperial Russia and France's ugly complicity in that persecution, according to the POF, stemmed less from racism than from antisocialism—from the two regimes' reactionary reflex against "the active participation of the youth and the workers of the Jews in the socialist and revolutionary movement."[196] At the same time, Russia's Jews and France's socialists were supposedly naturally united against reactionary Russia and bourgeois France. This intricate amalgam of antinomies served Guesdism well. The more sympathetically the Parti Ouvrier depicted suffering Russian Jewry, the more effectively the POF discredited the hated authorities in Paris and St. Petersburg, along with their despicable alliance.[197]

The Parti Ouvrier, indeed, came to believe that Jews, certainly in Russia but perhaps elsewhere as well, would someday play a starring role in that ultimate redemptive drama: the revolution against capital, the attainment of a postcapitalist utopia. Proletarian Jews would champion the coming revolution, Guesdists were sure, while its victory would redeem their race from millennia of degradation. According to *Le Socialiste*,

> [T]he socialist proletariat—in struggling for the emancipation of all the exploited, of all the oppressed—will put an end to the terrible suffering of that martyr nation that has given Spinoza to philosophy, Marx to socialism. It will be the great historical revenge of this people to contribute . . . by its energy and its revolutionary tenacity to freeing humanity from nationalist barbarism.[198]

In the Guesdists' political imaginary, a revolutionary alliance of history's victims—an alliance between workers exploited by capitalism, women oppressed by patriarchy, and Jews martyred by nationalism—would ensure socialism's impending victory. Fulfillment of these pariahs' previously unrealized potential would then guarantee socialism's historical superiority over capitalism. In the Parti Ouvrier's vision of the future, once socialist revolution had finally given workers, women, and Jews "the means to develop their abilities," they would "soon be in the first rank [of the new society]."[199] No wonder France's anti-Semites—pitilessly hierarchical in their social and gender values no less than in their racial prejudices—identified both Marxism and feminism as part of the "international Jewish conspiracy."

By the 1890s, then, once the Jewish proletariat had been fully recognized, the Parti Ouvrier's answer to the "Jewish question" had become utterly unequivocal:

> Whether Jew or Christian, once you're a worker, the capitalist system crushes you under the same burden. If one accepts the famous definition of Alphonse Karr, it has to be admitted that, within that race damned by the Church, the workers are . . . the Jews, and the bankers such as Hirsch and the Rothschilds are the Israelites. Let M. Drumont concern himself with the Israelites, without forgetting their Christian friends. As for us, we'll stick with the Jews.[200]

Some socialists (not Guesdists, of course!), the Parti Ouvrier sorrowfully admitted, had almost lost their footing in the anti-Semitic tide, "so violent had been the flood against the Jews." Nonetheless,

> the class war [has] recognized its own. With the international socialist workers' party are all the workers of the Jewish race, exploited in the East End of London, in the slums of New York, and elsewhere. . . . They bring their aspirations to our international congresses, and [those aspirations] are the same as those of all other socialists. The bankers and Jewish high society are identical, except perhaps for [the Jewish capitalists'] greater intelligence, to the Christian capitalists. One shouldn't make any distinction between [Jewish and Christian capitalists], and their fate must be the same.[201]

The POF thus doomed all bankers, including Christian bankers, while embracing all workers, including Jewish workers—having finally recognized that there were, indeed, such beings as Jewish workers.

At the fin de siècle, pogroms were not, unfortunately, confined to Kiev and Kichenev. France, too, suffered murderous ethnic violence, particularly throughout the trans-Mediterranean departments. The maniacal racial spasm that racked the country during the Dreyfus affair convulsed Algeria with extraordinary violence as inflamed colons mobilized fanatically behind anti-Semites; as mobs of French settlers rampaged through sullen Arab souks and centuries-old Jewish mercantile settlements, baying "La France aux Français!"; as Algeria's Sephardic Jews—alienated from the Arabic and Berber majority, repudiated by the European settlers—suffered pillage, rapine, and murder. This racist tumult troubled Guesdists greatly, not least because the Algerian colons, even at their most virulently anti-Semitic, avowed themselves leftists, even "socialists." Weirdly, having elected Drumont himself to the Chamber of Deputies, the Algerian French then repudiated their famous representative because he insisted on sitting on the right of the parliamentary hemicycle, rather than on its left![202] How did Guesdists respond, when confronted by this grotesque tragicomedy?

Outraged by Algeria's wave of racist atrocities, the POF reeled back in horror from what it described as "these repugnant and cowardly ferocities that dishonor . . . the name of France."[203] Guesdists vowed to combat

> the odious campaign carried out by the anti-Semites and nationalists against an entire category of our citizens, to the exclusive advantage of reaction and clerical capitalism. First [they'll destroy] the Jews, then freethinkers and socialists. We've already seen as much in Algiers, where Drumont's gangs of shady characters have murdered . . . one of our comrades, the citizen Arganaud.[204]

"First they'll come for the Jews, then for the Communists, then for. . . ." Already, by 1898, at least in Algeria, the Parti Ouvrier understood the cumulative logic of national socialism—the logic that would eventually murder so many Marxists, in conjunction with hecatombs of Jews.

Fighting fire with fire, the Guesdists counterattacked. Algerian anti-Semites, they raged, were not even French, but merely "a cosmopolitan whirlpool of Maltese, Spaniards, Italians, and Levantines."[205] Max Régis, Drumont's youthful second in Algiers and John the Baptist to twentieth-century "Algérie Française," was scathingly identified as "Massimiliano Régis" and his mongrel mob of supporters sardonically portrayed as "authentic products" of Drumont's "workshop La France aux Français."[206] These tactics, in retrospect, evoke qualms. Undermining the anti-Semites' nationalist credentials was one thing, the tacit appeal to "true" Frenchness in an Algerian context quite another.

The POF nonetheless nurtured an Algerian socialism blind to ethnic difference. Reporting on a regional socialist conference at Mustapha, for instance, where an anti-Semitic delegate had moved abrogation of the Crémieux Decree that had enfranchised Algeria's Jews, *Le Socialiste* rejoiced that the meeting had almost unanimously rejected the motion—a repudiation of anti-Semitism that supposedly demonstrated that "questions of religion and race had nothing to do with socialism."[207] Unfortunately, the delegates gathered at Mustapha did not really represent Algeria's working-class settlers, among whom the POF's inclusive and cosmopolitan doctrine failed miserably. A rueful Parti Ouvrier eventually came to view Algeria as emblematic of racism's triumph over socialism—on one occasion, for instance, characterizing anti-Semitic, ultranationalist, and anti-Guesdist Nancy as a "second Algiers."[208]

Nonetheless, at the turn of the century, the Parti Ouvrier still hoped that Algeria would someday come to its senses. "The Algerian proletariat," wrote Henri Ghesquière, one of Guesde's closest aides,

> incited by the clerical anti-Semites, on the one hand, and by the homilies of the bourgeois republicans, on the other, is divided; the hatreds . . . of nationality and of religion are very powerful; political, religious, and national passions have created savage, brutal, and bestial mentalities that divide the workers, throw them against each other so that proletarians, divided and maddened, pay with their blood for the divisions of which they are the victims. These hatreds will cease under the influence of socialism, and the proletarians of all nations and of all religions, finally reconciled, will march together . . . toward the Social Republic, which will make all men into equal and free brothers.[209]

Foreknowledge that the colons and Muslims of Algeria would eventually become "equal and free brothers" only on the model of Cain and Abel would have thoroughly dispirited a clairvoyant Ghesquière. Clairvoyance about the long-term relationship of twentieth-century Arabs and Jews would have disillusioned him completely.

In conclusion, what can legitimately be said of the Guesdists' engagement with fin de siècle racism, and particularly about their encounter with the French anti-Semites? The answer is clear: Guesdists were not racists, and were consistently anti-anti-Semitic. In the Parti Ouvrier's ideological paradigm, "blood" explained nothing. Guesdists reduced racial identities to insignificant epiphenomena of class, as they so reduced national identities, while discounting anti-Semitism as a distorted manifestation of class conflict, as they so discounted nationalism. According to the Parti Ouvrier's Marxist theory, racial identity, like national identity, lurked throughout history as treacherous but trivial "false consciousness." It had to be exposed, opposed, and extirpated, but, overall, was not to be taken very seriously.

Why, indeed, *should* Guesdists have taken race seriously, given their Marxist millenarianism? As limned in the Parti Ouvrier's messianic vision, the coming world revolution would efface whatever differences still divided Caucasians from Asians, blacks from whites, Jews from gentiles. Socialism would unify the "genre humain," melding it, the *Internationale*'s "human *race*," into a universal community, finally fused against all racial distinctions. True to Schiller's generous familial metaphor, "all men [and all women too!] would be brothers" in the cosmopolitan concord of communist humanity. Thus, just as racists sought to establish "blood brothership" within their particular race, so French Marxists aspired to the brotherhood of humanity as a whole. Socialism would extinguish "difference"—the difference between races no less than that between classes. The Guesdists' stance on racism and the "Jewish question" thus not only paralleled the POF's most cosmopolitan answer to the "national question," but corresponded to the Marxists' responses to the "religious question" and the "women's question." The socialist revolution, Guesdists were sure, would definitively resolve all these divisive questions, rendering them irrelevant, passé, and immaterial.

Given these universalist protocols, Guesdists welcomed Jews (like blacks or, given the opportunity, Algerians, Vietnamese, and "coolies") into their ranks, but repulsed Jews (or any others) who themselves repudiated universalism. At the entrance to the socialist enterprise, the billboards read "no racists need apply," with Jewish zealots barred as firmly as Aryan fanatics. Bemoaning the "arrogant" separatism of the Jews, the poisoned fruit of their atrocious suffering across the ages, Guesdists nonetheless anticipated Jewry's subsumption into socialist humankind:

> Victims or servants of every oppression, [the Jews] will never lose their distinct character except within a liberated humanity. In place of the leaguing of minds through murder, the only solution offered by the anti-Semites, we will unfailingly advocate unity through class solidarity, through aspiration, through hope—the superior unity that will inevitably be achieved through a collectivist society.[210]

French Marxists thus spurned the nascent Jewish ethnic politics of the fin de siècle. Zion, for Marxists, including Marxist Jews, meant the New Jerusalem of socialism, not a reclaimed Jerusalem in Palestine.[211] In principle, the humanistic POF welcomed Jews as humans, but not as Jews.

This Marxist hostility to "difference" fares badly today, when every passing postmodernist denounces humanism as masking Eurocentrism, heterosexism, patriarchalism, and classism (po-mo's most recent lexical barbarity).[212] Historians have raged against the Second International's antiracist protocols (voted with enthusiastic Guesdist support), which categorically condemned anti-Semitism, but which also denounced philo-Semitism—with both answers to the "Jewish question" faulted as irrational, inadmissible, and . . . racist.[213] Philo-Semitism racist! Confronted by this abomination, Zionists have rebelled against the Marxist tradition, thereby exemplifying today's clash between identity politics and Marxism. Just as radical feminists denounce socialist-feminists as misogynist because they refuse "Wominism," just as Black Power militants damn Marxists as racist because they disavow Black separatism, so Zionists condemn socialist cosmopolitans as anti-Semites because they reject Jewish particularism.

The Guesdists' universalism is thus the ultimate ground for their indictment as anti-Semites. The very occasional, usually ambiguous, and always unrepresentative "anti-Semitic" asides in the Parti Ouvrier's vast canon have been largely irrelevant to the case, compared to the much more fundamental charge that Marxism annuls Jewish identity—or, for that matter, any other racial, national, or religious identity. Philo-Semitic historians have bemoaned the ways in which, "since the end of the nineteenth century, Jews in many countries have confused their own emancipation with the emancipation of mankind as a whole by blindly enrolling in the socialist ranks." No wonder such historians can conclude that the POF, which advocated exactly such enrollment, fell into the arms of the anti-Semites "on the basis of class logic."[214] The Guesdists' conviction that "in the socialist army, there are neither Jews nor Christians, for there is no place there for religious or racial questions" thereby becomes, not the attack on racism it seems, but evidence of covert anti-Semitism—because it logically precludes "proclamations in favor of the Jewish race."[215]

For Jews, a self-chosen *positive* identity, even a self-chosen positive *racial* identity, has played a vital role in their long and heroic struggle against persecution.[216] Fin de siècle Jewish ethnonationalism certainly mustered in reaction to the period's rampant anti-Semitism, with Theodor Herzl's Zionist "proclamations in favor of the Jewish race" being as historically "rational" as the Parti Ouvrier's absolute antiracism. Then, as now, both Zionists and Marxists feared, hated, and fought the anti-Semites. But then, as now, they also feared, hated, and fought each other. In common with the anti-Semites, Jewish particularists denounced Marxist cosmopolitanism, while antiparticularist Marxists condemned *every* assertion of foundational ethnic identity, whether negative à la Drumont, or positive à la Herzl. Guesdists deplored ghettoization, whether imposed by anti-Semites or chosen by Jews.

There are many reasons for questioning Marxist cosmopolitanism. But, in accusing Marxists of anti-Semitism, philo-Semites run the absurd risk of assimilating *real* anti-Semites like Drumont to antiracist cosmopolitans like Guesde. Drumont acknowledged, even insisted on, Jewish particularity, and had no desire whatsoever to assimilate Jews into a common humanity. In this, he was utterly different from the POF's leader. Zionist militants, black power advocates, and postmodern multiculturalists who are fighting to conserve ethnic "difference" against today's capitalist (or yesterday's socialist) globalization should differentiate antiracists like Guesde, aspiring to the ultimate unification of the "genre humain," from racists like Drumont, striving for "La France aux Français." Inclusive cosmopolitanism, however inimical to ethnic identity, is one thing, genocidal exclusion quite another. For the sake of us all, they must be distinguished.[217]

CHAPTER 6

"A Class of Madmen": Marxists Confront National Socialism

The year 1882 marked a decisive moment in ideological history. Within the space of a few months, Europe witnessed the foundation of Jules Guesde's Parti Ouvrier and Paul Déroulède's Ligue des Patriotes—respectively, France's first Marxist party and the first of the paramilitary leagues that would mutate into "national socialism."[1] Few question the POF's role in the making of mass Marxism. But the first stirrings of fascism, that ideological earthquake, have also been recently traced to the seismic depths of the French fin de siècle. The Marquis de Morès's thuggish butcher boys of the Ligue Antisémitique, their gaudy cowboy-shirt uniform prefiguring and outdoing the black and brown to come, their ideals articulated in Morès's "doctrine du faisceau" (anticipating Mussolini's usage by decades), were genuine protofascists, even proto-Nazis. Edouard Drumont popularized the militant anti-Semitism that would shake the Third Republic during the Dreyfus affair, and then savage the world during the Third Reich. And Maurice Barrès, that modern "master of thought," high priest in the cult of "la terre et les morts," is now irretrievably implicated in the genesis of national socialism.[2] Marxist socialism and national socialism nascent together from the belly of the belle epoque—indeed a decisive moment!

This portentous conjunction has been noted,[3] but not explored. The oversight is unfortunate, as such exploration leads toward rich treasures of historical understanding. Ever since the inception of "Left" and "Right" in the revolutionary hemicycle of 1789, those ideological opposites have defined themselves by defying each other. Their historical meanings emerge from their "difference," that sacred word of contemporary hermeneutical divination. Divination of socialism and national socialism's intersecting, intertwining, and interlocking histories, dialectical understanding of their mutual conditioning, insight into their complex "unity of opposites"—such method offers a "dialogical" comprehension of Marxism and ultranationalism far more illuminating than exploration of those movements "in themselves."[4] Certainly the Parti Ouvrier's answer to the "national question" was formulated during its long war against national socialism,[5] while the national socialists' integral nationalism was shaped by their assault on Marxism.

How, then, did Guesdists make sense of the fin de siècle's "birth of fascist ideology"? They often interpreted the new Right as senselessness. In this Olympian mode, the Parti Ouvrier ridiculed the national socialists, whose politics, according to Guesdist caricature, consisted solely in "shrieking the word *patrie*, while rolling their "*r*'s and their eyes."[6] The Guesdists often returned to this comic device, on one notable occasion portraying "General" Cluseret, a Blanquist leader who had moved from social radicalism to ultranationalism, as "ce modèle des Frrrançais" who was about to embark on "une grrrande tournée [speaking tour] patrrriotique."[7] The medical Guesdist Pierre Bonnier, for his part, diagnosed the ultranationalists as "victims of patriotic fever," as "a class of the mad . . . that one identifies as the persecuted-persecutors"—an analysis conducted in the imaginary asylum housing the restrained and raving Paul de Cassagnac, Henri Rochefort, and Francis Laur.[8] Marxists thus equated ultranationalist politics with sadomasochistic madness long before the canonical work of Wilhelm Reich and Erich Fromm. Guesdists would have agreed with John Dunn's characterization of "a world of self-righteous nations" as constituting humanity as "a species of rational psychopaths."[9]

None of the new Right's heroes escaped such mockery. Paul Déroulède of the League of Patriots bore the brunt of Guesdist disdain. "Déroulédindon"[10] (Déroulède/turkey, or Déroulède the ninny) was routinely vilified as "a cretin by nature and a bad poet by vocation."[11] Some of this invective was genuinely funny, as with a knockabout "Letter to Paul Déroulède" published in *Le Socialiste*, which slyly commiserated with the ultranationalist leader on the day-to-day difficulties of "keeping one's eyes always toward the East," Déroulède's metaphorical guideline for remembering Alsace-Lorraine.[12] Boulanger himself, admittedly a soft target, was repeatedly reduced to a figure of fun, as with the POF's gleeful disclosure that the ubiquitous lithographs of the "brave general" had been manufactured . . . in Germany![13] Captain Marchand, for a brief moment Caesar to Paris's Rome, was spurned by Guesdists as a self-glorifying broker for Sudanese slave traders.[14] And Maurice Barrès himself, darling of the intellectual ultras, was contemptuously dismissed as one of "those souls who can transcend the narrow limits of their individualism only by attaining [the narrow limits] of the nation."[15] Ad hominem ruled. But Marxist barbs had a weightier point. The Parti Ouvrier ridiculed the ultranationalists' muddleheaded "cultural politics," mocking their "heroic" assaults on pubs that sold German beer, or their "epic" attacks on Wagnerian productions at the Opéra.[16] When safeguarding good beer and grand opera, the Parti Ouvrier genuinely shielded civilization against the barbarians.

The Guesdists would have liked to relegate ultranationalists to the lunatic fringe, but could not. Déroulède's Leaguers, after all, marshaled not only for comic opera assaults on the *Ring Cycle*, but for the seizure of power. History itself told against dismissal of ultranationalist politics. A hoary legacy of revolutionary barricades may have shadowed Paris's streets, but those cobblestones had also witnessed the triumphant tread of Louis Napoleon's lumpenproletarian "Society of 10 December," the protofascist mobilization that had first evoked Marx's prescient musings on ultranationalist demagoguery. As late as the 1880s, plebeian Bonapartism continued to bubble up as a subterranean source of the ascendant new Right. Even the Republican nationalism descendent from Michelet sometimes evinced a "blood and soil" fanaticism liable to national-socialist appropriation.[17]

Worse, France's socialist sects themselves proved sickeningly susceptible to ultranationalist contagion. Benoît Malon's protean "Integral Socialism" may have inspired Jaurès and Lucien Herr, but it also fostered Albert Regnard and Auguste Chirac's anti-Semitic "national socialism." And what of the Blanquists, those descendants of the most authentically "French" of France's many socialist traditions? Blanquism bifurcated during the 1890s, one remnant evolving toward Marxism and eventual merger with the Parti Ouvrier, but another devolving into a racist populism that, in parts of working-class Paris, even in revolutionary Belleville, merged seamlessly with the paramilitary Ligue des Patriotes. The resultant Parti Républicain Socialiste Français, violently anti-Semitic and ultranationalist, may have receded from historical memory, but, in its day, in the movement's Parisian strongholds, its leaders—Ernest Roche, Henri Rochefort, and Alfred Gabriel—utterly eclipsed the Parisian Guesdists and their Left-Blanquist ally Edouard Vaillant.[18] The "new" nationalism, ultranationalism, integral nationalism, national socialism—their terrifying ascendancy was no joke. Guesdists had to take them very seriously indeed.

And take them seriously they did. Guesdists obsessively followed the fortunes of their ultranationalist enemies, seeking to fathom the new Right's strengths and weaknesses, and thereby forestall its incursions into the POF's working-class domain. The ascendancy of French protofascism, however, disorientated the Parti Ouvrier. Whether on the defensive or on the attack, whether in theory or in practice, no coherent "party line" evolved from the POF's violent engagement against national socialism. Instead, Guesdists multiplied a kaleidoscopic array of conflicting understandings and contradictory strategies. These apparently haphazard yet systematically recurrent reactions to the new Right inflected the POF's historical development, reflected fundamental aporias in Marxism, and foreshadowed socialism's travails during the "era of fascism." They deserve scrutiny.

"Up against the Wall!": Guesdists Encounter the National Socialists

One scholarly reaction to the Parti Ouvrier's record has scrutinized the Guesdists as closet national socialists.[19] Marxists as cryptofascists? Surely not! Yet surprising similarities knotted the Parti Ouvrier and the ultranationalists together in the ideological tangle of the French fin de siècle. The POF's sometimes nationalist socialism could, on occasion, faintly echo the rhetoric of genuine national socialists.[20] More significantly, the two movements evolved similar critiques of liberalism. Guesde's extreme Left and Barrès's extreme Right both contended that the Third Republic had degenerated into a plaything for irresponsible bourgeois elites, and both Marxists and national socialists bemoaned "the condition of the working class" under Republican rule. At times, in their critiques of "the establishment," Marxist socialism and national socialism apparently melded into a unitary antiliberal front.

Beleaguered French liberals certainly concluded that the extremes that led from the Republican center toward left and right met at the other end of the ideological circlet, a conclusion that prefigured the twentieth-century theory of "totalitarianism."[21] Liberals discredited their national-socialist enemies by identifying them with the dreaded Marxists, while simultaneously defaming revolutionary socialists by equating them with the despised anti-Republican Right. Extreme Right equaled extreme Left! This contention utterly infuriated Guesdists, who responded in kind.[22] According to the Parti Ouvrier, Barrèsian ultras agreed with the liberals on everything that mattered. Ultranationalism and liberalism were both fronts for capitalism, the Parti Ouvrier argued, because national socialism, like liberalism, "denies or ignores the division of society into classes. It denies or doesn't wish to see the existence of exploiters and exploited."[23] Ultranationalism equaled liberalism! National socialists completed the polemical pattern. According to the new Right, liberalism and socialism were Siamese twins born from the depraved coupling of the Enlightenment with the French Revolution. From this parentage sprang all the ills of modernity. The rationalism of liberals and socialists debased spiritual ideals; their egalitarianism undermined healthy hierarchies; their cosmopolitanism disrupted communal solidarity. Liberalism equaled socialism![24]

An overly scrupulous historian might summarily dismiss all these tendentious equations. That would be a mistake. Liberals and fascists *have* allied against socialism. Think of Mussolini coming to power in coalition with Italy's liberals. Marxists and liberals *have* coalesced against fascism. Think of the popular-front dynamic that eventually forced even Stalin and Churchill into alliance. And fascists and Marxists *have* cooperated against ruling liberals.[25] Here we may think of the Parti Ouvrier. During the 1880s, France witnessed a particularly close symbiosis between the nationalist ultras and the ultras of anticapitalism. Despite their contempt for "Déroulèdindon," the Guesdists participated with Déroulède's Patriotes in the mass demonstrations of December 1887 against Jules Ferry. Assailed by national socialists and socialist nationalists, the beleaguered Ferry and his Opportunist ministry understandably viewed the revolutionary Right and the revolutionary Left as complicit, even as identical.

The period's ideologically indiscriminate anti-Opportunist agitation culminated in the Boulanger affair, as the Republic tottered under the assault of General Boulanger's massed supporters. Unlike other socialist factions, the Parti Ouvrier distanced itself from the fray. Yet troubling ambiguities undermined the Guesdists' supposedly evenhanded neutrality, ambiguities best represented by Lafargue's conviction, so distressing to the violently anti-Boulangist Engels, that Left Boulangism might be appropriated for socialist ends.[26] On the ground, in some of the POF's regional bastions, Guesdist susceptibility to Boulangism became even more obvious. The powerful Parti Ouvrier section in Bordeaux, for instance, succumbed without resistance to Boulangist temptation, agitating against foreign workers and aligning itself with the militarist Ligue des Patriotes. At the end of the affair, however, during the early 1890s, the Parti Ouvrier successful appropriated the Left Boulangist legacy—a triumph signified by the POF's association with Clovis Hugues, one of the most prominent Boulangists within the working-class movement. Lafargue, rather than Engels, had evidently best judged the socialist potential of Left Boulangism.[27] Yet the equivocal relationship between Guesdists and Boulangists also highlighted how easily ultranationalism could penetrate French socialism's still promiscuous body.

Promiscuous coupling sometimes led to sedate cohabitation. Guesdists in the 1889–93 Chamber of Deputies worked so closely with recently elected "Left Boulangists" that Marxists and "National Party" virtually merged. Tellingly, it was during this fleeting moment of connubial concord that Barrès effusively praised Guesde and Lafargue for their integrity and intelligence. Guesdist parliamentarians, for their part, sat amicably with Rochefort's anti-Semitic "Socialistes Patriotiques."[28] Liberals in the Chamber of Deputies—still terrified by their near-death experience during the Boulanger crisis, mud-spattered by the ongoing Panama scandal, fearing nemesis in the upcoming parliamentary elections—understandably equated the socialist Left and the left of the "National Party." This apparent symbiosis of Marxist socialism and national socialism recurred at the beginning of the twentieth century, in the aftermath of the Dreyfus affair, as intransigent Guesdists and integral nationalists assailed the alliance of Dreyfusard Opportunists, Radicals, and Ministerialist socialists that then governed France. Whether against Ferry, Constans, or Combes, Guesde and Barrès seemed as one, at least to liberal victims of their venom.

Further illustrating this apparent complicity, several prominent national socialists had begun their careers as associates of the POF. Pierre Biétry, before rising to leadership of the protofascist "Yellow" unions, worked closely with the POF in eastern France, his early militancy in the Franche-Comté vociferously acclaimed by *Le Socialiste*, which then referred to him as "our comrade Biétry."[29] And Georges Vacher de Lapouge, the internationally renowned advocate of proto-Nazi "scientific racism," first encountered politics as a Parti Ouvrier militant in Montpellier. Henri Vaugeois, the founder of the Action Française, had flirted with Marxism in his youth. Even Alexandre Zévaès, for a time Guesde's chosen successor, ended his political career in Gustave Hervé's postwar national-socialist movement.[30] Biétry, Vacher de Lapouge, Vaugeois, Zévaès—the POF can seem a seedbed of French national socialism. What affinities permitted these compromising connections?

Most obviously, both Marxists and national socialists attributed France's ills to the cash nexus, that noxious bourgeois tincture in which "money is everything."[31] This diagnosis of modernity's malaise, solidly founded on Marx's explorations in "commodity fetishism," suffused Guesdist polemic. The Parti Ouvrier bemoaned a world in which "everything is merchandise, everything can be bought and sold: ideas as well as manual labor, love as well as domesticity."[32] This corrosive critique of "commercial civilization," however, long antedated Marx. The romantic Conservatism born at the end of the eighteenth century had reviled capitalism's "economic rationalism," and this Conservative "culture critique" has continued unabated until the present. Throughout the nineteenth century, France's own Legitimists had cheered rebellion, even socialist rebellion, against the "Orleanist money-grubbers" who had overthrown the organic ancien régime. The fin de siècle monarchist workers' movement led by Firmin Bacconnier sustained this reactionary tradition, denouncing the market for reducing all human relations to the alienating abstractions of balance sheets and account books. In their turn, ideologues of the Action Française recuperated Bracconnier's paleoroyalist denunciation of bourgeois market society for their own neoroyalism, faithfully translating the tradition for twentieth-century national socialism.[33]

These Conservative critiques of commercialization could sometimes sound remarkably "Marxist." Hear Drumont denouncing the malignancies incurred when wealth, "concentrated in a small number of hands, governs as it pleases the economic life of whole peoples, enslaving its workforce and glutting itself on profits acquired without labor."[34] Amplifying Drumont's fury, the Anti-Semitic Congress of 1896 voted a resolution "totally rejecting capitalism, the modern form of [usury]."[35] France's venerable tradition of Catholic anti-Semitism further empowered this strange Conservative "Marxism." Listen to *La Croix* of 1886: "King Capital . . . capital freed from all limits, from all control . . . there is the site of corruption."[36] Secular ultranationalists seconded ultramontane vituperation. Barrès repeatedly employed quasi-Marxist invective, denouncing the ways in which the triumphant bourgeoisie had recreated man as a "slave to the relationship between labor and capital."[37] France's ruling Opportunists, he fumed, were simply "a financial society organized for the exploitation of France."[38] "Nationalism," proclaimed the great nationalist, "engenders socialism."[39] Maurras agreed: "We [of the Action

Française]," he affirmed, "are nationalistic, and consequently social."[40] "Left Maurrasians" like Thierry Maulnier have urged that their hero had indeed aligned himself with socialism.[41] No wonder France's bourgeois oligarchs indicted ultranationalism as being one with Marxist collectivism.

The national socialists' apparent anticapitalism emanated from profound sympathy with the worker, that "pariah of our great industrial cities, weighed down by the labor which consumes him, worn out before his time to enrich his master."[42] Drumont repeatedly affirmed such proletarian sympathies, testifying that "on every occasion, we have valiantly supported the cause of the persecuted, of the deprived, of the oppressed, of the exploited, of the humble, of the suffering."[43] Likewise, for Barrès, "to desert the cause of the disinherited" would have been "to betray the cause of the nation itself."[44] His program affirmed "the democratic interests of the workers, of the unfortunate, rather than . . . bourgeois oligarchy."[45] Even the socially conservative Ligue de la Patrie Française, otherwise a perfect expression of the more nationalist elements among that "bourgeois oligarchy," ensured that the "socialiste national" Giard sat on its directing committee—thereby supposedly bonding the LPF to the proletariat.[46] When pursuing this "ouvrieriste" strategy, France's ultranationalists might well have denominated themselves the Parti Ouvrier Français . . . had not the title of "French Workers' Party" already been taken by the Guesdists.[47]

The new Right's Conservative "anticapitalism" and empathy for the downtrodden impelled repeated national-socialist assaults on the Third Republic's free-enterprise establishment. Deploying a strategy characteristic of the Right since democracy's first stirrings, French ultranationalists elaborated a "democratic" attack on "liberal democracy." France's uncomprehending populace, ultras raged, had been cynically manipulated by liberals into a cruel travesty of popular government. In Drumont's mordant words, "[T]he proletariat, showing a remarkable blindness, works with its own hands to assure for the Bourgeoisie that political power . . . which the Bourgeoisie immediately uses against those who gave it to them."[48] This critique paralleled the Guesdists' own attacks on Republican politics, where hardly an issue of *Le Socialiste* passed without tirades against the "bourgeois Republic" and its proletarian dupes. No wonder the Action Français cheered Guesdist denunciations of liberalism's "Rights of Man and the Citizen," commenting enthusiastically (albeit mendaciously) that virtually no one on the Right would have dared employ such extreme language against the founding ideals of the French Republic.[49]

Establishment ideologues like Anatole Leroy-Beaulieu thus made few distinctions between extreme Right and extreme Left, predicting that national "socialism" would necessarily evolve into the real thing, into Marxist collectivism—a view sometimes shared by optimistic Guesdists. Assessing the Right's electoral triumph during 1900, Lafargue confidently forecast that ultranationalists,

> once they have witnessed [their leaders'] impotence, will turn to socialism. Far be it from us, therefore, to insult them and treat them as "savages." . . . Instead, we must redouble our efforts to propagate the emancipatory themes of revolutionary socialism. To work, comrades! Nationalism is one of the harbingers of socialist triumph![50]

Guesdists offered ultranationalists a "France, living by and for herself, freed from the capitalist system"[51]—the sole formula, according to French Marxists, that could author a genuine national socialism. "Totalitarianist" logic appears compelling. National socialism and Marxist socialism indeed seem alike.

This logic fails, however. No common *positive* identity yoked Marxists to national socialists. Drumont and Barrès may have episodically sympathized with Guesde and Lafargue's antiliberal passion, while Guesdists may have occasionally hoped that national-socialist antiliberalism would mutate into "real" socialism. But these conjunctions were more apparent than real. The Marxist Left and the ultranationalist Right shared little but hostility toward the ruling liberals. If nothing else, Guesdists, even at their most nationalist, remained internationalists, and were often enough genuinely cosmopolitan. National socialists—by contrast, and by definition—were not only nationalist, but *integrally* nationalist. They subordinated all other identities to ethnic identity, defined the national self against hostile others, and hunted down France's "enemies within," seeking to cleanse France of those like the Marxists who represented "alien doctrines." Guesdists understood this incompatibility. As self-conscious universalists, as disciples of a German theorist domiciled in England, French Marxists necessarily damned national socialism's absolute particularism, its conviction that "German truth and English truth have nothing to do with French truth, and . . . can poison us."[52] Guesdists would never, could never, avow Barrèsian "national egotism."[53]

The intensity of this conflict between class universalism and national particularity was, paradoxically, accentuated by surprising parallels between class and nation, and by similarities in their respective hegemonic projects. Both classes and nations, scholars have argued, may subsist without ideological consciousness (as Marx's prepolitical "classes in themselves" and in their national equivalent as the prepolitical "ethnies" explored by Anthony Smith),[54] and both require sustained political militancy to develop self-awareness and historical force. Modern history has thus manifested some movement, and a far greater number of missed moves, from "classes in themselves" to "classes for themselves," and a few transitions, and a vastly greater number of failed transits, from "ethnies" to nations. Barrès's nationalism and Guesde's Marxism thus fought each other as competing primary identities, as alternative hegemonic projects. For Barrès, the nation trumped all other identities, including class. For Guesde, class prevailed over all other allegiances, including that of the nation. Neither would tolerate a flaccid pluralism in which national and class identities coexisted without preordained hierarchy.[55] Nationalist particularism versus class cosmopolitanism—the conflict was irreconcilable.

Even the apparently shared antiliberalism of Marxists and ultranationalists actually diverged toward distant extremes, never meeting at any point on the ideological compass. French Marxists faulted the ruling Republicans for *betraying* the values of 1789. According to Guesdists, the coming socialist revolution would finally realize the ideals of "Liberty, Equality, and Fraternity" so sadly travestied by liberals. Marxism's "Social Republic," unlike the liberals' Third Republic, would be libertarian, egalitarian, and fraternal in ways impossible under capitalism. National socialists, for their part, condemned France's Republicans for *realizing* the ideals of the Great Revolution.[56] According to ultranationalists, "Liberty, Equality, and Fraternity" meant license, mediocrity, and treason. The coming "national revolution" would restore a healthy regime of authority, hierarchy, and community. Marxist socialism and integral nationalism: common antiliberalism? yes; commonality? no.

Once diverted from attacks on liberalism, once focused on each other, Guesdists and national socialists fought like cats and dogs.[57] Their fracas featured vividly in the POF's historical memory. Looking back on the Party's record from the perspective of its last days, French Marxists prided themselves particularly on "the struggle that [we have] sustained . . . against anti-Semitism and chauvinism."[58] This "antifascist" self-identity encompassed not only the Party's past, but its imagined future, where Guesdists foresaw a final battle between aspiring socialism and a decrepit capitalism defended by the reactionary Right. Some future Boulanger would seize power, intending to shore up the tottering social edifice, only to open the way to revolution.[59] Après le déluge, nous! Marxists and national socialists both presaged a fight to the death. According to the ultranationalists, Marxist socialism preyed upon France like a "poisoned beast whose bites had gangrened the social body," a beast that the ultranationalist Right would slaughter, "leaving its carcass to rot before the contemptuous people" while moving on to "disinfect the cities that [socialism] had occupied."[60] On the other side of the barricades, Guesdists dreamed of exterminating "the Régis, the Drumonts, and the Guérins," who would be put where they belonged: "up against the wall!"[61]

In the everyday politics of faubourg and estaminet, socialists and national socialists vied for the same constituency, the "popular masses." Ultranationalists entered this contest determined to tear the working class from socialism's embrace. Throughout national socialism's fraught history, from its violent birth during the 1880s until its bloody demise during the 1940s, its French champions fought to "nationalize" the proletariat.[62] Proletarians who worshipped in the cult of "la terre et les morts," they knew, forswore internationalist Marxism, while those enlisted in the Marxists' class war abjured ultranationalism.[63] For their part, Guesdists concluded that "national socialists" were both thoroughly false nationalists and thorough antisocialists. The ultranationalists' obsession with "the internal enemy" legitimated this conclusion. Much of their "socialism" amounted to little more than a "crude anti-Marxist device."[64] Barrès, for one, sometimes seemed more anti-Marxist than anti-German, or even anti-German *because* anti-Marxist, seeking to impose class collaboration "by means of hatred of our neighbors."[65] In their anti-Marxist persona, ultranationalists even discarded revanche. For all his integral nationalism, Drumont was indifferent to Alsace-Lorraine. For him, the Aryan peoples of France and Germany had been lured into war by Jewish high finance, and should unite against the greater racial enemy, including the Jewish Marxist enemy. According to Jules Lemaître of the Ligue de la Patrie Française, "[N]ationalism does not mean war. We have too much to do with enemies at home."[66] "Such patriots," the Guesdists fumed, "think of Revenge . . . only against their countrymen."[67] The warriors of national socialism supposedly trained solely for civil war.

If the national socialists' nationalism was fraudulent, the Parti Ouvrier concluded, then how much more so was their "socialism." The Guesdists could reach this dismissive conclusion because they defined socialism in their own interest, and, today, after a century of Marxist militancy, it is difficult not to concur with them. Socialism has become synonymous with the intertwining Labor, social-democratic, and communist movements. Like the Parti Ouvrier, these movements have construed socialism as the workers' cause in the class war fought between labor and capital. In their "minimum program," when on the defensive, such socialists have protected workers against capital's abuse. In their "maximum program," when on the offensive, they have aspired to total victory, to the "socialization of the means of production." Most scholarship today implicitly accepts this Marxist conception of "real socialism."

Yet things were less simple at the fin de siècle. Then, in France, any movement that doubted the verities of laissez-faire economics and sympathized with the poor could claim to be "socialist."[68] The Catholics who constructed "Christian socialism," the social liberals who turned themselves into the Parti Républicain Radical et Radical Socialiste, the ultranationalists and anti-Semites who first fabricated national socialism—all advocated class collaboration rather than class war, all defended the private ownership of the means of production, and yet all considered themselves to be authentically "socialist." Guesdists fought desperately to dispel this ideological ambiguity, categorically denying the socialist credential of Christian socialists, Radical Socialists, and national socialists. They succeeded. By the 1890s, "socialism" was increasingly identified with the POF's collectivist anticapitalism. As the new Right had always loathed collectivism, ultranationalists increasingly defined themselves against a "socialism" that they had once, before the Marxist ascendancy, claimed as their own—often, under the new circumstances, abandoning the very term.[69] The Parisian "national movement" that triumphed in 1900, for instance, was overtly antisocialist, in sharp contrast to its Boulangist predecessor of 1889, although the positive programs of the two movements differed very little. The League of Patriots, for its part, mobilized behind both Boulangists and anti-Dreyfusards, but, at the turn of century, had abandoned the inchoate radicalism of its Boulangist phase for sharply defined reaction . . . against socialism. And Barrès's successive election campaigns in Nancy contrast tellingly. As a Boulangist in 1889, he had violently challenged France's bourgeois oligarchy; as an anti-Dreyfusard in 1898, he directed his ire against Jews and Marxists.[70] By the turn of the century, the early border clashes between Marxist socialism and national socialism had escalated into total war. This battlefront between Marxism's socialism and the increasingly attenuated "socialism" of the national socialists warrants reconnaissance.

To begin with first principles, ultranationalists mocked Marxism's "materialism." In so doing, they claimed a noble legacy. From the romantic Restoration to the neoromantic fin de siècle, nationalist idealism repeatedly clashed with the hardheaded materialism of liberal or Marxist "economism." Nationalism had been born in revolt against the cosmopolitan rationalism of the Enlightenment, had been nurtured to maturity by prophets of romanticism such as Herder, and had metamorphosed into integral nationalism during the antipositivist rebellion of the belle epoque. The rift between the exalted Mazzini and the down-to-earth Marx exemplified this century-long clash of concepts. Despising the novel cult of the nation as much as he loathed traditional theology, Marx had derided Mazzini as "Theopompous."[71] As heirs to nationalist idealism, albeit heirs who would have horrified the humane Herder and Mazzini, Barrès and his followers thus detested Marx's French disciples, and were detested in return. The philosophical politics of Marxism and national socialism fundamentally contradicted each other. For Marxists, "material" reality determined the derivative domain of ideas and motives, while for Barrèsians, creative ideals and the heroic will forged reality itself.[72] National socialism strode forth as sublime ideal, as the embodied national will, not as a calculus of economic interest. The Dionysian élan of Nietzsche and Bergson animated the new nationalism, not the Apollonian analytics of Condorcet and Marx.

National socialists thus "put politics first." For the new Right, institutional debility accounted for France's social sickness, and a nationalist seizure of power would set the nation to rights. Déroulède's Ligue des Patriotes attributed France's crippling economic disorders to the Third Republic's perverse political order; Boulangists promised to assuage the "Great Depression" by revising the constitution; the leagues of the 1890s championed Bismarckian "state socialism." All ultranationalists invested their hopes in a hero who would intervene "from above" to solve "the social question."[73] Marxists repudiated this "primacy of politics." For the Parti Ouvrier, the Third Republic's inequities derived from capitalism's inequalities. Social revolution alone, Guesdists urged, could institute a just political order, or would even abolish politics altogether. Here lay a foundational difference between national socialism and Marxism: the providential politics of the national will versus the political economy of the labor movement. Barrès, for one, always emphasized the utter incompatibility between his "spiritual" nationalism and "materialist" Marxism, while Guesdists disparaged the new Right's ideology as "pure moral rhetoric."[74]

According to the Parti Ouvrier, the ultranationalists' moral rhetoric disguised neo-Conservatism, or masked a Conservatism with little of the "neo" about it. "Socialists" funded by business interests? "Revolutionaries" underwritten by the Duc d'Orléans? For skeptical Marxists, a self-advertised social-revolutionary movement subsidized by ironmasters and patronized by the royal pretender lacked a certain credibility. Guesdist skepticism should be endorsed. The national socialists of the belle epoque fought their ideological war not as socialists (as the term is today commonly understood) but as "Conservative revolutionaries." Theirs was the "national revolution" that would eventually furnish Europe's Nazis and fascists with intellectual rigor and institutional armature. Barrès thus had almost nothing in common with Karl Kautsky and Antonio Labriola, but much with Ernst Jünger and Giovanni Papini. Guesdists could convincingly affirm that the ultranationalists' "filthy polemics, their calls for violence and murder, are totally different from the methodical and reasoned preparation of the proletariat for an . . . inevitable social transformation."[75]

"Inevitable social transformation"? For French Marxists, history was going their way; modernity marched toward socialism. For national socialists, by contrast, the times tumbled toward a precipice; modernity threatened the world with decline, degeneration, and decadence.[76] The surging metropolitan world of tentacular cities, teeming masses, and world-spanning enterprise—the milieu of modernity, the subject of modernism—repelled, even terrified, ultranationalists. Unlike the sanguine Guesde, national socialists like Barrès feared and hated the new world of "industrial development which encloses the people in cities and creates an immense horde of workers."[77] Great cities, an "immense horde of workers"—exactly the milieu that Marxists counted on for their eventual historical triumph! Further exemplifying the ultranationalists' "reactionary socialism," as Marx had contemptuously characterized this mentality, even Biétry's "Jaunes," the national-socialist *labor* movement, abjured industrial society, nostalgically recalling the age of the *compagnonnages*, of artisanal workshops, of master and man joined in communion. This "national socialism," if it meant anything, meant "the reconciliation of ancient France with democracy,"[78] the reconciliation of "the people" with ancient aristocratic traditions, and perhaps with the ancient aristocracy itself.

Rather than following the Marxists confidently into cosmopolis, then, national socialists retreated sullenly toward an antique France of artisans rooted in tradition, peasants rooted in the soil, and elites rooted in their *pays*. In metahistorical terms, the belle epoque's ultranationalists were thus genuinely reactionary. They fought their ideological battles as revolutionary Conservatives, as reactionary modernists, as restorationists who aimed to repair the ancien régime with the tools of modernity.[79] Needless to say, the revolutionary Conservatives' reactionary metahistory in no way precluded fascination with the techniques and technologies of "modernization." France had to have the most modern artillery, Barrès et Cie urged their countrymen, but the guns' field of fire should defend a traditional "organic" society against cosmopolitan, egalitarian, and libertarian modernity—whether internal to France as socialist revolution, or external as globalizing capitalism. French protofascists exemplified a synthesis between reactionary ends and modern means. Even Drumont, for all his antimodernism, made brilliant use of the new media techniques of the second industrial revolution.[80]

This dissonance between the Parti Ouvrier's Marxist socialism and the ultranationalists' national socialism is best exemplified by the movements' emblematic thinkers: for the Guesdists, Karl Marx, one of the greatest theorists of modernity; for the national socialists, Pierre-Joseph Proudhon, the nineteenth century's most profound critic of the modern. Both social philosophers had criticized "modern times," but Marx had criticized them from within, faulting capitalism for failing to realize modernity's full potential, while Proudhon had rejected every aspect of the modern project, from industrialism to democracy, from cosmopolitanism to feminism. Barrès, Drumont, Biétry—all venerated the great antimodernist thinker from the Jura, while Sorel's turn to the Right from Marxist socialism toward national socialism explicitly discarded Marx in favor of Proudhon. By contrast, Guesdists detested every aspect of the Proudhonian legacy: its "mutualism," as opposed to their "collectivism"; its devotion to "the people," as opposed to their deification of the proletariat; its racist nationalism, as opposed to their humanist cosmopolitanism; its "family values," as opposed to their gender radicalism.[81] Marxist modernity versus Proudhonian antimodernity—a metahistorical chasm gaped between Guesdists and ultranationalists.

The French Marxists recognized this gap between their historical philosophy and that of the new Right. National socialists, Guesdists understood, hated modern capitalism not because it was capitalist, but because it was modern. Witness Joseph Sarraute, commenting confidently on Karl Lueger's menacing rise to power in Vienna:

> [I]n their rebellion against history, [the anti-Semitic Right] are attempting . . . to arrest social evolution and reverse it into the era of artisanal production. As socialists, [by contrast] we have no desire to clip the wings of progress. . . . We favor the utmost development of the productive forces: the source of well-being. It's in their increase, in their abundance, in their superabundance, that we'll discover . . . the arms and the soldiers necessary for the liberation of mankind. Modern industry separates us from the anti-Semites. All modern life, its material achievements and its mentality, separates them from us. They want to go back. We, forward![82]

According to the Parti Ouvrier, the supposedly "new" nationalism of the Right actually reeked of "putrefaction." It was no more than "the old France rotting."[83] Future versus past, progress versus reaction—what better distinction could be drawn between the Guesdists and the belle epoque's integral nationalists?[84]

"Financial Banditry": Class and Capital in Marxism and National Socialism

A better distinction can be drawn. Guesdists fought their battles as class warriors; France's protofascists as class collaborationists. In their foundational self-image, Guesdists identified themselves as "the men and the party of class conflict,"[85] while nationalists, even before the malign concoction of integral nationalism, disavowed class war. Nationalism's originating ideologues—from Fichte to Mazzini, from Herder to Michelet—all had condemned class conflict within the nation, all had affirmed "patriotic solidarity" between the classes. The national socialists of the belle epoque, however, enormously amplified this class collaborationist legacy. The belle epoque's protofascists fought desperately to unify their nation's nationals—whether worker or bourgeois, whether of the elite or the masses—against the foreign foe and against the "alien within."[86] For national socialists, war against "others" and solidarity with compatriots constituted a dialectical unity: war enforced solidarity, while solidarity empowered war. Driven by their hatred of the alien, spurred by their passion for community, ultranationalists detested class conflict as much as they loathed cosmopolitanism.

Without exception, luminaries of the new Right schemed to reestablish the amity between master and man sundered by liberal laissez-faire and socialist utopianism.[87] Barrès came to his anti-Semitism, as he had come to his ultranationalism, because ethnic identity politics appealed to *every* class, and thus reconciled labor to capital. Sorel's meteoric move from Marxism to national socialism was motivated by his insight that France's ethical renewal could come only from nationalist renaissance, rather than from syndicalist class war, given that nationalism could inspire anyone, while class conflict alienated everyone except the proletariat. Biétry devoted his enormous energies to constructing a "labor" movement that would work not only for labor, but for *all* the French, including employers. And Morès, in his persona as a "socialist gentleman,"[88] hoped to reconstruct France's long-lost unity by reconciling the working class to the aristocracy. National socialists of *every* variety—whether intellectual, proletarian, or aristocratic—based their ideal of national unity on class collaboration, and founded their program of class solidarity on ultranationalism.

To savor this redolent concoction of class collaboration and nationalism, attend to the anti-Semitic gathering where, Drumont enthused, "one could see, fraternally mixing with the workers, brought together with laboring men by an impulse of patriotism and justice, gentlemen of old family whose names evoke the most glorious pages of our history."[89] Aristocratic "gentlemen" and proletarian "laboring men" harmoniously united—a nationalist fraternity perfectly calculated to reduce any Marxist to apoplexy! The Parti *Ouvrier*, as the *Workers'* Party, confined its mission to the proletariat—excluding the bourgeoisie and the aristocracy from its comity, and neglecting, when not altogether ignoring, the peasantry and the petite bourgeoisie. National socialism rejected such social preference, organizing itself instead as a "broad church" open to every class. What the ultranationalists smugly characterized as their "practical socialism" (as opposed to the Marxists' "utopianism") was "practical" because it empowered collaboration between common people and the elite, between the masses and the aristocracy, between labor and capital.[90] Insofar as one's understanding of socialism implies class conflict, French protofascists should be conceived of not as "national *socialists*" but as "national *solidarists*"[91]—as crusaders for organic solidarity incarnate in a cohesive national community, as believers in a *Volksgemeinschaft* uniting all France's classes.

Militants of the new Right also praised themselves as "practical" because they abjured egalitarianism. In Maurras's canonical words, integral nationalists aimed to reestablish "the rules of hierarchy inscribed in the constitution of nature and the spirit"[92] whereby nature decreed the rule of the strong while spirit ordained the primacy of the select. Obeying the dictates of "realist" social science and the imperatives of idealist philosophy, the nationalist new order would be commanded by an "active upper class,"[93] by a resurgent aristocracy, albeit an aristocracy redefined to include the "healthy bourgeoisie." Elites would lead while the masses followed, capitalists would accumulate while laborers labored, management would command while the shop floor obeyed. When Maurras wrote that "a socialism that has been freed of democratic and cosmopolitan elements can fit nationalism like a well-made glove fits a beautiful hand,"[94] his image was unintentionally apt. Hands manipulate gloves, not vice versa. Maurras's antidemocratic national "socialism" gloved the mailed fist of the Conservative revolution.

That fist menaced the POF. The Parti Ouvrier, France's protofascists fumed, seduced proletarians from the national community, turning workers against their employers. This seduction had to be resisted, class war repudiated, Marxism smashed. Workers should realize that their misfortunes arose not from capitalism but from "capital [being] concentrated in the hands of a foreign race";[95] they should understand that their salvation lay not in the Parti Ouvrier's "collectivism" but in redistribution of Jewish wealth. The social war that national socialists fought was thus, most often, "war against the Jews."[96] Drumont exemplified this amalgam of anti-Semitism with anti-Marxism. Although he never found his Hitler, he always longed for "a man of the people, a socialist leader" who would achieve a "peaceful solution of the question of the proletariat" by convincing workers that "their real enemy was not their employers, but the Jews."[97] National socialism would then achieve its ultimate object, the "integration of the proletariat into the nation."[98] This project revolted French Marxists. The Parti Ouvrier ferociously contested all those "who wished to substitute 'class collaboration' for class conflict."[99] For Guesdists, class collaboration always manifested "conscious or unconscious . . . treason among workers."[100] "Treason" is here the operative word. Ultranationalists hated class war as treason against France; Marxists detested class collaboration as treason against the proletariat.

This radical opposition between Marxist socialism and national socialism became all the more evident once the movements' ideals manifested in practice. France's protofascists abhorred the Parti Ouvrier's own "practical" answer to the "social question": the "socialization of the means of production"—understood by national socialists, with some prescience, as an all-powerful state "acquiring a monopoly of the means of production, transport and exchange."[101] What was their alternative to Marxist "collectivism"? In sum, not much. At their most radical, national socialists recalled Proudhon's mutualism, particularly during the campaign for "la mine au mineurs" launched by the anti-Semitic luminary Francis Laur. In Laur's program, the state would have bought out the coal mines' plutocratic concessionaires (there was never any question of expropriation) and conferred the right to mine on the associated miners, who would thus become shareholders in their own enterprises. The Guesdists hated this idea. They dreaded a social order in which mutualist self-employers would evolve into stock-owning bourgeois. Worse yet, Guesdists fretted, worker proprietorship would disaggregate the working class. Steelworkers would fight with miners over the cost of coal, coal miners would struggle against forestry workers over the price of pit-props, foresters would brawl with metalworkers over the value of saws. According to a horrified Parti Ouvrier, worker-owned "corporative property . . . would lead to the same evils, the same disorder, as [capitalist] property."[102] French Marxists likewise condemned "profit-sharing," the most common national-socialist answer to the "social question." According to the Parti Ouvrier, profit-sharing merely bribed workers (with a small portion of the vast wealth they had themselves produced) into acceptance of capitalism. Ultranationalists like Alfred Gabriel happily agreed, advertising national-socialist profit-sharing as guaranteeing "a close alliance between labor and capital."[103] Again, war over class war utterly severed Marxists from ultranationalists.

When confronted by the national socialists' program, Guesdists mobilized their standard critiques of "reformism," arguing that such social reform was impossible under capitalism, or, if possible, would only prolong workers' misery. Prefiguring the charge of "social fascism" concocted by the Third International, the Parti Ouvrier equated the ultranationalists with the Third Republic's other "social reformist" movements. In *essence*, Guesdists suggested, national socialists differed not at all from Christian Democrats, Solidaristic Radicals, or "Ministerialist" socialists. All sought to save capitalism from its self-destructive dynamic, all hoped to "humanize" market society, all promoted class collaboration to achieve those ends. Social Catholics, social liberals, social democrats . . . and national socialists—all were the same, all were pernicious. This revolutionary reductionism should not be casually dismissed. In their opposition to class war, in their hostility to Marxist socialism, in their detestation of laissez-faire, the belle epoque's array of social reformers *were* similar, and even shared moments of communion. Barrès, after all, praised the reformist socialists associated with Benoît Malon because they, like Barrès's national socialists, "practically" opposed Marxist "utopianism."[104] Guesdists seized on such testimonials. National socialists, the Parti Ouvrier contended, were typical "bourgeois reformers" who "denied or did not wish to see the division of society into classes."[105]

The very different "utopias" imagined by Marxist socialists and national socialists further divided them. Guesdists dreamed a social order of universal freedom and empowerment based on common ownership of the means of production. After the workers' revolution, modernity's vast productive capacity would be "socialized," so that everyone became "coproprietors of all social wealth."[106] This collectivization of property ownership defined Marxist "collectivism." National socialists, however, valued, even venerated, the "private ownership of the means of production," and viewed the collectivist project with horror.[107] According to France's protofascists, "collectivism" epitomized degenerate democratization. A "social democracy" manifest in socialized production would destroy the economy's indispensable hierarchy, just as political democracy had ravaged the vital hierarchies of the polity. For French protofascists, proprietors' right to their property was sacrosanct, as was their right to "manage." There was nothing "collectivist" about this "national socialism." What then, if not collectivism, did the ultranationalist have to offer?

It is tempting to answer "little or nothing." In keeping with their "primacy of politics," national socialists prophesied a "national revolution" that would put things right without significant social fiddling or economic tinkering. As with an earlier national revolution, "everything [political] would have to change so that everything [socioeconomic] could remain the same." Insofar as the ultranationalists *did* envisage a nationalist political economy, they vacillated, much like their liberal enemies, between modernist celebration of entrepreneurial capitalists and reactionary nostalgia for widely dispersed proprietorship. In both visions, national "socialism," if it can be so described, lauded individual property ownership, thereby reinforcing the similarity between ultranationalists and liberals. The illusion that national socialists were genuinely socialist in any anticapitalist sense, the illusion that so frightened fin de siècle liberals and that still misleads liberal historians,[108] arose from the ultranationalists' repudiation of laissez-faire economics and their enmity toward "speculative" capital. Neither of these negations, however, challenged the private ownership of the means of production. Both were advanced to reinforce capitalism, not to overthrow it.

What about laissez-faire? As Adam Smith pointed out long ago, capitalists honor laissez-faire in the breach rather than in the observance. Collusion to fix prices, conspiracy to manage markets, machinations to dominate workers and manipulate consumers—these constitute the modus operandi of *real* capitalists. Certainly the behavior of French capitalists during the fin de siècle validated Smith's cynical realism rather than Paul Leroy-Beaulieu's hopeful naïveté (or mendacity). French entrepreneurs battened on protective tariffs, relied on public funding for vital infrastructure, and rejoiced in an "industrial policy" thinly disguised as armaments expenditure. The belle epoque's capitalists even gradually abandoned their lengthy love affair with individualized labor markets. The "nation," they proposed, should enforce labor peace by subordinating workers to the "national interest," manage the labor market by establishing national-corporatist linkages between labor and capital, and ensure a docile and plentiful labor force through national training schemes. The new Right enthusiastically seconded these proposals. Guesdists, however, despised them. National socialists, they contended, aimed not to liberate labor but to marshal workers into "forced labor in capitalist barracks."[109] National-socialist anticapitalism? The French ultranationalists were only anticapitalist in the fevered imagination of France's laissez-faire ideologues, or in the tales of market-fundamentalist historians. With their program of state-managed markets and corporativist labor relations, Barrès and his friends actually *exemplified* the capitalism that would prevail almost everywhere between the 1890s and the 1980s. Like the Christian Democrats and Solidarist Radicals, they were far more in tune with the capitalist times than were devout free-marketeers like Leroy-Beaulieu.

Nonetheless, for all their acceptance of capitalism, national socialists on rare occasions *did* bemoan the concentration and centralization of capital.

They sometimes worried about modernity's concentration of capital investment in titanic steel mills and vast engineering works, and occasionally fretted over its centralization of capital ownership in all-encompassing trusts and monopolistic corporations. When developing this antimodernist critique, however, ultranationalists dreamed only of curbing these monsters of capital, never of their nationalization. Despite his occasional rhetorical radicalism, in spite of his self-proclaimed "socialism," Barrès, for one, never proposed a single socialization, not even of the mines or the railways.[110] His "nationalists" would "nationalize" nothing. Even national-socialist labor leaders declined socializations. "We want to transform the status of wage-earners," Biétry insisted, "not in the direction of collectivism, but in the direction of the extension of individual property."[111] Whether this neo-Proudhonian project was to be achieved through expansion of small-scale enterprise or through employee share-ownership, there would be absolutely *no* tampering with the rights of private property. The contrast between ultra-Left and ultra-Right could not have been more stark. Marxists intended to abolish private ownership of the means of production; ultranationalists fought to preserve it, or even extend its domain.

In fact, most national socialists, most of the time, never thought of reversing capital's accelerating self-concentration and self-centralization, and often welcomed these trends. Instead of quixotically assailing the titanic blast furnaces at Le Creusot or denouncing the monstrous capital structure behind them, the new Right hailed their owners as heroes of national labor. Schneider of Creusot's steel and cannon, after all, armored France against her enemies. Concentrated enterprise, the centralization of capital investment, corporate capitalism—for the ultranationalists, these were not problems in themselves. Instead, large-scale capital supposedly took two radically different forms, one beneficent, the other malign. The beneficent form manifested in "productive" capitalists like the Schneiders, who constructed wealth-producing companies, furnished workers with livelihoods, and empowered the nation both economically and militarily. The malignant form manifested in "speculative" capitalists like the Rothschilds, who inflicted misery on workers and consumers, provoked periodic economic crises, and dilapidated the national economy. For ultranationalists, this distinction between producers and parasites was both economic and ethnic—convinced as national socialists were that "national capital is being rapidly soaked up by [Jewish] exploiters."[112] The distinction between "good" and "bad" capitalists thus reinforced the Right's "blood and soil" fanaticism. "Productive capital" was French; "speculative capital" was Jewish.[113]

Distinctions between productive and unproductive capital, between heroic entrepreneurs and parasitic speculators, between "national French capital" and "cosmopolitan Jewish capital," resonated in fin de siècle France. Like small businessmen everywhere during the deflationary decades of the triumphant gold standard, French petits bourgeois believed, in the resonant words of William Jennings Bryan, that they were being "crucified on a cross of gold." Hard-pressed farmers, near-bankrupt tradesmen, overborrowed shopkeepers—all believed that predatory financiers, "les gros," ruthlessly manipulated the credit system against small businessmen, "les petits." Given this mentality, advocacy of "free silver," that now-forgotten slogan of revolutionary monetarism, recurred in ultranationalist programs. Monetize silver, "funny money" fanatics advised, and credit would inflate, interest rates plummet, and business boom. Only the "yellow international of gold," that cosmopolitan Jewish cabal, would suffer. Nor was this credit chiliasm restricted to ill-educated peasants and hysterical petits bourgeois. Some of the time's most influential industrialists reviled the all-powerful credit conspiracy that supposedly ruled France. According to the well-funded publicists and economists of "national economics," the *haute banque*'s investment strategies reflected the pernicious cosmopolitanism of a Jewish financial elite. Parisian investment banks led by the rue Lafitte allegedly discriminated against national producers, favored foreign speculations, and thereby drained France of her substance. As for agriculture, France's increasingly desperate landowners eagerly seconded the time's anti-Semitic and ultranationalist political economy. They attributed declining agricultural prices and collapsing rent-rates to the machinations of the urban (read Jewish) financiers whose speculations had created the fin de siècle's long agricultural depression, and who now preyed on its victims by offering extortionate loans that led only to foreclosure.[114] The paranoia of peasants and petits bourgeois, the ambitions of French industrialists, the despair of French agrarians—all empowered the national-socialist indictment of "parasitic" capital.

The national socialists' distinction between "the gilded Bourgeoisie which has entered into the Jewish system" and that "other part of the Bourgeoisie, the worthiest and the most French, which works for its living"[115] sundered them irrevocably from French Marxists. Ultranationalists not only lauded "working capital" as opposed to "speculative capital,"[116] but campaigned vigorously against the Marxist socialism that conflated the two. "What enemy is socialism always pointing out to the proletariat?" the new Right angrily demanded. It was "capital." Yet who was the proletariat's *real* enemy? It was "the Jew."[117] National socialists reviled the Marxists who indiscriminately attacked capital, given that, freed from Jewry, "capital would once more become an instrument of labor rather than of speculation."[118] France's proto-fascists explicitly repudiated the "Jewish" socialism of the POF because "we [national socialists] attack international finance so that we may have France for the French."[119] *La France aux Français!* That epochal slogan promised France to French workers, but also to French capitalists.

Guesdists, for their part, despised the national-socialist distinction between malignant-because-parasitic Jewish speculators and beneficent-because-productive French entrepreneurs. Well aware that the triumph of "France for the French!" meant defeat for "Workers of the World, Unite!" the Parti Ouvrier counterattacked violently, reviling the national-socialist equation of "Jew" with "speculator," while denouncing the ultranationalists' attribution of all capitalism's ills to "cosmopolitan finance capital." For Guesdists, the "France of the French" so lauded by nationalists spawned its own predators and parasites. "All speculators," Lafargue asserted disdainfully, "whatever their nationality, race, or color, share identical interests [and] belong to the yellow international. . . . The Bontoux and the Rothschilds may be of different races and religions . . . but they are in total accord when it comes to appropriating capital."[120] According to a contemptuous Parti Ouvrier, national socialists sought only to aid one cabal of speculators against another. The ultranationalists' ethnic biases validated this accusation. When the POF, for instance, proposed an impost on financial transactions that would replace regressive consumption taxes, the Parti Ouvrier was assailed by ultras of the Ligue Antisémitique. The proposed tax, they raged, would disadvantage good French bankers and brokers. *Le Socialiste* responded sardonically: "[S]o it's only French and Christian financiers who have the right to steal from the French and the Christians!"[121] For Marxists, there could be no such double standard. *All* finance, indeed all *capital*, was theft, whatever its ethnic or religious allegiance. As if "Aryan" banks charged lower interest rates than Jewish ones! "There are some journals," Lafargue sneered, "that imagine that you can moralize finance. The anti-Semites are among their number; according to them, if it weren't for the Jews, Christian financiers, who are as sweet and simple as tender doves, wouldn't . . . rip off anyone."[122] Lafargue's Marxism conclusively demonstrated that, whether one borrowed from Jewish Rothschild or gentile Crédit Lyonnais, interest rates would be equally onerous, debt collection just as ruthless, foreclosure no less brutal.

Overall, then, Guesdists attributed the discontents of modernity to capital in general, not to cosmopolitan finance in particular, and certainly never to the Jews specifically. The Parti Ouvrier disavowed the national socialists' attribution of social disorder and economic malignancy to Jewry, even if "Jewry" meant, as it so often did during the nineteenth century, speculation and usury rather than ethnicity and religion. "The capitalist, for a socialist worker, is neither Jew nor Catholic," Charles Bonnier insisted. "He is not even a man or an individual; he is the representative of a system that must be destroyed."[123] In both theory and practice, this priority to social system rather than to identity politics dug an impassable abyss between Marxist socialism and national socialism, radically separating the Guesdists' program of socializing the means of production from the ultranationalists' strategy of "ethnic cleansing."

Insofar as national socialists *did* advance a rudimentary political economy, the Parti Ouvrier denounced them for demonizing finance capital. According to the Marxists' own economic theory, finance hardly mattered. It exploited only exploiters, and the Parti Ouvrier held no brief for the industrialists, agrarians, and petits bourgeois despoiled by financial speculation. What about the workers? During their sorry lives, France's proletarians, the *real* victims of capitalist exploitation, would never encounter Rothschild. "Those who attack financial exploitation," scoffed Alexandre Zévaès, "are not workers, but those who live off the workers. How often, on the highroads of the stock exchange, where our great financiers practise their banditry, do you find a single worker?"[124] Propertyless proletarians could safely ignore the fratricidal battle between profit and interest, supposedly the real agenda governing the national-socialist campaign against "Jewish speculation." "High finance," Guesdists contended, "intervenes only in order to steal from the thieves of proletarian labor. Thus . . . anti-Semitism, even as antifinance, doesn't have the slightest chance of making inroads into the mass of the dispossessed."[125] Workers would war against capital, whether industrial capital or finance capital.

When the Parti Ouvrier did deign to notice conflict between interest and profit, Guesdists took a sour pleasure in the carnage inflicted among French property owners by speculators. From the embittered perspective of the factory floor, Guesdists were sure, workers would see that, as the "exploiters of our exploiters, vampires upon the vampire class, the masters of money are . . . the avengers of labor."[126] There was considerably more to Guesdist enthusiasm for finance capital, however, than mere *Schadenfreude*. French Marxists were certain that the awesome predators of global finance unwittingly impelled the world's economic ecology toward postcapitalism. The bloody logic of capital, they argued, spelled social death for *les petits*, who fled helplessly before the ravening banks and brokerages that drove history toward the full development of capitalism and hence toward the socialist succession. Confident in their "scientific socialism," Guesdists mocked national-socialist proposals to stem this exterminationist logic with "free credit."[127] "To hope to decentralize finance," Guesde taunted, "is as sensible as wishing to arrest . . . the tides of the ocean."[128] The King Canutes of national socialism would soon be submerged by the waves of money they sought to check.

Guesdists, for their part, had no desire whatsoever to build breakwaters against capitalism's tidal waves. Globalizing finance ruined the petite bourgeoisie, destroying that "shock absorber"[129] class situated between labor and capital and forcing petits bourgeois into the all-encompassing proletariat. Without a "middle class" between itself and its working-class enemy, a minuscule bourgeoisie would one day cower defenseless before socialist revolutionaries. Better yet, finance capitalists "socialized the means of production" even *before* the revolution. By concentrating production and centralizing capital on a global scale, financiers were erecting the infrastructure of utopia. In the Parti Ouvrier's metahistorical vision, the "economic concentration that is occurring in a feudal form, to the benefit of a few, can, and will, finish in a social form benefiting all."[130] In the Parti Ouvrier's historical imaginary, national socialists represented those about to be expropriated by finance capital, while Guesdists represented proletarians who had already been expropriated, who had no desire whatsoever to cling to an effervescent present or retreat toward an irretrievable past and who instead aspired to a transcendent future. Unlike the new Right, the Parti Ouvrier would not swim against the tide. Capitalism's currents bore the working class straight toward the shores of socialism.

"M. Déroulède, Russian Agent": National Socialism as Conspiracy

Overall, then, Guesdists hated the national socialists, denouncing them at every turn, when not dismissing them as madmen. But the Parti Ouvrier still needed to explain *why* national socialism existed at all, even as madness. Irrationality, after all, demands rational explanation. What, then, accounted for the upsurge of ultranationalist and anti-Semitic militancy that had so unexpectedly interrupted history's smooth movement from bourgeois liberalism to working-class socialism? This question troubled Guesdists. From their Marxist perspective, national socialism's vaporous ideology, no sooner floated, should have evaporated in the furnace heat of capitalist globalization. Given that ultranationalism lacked substance of its own, the Parti Ouvrier concluded, it must survive solely as false consciousness designed to mislead the masses. "Designed"? According to the Guesdists' favorite interpretation of national socialism, the movement endured only as an antisocialist conspiracy.[131]

But *whose* conspiracy? Guesdists blamed the bourgeoisie. In their denunciations of ultranationalism, its venal ideologues—some selling themselves to bourgeois bidders, others mad and manipulated—were subsidized to concoct fantasies that would divert workers from socialism. This conspiracy theory of national socialism, for French Marxists, elegantly explained anti-Semitism. According to Guesde,

> *"Le juif, voilà l'ennemi"* offered by those salesmen of speech more or less free [a dig at Drumont's *Libre Parole*], has emerged from the same pack of tricks as *"le cléricalisme, voilà l'ennemi."* . . . While the proletariat, like a dog with a bone, devours the priest and the Semite, it will leave in peace . . . the owners of the mines, the factories, the soil, and the other means of production.[132]

In this interpretation, national socialists served capital by deflecting workers from the deadly-serious war between capital and labor toward a farcical battle "between those with foreskins and those without."[133]

Guesdists applied the same reductive logic to Caesarism, attributing it to capital's frantic erection of barricades against the forward march of labor.[134] French Marxists here recalled Marx's musings on "Bonapartism," thereby foreshadowing what would become, two generations later, one of the best analyses of fascism. In this interpretation of the ultranationalist ascendancy, Bonapartism surged forth from "the bourgeois and capitalist regime" as "regularly and unalterably as the flux and reflux of the tides."[135] Just as the Thermidorean bourgeois had commissioned Napoleon Bonaparte against renascent Jacobinism, just as the bourgeois of the Second Republic had engaged Louis Napoleon against insurgent radicals, so the bourgeois of the Third Republic sought their own savior. French workers were to be seduced from socialism by a charismatic "man on horseback," or, if unseduced, would be ridden down.[136]

On rare occasions, however, Guesdists nuanced this instrumental interpretation of French protofascism, admitting that the ultras might seize some autonomy from their capitalist patrons. The Parti Ouvrier followed the Marx of the *Eighteenth Brumaire of Louis Bonaparte* in suggesting that a "man on horseback" might someday ride to his own purpose. The regnant bourgeois, Guesdists gloated, would have no one but themselves to blame if one of their bloody antisocialist protégés ran wild, trampling bourgeois and proletarians alike as he careered toward glory.[137] French Marxists, however, never once suggested that a Bonapartist horseman might override the logic of capital. Like Marx confronted by the Second Empire, like interwar Marxists facing fascism, Guesdists assumed that a national-socialist "Napoleon IV" would be no less subject to capital logic than the liberals he displaced. A successful "national revolution" against the "bourgeois Republic," Guesdists assumed, would simply substitute one form of bourgeois governance for another.

Historians have harshly criticized the Parti Ouvrier for reducing the anti-Semitic Right to mere bourgeois manipulation, and conspiracy theory, in itself, certainly fails to explain protofascism.[138] Nonetheless, this Guesdist viewpoint made some sense. For all Boulanger's plebeian bluster, his ensnarement by a plutocratic cabal soon became public knowledge. Despite its populist rhetoric, the Ligue des Patriotes quite evidently depended on the largess of a few indulgent millionaires. And, most tellingly, Biétry's national-socialist labor movement survived on subsidies from self-interested employers. Threatened by the "forward march of labor," frightened bourgeois indeed rushed to purchase ultranationalist insurance-policies. Guesdists were thus hardly surprised when Paul Leroy-Beaulieu of the *Economiste Français*, the house organ of French capitalism, hailed the ultranationalist victory in Paris during 1900.[139]

Bourgeois investment in ultranationalism had paid off. The world capital of revolution had been retaken from the Left.

French Marxists were sure, however, that ultranationalist insurance-agents faced bankruptcy. Had not Boulanger's working-class constituency abandoned him, as soon as his compromising connections had been revealed? Had not Biétry's "Yellow" labor movement collapsed into scandal, once its corrupt "company unionism" had become evident? This critique deserves respect. Reliance on bourgeois backers *did* confound the belle epoque's national socialists, as similar dependency would later frustrate the Strassers and Labriolas of radical fascism. Torn between the conflicting interests of proletarian supporters and plutocratic underwriters, national socialists suffered ideological whiplash, at one moment seducing workers by denouncing capitalism, at the next soliciting capitalist subvention by praising free enterprise.[140] National socialists would always struggle to reconcile their elitism with their populism, their Conservative authoritarianism with their radical passions, their bourgeois backers with their plebeian followers. In most places, at most times, they have, fortunately, failed these tests.

Whatever the national socialists' covert intimacies with France's bourgeoisie, they nonetheless fully intended to overthrow the much-hated "bourgeois Republic." Even the most conspiracy-minded Marxists had difficulty viewing the tumultuous events of 1888 and 1898 as mere pantomimes scripted by capitalism's playwrights. The Parti Ouvrier therefore originated an alternative conspiracy theory. National socialism, Guesdists urged, was a front, not for the bourgeoisie, but for aristocratic reaction.[141] The new Right fronted for the old Right. "At the head of every anti-Semitic demonstration," a suspicious POF alleged, marched "the royalists . . . and the clericals."[142] The Parti Ouvrier repeatedly instanced the Marquis de Morès, that erratic crusader for aristocratic ultranationalism, as exemplifying such leadership. At the same time, in Berlin, Pastor Stöcker's court reactionaries pioneered the German anti-Semitic movement; in Russia, the antiquated czarist autocracy patronized pogroms; in Austria, anti-Semitism originated with the Prince of Lichtenstein's ultras.[143] Wherever anti-Semitism rode forth, whether coursing down Parisian boulevards or lurking through Bohemian forests, it had supposedly been dispatched from chateaux crumbling on the remote borders of modernity. In fin de siècle Vienna no less than in belle epoque Paris, national socialism exploded as a final feudal insurgency backed by "large landed property that has been relegated to the margins by the triumph of industry."[144]

Further embellishing this already baroque polemical construction, Guesdists ascribed ultranationalism to clerical conspiracy. "France for the French!" the Parti Ouvrier alleged, really meant "France for Rome!"[145] This charge found a ready audience in the fevered political climate of the fin de siècle. Some national-socialist ideologues like Drumont were indeed deeply devout, if only because Catholicism represented their beloved "old France." Others like Barrès and Maurras attacked Republican anticlericalism because it divided France, supposedly enfeebling the nation against foreign foes while empowering its insidious Semitic enemy. Both the religious Drumont and the atheist Maurras, however, hoped that Catholic Integralism's ascendancy would launch integral nationalism's hegemony. At the same time, just as the new nationalists rediscovered the old faith, so traditionalist Catholics discovered national socialism. Emergent "Social Catholicism" mimicked the new Right, not least in its anti-Semitism and chauvinism. Given that the editorial team at *Le Socialiste* closely followed both the Assumptionists' anti-Semitic *La Croix* and Drumont's clerical *Libre Parole*, the Parti Ouvrier understandably made few distinctions between Christian Democrats such as the Abbé Garnier and Drumontists such as Morès.[146] Garnier's Union Nationale, after all, had enthusiastically aligned itself with the anti-Semitic leagues, which in turn battened on traditional Catholic anti-Judaism.[147] Given these alignments, Guesdists mordantly suggested that fanatics for France like Drumont and Morès actually served "the Black International, Catholic and Roman,"[148] while integral nationalists like Barrès actually "took orders from an Italian"[149]—points that cynically mobilized France's traditional Gallican nationalism against the ultras, whether ultramontane or ultranationalist. According to the Parti Ouvrier, the covertly clerico-aristocratic new Right deviously worked to resurrect the ancien régime.

This polemic foreshadowed theories that emphasize continuity between nineteenth-century "reactionaries" and twentieth-century fascists. The time's ultra-Conservative politics validated such understanding. At the fin de siècle, the traditional Right's monarchs by divine right metamorphosed into the new Right's charismatic leaders; the traditionalists' hereditary aristocracy mutated into the national socialist's racial elite; the old Right's dogma of religious communion evolved into the ultranationalists' myth of ethnic belonging. The ancient ideology of authority, hierarchy, and community still beset liberty, equality, and fraternity, but the Right's reactionary convictions had been retooled for a modernity of mass politics, capitalist industrialization, and secular identities.[150] Nonetheless, this theorization of the new Right, for all its inherent credibility, posed a serious problem. It patently contradicted the Parti Ouvrier's portrayal of ultranationalism as a carefully concocted "bourgeois ideology." How could Drumont and Barrès possibly represent both capitalism *and* neofeudalism? With some contortion, Guesdists resolved this apparent contradiction. They argued that the bourgeoisie, in its senescence, had retreated into the authoritarianism, elitism, and dogma that typified the ancien régime's bankrupt legatees.[151] Historically transcended bourgeois thus joined backwoods nobles in a common front against modernity. Capitalist reaction against socialism, for Marxists, thus melded into the real thing, into the "Reaction" of the traditional counterrevolution.

The Parti Ouvrier reinforced its reduction of national socialism to conspiracy with a final "discovery." Ultranationalists, the POF alleged, were paid agents of imperial Russia. They were not so much on the Right as from the East. The leader of the Ligue des Patriotes, for instance, was repeatedly named and shamed as "M. Déroulède, Russian agent,"[152] while the anti-Semitic leagues, for all their shrieking of *La France aux Français!* allegedly owed their true allegiance to "the fatherland of the knout."[153] That national socialists worked for the Russian embassy, the Parti Ouvrier contended, confirmed that they were stooges of the bourgeoisie *and* puppets of the reactionaries. Russia, after all, served "the bourgeois Republic" as an economic dependency and military ally, while simultaneously flaunting itself as the last "ancien régime." Nationalist zealots thus stood nakedly revealed as agents of capital, reaction . . . and a foreign power.

These interpretations of national socialism as a proxy for antisocialism comforted embattled Guesdists, whether they portrayed the new Right as a bourgeois front organization, as a tool of reactionaries, or as the Parisian branch of the czarist secret police. Russia, French Marxists believed, would inevitably succumb to modernity; St. Petersburg's French agents were doomed by the metahistorical fate that hung over the czar. France's own nobles and clergy could hardly hide from history; their national-socialist protégés would also be trodden down by progress. And capitalism itself confronted world-historical defeat; bourgeois subsidy would not for long sustain ultranationalists. The new Right's ramshackle edifice of lies, illusions, and corruption would soon "collapse under the derision of the masses," the masses "that were in revolt against the [capitalist] present, not in favor of the feudal past, but in favor of the socialist future."[154]

"Stupidly Nationalist": The Guesdist Class Analysis of National Socialism

This self-confidence nonetheless faltered before daunting reality, as hundreds of thousands of the fin de siècle French mobilized behind ultranationalism. The membership of the Ligue des Patriots, for instance, far outnumbered recruitment into the Parti Ouvrier, with the LdP's effectives estimated at over 200,000 in 1887.[155] Barrès' triumphs in the industrial northeast humiliated the Parti Ouvrier, which vaunted itself as representing the entire French proletariat. And the explosive growth of Biétry's Jaunes eclipsed the Guesdists' own labored efforts to popularize Marxist syndicalism. Guesdists may have mocked anti-Semitic ultranationalism as the "socialism of fools," but they still needed to explain why so many of their fellow citizens were so foolish. In seeking to answer this question, Guesdists applied the penetrating logic of Marxist class analysis.

French Marxists usually began such analyses by stressing that the new nationalism appealed to losers. Exploiting Barrès's own imagery of "uprootedness," the Parti Ouvrier asserted that national socialism attracted capitalism's "déracinés."[156] These wretched victims of modernity had been torn from accustomed routines and customary communities, had withered in the late-capitalist world of high technology, high finance, and high exploitation, and now, lost and terrified, surrendered helplessly to ultranationalist irrationality. The time's ever-increasing horde of "uprooted"—a sad residue of urban drifters, disorientated peasants, and hard-pressed shopkeepers—ensured that the national-socialist constituency would, for a time, "grow by leaps and bounds," as modernity's victims, "even leaving aside the students of the Lycée of Nancy [a sneering reference to the protagonists of Barrès's *Les Déracinés*]," included all those "who have lost their footing and no longer can understand anything about the present."[157] Members of the ruling class themselves might join this unhappy throng. "Aged and stupefied by luxury," *Le Socialiste* suggested contemptuously, decadent bourgeois succumbed to ultranationalism as easily as did bankrupt petits bourgeois. Bewildered by the globe-spanning economy that funded their parasitism, bilked by capital's peak predators, doomed by capitalism's ultimate socialist logic, bourgeois ran mad, becoming "stupidly Nationalist."[158] According to this interpretation, national socialism was anything but a cunning bourgeois plot. Instead, insofar as the new Right recruited among the wealthy, it represented the bourgeoisie's nightmare struggle to escape the (self-)destructive logic of its own mode of production.

Nonetheless, Guesdists had difficulty in identifying a genuine bourgeois constituency for the new Right. The French ruling class, after all, continued in its vast majority to support Orleanist or Republican liberalism. One element of the capitalist elite, however, validated Guesdist political sociology: bourgeois young people, and particularly the young men of the lycées, the faculties, and the *grandes écoles*. The gilded youths of the Latin Quarter flocked to fin de siècle national socialism, confirming, according to the POF, their status as "the most reactionary part"[159] of the bourgeoisie. The new Right, in turn, enthusiastically welcomed youth's adherence. Having reluctantly concluded that workers were too burdened to sustain the national revolution, Barrès eventually turned to what he described as the "proletariat of graduates,"[160] investing his hopes in the angry young men of the schools who enjoyed the time, income, and energy necessary for unrestrained militancy. Not for nothing did Barrès become known as "the prince of youth."[161] Given the Guesdists' characteristic disdain for "bourgeois students," French Marxists relished this identification of national socialism with a rowdy, raucous, and irresponsible constituency. Whether escorting naked "models" to artists' balls or assaulting their leftist teachers, the scapegrace young bourgeois of the Boul' Mich', Guesdists sneered, perfectly personified the decadence and irrationality of their class.

Yet national socialism, as a *mass* movement, could hardly be built on bourgeois foundations. France's wealthy elite was too small, and too cosseted, to fill the streets with marching millions. The Parti Ouvrier itself always emphasized just how few the capitalists were who ruled France. So, if not a congeries of decadent bourgeois, who *were* the national socialists? Turning from the rarefied heights of French society to its teeming depths, Guesdists discovered national socialism's true constituency in the twilight world of "lumpenproletarians." According to the French Marxists' social paradigm, following Marx's own dubious usage, the lumpenproletariat swarmed as an inchoate mass of "marginals," a residual "class" composed of servants, prostitutes, criminals, and beggars. And, just as Marx had attributed the street-fighting ferocity of popular Bonapartism to these "lackeys," paupers, and felons, so Guesdists identified the outcasts of bourgeois society as the natural constituency of thuggish national socialism. To the intensely "respectable" Guesdists, nothing seemed more natural than that the mad and bad of the National Movement should consort with the vicious *apachés* of the Parisian slums. Confronted by murderous anti-Semites storming through the streets, *Le Socialiste* relegated their exploits to the crime page: they were nothing but a "gang of thugs and pimps."[162]

Unfortunately for Guesdist theory, attributing national socialism's mass militancy to the criminal underclass, a tiny proportion of the population, lacked sociological credibility. The attribution, however, well served Guesdist polemic. The hardworking, self-improving, "respectable working class" to which the POF appealed, and which appealed to the POF, detested the netherworlds of crime and dependency. Catering to its constituency, the Parti Ouvrier systematically vilified "those milieus" and willingly relegated "the beings who belong there" to the nationalists, who in turn willingly accepted them. Barrès reveled in the louche vitality and picaresque imagination of Paris's criminal Bohème. Exploiting this compromising connection, *Le Socialiste* assured its disgusted readership that Barrès's new Right recruited its followers among "the pimps and prostitutes of the Moulin-Rouge."[163]

Nonetheless, Guesdists still had to explain the vast crowds that acclaimed Boulanger, the militant masses who cheered the anti-Dreyfusards, the flood of recruits into Biétry's national-socialist labor movement. All could not be pimps, prostitutes, and "apachés." But they might still be "lumpenproletarians," given the indiscriminate inclusiveness of that identity. What of the "lackeys" in Marx's omnibus characterization of the lumpenproletariat? At the fin de siècle, servants indeed constituted a mass constituency for the taking. The belle epoque's myriad maids, housekeepers, and cooks almost matched factory workers in numbers. And servants did gravitate toward ultranationalism, while shunning socialism. Biétry's Jaunes, typically, recruited heavily "below stairs." Because of their extreme dependency, and because of their frequent ill-treatment, France's isolated and alienated servants subscribed with particular enthusiasm to anti-Semitism. Drumont et Cie proliferated gratifying invective against wealthy Jews, but stopped short of the too-dangerous Marxist critique of employers in general. The gestural politics of the new Right thus sold well to the servant classes, who could afford nothing better. Overall, then, the Guesdists' relegation of national socialism to the politics of "lackeys"[164] carried some weight as political sociology. And, as polemic, relegating ultranationalism to the servants' quarters effectively discredited the new Right among France's industrial workers, who detested service and despised servants.[165]

Seeking national socialism's mass base beyond France's slums and sculleries, inquisitive Guesdists toured the countryside. They had long contended that the new Right served aristocratic reaction. But the Parti Ouvrier went further, suggesting that an army of Sancho Panzas trotted behind ultranationalist Don Quixotes. The lords of national socialism, according to the POF, recruited their retinues among ignorant peasants from "remote villages."[166] Why? Because, according to *Le Socialiste*, "the Jew is equated [by the most backward peasants] with the usurer."[167] Anti-Semites thus tapped a receptive audience of bumpkins when they blamed rural misery on the Jews, even if "the Jews," to ignorant peasants, meant moneylenders rather than an ethnicity. Peasant simplicity, according to the Parti Ouvrier, succumbed easily to national-socialist blandishment.

This version of Guesdist political sociology rang true. In their populist persona, national socialists traced France's essential "populace" to the village, thereby amplifying nationalism's long-entrenched "folklorism." National socialists glorified country life, while contrasting it to the "rootlessness" of the predatory Jews who supposedly ruled the ascendant metropolis. The verdant hills of the Vosges, the pleasant valleys of the Meuse and the Moselle, the ancient *paysages* of Lorraine—their fields and villages, according to Barrèsians, embodied *la France profonde*, promising authenticity to a forlorn nation that had sold its soul to the Semites. These Arcadian panegyrics resonated among the troubled fin de siècle peasantry. Biétry's Yellow unions recruited massively among agricultural workers, among the rural proletarians who stubbornly refused socialist mobilization. No wonder the Guesdists contemptuously reduced national socialism to the archaic peasant mentality that Marx had vilified as the "idiocy of rural life."[168]

Nonetheless, when French Marxists diagnosed the national-socialist rot that gangrened French politics, they most often traced it to the decomposing middle class. Given that national socialism was essentially antimodern, the Parti Ouvrier concluded, it would necessarily attract that most antimodern of modern classes, the petite bourgeoisie. Shopkeepers doomed by the department store, artisans condemned by the factory, all the "independent" small businessmen destined to bankruptcy by large-scale capitalism—this multitude of losers supposedly constituted the new Right's *real* mass constituency. This theory achieved some credibility. Certainly many petits bourgeois championed the time's ugly xenophobia. During the belle epoque's economic and social crises, as prices fell and markets contracted, failing small businessmen blamed "alien others" for their plight. How could a shopkeeper compete with the ragged foreigners huckstering their cut-rate goods on every sidewalk? How could French cobblers and tailors survive when starveling East European immigrants so undercut their prices? To marginal small businessmen, *La France aux Français!* sounded more like a commercial strategy than a political slogan.[169]

More significantly, petit-bourgeois victims of modernity snapped up the anti-Semitic red-herring trailed across their road to oblivion. Admittedly, the Parti Ouvrier frequently linked the anti-Semitic new Right with the petits bourgeois of backward central and eastern Europe, rather than with the French middle class. Informed of Karl Lueger's triumph in Vienna, for instance, *Le Socialiste* reflected that

> the mounting victories of the anti-Semitic league are easily explicable. That league is the refuge of the continuously expanding number of the defeated from small industry and trade. Appropriated by the Don Quixotes of that league . . . the [petit-bourgeois] victims of the battle against capital adopt this transitory form [of politics] before their complete enlightenment, the consequence of which will be enlistment in the proletarian army.[170]

There were even rare occasions when the POF suggested that French petits bourgeois, unlike their fellows in Austria or Germany, would repudiate anti-Semitic ultranationalism altogether, if only because,

> having seen the Catholic Rouvier succeed the Jew Raynal, the freethinker Burdeau succeed the Protestant Ribot, having seen, in a word, the races succeed each other in power . . . without the establishment changing in the slightest or its own situation change at all, [the French petite bourgeoisie] isn't going to swallow the anti-Semitic line.[171]

More often, however, the Parti Ouvrier attributed the new Right's racist popularity in Paris and Lorraine, no less than in Vienna and Hesse, to the "malaise of a class . . . being expropriated, the petite bourgeoisie."[172]

Here, at the intersection of anti-Semitic ultranationalism and middle-class malaise, the Parti Ouvrier engaged one of the fundamental dynamics in modern French politics: the rupture of "the People" of 1792 and 1848 into a proletariat and a petite bourgeoisie, and the political devolution of some elements of the latter from nineteenth-century Jacobinism toward twentieth-century fascism.[173] Certainly fin de siècle petits bourgeois often blamed Jewry for the commercial concentration that threatened their entrepreneurial existence, although the great Parisian department stores they feared most had all been founded by good Catholics.[174] Barrès thus aimed his rather opportunistic anti-Semitism squarely at the petite bourgeoisie, which he insightfully characterized as "ferociously dedicated to private property [and thus hating the Marxists who challenged personal-property ownership], but jealous of the great fortunes [and thus detesting the Jews who personified plutocracy]."[175] The Ligue des Patriotes, during its final national-socialist metamorphosis, also recruited its most fanatical supporters among Parisian petits bourgeois, mobilizing them against Marxism, against the foreign foe . . . and against the Jews. Insofar as its obscure political sociology can be discerned, the Ligue Antisémitique Française likewise mustered petits bourgeois, with its "shopkeeper socialism" directed against department stores, but also against consumer cooperatives—socialist associations supposedly "in cahoots with the German collectivism [i.e., Marxism] which is dominated by Jews scheming to gain control of our commerce."[176] Jules Guérin himself—thuggish leader of the LAF, bankrupt oil refiner, and self-proclaimed victim of the petroleum trust—perfectly personified the tormented small businessmen whose disempowerment by capital, according to the POF, empowered the new Right.[177]

Did a common hostility toward large-scale capitalism align petit-bourgeois national socialists with the Guesdists, as has been alleged?[178] Not at all. In the Guesdists' own words, although anti-Semites, "at first sight," seemed to share a common cause with Marxists ("opposition to the large-scale plutocracy that is sweeping up all small-scale capital and small-scale savings"), the two movements, "in reality," were separated by "enormous differences."[179] On the one hand, exploiting the roiling hatreds and unrealistic hopes of an "agonized and expiring petite bourgeoisie,"[180] national socialists reviled and resisted mercantile concentration, interpreting it as a perverse consequence of Jewish malignancy. On the other hand, embodying the rationality of history, Marxists *welcomed* the concentration and centralization of merchant capital. At the very least, the Parti Ouvrier, representing working-class consumers, enthusiastically embraced the belle epoque's "modernization of retailing." Cooperatives and chain stores meant cheaper prices, even if they meant fewer shopkeepers.[181] As the POF's leader in Nantes, Charles Brunellière, half-jokingly suggested, workers would never subscribe to the shopkeepers' anti-Semitism. Why? Because workers' wives had "pointed out to them that, the more big stores there are, the lower the cost of living!"[182] More seriously, Guesdists believed that the "disappearance of the middle class" constituted "a necessity for the collectivist transformation of society."[183] Obliteration of the petite bourgeoisie would remove the "tampon"[184] that had hitherto cushioned the bourgeoisie against working-class insurgency, while simultaneously swelling socialism's proletarian constituency. National socialists stood athwart this process of proletarianization; Marxists cheered it on.

Guesdists thus understood the force and futility of middle-class national socialism. It reflected the "naturally" irrational politics of a class in its death agony. But could the Parti Ouvrier engage with this terminally ill middle class and its deathbed hallucinations? Some Guesdists despaired of petits bourgeois. "One could not," according to Charles Bonnier, "ask for reason among those who are doomed to the abyss."[185] Other Guesdists, sometimes even the same Guesdists in other circumstances, were more sanguine. Bonnier, having dismissed the petite bourgeoisie in 1899, only a year later speculated that the POF might have gained its votes during the Parisian municipal elections of 1900, if only socialist stupidities had not pushed the middle class toward ultranationalism.[186] Whatever the Parti Ouvrier's strategy, however, it consistently emphasized the fundamental distinction between rationalist Marxism and irrationalist national socialism, its irrationality born of the petite bourgeoisie's convulsive death throes.

Finally, what about ultranationalism among workers? Marxists of the Second and Third Internationals sometimes denied its very possibility. As the "universal class," proletarians supposedly had no need for nationalist false-consciousness, and certainly no need for national socialism. Marx himself, however, had reluctantly recognized working-class vulnerability to nationalism, and the politics of the fin de siècle confirmed his forebodings.[187] France's ultranationalists had no intention of nationalizing the means of production, but they had every intention of "nationalizing" the working class. As Barrès summed up his ultimate purpose, national socialism was intended to "bind [the workers] to the idea of the nation."[188] When France's protofascists cried out to workers, "[Y]our only enemy is the Jew. Let's hang him from the nearest lamppost!"[189] they expected to be heard.

And workers were listening.[190] Paulin Méry's violently anti-Semitic Ligue pour la Défense du Travail National recruited successfully among Parisian proletarians, particularly in the industrial northeast of the city, a congested and polluted terrain that should have been a Guesdist bastion, but was not. Even in Lille, the Parti Ouvrier's strongest citadel, working-class ultranationalism challenged Guesdism. Not all France's workers, it transpired, adored modernity, championed egalitarianism, and spurned capitalism. Some, instead, mourned the corporatist past, embraced the hierarchical fanaticism of integral nationalism, and admired their boss, or themselves aspired to property ownership. The butchers of La Villette—a cohesive community of masters and men, and the storm troopers of the LAF—exemplified the resultant working-class national socialism. Beyond the capital, Barrès' national-socialist constituency in

Nancy remained a standing rebuke to the POF's hegemonic pretensions. And Biétry's Jaunes spectacularly manifested an anti-Marxist working-class mentality of class collaboration, ultranationalism, and anti-Semitism.[191] In the mines, on the railways, among Lorraine's steelworks, and certainly throughout France's myriad artisanal workshops, millions of workers opted for national solidarity with French capitalists rather than for class solidarity with the workers of the world, and many thousands opted for national socialism at its most extreme.

In any case, who were "the workers"? Did the term designate horny-handed "sons of labor," the archetypical manual laborers of mine and factory? Or, as Marxist theory insisted, did the working class encompass service, technical, and clerical employees? If it did, then national socialism could aspire to a massive working-class constituency. The commercial revolution's expansion of retailing and finance, the second industrial revolution's proliferation of managerial and clerical labor, the state's multiplication of civil servants—all vastly inflated the fin de siècle "white-collar" working class. Marxists hoped that sales assistants, bank clerks, technicians, bookkeepers, customs officers, and postmistresses would recognize themselves as proletarians and enlist in the class war. But these hopes were dashed. Like the traditional petite bourgeoisie, white-collar workers mobilized more in favor of the nationalist Right than the socialist Left.[192]

Did Guesdists recognize this broader proletarian susceptibility to national socialism? Not for a moment. The Parti Ouvrier *knew* that workers abjured the "socialism of fools." Petits bourgeois could be foolish; peasants were fools by definition; but workers, also by definition, were wise. Where anti-Semitic nationalists attained power, as in Vienna, Guesdists blithely dismissed their victories. Once Austrian workers were enfranchised, the POF predicted, Lueger and company would slink back into their rat holes.[193] Elsewhere, closer to home, in Lorraine or at La Villette, where such excuses would not suffice, the Parti Ouvrier largely ignored working-class ultranationalism. Solicited by Drumont or Barrès, Guesdists assumed, workers would "simply shrug their shoulders" and dismiss the "ridiculous idea" that capitalism's inequities and inequalities could be attributed to "the presence on French soil of a few thousand Israelites."[194] Nonetheless, working-class national socialism continued to advance into the French political culture. The Parti Ouvrier's stubborn avoidance of a "reality check" represented a troubling triumph of doctrinal optimism over sociological realism.

So, according to the Parti Ouvrier, "who *were* the [proto]fascists?"[195] Were they the unruly offspring of the haute bourgeoisie, rioting through the Latin Quarter before settling down in daddy's business? Did they slink forth from Montmartre's sinister underworld, pimps and thugs for hire whenever reactionaries sought rent-a-crowds? Might they have emerged blinking from the benighted countryside, decayed aristocrats leading village simpletons back to the Dark Ages? Or were they a stampeding herd of frenzied petits bourgeois, lemmings doomed to drown in metahistorical oblivion? The Parti Ouvrier advanced one theory after another to account for the fin de siècle's upsurge of ultranationalism, but never managed to synthesize these apparently contradictory interpretations. Taken as a whole, however, the Guesdists' dispersed analyses suggest a more fruitful sociology of national socialism, although one never fully realized by the Parti Ouvrier itself.

If the POF had advanced all its sociological interpretations of ultranationalism simultaneously, the resultant composite would have demonstrated that *every* class could succumb to the new Right, albeit in different ways and for different reasons. Encountering ultranationalism's amalgam of elitism and populism, for instance, bourgeois and aristocrats would embrace the elitism, peasants and petits bourgeois the populism. Offered "reactionary modernism," bourgeois and the "new working class" of technicians and employees would empathize with the modernism, and aristocrats, peasants, and petits bourgeois with the reaction. Enticed by corporatism, capitalists would delight in its labor discipline, proletarians in its solidarity. The fin de siècle's protean new Right would thus have appeared as a universal creed, as a catchall movement. This all-inclusiveness might, at first sight, have rendered Marxism superfluous—since national socialism, apparently, emerged without reference to class.[196] Guesdists, however, could have accepted that the new Right indeed occurred across the class spectrum, but could then have used their Marxism to explicate the varied national socialisms emergent in different class contexts. The ultranationalism of the haut-bourgeois Ligue de la Patrie Française, for instance, might have been contrasted with that of the plebeian Jaunes, thereby elucidating both the cross-class coherence of the new Right and its internal contradictions. Unfortunately, this rewarding political sociology lurked latent in the Guesdists' confused engagement with ultranationalism, but ultimately failed to materialize.[197]

In sum, how did the Guesdists understand the fin de siècle's nascent new Right? Confusedly. At their most insouciant, French Marxists dismissed ultranationalists as lunatics. At other times, the Parti Ouvrier sympathized with national-socialist antiliberalism. Most often, however, the POF reviled ultranationalism as antisocialism. Even in this dominant mode, however, the Guesdists were inconsistent. Was national socialism merely an antisocialist plot? Or did ultranationalism embody its own ideological purpose? Guesdists oscillated between these conflicting "heteronomic" and "autonomic" interpretations of the new Right. Nor was this oscillation their only confusion. If national socialism was a plot, who had contrived it? The bourgeoisie? Or aristocratic reactionaries? The Parti Ouvrier advanced both conspiracy theories, without much effort to reconcile their evident contradiction. On the other hand, if ultranationalism genuinely represented some of the French, who were they? The bourgeoisie? The lumpenproletariat? The peasantry? The petite bourgeoisie? One after another, the Parti Ouvrier attributed the new Right to these classes, but without any serious attempt to synthesize the attributions.

The intensity and frequency of these themes shifted across the decades. The Parti Ouvrier's war against ultranationalism was understandably more intense at the peak of the Dreyfus affair than during the 1880s' mobilization against the Opportunists, and Guesdist hatred of national socialism necessarily escalated during the 1890s as the national socialists themselves became more hostile to the ascendant Marxists. Nonetheless, the content and pattern of Guesdist polemic remained constant. French Marxists despised ultranationalism even while tacitly tolerating it during the campaign against Ferry; they trashed its metahistorical solidity even while fighting it in the streets during 1898. The Guesdists' conflicted discourse, indeed, reiterated that of Marx confronting Bonapartism, and foreshadowed that of interwar Marxists struggling against fascism.[198] These continuities suggest structural rather than conjunctural explanation. Such explanation is ready to hand: French Marxists vacillated over national socialism because they were confused about ethnic identity. At their most dogmatic, Guesdists dismissed ethnicity as a misty revenant from the dead past, and thus relegated ultranationalism's acolytes to history's capacious wastebasket. Alternatively, in the Guesdists' (often justified) paranoid mode, they attributed national identity to capitalist manipulation, and thus contested national socialism as a ruling-class plot. Finally, at their most perceptive, French Marxists accepted nationalism as inherent in capitalist modernity, and thus strove to appropriate the national socialists' authentic constituency for the POF's own (rather inauthentic) socialist nationalism. Guesdists leaped with impressive agility among these mutually contradictory alternatives. Many of their consequent insights into the origins, character, and potential of protofascism were profound, and foreshadowed some of the most brilliant interwar theories of fascism. But these insights failed to cohere. Given Marxism's perplexity about ethnicity, the Parti Ouvrier necessarily lacked systematic understanding of embryonic national socialism, or a coherent strategy of engagement with its militants.

Conclusion

Like all ideological paradigms, Marxism has sparked dazzling illumination among its adepts, but also inflicted ignorance and incomprehension. The doctrine's perception of nationalism has exemplified this dialectic between blindness and brilliance. From Marx and Engels themselves, through their disciples during Marxism's century-long ascendancy, until today's remnant faithful, Marxists' insights into ethnicity have been focused and penetrating, but also one-eyed, figured through "the vision of a Cyclops."[1] Their focus and penetration, however, have been impressive indeed. No other school of thought has so clearly highlighted the nexus between ethnic identity and capitalist modernity. The "combined and uneven development" of the world market, spatial patterns of exploitation and exclusion ("the only thing worse than being exploited by capital," as East European used to say, "is *not* being exploited by capital"), the intricate geography of class domination, class rebellion, and class collaboration—all have determined modernity's experience of ethnicity, and all have been best illuminated by Marxists. Yet Marxism's penetrating focus has depended on blinkered vision. Governed by their ideological partis pris, Marxists have all too often reduced ethnicity to class, neglected the "inter"national dynamics of the world system, and underestimated nationalism in its contest with socialism. The "grandeur and misery" of Marxism's answers to the "national question" have constituted an organic whole, with the miseries inherent in the grandeur.

How well did Guesdists, for their part, answer that national question? In many respects, very well indeed. Because their cosmopolitanism awarded critical detachment, they understood nationhood far better than nationalist contemporaries who took the nation-state for granted. French Marxists knew that nations were "constructed"—that they were neither the free choice of free citizens nor primordial entities emergent from the historical abyss. Not for Guesdists Renan's liberal "everyday plebiscite" in favor of nationality; not for them Barrès's mystic pulsations from *la terre et les morts*. Better yet, Guesdists engaged with "globalization"—building on the *Manifesto*'s prescient portrayal of how "national one-sidedness and narrow-mindedness become more and more impossible."[2] As heir to Marx's dialectics, the Parti Ouvrier knew that the apparently independent national elements of the world-system actually defined each other, that the international whole determined its national parts, and that the whole might some day subsume its ephemeral national moments altogether. Best of all, however, French Marxists fully understood how motherlands and fatherlands could abuse their offspring. At the beginning of the twentieth century, Guesdists already anticipated Verdun, already feared fascism. The Parti Ouvrier's vision of nationhood could be brilliant indeed.

Yet the Parti Ouvrier's understanding of ethnic identity also generated systematic ambiguities, absences, and contradictions—many of which had characterized Marx's own conflicted interpretation of ethnicity, some of which have persisted until today's protracted "death of Marxism." Most fundamentally, Guesdists never reconciled Marxism's alternative understandings of nationhood. On the one hand, French Marxists insisted that modernity doomed every particularism, including nationality. Capitalism supposedly debilitated national economics, undermined national polities, and obliterated national cultures. In this formulation, capital constructed cosmopolis. On the other hand, the Parti Ouvrier contended that capitalism engendered a multitude of divisive particularisms, including warring nations. At the least, Guesdists argued, bourgeois brainwashed their subjects into racial exclusion and nationalist aggression, thereby accomplishing that "divide and rule" so vital to ruling-class hegemony. At the most, capitalism demanded national embodiment—capital's only conceivable institutional incarnation. In this formulation, the bourgeoisie marched across the world as the all-conquering nation-state. So, which was it to be? Global uniformity or divisive particularism? A more dialectically sophisticated Marxism than that of the Guesdists might have synthesized these alternatives. But such a synthesis had remained beyond Marx's impressive grasp, and still nonpluses Marxists today. The Guesdists' confusion at the fin de siècle is understandable. Then, as now, cosmopolis and conflict intersected in kaleidoscopic disarray—daunting the most sensitive theorization.

As in theory, so in practice. Like Marxists before and since, Guesdists oscillated dizzyingly between abstract cosmopolitanism and grounded socialist nationalism—the former empowered by the obvious absurdities of nationalist exclusion, the latter by the inescapable realities of the belle epoque. At one extreme, French Marxists simply denied ethnicity's relevance, confident that socialists could ignore nationhood and race. Capital's ruthless reduction of all humankind—Jew or gentile, black or white, French or German—to the common denominators of capital and labor would supposedly consign races and nations to the historical dustbin. This classic conviction, so often mocked, deserves respect. At the least, the Parti Ouvrier demonstrated that France's nation-state had been recently born, suggested that it might soon die, and offered insight into the nexus between the capitalist world-system and its (fleeting?) national embodiments. Neither the liberals' civic nationalism nor the protofascists' ethnic chauvinism attained such acuity.

Yet Guesdists had great difficulty in sustaining socialist cosmopolitanism, however acute it may have been "in theory." The POF's constituency—the sober, self-improving, militant working class of France's grimy industrial towns—had been systematically subjected to the fin de siècle's "nationalization of the masses," and had, to some extent, succumbed. "Subjected," from the Guesdists' perspective, was exactly the right word. According to the Parti Ouvrier in its cosmopolitan mode, proletarian nationalism represented false consciousness. How so? Still representative of the nineteenth century, French Marxists ignored the embryonic "culture industry" and neglected the nascent welfare state—"ideological state apparatuses" that would soon drive the pulsing heart of popular nationalism. Yet Guesdists already knew that France's recently established system of universal primary education indoctrinated children with unthinking national identity, and the Parti Ouvrier fully understood the malign ultranationalist workings of "social imperialism." Guesdists desperately hoped that proletarians would see through the bourgeoisie's nationalizing propaganda. But French Marxists nonetheless had to withstand the tidal waves of popular nationalism that flooded across their time, and were sometimes swept away.

Worse yet, from the Guesdists' cosmopolitan perspective, the "national economics" that challenged both Marxism and Manchesterian liberalism appealed mightily to workers. As pioneered by Mélinistes and Barrèsians, protectionism promised to protect both the "national bourgeoisie" *and* France's proletarians. Economic dikes, nationalists pledged, would be erected against the worldwide flood of labor that threatened French workers with catastrophic inundation—by an influx of footloose Italians and Belgians at the fin de siècle, by East Asian "coolies" or even American monkeys during the upcoming twentieth century. At the same time, economic nationalists guaranteed that workers would profit from protective tariffs—with their jobs defended and their wages maintained against foreign competition. When offered the choice between hardheaded national economics and Marxism's dimly imagined global commonwealth, many workers understandably chose the former. Guesdists bitterly criticized labor exclusion and trade protection, but nonetheless sometimes advanced their own shamefaced national economics. Seeking to outbid Barrès, they then contended that their socialism alone could defend the French economy against piratical global capitalism.

Finally, Guesdists occasionally succumbed to economic nationalism because their own socialism empowered nationhood—in foreshadowed practice, if not in theory. The Parti Ouvrier's practical goal, the "*socialization* of the means of production," when imagined by Guesdists, always degenerated into the "*nationalization* of the means of production." Marxism's cosmopolitanism may have pointed toward a worldwide socialization of global capital by the united "workers of the world." But, like Marx himself and all Marxists since,

Guesdists had absolutely no idea how such a project might be implemented. When they envisioned a socialist "transformation of the means of production," their vision instead evoked a *French* revolution that would "nationalize" *France's* capital. Long before Stalin's Soviet Union, "socialism in one country" lurked within the Guesdists' cosmopolitan dreams, foreshadowing a "national socialism" far more authentic than the Barrèsians' fatuous fakery.

So, when cosmopolitanism failed them, how did Guesdists respond? With "Vive la France!" Appropriating nationhood rather than resisting it, driven by the "socialist nationalism" implicit in their own project, French Marxists sometimes manifested a patriotism more worthy of Blanqui than of Marx.[3] In this mode, Guesdists sought to embody *La Grande Nation.* The First Republic's triumphs, they were sure, foreshadowed the victories they themselves would someday win—as the world once again looked to Paris for revolutionary inspiration. Cozily wrapped in both the *tricolore* and the red flag, French Marxists thus weathered the nationalist tempests of the Boulanger and Dreyfus affairs, warmed by the conviction that Marxist socialism alone incarnated "true France." Paradoxically, however, this episodic nationalism never muffled the affirmation that "workers have no fatherland."

Overall, then, Guesdists subscribed to incompatible programs, ranging from idealistic cosmopolitanism to pragmatic socialist nationalism—switching erratically from one alternative to the other. Within single articles, as polemic shifted from denouncing enemies to seducing compatriots, journalists could move from indicting nationhood as pernicious false consciousness to vaunting socialism as France's national salvation. One decisive determinant stabilized this otherwise self-contradictory amalgam of ultracosmopolitanism and socialist nationalism: a continuity of hatreds. From the Guesdists' jaundiced perspective, they confronted the same intolerable regime in 1905 as they had in 1882 (the much-detested "bourgeois republic"), just as they continued to experience the same iniquitous international order (a pandemonium of imperialist powers). Here the obvious historical contrast is with Guesdism's heir: the French Communist Party (PCF). Communists, like Guesdists, combined cosmopolitan antinationalism with vehement socialist nationalism, but their periodic oscillations from one alternative to the other were far more extreme than anything evident in the POF's history. Why? Because the PCF's international and domestic circumstances themselves changed so dramatically—ranging from the sectarian cosmopolitanism of the Comintern's "Third Period" (when "socialist nationalism" became an oxymoron) to the ultrapatriotism of the resistance years (when cosmopolitanism seemed a swear word).[4] Contrast the Communists' France of 1928 with that of 1942!

Guesdists suffered nothing equivalent. The Parti Ouvrier experienced, at the most, the Third Republic's transition from appeasement of Germany during the 1880s to alliance with Russia during the 1890s. For Guesdists, however, nothing much had changed, given that they despised Nicholas's "empire of the knout" at least as much as they detested Bismarck's Reich. Whether their polemics were launched during the 1880s or during the 1890s, French Marxists, in their cosmopolitan mode, denounced the "bourgeois republic" for imperialism, militarism, and warmongering, while, at the same time, as socialist nationalists, indicting the Republic for supinely abandoning the national interest (whether to placate Berlin or to please St. Petersburg). The only inflection of this discourse evolved from the POF's electoral successes during the early 1890s, when the Guesdists' liberal enemies and socialist competitors took to accusing the ascendant Parti Ouvrier of pro-German treason. In response, Guesdists understandably accentuated their socialist nationalism (redenominating themselves as the Parti Ouvrier *Français*, among other things). Nonetheless, such socialist nationalism had been readily evident during the 1880s, long before this inflection, while the Party's ultracosmopolitanism was hardly eclipsed during the 1890s. Overall, neither internal nor external circumstances between 1882 and 1905 changed sufficiently to substantially modify the POF's intricate answer to the "national question"—an answer characterized by consistent ambiguity and internal contradiction rather than "development," or even by the disorientating fluctuations experienced by twentieth-century Communists.

The Parti Ouvrier, however, was consistent only in its inconsistency. It never conceived a "nationalist internationalism," much less a "national cosmopolitanism."[5] Bedeviled by self-contradiction, misled by a reductionist class theory, Guesdists ended by grossly misjudging nationalism's force, most obviously during their war against the belle epoque's rampant racism and nascent national socialism—a misjudgment that foreshadowed both Marxism's near-fatal errors of the 1930s and the "death of Marxism" at our own "End of History."

If Guesde could be resurrected to witness Marxism's death throes, how might he respond? Unable to opt for a vanishing Marxist socialism, would he subscribe to the bourgeois antiglobalism of Le Pen? Most certainly *not*. He had detested Barrès's very similar "préférence nationale," and had particularly hated the Barrèsians' Le Penist preference for national capitalists. Would a revenant Guesde opt instead for the anarchism of today's "deep Green" antiglobalization movement? Perhaps. But perhaps not—given that he had always favored globalizing modernity, and had abhorred the belle epoque's own anarchists. Instead, forced to chose between today's ideological contestants, Guesde might well side with liberal champions of global capitalism, as Marx himself had done when choosing between globalization and its parochial enemies.[6] Whatever his choice, however, a resurrected Guesde, surveying our twenty-first century, would despair for us—deprived as we have been of the globalizing socialism for which his Parti Ouvrier had once fought so bravely.

Appendix A
Ideology and Terminology

Terminology in the study of ideology is itself ideological. A term, after all, can mean different things, depending on time, place, and provenance. What, for instance, is a "liberal"? To today's American "conservative," the word describes a softhearted (not to mention softheaded) believer in "social engineering," if not "socialism"—someone who would be characterized as a social democrat on the other side of the Atlantic. To a continental European, by contrast, a liberal is a true believer in the free market and the minimal state. Without clear definition, confusion reigns unchecked. It thus behooves a scholar writing about ideological conflict in the alien past, and within the intricate French political culture, to clarify his terms.

Here, at the moment of definition, there is a temptation to play Humpty Dumpty, and decree meaning. As Humpty instructed Alice, "[W]hen *I* use a word, it means just what I choose it to mean." This study, however, uses terms that have been defined in relation to each other, and its terminological *framework* thus needs explication. This ideological frame has been constructed, first, around the definitive "difference" between liberals and Conservatives—the all-important (although often denied) conflict between historical Left and Right.[1] "Liberals" and "Conservatives"? These are both conflicted terms, and emphatically in need of definition. First, then, in this book "liberalism" designates the ur-ideology of modernity—the political convictions of those who have fought for "liberty, equality, and fraternity," for the "rights of man and the citizen," for the ideal "that all men are created equal" and that all men (and perhaps all women, too) have an equal right to "life, liberty, and the pursuit of happiness."[2]

When considering the Third Republic during the belle epoque, one might designate such liberals as "Republicans"—a term that usefully amalgamates defenders of the time's status quo (the "Opportunists" of the 1880s) with the more radical "Radicals," who believed that the project initiated in 1789 still had some way to go before its full Republican realization. France, like Wilhelmine Germany, or for that matter Edwardian England and Giolittian Italy, was torn between moderate liberals (why not think of them as "National Liberals," after their German counterparts?) and radical liberals (the self-designation "Radical," too, recurs across the continent)—although both French factions claimed the Republic as their own.

Unfortunately for terminological convenience, "liberal" during the Third Republic did not equal "Republican." Not all liberals supported the Republic; not all Republicans were liberals. Those among the French who waxed nostalgic for the Orleanist *juste milieu* maintained their traditional royalism—looking across the channel for their model of the perfect liberal polity, complete with a property suffrage and a constitutional monarchy. At the same time, Maurice Barrès and his protofascist followers were determinedly Republican, but also violently antiliberal. This book perforce uses the term "liberal" to designate those (including Orleanists, Opportunists, and Radicals) who favored a polity where free men (and perhaps free women) strove together within free institutions . . . for free enterprise.

"Free enterprise" . . . Marxists, too, were Republicans, but decidedly *not* liberals, or at least not liberals if liberalism meant supporting "free enterprise" (aka capitalism). Instead, Marxists designated themselves as "socialists" or "collectivists." More conflicted terms! France had many varieties of "socialism," and ideological wars were fought over copyright on the concept. Throughout much of the nineteenth century, a socialist might have been anyone with a vague commitment to "social justice" or an uneasy sense that free markets failed to guarantee the "economic harmonies" worshipped by laissez-faire orthodoxy. Aristocratic Conservatives, Christian Democrats, even Radical liberals all claimed socialist credentials—until the advent of the Parti Ouvrier. Marxism's ascendancy during the 1890s altered the terminological terrain, as "socialism" came to designate the "socialization of the means of production": that revolutionary ideal which French Marxists called "collectivism."

The advent of collectivism constituted the decisive rupture between liberals and socialists, albeit a rupture prefigured many times since Babeuf's "Conspiracy of Equals." At that ruptural moment, Marxists arrogated the French Revolution's legacy—pledging to realize "liberty, equality, and fraternity," but assailing the liberal attempt to marry these ideals to capitalism's economic tyranny, inequality, and exclusion. The promise of 1789, the POF vowed, would soon be realized—but only through another world-historical revolution, this time against "bourgeois liberalism." French Marxists were thus on the Left, like liberals, and like most liberals embraced the Republic, albeit a "Social Republic." As "collectivists," however, Marxists were not scions of France's squabbling liberal family.

The terms "collectivist," "Guesdist" (after Jules Guesde, the POF's most prominent leader), "Parti Ouvrier," "POF" (Parti Ouvrier Français—as the movement eventually came to be known), and "French Marxist" designate for our purposes the same ideological milieu: a militantly antiliberal socialist Left, the French Marxism of the belle epoque. These terminological equations in no way denigrate the many non-Guesdists who also appropriated Marxism: luminaries like Edouard Vaillant, who deployed Marx's concepts with such skill; Benoît Malon, who incorporated Marx into his syncretist socialism; or Jean Jaurès, who so respected the sage of the British Museum. The POF, however, alone among France's several socialist parties, self-consciously identified itself as "Marxist," and as nothing else. The nation's other socialist movements—Vaillant's insurrectionary "Blanquists," Malon's Lib-Lab "Integral Socialists," Jaurès's eclectic "Independents"—claimed other legacies and criticized aspects of Marx's work, unlike the unconditionally Marxist Parti Ouvrier.

So much for the Left—those who observed the precepts of the French Revolution, from the most moderate defenders of bourgeois-liberal order to the most extreme socialist revolutionaries. What about the rebellious Right? What about the Third Republic's "Conservative revolutionaries"? The term "revolutionary Conservative" may seem oxymoronic, but only if the "conservative" (lowercase *c*), defined as a defender of the status quo (*any* status quo—whether liberal, socialist, or Conservative), is confused with the "Conservative" (capital *C*), conceived as an adherent of Conservatism—that very specific antiliberal and anticollectivist ideology of authority, hierarchy, and (exclusive) community. The latter is the ur-ideology of premodernity; the defining "Other" of the Left.

Confusion between "conservatism" and "Conservatism" is particularly characteristic of the English-speaking world, if only because liberalism is there so completely hegemonic, and Conservatism as an antiliberal ideology so vestigial. Ultraliberals in the United States identify themselves as Conservatives, when they are really conservatives (lowercase *c*) defending the liberal status quo against America's hapless social democrats (who have come to be identified, to confuse matters further, as "liberals"). Across the Atlantic, the British Conservative Party has long been thoroughly liberal, and therefore (in the context of Britain, that first hegemon of global liberalism) "conservative" rather than "Conservative." As a consequence, in these heartland societies of today's neoliberal world-order, and in hegemonized satellite-societies like Australia, it has become virtually impossible to conceptualize, or even recognize, "Conservatism" as antiliberal ideology.[3] Indicatively, Steven Holmes, in his admirable *Anatomy of Antiliberalism*, devotes an entire book to criticizing the politics of authority, hierarchy, and community, but can find no name for this obviously Conservative political tradition other than "non-Marxist antiliberalism."[4] The book at hand is more positive, calling a spade a spade, and a Conservative a Conservative—even, or particularly, when that Conservative was a Conservative Revolutionary, as Conservatives had to be under the conservatively (note the lowercase *c*) liberal Third Republic.[5]

The antiquated Legitimist Right that, at the end of the nineteenth century, still lurked through the Breton Bocage hardly concerns this book. The "new Right" or new Conservatism nascent at the fin de siècle (albeit prefigured by Bonapartism) takes center stage, however—dedicated as it was to charismatic Caesarism rather than to divine-right monarchy, to racial elites emergent from the people rather than to hereditary aristocracy, and to the ethnicized nation rather than to Christendom. Terminology is here a fraught issue. While fully cognizant of contemporary variations in meaning, this book equates France's new Right, best characterized as a "national socialism,"[6] with the fin de siècle's "integral nationalism," "new nationalism," and "ultranationalism."

The anti-Semitic and chauvinist sects of the French fin de siècle are, then, understood not only as "national-socialist," but as genuinely fascist, or at least as genuinely protofascist. Fascism as a full-fledged phenomenon obviously emerged only as the "totalitarian" consequence of total war, and evolved into maturity only through civil war between Bolshevism and anti-Bolshevism—thus manifesting in its full horror only during the terrible years between 1914 and 1945.[7] But France, after her own *année terrible* of 1870–71, prefigured that era. The shock of defeat in the Franco-Prussian War portended the malign Central European legacy of 1918; the brutal repression of the Commune augured the counterrevolutionary "White" terror of the "Red Years." Those on the ultranationalist Right who played to fin de siècle France's ethnic chauvinism and political paranoia (fortunately still largely confined to ultranationalist Paris and the traumatized borderlands) foreshadowed the black and brown terrors to come. Their militancy inaugurated the Noltean "Era of Fascism."[8]

This "national socialism" should be kept clearly distinct from the Marxist Left's occasional "socialist nationalism." Socialist nationalists may have traduced Marx's cosmopolitanism, but they still pursued the class war against capitalism and aspired to a collectivist "Social Republic." National socialists, by contrast, fought for a "national community" that would authoritatively bind master and man together in hierarchical harmony. Class conflict versus class collaboration, egalitarianism versus hierarchy—despite their common hatred of the ruling liberals, socialist nationalists and national socialists resided at opposite extremes on the ideological spectrum, on the extreme Left and on the extreme Right, respectively.

Here, then, is the terminological framework of this book: a fundamental dichotomy between liberal Left and Conservative Right, with the liberals challenged on their own left by insurgent collectivists and the Conservatives giving birth to national socialism. These warring ideologies offered conflicting answers to the insistent "national question"—answers that decisively determined Marxism's fraught encounter with French nationhood during the belle epoque.

Appendix B
Bibliographical Note

The primary sources for this book are constituted by the Parti Ouvrier's public discourse between 1882 and 1905. That means, above all, the Party's official weeklies—first *L'Egalité* and then *Le Socialiste.* Other newspapers to which the POF's leadership contributed as national spokespersons for their movement have also been consulted, particularly *Le Cri du Peuple,* as well as periodicals such as *L'Ere Nouvelle* and *Le Devenir Social.* The *Bulletin Mensuel de la Fédération Nationale des Elus du POF* offers the Parti Ouvrier at its most "reformist," while the *Bulletin Mensuel de la Fédération Nationale des Syndicats et Groupes Corporatifs Ouvriers de France* allows insight into its syndicalism.

There is a large pamphlet literature associated with the POF. These works have been consulted insofar as they were distributed through the Bibliothèque du Parti Ouvrier Français and were advertised in the Party's national press. Records of party congresses are invaluable sources for the POF's most official viewpoint, while speeches in the Chamber of Deputies allowed some of the movement's "loose cannons" to express views never allowed into more "party line" venues.

The texts of Marx and Engels offer a benchmark in any study of Marxist discourse. Citations of the "masterworks" have been consolidated as references to the now definitive English-language *Collected Works.*

The conceptual and contextual works that have sustained this book are listed in the bibliography.

Notes

Introduction

1. See the acerbic commentary on Simon's views in J. G. [Jules Guesde], "Patriotisme de classe," *Le Socialiste*, 26 September 1891. Guesde quotes Simon, but does not, unfortunately, identify the cited text.

2. S. Bloom, *The World of Nations: A Study of the National Implications in the Work of Karl Marx* (New York: Columbia University Press, 1941), still one of the best studies of "Marxism and nationalism."

3. N. Poulantzas, *State, Power, Socialism* (London: New Left Books, 1978), p. 93. For "evasion," see B. Anderson, *Imagined Communities: Reflections on the Origins and Spread of Nationalism* (London: Verso, 1983), p. 13; and for "historical failure," T. Nairn, "The Modern Janus," *New Left Review*, no. 94 (1975): 3. All three indictments originate with scholars sympathetic to Marxism.

4. According to the great Marxist historian Eric Hobsbawm in his "Reflections on Nationalism," in *Imagination and Precision in the Social Sciences*, ed. T. Nossiter, A. Hanson, and S. Rokkan (London: Faber and Faber, 1972), p. 386.

5. A. Wright, "Socialism and Nationalism," in *The Nation State*, ed. L. Tivey (Oxford: Robertson, 1981), p. 149. For Marx's typically abortive plan to expand his work beyond the analysis of capitalism to the study of nationalism, see H. Davis, *Toward a Marxist Theory of Nationalism* (New York: Monthly Review Press, 1978), p. 1. There is a representative critique of Marx in S. Avineri, "Marxism and Nationalism," in *The Impact of Western Nationalism*, ed. J. Reinharz and G. Mosse (London: Sage, 1992), p. 284.

6. For the supposedly disabling commitment to world history, see J. Petras, "Marx and Engels on the National Question," *Journal of Politics* 33 (1971): 799–802. Critique of the critiques of classical Marxist understandings of nationalism may be found in M. Löwy, "Marxism and the National Question," in *Revolution and Class Struggle: A Reader in Marxist Politics*, ed. R. Blackburn (London: Harvester, 1978), pp. 136–60; T. Purvis, "Marxism and Nationalism," in *Marxism and Social Science*, ed. A. Gamble, D. Marsh, and T. Tant (London: Macmillan, 1999), pp. 217–28; I. Cummins, *Marx, Engels and National Movements* (London: Croom Helm, 1980), pp. 171–72; S. Milner, *The Dilemmas of Internationalism: French Syndicalism and the International Labour Movement, 1900–1914* (New York: Berg, 1991), pp. 2–3; and M. Forman, *Nationalism and the International Labor Movement: The Idea of the Nation in Socialist and Anarchist Theory* (University Park: Pennsylvania State University Press, 1998), esp. p. 167.

7. C. Herod, *The Nation in the History of Marxian Thought: The Concept of Nations with History and Nations without History* (The Hague: Martinus Nijhoff, 1976); and R. Rosdolsky, *Engels and the "Nonhistoric" Peoples: The National Question in the Revolution of 1848* (Glasgow: Critique Books, 1986). For defense of the concept, see S. Meznaric, "A Neo-Marxist Approach to the Sociology of Nationalism, Doomed Nations and Doomed Schemes," *Praxis International* 7 (1987): 79–89; and for critique, E. Nimni, "Marx, Engels, and the National Question," in *The Rights of Minority Cultures*, ed. W. Kymlicka (Oxford: Oxford University Press, 1995), pp. 57–75. The best overview of the Marxist engagement with national liberation struggles is W. Connor, *The National Question in Marxist-Leninist Theory and Strategy* (Princeton, N.J. Princeton University Press, 1984), although the study neglects non-Communist Marxist traditions.

8. For the central importance of the Second International to our understanding of the Marxist engagement with nationalism, see A. Kriegel, "La IIe Internationale devant les questions nationales en Europe (1889–1914)," in *Le Pain et les roses: Jalons pour une histoire des socialismes* (Paris: Presses Universitaires de France, 1968), pp. 79–94; B. Jenkins and G. Minnerup, *Citizens and Comrades: Socialism in a World of Nation States* (London: Pluto Press, 1984), p. 42; and C. Weill, *L'Internationale et l'autre: Les Relations inter-ethniques dans la IIe Internationale (Discussions et débats)* (Paris: Arcantère, 1987).

9. G. Haupt, "Les Marxistes face à la question nationale: L'Histoire du problème," in *Les Marxistes et la question nationale, 1848–1914*, G. Haupt, M. Löwy, and C. Weill (Paris: François Maspero, 1974), pp. 28–29.

10. Kriegel, "La IIe Internationale devant les questions nationales en Europe (1889–1914)," p. 82.

11. R. Debray, "Marxism and the National Question," *New Left Review*, no. 105 (1977): 31. Shlomo Avineri uses the same astronomical metaphor in his "Marxism and Nationalism," *Journal of Contemporary History* 26 (1991): 638. For critique of the Second International on the "national question," with particular emphasis on Bauer's brilliant but failed intervention, see E. Nimni, *Marxism and Nationalism: Theoretical Origins of a Political Crisis* (London: Pluto, 1991).

12. Debray, "Marxism and the National Question," p. 31.

13. For the distinction, V. Fisera and G. Minnerup, "Marx, Engels and the National Question," in *Socialism and Nationalism*, ed. E. Cahm and V. Fisera (Nottingham: Spokesman, 1978), vol. 1, p. 7.

14. J. Cocks, *Passion and Paradox: Intellectuals Confront the National Question* (Princeton, N.J.: Princeton University Press, 2002), p. 22.

15. See, for instance, P. Ludz, "Socialism and the Nation," in *The Socialist Idea: A Reappraisal*, ed. L. Kolakowski and C. Hampshire (London: Quartet Books, 1974), p. 139.

16. See, for instance, A. Yaari, *Le Défi national: Les Théories marxistes sur la question national à l'épreuve de l'histoire* (Paris: Editions Anthropos, 1978); and Weill, *L'Internationale et l'autre*. For the centrality France should have in any study of national-

ism, see S. Hoffmann, "The Nation: What For? Vicissitudes of French Nationalism, 1871–1973," in *Decline or Renewal? France since the 1930s* (New York: Viking Press, 1974), p. 403; and Brian Jenkins's important study *Nationalism in France: Class and Nation since 1789* (London: Routledge, 1990), p. 12.

17. For discussion of this conflict between liberal nationalism and its nationalist critics, see S. Hazareesingh, *Political Traditions in Modern France* (Oxford: Oxford University Press, 1994), chap. 5.

18. "Liberal"? Terminology is all-important in historical studies of ideology, and always conflicted. See appendix A of this book for an explanation and justification of such use of terms.

19. C. Willard, *Le Mouvement socialiste en France (1893–1905): Les Guesdistes* (Paris, Editions Sociales, 1965), and R. Stuart, *Marxism at Work: Ideology, Class, and French Socialism during the Third Republic* (Cambridge: Cambridge University Press, 1992), provide an institutional history of the Party (the former work) and a study of its ideological paradigm (the latter).

20. There is a brief and unsatisfactory discussion in Willard, *Le Mouvement socialiste en France*, pp. 198–212. Only one of the many studies on the relationship between Marxism and nationalism even mentions the POF—and then only in relation to the party's principled opposition to colonialism! H. Davis, *Nationalism and Socialism: Marxist and Labor Theories of Nationalism to 1917* (New York: Monthly Review Press, 1967), p. 103.

21. For the relationship between narrative and analysis, see W. Dray, "Narrative versus Analysis in History," in *Rationality, Relativism and the Human Sciences*, ed. J. Margolis, M. Krausz, and R. Burian (Dordrecht: Nijhoff, 1986), pp. 23–42.

22. Claude Willard, in his *Les Guesdistes*, argues that cosmopolitanism dominated the early sectarian phase of the POF's history, giving way to nationalism during the reformist mid-1890s, only to be revived against the Ministerialists at the turn of the century. Willard, *Les Guesdistes*, pp. 63–67; 202–5. This periodization is too absolute, and fails to indicate the strong nationalist dimension of the Party during the 1880s and during the Ministerialist crisis, and the continuing cosmopolitanism of the mid-1890s. For a more nuanced argument that the Guesdists became increasingly favorable to the nation after 1893, see E. Cahm, "Le Mouvement socialiste face au nationalisme au temps de l'Affaire Dreyfus," *Bulletin de la Société des Etudes Jauresiennes*, no. 79 (1980): 5.

23. For the distinction, see H. White, "The Value of Narrativity in the Representation of Reality," *Critical Inquiry* 7 (1980): 6. If one prefers a more complex definition of "narrative" than a chronological ordering of events (with its implication of the *post hoc, ergo propter hoc* logical error), then my work might be characterized as "more an anatomizing narrative of character [in this case, the character of Marxism] than a sequential narrative of action." A. Megill, "Recounting the Past: 'Description,' Explanation and Narrative in Historiography," *American Historical Review* 94 (1989): 646.

24. K. Marx and F. Engels, *Manifesto of the Communist Party* [1848], in K. Marx and F. Engels, *Collected Works* (London: Lawrence and Wishart, 1976) 6: 502.

25. J. Guesde, preface to J. Vingtras, *Socialisme et patriotisme* (Lille, 1900), p. 3. All translations from Guesdist texts are by the author, unless otherwise indicated.

26. P. Lafargue, "Socialisme et patriotisme," *Le Socialiste*, 20 August 1887.

27. C. Bonnier and P. Bonnier, "La Crise du nationalisme," *Le Devenir Social*, nos. 11–12 (1897): 911–12.

28. "Protection et libre échange," *Le Socialiste*, 10 July 1886.

29. Account of speech by Ferroul, "Le Parti Ouvrier en France—Caudebec-les-Elbeuf," *Le Socialiste*, 29 January 1893.

30. Report of a speech by Guesde, "Une Triple manifestation," *Le Socialiste*, 24 June 1893.

31. Petras, "Marx and Engels on the National Question," p. 797.

32. "La Semaine," *Le Socialiste*, 7 November 1892.

33. J.M. [Massard], "La Théorie des races," *L'Egalité*, 14 May 1882.

34. "Le Traître Dreyfus," *Le Reveil du Nord*, 11 November 1896, cited in Willard, *Le Mouvement socialiste en France*, p. 410.

35. J. Guesde, "L'Epargne et ses caisses," *Le Salariat*, 25 May 1890, cited in Y. Marec, "Le Socialisme et l'épargne: Réactions de Jules Guesde," *Revue d'Economie Sociale*, no. 5 (1985): 48.

36. P. Lafargue, "Juifs et socialistes," *Le Cri du Peuple*, 2 October 1886.

37. T. Nairn, *The Breakup of Britain: Crisis and Neo-Nationalism* (London: New Left Books, 1981), p. 347.

38. Paul Lafargue, "Nationalisme et socialisme," *Le Socialiste*, 27 May 1900.

39. J. Phalippou, "En Algérie," *Le Socialiste*, 20 November 1898.

1. "For Us the World!": The Guesdists against the Nation

1. "Cosmopolitanism" and "internationalism" differ fundamentally, albeit the terms are often used interchangeably (the Guesdists themselves frequently used the latter term when they patently meant the former). Cosmopolitanism is opposed to nationalism; "inter"nationalism is founded upon it, as demonstrated by Craig Calhoun's point that "our very word 'international' suggests not the absence of nations but their primacy." C. Calhoun, *Nationalism* (Buckingham: Open University Press, 1997), p. 26. For an elaboration of the cosmopolitanism/internationalism confusion within Marxism, see R. Munck, *The Difficult Dialogue: Marxism and Nationalism* (London: Zed Press, 1986), p. 172. Marx himself tended to see internationalism as a transition toward cosmopolitanism, according to the analysis in J. Petras, "Marx and Engels on the National Question," *Review of Politics* 33 (1971): 811.

2. For nationalism and "enracinement" ("rootedness" is an inelegant translation of this powerful term), see P. Barral, "La Patrie," in *Histoire des droites en France*, vol. 3,

Sensibilités, ed., J.-F. Sirinelli (Paris: Gallimard, 1992), pp. 109–15. For critique of Marxism's episodic cosmopolitanism, indicted as alienating socialists from workers' own natural "grounding," see S. Avineri, "Marxism and Nationalism," *Journal of Contemporary History* 26 (1991): 654–55; and M. Freitag, "Théorie Marxiste et question nationale: Autopsie d'un malentendu," *Pluriel-Débat*, no. 26 (1981): 3–37.

3. K. Marx and F. Engels, *Manifesto of the Communist Party* [1848], in *Collected Works* (London: Lawrence and Wishart, 1976), 6: 497. For a representative Guesdist appropriation of this injunction, see Geva, "Emigration et immigration," *Le Socialiste*, 27 January 1894.

4. M. Rustin, "Place and Time in Socialist Theory," *Radical Philosophy*, no. 47 (1987): 32—a critique of this Marxist project.

5. Paul Lafargue, "Socialisme et patriotisme," *Le Socialiste*, 20 August 1887.

6. It has been suggested that Marx—son of a converted Jew, child of the nationally ambiguous Rhineland, lifelong exile—systematically underestimated the appeal of national identity because of his own shallow national roots. V. Kiernan, "On the Development of a Marxist Approach to Nationalism," *Science and Society* 34 (1970): 93. There is linkage between this biographical explanation of Marxist cosmopolitanism and more fundamental determinations in Z. Pelczynski, "Nation, Civil Society, State: Hegelian Sources of the Marxian Non-Theory of Nationality," in *The State and Civil Society: Studies in Hegel's Political Philosophy*, ed. Z. Pelczynski (Cambridge: Cambridge University Press, 1984), p. 262.

7. Mathilde Guesde was fluent in five languages. C. Willard, *Jules Guesde: L'Apôtre et la loi* (Paris: Editions Ouvrières, 1991), p. 26.

8. When asked about his origins, Lafargue allegedly once responded, "I am proudest of my Negro extraction." Cited in the editor's introduction to P. Lafargue, *Socialism and the Intellectuals*, New York edition (1967), and quoted in Leslie Derfler's invaluable *Paul Lafargue and the Founding of French Marxism, 1842–1882* (Cambridge: Mass.: Harvard University Press, 1991), p. 15.

9. "Le Parti Ouvrier en France—Tourcoing," *Le Socialiste*, 19 December 1891—an account of one of Lafargue's incessant speaking tours. The correspondent on such occasions was usually the traveling speaker himself.

10. See, for instance, Geva, "L'Internationalisme," *Le Socialiste*, 19 February 1887. Indeed, the Guesdists repeatedly emphasized that the Commune—that iconic focus of French leftist identity—had been thoroughly cosmopolitan, animated as it was by such figures as "Franckel, Dombrowsky, Wrobelensky, Cipriani, and other cosmopolitan heroes." For this list (including the misspelling of Leo Frankel's name), see ibid. In fact, the Commune had been, as much as anything, a nationalist reaction against a defeatist government, and many of its survivors, not least the Blanquists who best incarnated the Communard legacy, evolved toward protofascism, not toward cosmopolitan Marxism.

11. For the many Belgians in the POF, see C. Strikwerda, "Regionalism and Internationalism: The Working-Class Movement in the Nord and the Belgian Con-

nection, 1871–1914," *Proceedings of the Western Society for French History* 12 (1984): 221–30; D. Gordon, *Liberalism and Social Reform: Industrial Growth and Progressiste Politics in France, 1880–1914* (Westport, Conn.: Greenwood Press, 1996), pp. 36–37; and G. Noiriel, *Le Creuset français: Histoire de l'immigration, XIXe–XXe siècles* (Paris: Seuil, 1988), p. 331. The border between France and Belgium had little experiential reality, according to T. Baycroft, "Changing Identities in the Franco-Belgian Borderland in the Nineteenth and Twentieth Centuries," *French History* 13 (1999): 417–38, with particular comment on the intermingling of border socialisms on p. 425.

12. Y. Lequin, "'Métissages Imprudents,'" in *Histoire des Etrangers et de l'Immigration en France*, ed. Y. Lequin (Paris: Larousse, 1992), p. 383.

13. "Le Parti Ouvrier en France—Savoie," *Le Socialiste*, 29 July 1900. Pierre Milza, in his "Le Racisme anti-Italien en France: La Tuerie d'Aigues-Mortes (1893)," *L'Histoire*, no. 10 (1979): 30, has claimed that anti-Italian prejudice was rife in the French socialist press. This was certainly *not* the case in the POF's journals. For an instance of Italian language material in the Guesdist press, see "Operai italiani," *Le Socialiste*, 17 July 1886—published at the peak of the Great Depression's anti-immigrant agitation.

14. See, for example, the five contributions listed for 31 July 1886, of which *three* are non-French (Benevento, Geneva, and "Italy"). *Le Socialiste*, 31 July 1886. The Guesdists made no secret of the particularly large sums obtained from the SPD.

15. Although there is no evidence that they were able to help a certain "Mac Corm," who had written from Massachusetts asking the POF to propagandize strikebreaking French Canadian mill workers in his town! "Un Appel," *Le Socialiste*, 13 November 1886.

16. B., "Union internationale," *Le Socialiste*, 19 October 1890.

17. "20me Anniversaire du 18 mars," *Le Socialiste*, 25 March 1891.

18. "Le Parti Ouvrier en France—Paris," *Le Socialiste*, 11 December 1892.

19. "Mouvement social—France," *Le Socialiste*, 12 September 1885.

20. On one occasion, humiliated Guesdists were forced to call the police to protect their German guests! R. Baker, "A Regional Study of Working-Class Organization in France: Socialism in the Nord, 1870–1924" (Ph.D. thesis, Stanford University, 1967), p. 84 (on the Lille Congress of 1890).

21. "Vive l'Internationale!" *Le Socialiste*, 17 June 1900.

22. For the ambiguous meaning of *pays*, see E. Weber, *Peasants into Frenchmen: The Modernization of Rural France, 1870–1914* (Stanford, Calif.: Stanford University Press, 1976), p. 45.

23. J.M., "Pan-latins, pan-germains et pan-compagnie," *L'Egalité*, 7 May 1882. The most obvious explanation for this hostility relates to the southern regionalists' Proudhonian federalism—a long-standing Marxist bête noire. For their Proudhonianism, see V. Nguyen, "Aperçus sur la conscience d'Oc autour des années 1900," in *Régions et régionalisme en France du XVIIIe siècle à nos jours*, ed. C. Gras and G. Livet (Paris: Presses Universitaires de France, 1977), pp. 241–55.

24. For Marx and Engels's own qualms about such sham cosmopolitanism, see Marx's letter to Engels, 20 June 1866, where Marx scathingly denounces the young (and still non-Marxist) Lafargue, whose "denial of nationalities" implied "their absorption by the model French nation." Karl Marx and Frederick Engels, *Collected Works* (London: Lawrence and Wishart, 1987), 42: 287. For analyses of the ways in which overt cosmopolitanism may well conceal covert metropolitan imperialism, see T. Nairn, "Internationalism and the Second Coming," in *Mapping the Nation*, ed. G. Balakrishnan (London: Verso, 1996), pp. 271–72; and M. Walzer, "The New Tribalism: Notes on a Difficult Problem," in *Theorizing Nationalism*, ed., R. Beiner (Albany: SUNY Press, 1999), p. 205. It has been suggested that Otto Bauer's reconceptualization of the Marxist approach to nationality offered a genuine "multiculturalism" similar to that advanced for liberalism by such contemporary thinkers as Walzer and Charles Taylor. E. Nimni, "Introduction for the English-Language Audience," in O. Bauer, *The Question of Nationalities and Social Democracy* (Minneapolis: University of Minnesota Press, 2000), pp. xv–xlvi. The Guesdists, unfortunately, manifested no such "Bauerian" insights.

25. For such a "regionalist socialism," see M. Keating, "Do the Workers Really Have No County? Peripheral Nationalism and Socialism in the United Kingdom, France, Italy and Spain," in *The Social Origins of National Movements: The Contemporary West European Experience*, ed. J. Coakley (London: Sage, 1992), pp. 62–80. On the dialectic between local and national allegiance, see P. Sahlins, *Boundaries: The Making of France and Spain in the Pyrenees* (Berkeley: University of California Press, 1989), esp. pp. 269–74; and, for the ways in which the *pays* continued to be the real *patrie* for many French well into the Guesdists' period, see Weber, *Peasants into Frenchmen*, chap. 7. The ideological polyvalence of regionalism is discussed in A.-M. Thiesse, "L'Invention du régionalisme à la Belle Epoque," *Le Mouvement Social*, no. 160 (1992): 25; and P. Vigier, "Régions et régionalisme en France au XIXe siècle," in *Régions et régionalisme en France du XVIIIe siècle à nos jours*, ed. C. Gras and G. Livet (Paris: Presses Universitaires de France, 1977), pp. 161–75 (although Vigier concludes that Conservative traditionalism tended to prevail, p. 174). For the POF's largely provincial implantation, see C. Willard, *Le Movement socialiste en France (1893–1905): Les Guesdistes* (Paris: Editions Sociales, 1965), pp. 249–50.

26. For the power of the Right's synthesis of the "petite patrie" of the *pays* with the "grande patrie" of the nation, see H. Lebovics, "Creating the Authentic France: Struggles over French Identity in the First Half of the Twentieth Century," in *Commemorations: The Politics of National Identity*, ed. J. Gillis (Princeton, N.J.: Princeton University Press, 1994), p. 241; and T. Todorov, *On Human Diversity: Nationalism, Racism, and Exoticism in French Thought* (Cambridge, Mass.: Harvard University Press, 1993), p. 231.

27. On the localism of the turn-of-the-century ultranationalists, see G. Putnam, "The Meaning of Barrèsisme," *Western Political Quarterly* 7 (1954): 177–78. As for the Parti Ouvrier, even its many local newspapers reproduced the unrelievedly "national" and global perspective of *L'Egalité* and *Le Socialiste.* There is a quasi-Guesdist critique of the (supposedly illegitimate) conflation of the "imagined community" of the nation with the "experienced community" of the locality in J. Rée, "Internationality," *Radical*

Philosophy, no. 60 (1992): 10–11; and J. Rée, "Cosmopolitanism and the Experience of Nationality," in *Cosmopolitics: Thinking and Feeling Beyond the Nation*, ed. P. Cheah and B. Robbins (London: University of Minnesota Press, 1998), pp. 82–83. See, in turn, the useful "anti-Guesdist" critique of Rée in R. Poole, "On National Identity: A Response to Jonathan Rée," *Radical Philosophy*, no. 62 (1992): 14–19.

28. There is a wise lament for the disjuncture between cosmopolitan socialists and their putative constituency's "lived and worked and placeable social identities" in R. Williams, "The Culture of Nations," in *Towards 2000* (London: Penguin, 1983), pp. 195–97.

29. O. Milza, *Les Français devant l'immigration* (Brussels: Editions Complexe, 1988), pp. 19–20.

30. The localism of the French working class is stressed in B. Moss's important *The Origins of the French Labor Movement, 1830–1914: The Socialism of Skilled Workers* (Berkeley: University of California Press, 1976). For the roots of proletarian regionalism in the capitalist political economy otherwise understood by Guesdists as a homogenizing force, see the study in W. Brustein, "A Regional Mode-of-Production Analysis of Political Behavior: The Cases of Western and Mediterranean France," *Politics and Society* 10 (1981): 355–98. There is a fascinating discussion of the sometimes nearly hermetic boundaries between locals and French migrants to their locality in Weber, *Peasants into Frenchmen*, pp. 281–82.

31. For the dismayed response of the POF to the Broussists' proposal, see "Le Droit du logement," *Le Socialiste*, 26 December 1885, with its bitter attack on Brousse. See H. Ghesquière, "Unité et fédéralisme," *Le Socialiste*, 30 March–6 April 1902 for a powerful critique of localism in general.

32. Paul Grados, "Intérêts de quartier," *Le Socialiste*, 8–15 May 1904. One of the most subtle examinations of such cosmopolitanism has indeed emphasized that "universality . . . arises out of estrangement"—a brilliant, if unwitting, summation of the Marxist understanding of the proletarian "universal class." Z. Bauman, "Strangers: The Social Construction of Universality and Particularity," *Telos*, no. 78 (1988–89): 26.

33. "La Guerre moderne," *Le Socialiste*, 9 February 1896. For critique of such abstract cosmopolitanism, see H. Putnam, "Must We Choose between Patriotism and Universal Reason?" in *For Love of Country: Debating the Limits of Patriotism*, ed. J. Cohen (Boston: Beacon Press, 1996), pp. 91–97; D. Miller, "In What Sense Must Socialism Be Communitarian?" *Social Philosophy and Policy* 6 (1988/9): 51–73, esp. pp. 67–70; E. Laclau, "Universalism, Particularism, and the Question of Identity," in *The Politics of Difference: Ethnic Premises in a World of Power*, ed. E. Wilmsen and P. McAllister (Chicago: University of Chicago Press, 1996), pp. 45–58; and G. Cohen, *History, Labour and Freedom* (Oxford: Clarendon, 1988), pp. 145–46.

34. As argued in C. Weill, introduction to *La Question des nationalités et la social-démocratie*, by O. Bauer (Montreal: Guérin, 1987), 1: 3.

35. T. Eagleton, "Nationalism: Irony and Commitment," in *Nationalism, Colonialism, and Literature*, by T. Eagleton, F. Jameson, and E. Said (Minneapolis: University of Minnesota Press, 1990), p. 27. For the philosophical foundation of such "medi-

ated universalism," see F. Dallmayr, "Polis and Cosmopolis," in *Margins of Political Discourse* (Albany: SUNY Press, 1989), pp. 1–21.

36. One of the dictums of Enlightenment, and Marx's favorite maxim, according to his "Confession." D. McLellan, ed., *Karl Marx: Interviews and Recollections* (London: Macmillan, 1981), p. 167. There is a useful critique of the dictum and its associated "abstract cosmopolitanism" in Kai Nielsen's "Socialism and Nationalism," *Imprints* 2 (1998): 215. For the Enlightenment's incompatibility with nationalism, see J. Schwarzmantel, *The Age of Ideology: Political Ideologies from the American Revolution to Postmodern Times* (New York: Macmillan, 1998), pp. 131–33.

37. M. Cohen, "Rooted Cosmopolitanism: Thoughts on the Left, Nationalism, and Multiculturalism," *Dissent*, Fall 1992, p. 480.

38. Pelczynski, "Nation, Civil Society, State," pp. 262–78.

39. For critique of Guesdist political thought, see R. Stuart, *Marxism at Work: Ideology, Class and French Socialism during the Third Republic* (Cambridge: Cambridge University Press, 1992), chaps. 7 and 8.

40. France, after all, had endowed Marx with his own very occasionally positive paradigm of "the nation" as a polity constructed upon inclusive citizenship rather than exclusive ethnicity—as a nation-state based upon civic participation rather than "Volkish" belonging. M. Forman, *Nationalism and the International Labor Movement: The Idea of the Nation in Socialist and Anarchist Theory* (University Park: Pennsylvania State University Press, 1998), p. 55. For the French Republican tradition of civic nationality embodied in *jus soli* as opposed to ethnic nationality as embodied in *jus sanguinis*, see R. Brubaker, *Citizenship and Nationhood in France and Germany* (Cambridge, Mass.: Harvard University Press, 1992). Brubaker (pp. 98–102) emphasizes, however, that the ultranationalists of the fin de siècle attempted to swing France towards a "Teutonic" conception of a *jus sanguinis*. See also R. Brubaker, "De l'immigré au citoyen: Comment le *jus soli* s'est imposé en France à la fin du XIXe siècle," *Actes de la Recherche en Sciences Sociales*, no. 99 (1993): 3–25, esp. p. 13. For a critique of the aporias inherent in the French tradition of Republican universalism, which could become as effectively exclusionary as any "blood and soil" nationalism, see M. Silverman, *Deconstructing the Nation: Immigration, Racism and Citizenship in Modern France* (London: Routledge, 1992), esp. chap. 1.

41. For a general indictment of the Left along these lines, see M. Viroli, *For Love of Country: An Essay on Patriotism and Nationalism* (Cambridge, Mass.: Clarendon, 1995), p. 15.

42, P. Lafargue, "Patriotes bourgeois," *Le Socialiste*, 14 December 1890. For a discussion of Marx's own intense cosmopolitanism, "the hallmark of his political activity," see A. Gilbert, "Marx on Internationalism and War," *Philosophy and Public Affairs* 7 (1978): 346–69. The cosmopolitan, as opposed to "inter-national," nature of Marx and Engels's ideological identity is further emphasized in M. Löwy, *Fatherland or Mother Earth? Essays on the National Question* (London: Pluto Press, 1998), chap. 1.

43. Geva, "Les Ouvriers étrangers," *Le Socialiste*, 20 November 1886.

44. Republication of a speech given by Guesde in 1892, "Duperie et réaction," in *Le Socialiste*, 31 July 1898.

45. Bernard, "La Cure du patriotisme en Alsace-Lorraine," *Le Socialiste*, 14 January 1891.

46. "Vive la paix!" *Le Socialiste*, 28 January 1888.

47. C.B., "La Peste chauvine," *Le Socialiste*, 26 March 1899.

48. P. Lafargue, "Juifs et socialistes," *Le Cri du Peuple*, 2 October 1886.

49. P. Lafargue, "Patriotisme bourgeois," *Le Socialiste*, 15 October 1887.

50. Paul Lafargue, "Qu'est ce que la patrie?" *Le Socialiste*, 8 October 1887. There is a provocative alignment of eighteenth-century "bourgeois" cosmopolitanism with nineteenth-century "proletarian" cosmopolitanism in M. Ishay, *Internationalism and Its Betrayal* (London: University of Minnesota Press, 1995), p. xxiii.

51. Paul Lafargue, "Socialisme et patriotisme," *Le Socialiste*, 20 August 1887.

52. J. Guesde, preface to *Socialisme et patriotisme*, by J. Vingtras (Lille, 1900), p. 3. For Guesdists operating in this cosmopolitan mode, "internationalism" did not, as the word suggests, imply a community of nations, but rather a community against nations—a usage similar to that deployed by Marx and Engels in much of their work. Löwy, *Fatherland or Mother Earth?* p. 20.

53. G. Crépin, "Leur patriotisme," *Le Socialiste*, 14 August 1886.

54. B., "Les Vêpres d'Aigues-Mortes," *Le Socialiste*, 6 January 1894.

55. Dr. Z. [Pierre Bonnier], "Les Dégénérés," *Le Socialiste*, 26 September 1891.

56. "B." [Charles Bonnier], "Nationalisme politique et nationalisme économique," *Le Socialiste*, 11–18 September 1904 (the original quotation in English). Bonnier enjoyed using his considerable linguistic skills, occasionally with unfortunate results.

57. P. Lafargue, "Qu'est-ce que la patrie?" *Le Socialiste*, 8 October 1887. It is certainly not the case, as alleged by some historians of nationalism and socialism (see, for instance, M. Winock, "Socialisme et patriotisme en France [1891–1894]," *Revue d'Histoire Moderne et Contemporaine* 20 [1973]: 415), that only the more "anarchisant" and anti-Marxist elements of the French Left spurned their nation.

58. P. Lafargue, "Qu'est-ce que la patrie?" *Le Socialiste*, 8 October 1887.

59. Ibid.

60. P. Lafargue, "La Campagne patriotarde—Le Drapeau tricolore et le drapeau rouge," *Le Socialiste*, 24 June 1893.

61. Z., "La Saint Romanof [*sic*]," *Le Socialiste*, 28 July 1895.

62. "Leur fête," *Le Socialiste*, 15 July 1891.

63. "Le Parti Ouvrier en France: XVIIIe Arrondissement," *Le Socialiste*, 14–21 September 1902.

64. P. Lafargue, "Patriotes bourgeois," *Le Socialiste*, 14 December 1890.

65. P. Lafargue, *La Religion du capital* (Paris, 1887), p. 22.

66. P. Lafargue, "Socialisme et patriotisme," *Le Socialiste*, 20 August 1887.

67. P. Lafargue, *Le Patriotisme de la bourgeoisie* (Paris, n.d.), p. 9.

68. *XVIe Congrès National du Parti Ouvrier Français tenu à Montluçon du 17 au 20 Septembre 1898* (Paris: 1898), p. 27.

69. B., "L'Affaire de Kiel," *Le Socialiste*, 16 June 1895.

70. J. Guesde, "L'Ecole de la grève," *L'Egalité*, 12 March 1882.

71. J. Phalippou, "L'Internationalisme de l'or," *Le Socialiste*, 18 February 1900. For the importance of Leroy-Beaulieu, see D. Warshaw, *Paul Leroy-Beaulieu and Established Liberalism in France* (De Kalb: Northern Illinois University Press, 1991).

72. "L'Internationale jaune," *Le Socialiste*, 27 May 1900.

73. "La Semaine," *Le Socialiste*, 31 January 1897. There was an running commentary on *L'Economiste Français* across decades of Guesdist journalism, recapitulating Marx's own sustained engagement with the London *Economist.*

74. Gabriel Deville, "Les Syndicats professionnels," *L'Egalité*, 9 July 1882.

75. There is a analysis of this recurrent Marxist argument in I. Wallerstein, "The Ideological Tensions of Capitalism: Universalism versus Racism and Sexism," in *Race, Nation, Class: Ambiguous Identities*, by E. Balibar and I. Wallerstein (London: Verso, 1991), pp. 29–36, and see esp. p. 31.

76. Marx and Engels, *Manifesto of the Communist Party* [1848], *Collected Works* 6: 487–88. This passage was repeatedly cited by the Guesdists.

77. Report of a speech by Guesde, "Une Triple Manifestation," *Le Socialiste*, 24 June 1893.

78. Edouard Fortin, "Politique et économie," *Le Socialiste*, 27 January–3 February 1901.

79. J. Guesde, "L'Ecole de la grève," *L'Egalité*, 12 March 1882.

80. "La Semaine," *Le Socialiste*, 1 April 1900. For Motte, his anti-Guesdist nationalism, and the Union Sociale, see D. Gordon, "Liberalism and Socialism in the Nord: Eugène Motte and Republican Politics in Roubaix, 1898–1912," *French History* 3 (1989): 312–43.

81. C. Bonnier and P. Bonnier, "La Crise du nationalisme," *Le Devenir Social*, nos. 11–12 (1897): 908. For elaboration of this theme, see Lafargue's groundbreaking *Les Trusts américains: Leur Action économique, sociale, politique* (Paris: 1903).

82. Alexandre Zévaès, "Nationalisme et internationalisme," *Le Socialiste*, 31 January 1897.

83. Henry Nivet, "De Plus fort en plus fort," *Le Socialiste*, 8–15 December 1901.

84. Ed. Fortin, "Concurrence et salariat," *Le Socialiste*, 6 October 1895.

85. Paul Lafargue, "La Production capitaliste," *L'Egalité*, 30 July 1882.

86. Ed. Fortin, "Deux conférences," *Le Socialiste*, 10 November 1887.

87. For the Guesdists' historicization of property forms, see Stuart, *Marxism at Work*, pp. 69–70. For their equivalent historicization of the family, see R. Stuart, "Whores and Angels: Women and the Family in the Discourse of French Marxism, 1882–1905," *European History Quarterly* 27 (1997): 342–44.

88. Bonnier and Bonnier, "La Crise du nationalisme," pp. 912–13.

89. B., "Le Frisson," *Le Socialiste*, 6 January 1895. There are interesting prefigurings in Guesdist discourse of the current debate between "primordialists" and "modernists" over the modernity or otherwise of national identity and nationalist politics—where the Guesdists would have been solidly on the Gellnerite-Hobsbawmian side. For the antinationalist utility of the "countermyth" of nations' modernity, see A. Smith, "Nationalism and the Historians," in *Mapping the Nation*, ed. G. Balakrishnan and B. Anderson, p. 192.

90. The best expressions of this metahistorical understanding of "patriotic" identity may be found in Charles Bonnier's "Parti Ouvrier et patriotisme," *La Jeunesse Socialiste*, no. 9 (1895): esp. 456–60; and J. Vingtras, *Socialisme et patriotisme* (Lille: 1900), esp. pp. 8–15. It nonetheless suffuses less systematic Guesdist texts.

91. P. Lafargue, "Origine de la propriété foncière en Grèce," *Le Devenir Social*, April 1995, pp. 42–47.

92. "La Patrie," *Le Socialiste*, 13 March 1886.

93. Bonnier and Bonnier, "La Crise du nationalisme," p. 899.

94. Report of a speech by Zévaès, "Le Parti Ouvrier en France—Mauriac," *Le Socialiste*, 25 August 1895. This long-running rubric—"Le Parti Ouvrier en France"—in the Guesdists' official newspaper is itself indicative of the POF's cosmopolitanism: not news of "the French Workers' Party," but rather news of "the [universal] Workers' Party *in* France."

95. J. Guesde, *Le Collectivisme: Conférence de Jules Guesde à la Société d'Etudes Sociales et Politiques de Bruxelles sous la présidence de M. Montefiore Levy, Sénateur, le 7 mars 1891* (Lille, 1891), p. 18.

96. B., "Les Polonais," *Le Socialiste*, 23 January 1892.

97. Bonnier and Bonnier, "La Crise du nationalisme," pp. 914–15.

98. Ed. Fortin, "Concurrence et salariat," *Le Socialiste*, 6 October 1895. For discussion of this symbiosis between capitalist cosmopolitanism and its proletarian equivalent as central to Marxism, see I. Deutscher, "On Internationals and Internationalism," in *Marxism in Our Time* (Berkeley, Calif.: Ramparts Press, 1971), pp. 96–99.

99. Vingtras, *Socialisme et patriotisme*, pp. 16–17.

100. E. F., "La Dernière marche funèbre," *Le Socialiste*, 10 April 1886.

101. "La Patrie," *Le Socialiste*, 13 March 1886.

102. Edouard Fortin, "Le Courant d'emigration," *Le Socialiste*, 27 October 1895. "Sans-patrie" was the derogatory nationalist epithet for those such as the Guesdists who repudiated nationalism.

103. Ibid.

104. Bonnier and Bonnier, "La Crise du nationalisme," p. 908.

105. M. Walzer, *Obligations: Essays on Disobedience, War and Citizenship* (Cambridge, Mass.: Harvard University Press, 1970), p. 191, cited in Viroli, *For Love of Country*, p. 15.

106. Ed. Fortin, "Deux conférences," *Le Socialiste*, 10 November 1887 (stress in original). The Guesdists never confronted the logic by which the transcendence of the national state demanded the creation of a cosmopolitan state—cosmopolitan identities needing state embodiment to thrive no less than do nations. For this critique of antinationalist thought, see N. Stargardt, "Beyond the Liberal Idea of the Nation," in *Imagining Nations*, ed. G. Cubitt (Manchester: Manchester University Press, 1998), pp. 31–32.

107. A. Delon, *La Revue Philosophique et le socialisme intégral* (Lille, n.d.), p. 730. For Marxism's ideal of "Europeanism," see R. Berki, "Marxism and European Unity," in *European Unity in Context*, ed. P. Stirk (London: Pinter, 1989), pp. 41–64.

108. C. Bonnier, "Election globale," *Le Socialiste*, 27 April–4 May 1902.

109. Paul Lafargue, "Socialisme et patriotisme," *Le Socialiste*, 20 August 1887.

110. For this comparison, see P. Lafargue, "Les Luttes de Classes en Flandre," *L'Egalité*, 22 January and 29 January 1882.

111. For development of this comparison, see Ed. Fortin, "Deux conférences," *Le Socialiste*, 10 November 1887. This argument for internationalism is discussed in J. Talmon, *The Myth of the Nation and the Vision of Revolution: The Origins of Ideological Polarisation in the Twentieth Century* (London: Secker and Warburg, 1981), pp. 24–25. The geographical impossibility of an isolated socialist revolution are forcefully driven home in D. Harvey, *Spaces of Hope* (Edinburgh: Edinburgh University Press, 2000), p. 33.

112. See, for an early instance, J. Guesde, "Tant mieux," *Le Cri du Peuple*, 9 September 1884.

113. B., "Fédération," *Le Socialiste*, 3 June 1891.

114. As beautifully demonstrated in M. Nussbaum, "Patriotism and Cosmopolitanism," in *For Love of Country: Debating the Limits of Patriotism*, ed. J. Cohen (Boston: Beacon Press, 1996), pp. 2–17, with her reply to nationalist critics, pp. 131–44. There is a sustained defense of Marxist cosmopolitanism in W. Breckman and L. Trägårdh, "Nationalism, Individualism, and Capitalism: Reply to Greenfeld," *Critical Review* 10 (1996): 389–407. They criticize what is indeed a thoroughly tendentious presentation of Marx and Marxism in L. Greenfeld, "The Worth of Nations: Some Economic Implications of Nationalism," *Critical Review* 9 (1995): 555–84. For a salutary critique of "post-Marxist" genuflections to nationalist arrogance, see F. Halliday, "Bringing the 'Economic' Back In: The Case of Nationalism," *Economy and Society* 21 (1992): 483–89.

2. "Dupes of Patriotism": Nationalism as Bourgeois Hegemony

1. C. Vogler, *The Nation State: The Neglected Dimension of Class* (Aldershot: Gower, 1985), p. xii. For a particularly powerful account of the nation's continuing vitality, see M. Mann, "Nation-States in Europe and Other Continents: Diversifying, Developing, not Dying," in *Mapping the Nation*, ed. G. Balakrishnan and B. Anderson (London: Verso, 1996), pp. 295–316.

2. C. Calhoun, "Social Theory and the Politics of Identity," in *Social Theory and the Politics of Identity*, ed. C. Calhoun (Oxford: Blackwell, 1994), pp. 26–27.

3. See, for instance, a profoundly discouraged Engels writing to Paul Lafargue, 4 February 1889, during the Boulangist crisis, in *Friedrich Engels, Paul et Laura Lafargue: Correspondance* (Paris: Editions Sociales, 1956), 2: 209. For a rehearsal of nationalism as a forceful (and successful) alternative to French socialism during the Guesdists' period, see J. Howorth, "French Workers and German Workers: The Impossibility of Internationalism, 1900–1914," *European History Quarterly* 15 (1985): 74. More generally, see R. Szporluk, *Communism and Nationalism: Karl Marx versus Friedrich List* (Oxford: Oxford University Press, 1988), pp. 164–65, where Szporluk emphasizes nationalism's success in fusing "theory and practice—something that Marxism has been much less successful in accomplishing, since to this day the proletariat has not become that universal and philosophical class Marx had expected it to become."

4. "Un Nouveau combattant," *Le Socialiste*, 16 July 1899.

5. See, for instance, the pathetic commentary on an abortive rally in "Le Parti Ouvrier en France—Nancy," *Le Socialiste*, 4 December 1898. For the xenophobia of the mining basin, and its consequent impermeability to socialism, see D. Gordon, *Liberalism and Social Reform: Industrial Growth and Progressiste Politics in France, 1880–1914* (Westport, Conn.: Greenwood Press, 1996), chap. 5.

6. "Le Parti Ouvrier en France—Meurthe-et-Moselle," *Le Socialiste*, 29 October 1899.

7. W. Serman, "The Nationalists of Meurthe-et-Moselle, 1888–1912," in *Nationhood and Nationalism in France from Boulangism to the Great War, 1889–1918*, ed. R. Tombs (London: HarperCollins Academic, 1991), p. 121.

8. Although one should not overestimate "Revanche" as an issue in the broader French political culture, according to J.-J. Becker, *1914: Comment les français sont entrés dans la guerre* (Paris: Presses de la Fondation Nationale des Sciences Politiques, 1977), pp. 53–62.

9. "La Proposition Boyer," *Le Socialiste*, 8 January 1887.

10. See, for instance, B., "Les Polonais," *Le Socialiste*, 23 January 1892. For the predominant rightist politics of the Alsatians, see M. Anderson, *Conservative Politics in France* (London: Allen and Unwin, 1974), pp. 110–16.

11. Jules Guesde, "Vive l'Internationale!" *Le Socialiste*, 14 May 1899.

12. Paul Lafargue, "Qu'est-ce que la patrie?" *Le Socialiste*, 8 October 1887.

13. Bernard, "La Revanche," *Le Socialiste*, 27 May 1893.

14. There is an extended polemic to this effect in *La Démocratie socialiste allemande devant l'histoire* (Lille, 1893).

15. See, for instance, "Entendez-vous," *Le Socialiste*, 12 February 1893.

16. Paul Lafargue, "La Campagne patriotarde—L'Alsace-Lorraine," *Le Socialiste*, 3 June 1893. Lafargue may well have derived the thesis from his father-in-law, who had argued the same case. K. Marx, *The Civil War in France* [1871], in *Collected Works*, by Karl Marx and Frederick Engels (London: Lawrence and Wishart, 1986), 22: 347.

17. Paul Lafargue, "L'Alsace-Lorraine," *Le Socialiste*, 11 March 1891.

18. P.L., "La Neutralisation de l'Alsace," *Le Socialiste*, 18 March 1891.

19. Paul Lafargue, "L'Alsace-Lorraine," *Le Socialiste*, 11 March 1891.

20. "La Semaine," *Le Socialiste*, 22 February 1895. A parody of the nationalist imperative to "speak of [Revanche] never, but think of it always."

21. J. G., "Vive l'Internationale!" *Le Socialiste*, 16 October 1892. Significantly, despite Marx and Engels's support for German unification (supposedly necessary for the advance of German capitalism, and therefore for the eventual triumph of German socialism), they refused to endorse Bismarck's annexation of Alsace-Lorraine. B. Jenkins and G. Minnerup, *Citizens and Comrades: Socialism in a World of Nation States* (London: Pluto Press, 1984), p. 17.

22. *Journal Officiel, Chambre des Deputés*, 20 February 1897.

23. "Paix et guerre," *Le Socialiste*, 25 December 1886.

24. C. Bonnier and P. Bonnier, "La Crise du nationalisme," *Le Devenir Social*, nos. 11–12 (1897): 911.

25. G. Crépin, "Leur patriotisme," *Le Socialiste*, 14 August 1886.

26. Bonnier and Bonnier, "La Crise du nationalisme," pp. 911–12. For a recent expression of the same plaintive question, see M. Löwy, "Why Nationalism?" *Socialist Register*, 1993, p. 125.

27. For an enumeration, see M. van der Linden, "The National Integration of European Working Classes (1871–1914): Exploring the Causal Configuration," *International Review of Social History* 33 (1988): 285–311.

28. Both explanations, of course, ignore the possibility that nationalism fulfills a fundamental human need for identity—one that can be appropriated for class purposes, but one that does not derive from the mode of production. See G. Cohen, *History, Labour and Freedom* (Oxford: Clarendon, 1988), p. 144. There is a good critique of attributing a "false consciousness" model to Marx's understanding of proletarian nationalism in J. Cocks, *Passion and Paradox: Intellectuals Confront the National Question* (Princeton, N.J.: Princeton University Press, 2002), pp. 24–25.

29. G. Kitching, "Nationalism: The Instrumental Passion," *Capital and Class* 29 (1985): 99.

30. Paul Lafargue, "Qu'est-ce que la patrie?" *Le Socialiste*, 8 October 1887 (stress in the original). For the Guesdists' dismissal of religion as "false consciousness," see R. Stuart, "Marxism and Anticlericalism: The Parti Ouvrier Français and the War against Religion, 1882–1905," *Journal of Religious History* 22 (1998): 287–303.

31. The concept is, of course, Althusser's. L. Althusser, "Ideology and Ideological State Apparatuses," in *Lenin and Philosophy and Other Essays* (London: New Left Books, 1971), pp. 121–73.

32. As pointed out in E. Hobsbawm, "Reflections on Nationalism," in *Imagination and Precision in the Social Sciences*, ed. T. Nossiter, A. Hanson, and S. Rokkan (London: Faber and Faber, 1972), p. 390. The Guesdists, of course, had the greatest difficulty in incorporating the family into their Marxist categories, which may help to explain their complete inability to understand, counter, or exploit the appeal of the nationalists' familial metaphors. For the Guesdists' inability to theorize the family, see R. Stuart, "Whores and Angels: Women and the Family in the Discourse of French Marxism, 1882–1905," *European History Quarterly* 27 (1997): 339–70.

33. B. Parekh, "Politics of Nationhood," in *Nationalism, Ethnicity and Cultural Identity in Europe*, ed. K. von Benda-Beckmann and M. Verkuyten (Utrecht: European Research Centre on Migration and Ethnic Relations, 1995), p. 123; B. Anderson, *Imagined Communities: Reflections on the Origins and Spread of Nationalism* (London: Verso, 1991), p. 131; and A. Smith, "National Identity and Myths of Ethnic Descent," *Research in Social Movements, Conflict and Change* 7 (1984): 95–130.

34. K. Marx and F. Engels, *The Communist Manifesto* [1848], in *Collected Works* (London: Lawrence and Wishart, 1976), 6: 502.

35. For the "maternalism" of nationalist welfare-state policies, see G. Eley and R. Suny, "Introduction: From the Moment of Social History to the Work of Cultural Representation," in *Becoming National*, ed. G. Eley and R. Suny (New York: Oxford University Press, 1996), p. 26; and G. Eley, "Culture, Nation and Gender," in *Gendered Nations: Nationalisms and Gender Order in the Long Nineteenth Century*, ed. I. Blom, K. Hagemann, and C. Hall (Oxford: Berg, 2000), pp. 32–33. Karen Offen has elaborated this insight for France in her "Depopulation, Nationalism, and Feminism in Fin de Siècle France," *American Historical Review* 89 (1984): 648–77.

36. R. Gibson, "The Intensification of National Consciousness in Modern Europe," in *Nations, Nationalism and Patriotism in the European Past*, ed. C. Bjørn, A. Grant, and K. Stringer (Copenhagen: Academic Press, 1994), p. 185.

37. G. Deville, "L'Etat et le socialisme," *Le Socialiste*, 26 May 1895. For critique of the nation-state equation, see D. Miller, *On Nationality* (Oxford: Clarendon, 1995), p. 18.

38. Paul Lafargue, "Propos socialistes," *Le Socialiste*, 11 March 1891.

39. This equation is illuminated in E. Weber, *Peasants into Frenchmen: The Modernization of Rural France, 1870–1914* (Stanford, Calif.: Stanford University Press,

1976), p. 51—describing traditional peasant hostility towards "France," but a thesis nonetheless applicable to significant elements of the fin de siècle working class, according to D. Tartakowski, "Le Mouvement ouvrier français et l'état de la Commune à la Première Guerre Mondiale," *Cahiers d'Histoire de l'Institut des Recherches Marxistes*, no. 11 (1972): 18.

40. S. Hoffmann, "The Nation: What For? Vicissitudes of French Nationalism, 1871–1973," in *Decline or Renewal? France since the 1930s* (New York: Viking Press, 1974), pp. 404–6.

41. For the fruitfulness of this maneuver in the hands of the Right, see H. Lebovics, "Creating the Authentic France: Struggles over French Identity in the First Half of the Twentieth Century," in *Commemorations: The Politics of National Identity*, ed. J. Gillis (Princeton, N.J.: Princeton University Press, 1994), p. 241; and S. Hazareesingh, *Political Traditions in Modern France* (Oxford: Oxford University Press, 1994), pp. 129–30.

42. J. Breuilly, *Nationalism and the State* (Manchester: Manchester University Press, 1982), p. 382. For the hyphen metaphor, see P. Cheah, "The Cosmopolitical—Today," in *Cosmopolitics: Thinking and Feeling beyond the Nation*, ed. P. Cheah and B. Robbins (London: University of Minnesota Press, 1998), p. 28.

43. There is a discussion of this maneuver as "radical patriotism" in P. Ward, *Red Flag and Union Jack: Englishness, Patriotism and the British Left, 1881–1924* (Woodbridge: Boydell Press, 1998), p. 4.

44. According to Barrès, as cited in Z. Sternhell, *Naissance de l'idéologie fasciste* (Paris: Fayard, 1989), p. 11. The elitist Barrès, however, had no intention whatsoever of abolishing humility and disadvantage.

45. R. Talmy, *Le Syndicalisme chrétien en France, 1871–1930: Difficultés et controverses* (Paris: Bloud et Gay, 1965), pp. 74–79; and S. Elwitt, *The Third Republic Defended: Bourgeois Reform in France, 1880–1914* (Baton Rouge: Louisiana State University Press, 1986), pp. 170–216.

46. Election poster placarded in favor of Jules Lemaître, cited in D. Watson, "The Nationalist Movement in Paris, 1900–1906," in *The Right in France, 1890–1919*, ed. D. Schapiro (London: Chatto and Windus, 1962), p. 63. For the inclusive logic of nationalism, see D. Miller, "The Nation-State: A Modest Defence," in *Political Restructuring in Europe*, ed. C. Brown (London: Routledge, 1994), pp. 142–43; and D. Miller, "In What Sense Must Socialism Be Communitarian?" *Social Philosophy and Policy* 6 (1988/9): 51–73.

47. M. Barrès, *Mes Cahiers* (Paris: 1929–57), cited in Z. Sternhell, "National Socialism and Anti-Semitism: The Case of Maurice Barrès," *Journal of Contemporary History* 8 (1973): 52.

48. Barrès's electoral program of 1898, cited in S. Wilson, *Ideology and Experience: Anti-Semitism in France at the Time of the Dreyfus Affair* (London: Associated University Presses, 1982), p. 637.

49. Their other motivation, of course, was national solidarity during war, an incentive enforced by the working class's importance during sustained mass conflict.

The current implausibility of mass warfare, along with the end of the "Red threat," accounts for our neoliberal elite's willingness to dismantle the welfare state, and with it much of the nation state's popular legitimacy. For the French national socialists and the construction of the modern welfare-state, see R. Soucy, *Fascism in France: The Case of Maurice Barrès* (Berkeley: University of California Press, 1972), pp. 237, 243; and R. Griffiths, "Anticapitalism and the French Anti-Parliamentary Right, 1870–1940," *Journal of Contemporary History* 13 (1978): 733. The general point about the centrality of the welfare state to modern nationalism is made in G. Noiriel, "La Question nationale comme objet de l'histoire sociale," *Genèses*, no. 4 (1991): 92.

50. For this dynamic from the workers' perspective, see G. Friedman, "The State and the Making of the Working Class: France and the United States, 1880–1914," *Theory and Society* 17 (1988): 403–30; M. Weitz, "Varieties of Class-Collaborationist Ideology in the French Labor Movement before World War I" (Ph.D. thesis, City University of New York, 1977); and F. Caron, "Essai d'analyse historique d'une psychologie du travail," *Mouvement Social*, no. 50 (1965): 3–40. For this process from the perspective of the "bourgeois reformers," see Elwitt, *Third Republic Defended*; and J. Stone, *The Search for Social Peace: Reform Legislation in France, 1890–1914* (Albany: SUNY Press, 1985).

51. G. Friedman, "Capitalism, Republicanism, Socialism and the State: France, 1871–1914," *Social Science History* 14 (1990): 151–74. And see the challenge to France's alleged social-welfare backwardness in P. Nord, "The Welfare State in France, 1870–1914," *French Historical Studies* 18 (1994): 821–38, which stresses the ideology of "solidarity" that animated the Republic's nascent welfare state. It is worth stressing, however, that "participation" in social institutions has not automatically generated "integration" into the bourgeois nation-state. For this valuable point, see B. Jenkins, *Nationalism in France: Class and Nation since 1789* (London: Routledge, 1990), p. 111; and J. Julliard, "Les Ouvriers dans la société française: Intégration et autonomie," in *Histoire Sociale, Sensibilités Collectives et Mentalités: Mélanges Robert Mandrou* (Paris: Presses Universitaires de France, 1985), pp. 423–30.

52. Millerand's project is analyzed in L. Derfler, *Alexandre Millerand: The Socialist Years* (The Hague: Mouton, 1977). For Guesdist antireformism, see R. Stuart, *Marxism at Work: Ideology, Class and French Socialism during the Third Republic* (Cambridge: Cambridge University Press, 1992), chap. 8.

53. Henri Pécry, "A Propos d'usuriers," *Le Socialiste*, 5 February 1895. For this dogmatism as characteristic of the Marxist antinational tradition, see E. Benner, *Really Existing Nationalism: A Post-Communist View from Marx and Engels* (Oxford: Clarendon, 1995), pp. 218–19; and G. Balakrishnan, "The National Imagination," *New Left Review*, no. 211 (1995): 57.

54. See, for instance, P. Larlat-Bénaben, "Que peut-on attendre des réformes?" *Bulletin Mensuel de la Fédération Nationale des Elus du POF*, no. 22 (1 September 1901).

55. "République et propriété," *Le Socialiste*, 19 June 1886. For discussion of this thesis and its inadequacies, see R. Miliband, "State Power and Class Interests," in *Class Power and State Power* (London: Verso, 1983), pp. 63–78. With specific reference to

the French Marxists, see T. Judt, *Marxism and the French Left: Studies in Labour and Politics in France, 1830–1981* (Oxford: Clarendon, 1986), p. 47.

56. Speech by the miners' leader Emile Basly, cited in J. Michel, "Syndicalisme minier et politique dans le Nord-Pas-de-Calais: Le Cas Basly (1880–1914)," *Mouvement Social*, no. 87 (1974): 14.

57. J. Guesde, "Efforts perdus," *Le Cri du Peuple*, 14 January 1884.

58. P. Lafargue, "La Journée légale de travail réduite à huit heures," *L'Egalité*, 12 March 1882. For the Guesdists' absolute focus on class conflict, see Stuart, *Marxism at Work*, chap. 3. In this sense, the Guesdists reflected a characteristic aporia in modern political thought: the inability to accept the reality and legitimacy of all three of modernity's dimensions in state, nation, and class. Conservatives like Carl Schmitt have hypostatized the state and thereby delegitimated democratic nationalism and social democratic class identity; nationalists like Mazzini have delegitimated the "rule of law" and class identity in favor of national community; while Marxists like the Guesdists have delegitimated the state and the nation in favor of class. Few, if any, modern political thinkers have managed all three registers of political reality. R. Berki, *State, Class, Nation* (Hull: Hull University Press, 1986), pp. 3–4.

59. Le Conseil National of the Fédération Nationale des Syndicats (the Guesdists' trade union organization), "Appel aux travailleurs de France," *Bulletin Mensuel de la Fédération Nationale des Syndicats et Groupes Corporatifs Ouvriers de France*, no. 3 (25 July 1890).

60. The Guesdist press was replete with commentary on "journaux d'opinion" like *La Libre Parole* or *La Croix*, and Guesdists editors obviously followed weeklies and monthlies like *L'Economiste Français*, but there are virtually no references in the Guesdist canon to *any* of the mass newspapers of the period. For the construction of a genuine "public sphere" extending into even the most remote villages through journals like the *Petit Parisien*, see Weber, *Peasants into Frenchmen*, pp. 468–69.

61. R. Miliband, *Divided Societies: Class Struggle in Contemporary Capitalism* (Oxford: Clarendon, 1989), pp. 146–47.

62. For the centrality of "national" educational systems in creating modern nationalism, see E. Gellner, *Nations and Nationalism* (Oxford: Blackwell, 1983), pp. 50–61, 134–43. On the instance of France, see S. Elwitt, *The Making of the Third Republic: Class and Politics in France, 1868–1884* (Baton Rouge: Louisiana State University Press, 1975), chap. 5; Weber, *Peasants into Frenchmen*, pp. 332–36; and particularly S. Citron, *Le Mythe national: L'Histoire de France en question* (Paris: Editions Ouvrières, 1987).

63. Z. Bauman, "Soil, Blood and Identity," *Sociological Review* 47 (1992): 682.

64. Cited in J.-P. Azéma and M. Winock, *La IIIe République (1870–1940)* (Paris: Hachette, 1976), p. 149.

65. E. Weber, *The Nationalist Revival in France, 1905–1914* (Berkeley: University of California Press, 1959).

66. Account of a speech by Constans, "Le Socialisme à la chambre," *Le Socialiste*, 31 January–7 February 1904.

67. Paul Lafargue, "Nationalisme et socialisme," *Le Socialiste*, 27 May 1900.

68. G. Eley, "Defining Social Imperialism: Use and Abuse of an Idea," *Social History* 1 (1976): 265–84. The concept has been nuanced, reinforced with the concept of "national economics," and translated from Germany to France in H. Lebovics, *The Alliance of Iron and Wheat in the Third Republic, 1860–1914: The Origin of the New Conservatism* (Baton Rouge: Louisiana State University Press, 1988).

69. G. Haupt, "Les Marxistes face à la question nationale: L'Histoire du problème," in *Les Marxistes et la question nationale, 1848–1914*, by G. Haupt, M. Löwy, and C. Weill (Paris: François Maspero, 1974), pp. 18–19; and R. Munck, *The Difficult Dialogue: Marxism and Nationalism* (London: Zed Press, 1986), pp. 15–21. For the counterrevolutionary dimension of this dynamic, see J. Talmon, *The Unique and the Universal: Some Historical Reflections* (London: Secker and Warburg, 1965), pp. 39–40.

70. R. Brubaker, "De l'immigré au citoyen: Comment le *jus soli* s'est imposé en France à la fin du XIXe siècle," *Actes de la Recherche en Sciences Sociales*, no. 99 (1993): 16. The French Marxists, however, never confronted anything equivalent to the disaster inflicted on the British Left by Tory imperialists during the Boer War. See the discussion of the resultant Anglo-Marxist ideological contortions in M. Taylor, "Patriotism, History and the Left in Twentieth-Century Britain," *Historical Journal* 33 (1990): 975–76.

71. J. Guesde and P. Lafargue, *Programme du Parti Ouvrier: Son Histoire, ses considérants, ses articles* (Paris: n.d.), p. 93.

72. G. Crépin, "Leur patriotisme," *Le Socialiste*, 14 August 1886.

73. See the analyses of this transformation in T. Ziolkowski, "Le Nationalisme en France, 1890–1914," *Cahiers d'Histoire et de Politique International*, no. 7 (1987): 87–88; and W. Irvine, "Royalists and the Politics of Nationalism," in *Nationhood and Nationalism in France from Boulangism to the Great War, 1889–1918*, ed. R. Tombs (London: HarperCollins Academic, 1991), p. 117. Eric Cahm argues convincingly that a warmongering conservative nationalism existed throughout the nineteenth century. E. Cahm, *Péguy et le Nationalisme Français: De l'Affaire Dreyfus à la Grande Guerre* (Paris: Cahiers de l'Amitié Charles Péguy, 1972), pp. 13–14.

74. "A l'œuvre!" *Le Socialiste*, 22 January 1887.

75. A. Gouldner, *The Two Marxisms: Contradictions and Anomalies in the Development of Theory* (New York: Macmillan, 1980), chap. 13.

76. See, for instance, S. Amin, *Imperialism and Unequal Development* (London: Monthly Review Press, 1977).

77. "Patriotisme," *Le Socialiste*, 24 July 1886—a reference to the conquest of Tonkin.

78. B., "La Politique coloniale," *Le Socialiste*, 26 May 1895.

79. Ibid.

80. "Mouvement social—France," *L'Egalité*, 6 August 1882—in support of Arabi's "national bourgeois" endeavor to liberate Egypt from British and French financial imperialism. Such support for "national liberation" movements has always compromised Marxist cosmopolitanism, according to M. Löwy, *Fatherland or Mother Earth? Essays on the National Question* (London: Pluto Press, 1998), pp. 58–60.

81. "Autre méthode," *Le Socialiste*, 10 June 1893.

82. V. Kiernan, *Marxism and Imperialism* (London: Edward Arnold, 1974), p. 7. See also J. Blaut, *The National Question: Decolonising the Theory of Nationalism* (London: Zed, 1987), esp. p. 190.

83. P. Lafargue, in *Idéalisme et matérialisme dans la conception de l'histoire: Conférence de Jean Jaurès et réponse de Paul Lafargue*, by J. Jaurès and P. Lafargue (Paris: 1895), p. 33.

84. Paul Lafargue, "Une Enquête sur Fourmies," *Le Socialiste*, 17 June 1891.

85. Lafargue, in Jaurès and Lafargue, *Idéalisme et matérialisme dans la conception de l'histoire*, p. 34. The Guesdists repeatedly argued that war was good for business. See, for instance, the discussion of war loans, military contracts, and postwar reconstructions in G. Crépin, "Leur patriotisme," *Le Socialiste*, 14 August 1886.

86. Manifesto of 17 June 1893, in *Onze ans d'histoire socialiste: Aux travailleurs de France, Le Conseil national du Parti ouvrier français* (Paris: 1901), p. 47.

87. C. B., "La Peste chauvin," *Le Socialiste*, 26 March 1899.

88. Ibid.

89. "Vive la paix!" *Le Socialiste*, 28 January 1888.

90. "A l'œuvre!" *Le Socialiste*, 22 January 1887.

91. J. Guesde, "Tant mieux," *Le Cri du Peuple*, 9 September 1884.

92. Jules Guesde, "Le Congrès de Bruxelles et le militarisme," *Le Socialiste*, 2 September 1891.

93. "Variété: Les Chemins de fer chinois et le prolétariat européen," *Le Socialiste*, 15 January 1887.

94. There is a useful dissection of this equation in K. Walz, *Man, the State and War* (New York: Columbia University Press, 1959), p. 127. The Guesdists' theses on war were far more complex and elaborate than is admitted by Claude Willard in *Le Mouvement Socialiste en France (1893–1905): Les Guesdistes* (Paris: Editions Sociales, 1965), p. 208.

95. "La Guerre moderne," *Le Socialiste*, 9 February 1896.

96. This complex argument is most fully developed in Bonnier and Bonnier, "La Crise du nationalisme," pp. 915–19.

97. Thereby demonstrating that warlike capitalism was not only moribund, but in terminal decline. Untitled (column 3, p. 1), *Le Socialiste*, 24 April 1886.

98. Lafargue, in Jaurès and Lafargue, *Idéalisme et matérialisme dans la conception de l'histoire*, p. 34. See P. Nord, "Social Defence and Conservative Regeneration," in

Nationhood and Nationalism in France from Boulangism to the Great War, 1889–1919, ed. R. Tombs (London: HarperCollins Academic, 1991), pp. 213–14 for the genuine nexus between defense spending and bourgeois belligerence in France.

99. Paul Lafargue, "La Finance," *Le Socialiste*, 10 November 1887.

100. For this argument, see, for instance, Charles Verecque, "Les Expéditions coloniales ou commerciales," *Le Socialiste*, 16 September 1900.

101. Paul Lafargue, "Propos socialistes," *Le Socialiste*, 4 March 1891. For the tension in Marxism between this thesis and the alternate conviction that the capitalist world market transcends all parochial conflicts, see R. Berki, "Marxism and European Unity," in *European Unity in Context*, ed. P. Stirk (London: Pinter, 1989), p. 41.

102. Paul Lafargue, "Au Comité des Associations Populaires Milanaises," *Le Socialiste*, 15 April 1891.

103. For the difficulties encountered by Marx and Marxism when confronted by international conflicts, see J. McMurtry, *The Structure of Marx's World View* (Princeton, N.J.: Princeton University Press, 1978), pp. 87–88; and I. Wallerstein, "Class Formation in the Capitalist World-System," in *The Capitalist World-Economy* (Cambridge: Cambridge University Press, 1979), pp. 222–30.

104. Marx's own tendency to subordinate "real" wars to class war reflected the general international tranquility of the nineteenth century, according to A. Linklater, *Beyond Realism and Marxism: Critical Theory and International Relations* (London: Macmillan, 1990), p. 52.

105. A. Mayer, "Internal Causes and Purposes of War in Europe, 1870–1956," *Journal of Modern History* 41 (1969): 291–303. For Marx and Engels as theorists of international relations, see W. Gallie, *Philosophers of Peace and War: Kant, Clausewitz, Marx, Engels, and Tolstoy* (Cambridge: Cambridge University Press, 1975), chap. 4, with pp. 71–72 suggesting that Marxism was the precursor of today's "new diplomatic history."

106. For a sustained critique of such Marxist blindness, see A. Giddens, *The Nation-State and Violence: Volume Two of a Contemporary Critique of Historical Materialism* (Cambridge: Polity, 1985), esp. pp. 232–35.

107. For the role of the military in constructing barriers against socialism—both as a counterrevolutionary force and as an antisocialist "school of nationalism," see V. Kiernan, "Conscription and Society in Europe before the War of 1914–1918," in *History, Classes and Nation-States: Selected Writings of V. G. Kiernan* (Cambridge: Polity, 1988), pp. 166–85.

108. Paul Lafargue, "Socialisme et patriotisme," *Le Socialiste*, 20 August 1887.

109. Paul Lafargue, "La Campagne patriotarde—Les Sans patrie," *Le Socialiste*, 17 June 1893.

110. Charles Verecque, "Militarisme et socialisme," *Le Socialiste*, 1 October 1899.

111. Louis Dubreuilh, "Le Conscrit," *Le Socialiste*, 29 March–5 April 1903.

112. "Olivier Pain," *Le Socialiste*, 5 September 1885.

113. Ibid.

114. R. Soucy, "Barrès and Fascism," *French Historical Studies* 5 (1967): 88.

115. For French nationalist advocacy of the army as model for the broader social order, and as antidote to socialist egalitarianism, see P. Levillain, "Les Droites en République," in *Les Droites Françaises: De la Révolution à nos Jours*, ed. J.-F. Sirinelli (Paris: Gallimard, 1992), pp. 341–42; J.-P. Rioux, *Nationalisme et conservatisme: La Ligue de la Patrie Française* (Paris: Editions Beauchesne, 1977), p. 45; S. Berstein, "La Ligue," in *Histoire des droites en France*, vol. 2, *Cultures*, ed. J.-F. Sirinelli (Paris: Gallimard, 1992), p. 71; and R. Girardet, *Le Nationalisme français, 1871–1914* (Paris: A. Colins, 1966), p. 23.

116. Jules Guesde, "Pas d'illusion," *Le Socialiste*, 30 July 1887.

117. For the LdP's anti-Marxist militarism, see R. Soucy, *French Fascism: The First Wave, 1924–1933* (New Haven, Conn.: Yale University Press, 1986), p. 4.

118. "La Semaine," *Le Socialiste*, 7 January 1899.

119. J. Düffler, "Bonapartism, Fascism and National Socialism," *Journal of Contemporary History* 11 (1976): 109–28; and F. Adler, "Thalheimer, Bonapartism, and Fascism," *Telos*, no. 40 (1979): 424–39.

120 Charles Verecque, "Militarisme et socialisme," *Le Socialiste*, 1 October 1899.

121. Weber, *Peasants into Frenchmen*, chap. 17.

122. An occasion lovingly recalled in Bonnier and Bonnier, "La Crise du nationalisme," p. 910.

123. "Inauguration," *Le Socialiste*, 29 November 1896. There are no further references to this movement in the party press, which suggests that it was abortive.

124. Even the above-mentioned "Groupes des Anciens Militaires, Adhérents au Parti" stressed its members' suffering as conscripts and as victims of bourgeois militarism, rather than the glory of their service.

125. "Bulletin municipal—Lille," *Le Socialiste*, 27 December 1896. For the Guesdists' municipal support for reservists' families, see C. Verecque, "Le Pouvoir Communal," *Bulletin Mensuel de la Fédération Nationale des Elus du Parti Ouvrier Français*, no. 3 (1 February 1900): 1–2.

126. It is widely assumed in the literature on "nationalism and the working class" that the mere attainment of citizenship "nationalizes" the proletariat—a highly dubious assumption, given the abstractness of "citizenship" as experience. The "nationalization of the masses" depended upon filling the empty signifier of citizenship with the experiential realities of health, education, and welfare, and with at least the illusion of a state that cared for workers as it cared for its elites. For the citizenship-nationalization equation, see, for instance, E. Hobsbawm, "Working-Class Internationalism," in *Internationalism in the Labour Movement, 1830–1940*, ed. F. van Holthoon and M. van der Linden (Leiden: Brill, 1988), 1: 11.

127. R. Munck, "Marxism and the Nation," in *Marx@2000: Late Marxist Perspectives* (London: Macmillan, 2000), pp. 118–37 (with a Foucaldian genuflection on p. 137) is a particularly cringing instance of post-Marxist surrender to Nietzschean identity politics.

3. "National Economics": Protection, Migrant Labor, and French Marxism

1. M. Löwy, "Why Nationalism?" *Socialist Register*, 1993, pp. 125–26. For the "naturalness" of nationalism, see G. Eley and R. Suny, "Introduction: From the Moment of Social History to the Work of Cultural Representation," in *Becoming National*, ed. G. Eley and R. Suny (New York: Oxford University Press, 1996), p. 11; A. Giddens, *A Contemporary Critique of Historical Materialism: Power, Property and the State* (London: Macmillan, 1981), esp. chap. 8; and I. Wallerstein, "The Construction of Peoplehood: Racism, Nationalism, Ethnicity," *Sociological Forum* 2 (1987): 387.

2. For this argument, see E. Hobsbawm, "Ethnicity and Nationalism in Europe Today," in *Mapping the Nation*, ed. G. Balakrishnan and B. Anderson (London: Verso, 1996), pp. 264–65; I. Wallerstein, postscript to *Race, Nation, Class: Ambiguous Identities*, by E. Balibar and I. Wallerstein (London: Verso, 1991), pp. 230–31; and P. James, "Marx and the Abstract Nation," *Arena*, no. 1 (1993): 177.

3. For the contrast between national labor and cosmopolitan capital, see C. Vogler, *The Nation State: The Neglected Dimension of Class* (Aldershot: Gower, 1985), pp. 24–36; and B. Jenkins and G. Minnerup, *Citizens and Comrades: Socialism in a World of Nation States* (London: Pluto Press, 1984), pp. 22–23.

4. There is a summation of this issue in P. Anderson, "Internationalism: Metamorphoses of a Meaning," Sanford S. Elberg Lecture in International Studies, University of California, April 2001, available at http://globetrotter.berkele.edu/Elberg/Anderson. On Marx and Engels's views, see J. Schwarzmantel, *Socialism and the Idea of the Nation* (New York: Harvester, 1991), pp. 60–61; and, on the relevant Marxist theory more generally, P. Lekas, "The Supra-Class Rhetoric of Nationalism: An Introductory Comment," *East European Quarterly* 30 (1996): 271–72. Shlomo Avineri makes a convincing case that Marx had two theories of nationalism, that of the *Manifesto*, which relegated it to premodern obsolescence, and that of his texts during the later nationalist mid-century, which identified it as a necessary superstructural feature of capitalism. S. Avineri, "Toward a Socialist Theory of Nationalism," *Dissent*, Fall 1990, pp. 447–48. See also A. Colás, "Putting Cosmopolitanism into Practice: The Case of Socialist Internationalism," *Millennium: Journal of International Studies* 23 (1994): 518–19.

5. For the conflict between Marxist class war and "national economics," see R. Szporluk, *Communism and Nationalism: Karl Marx versus Friedrich List* (New York: Oxford University Press, 1988), which is a far broader analysis than its title indicates. There is a discussion of "national economics" as an antisocialist strategy, pp. 193–204.

6. A point made by Adam Przeworski in his "Material Interest, Class Compromise, and the Transition to Socialism," *Politics and Society* 10 (1980): 133–37. For the issue in the French context of the fin de siècle, see M. Perrot, *Les Ouvriers en grève: France, 1871–1890* (Paris: Mouton, 1974), 2: 443. For the Guesdists' period in general, see M. van der Linden, "The National Integration of European Working Classes (1871–1914): Exploring the Causal Configuration," *International Review of Social History* 33 (1988): 285–311.

7. "A real and theoretical object with an admissible transhistorical irreducibility," in Nicos Poulantzas's characteristically lucid and concise formulation. N. Poulantzas, *State, Power, Socialism* (London: New Left Books, 1978), p. 109. For discussion of such concessions to nationalism, see M. Löwy, "Fatherland or Mother Earth? Nationalism and Internationalism from a Socialist Perspective," *Socialist Register*, 1989, pp. 217–18; and Vogler, *Nation State*, p. x.

8. J. Ehrenreich, "Socialism, Nationalism and Capitalist Development," *Review of Radical Political Economics* 15 (1983): 8. See also I. Wallerstein, "Class Formation in the Capitalist World-System," in *The Capitalist World-Economy* (Cambridge: Cambridge University Press, 1979), pp. 224–30.

9. A. Kahan, "Nineteenth-Century European Experiences with Policies of Economic Nationalism," in *Economic Nationalism in Old and New States*, ed. H. Johnson (Chicago: University of Chicago Press, 1967), pp. 17–29; and T. van Tijn, "Nationalism and the Socialist Workers' Movement," in *Internationalism in the Labour Movement, 1830–1940*, ed. F. van Holthoon and M. van der Linden (Leiden: Brill, 1988), 2: 613.

10. Marx's later works prefigured this transition between unmediated cosmopolitanism and an equivocal internationalism, according to Szporluk, *Communism and Nationalism*, pp. 176–77. Shlomo Avineri comments on the ironic similarity of classical liberal and classical Marxist cosmopolitanism. S. Avineri, "Toward a Socialist Theory of Nationalism," *Dissent*, Fall 1990, p. 456. See also E. Hobsbawm, "Working-Class Internationalism," in *Internationalism in the Labour Movement, 1830–1940*, ed. F. van Holthoon and M. van der Linden (Leiden: Brill, 1988), 1: 5–6.

11. On "Listian" national economics and its associated social and political program, see Szporluk, *Communism and Nationalism*. For the Central European emergence of this program, see H. Lebovics, "'Agrarians' versus 'Industrialisers': Social Conservative Resistance to Industrialism and Capitalism in Late Nineteenth Century Germany," *International Review of Social History* 12 (1967): 31–65—an argument that has been expanded by Lebovics's work on equivalent but weaker trends in France during the same period. H. Lebovics, *The Alliance of Iron and Wheat in the Third French Republic, 1860–1914: Origins of the New Conservatism* (Baton Rouge: Louisiana State University Press, 1988). Lebovics's argument is prefigured in M. Smith, *Tariff Reform in France, 1860–1900: The Politics of Economic Interest* (Ithaca, N.Y.: Cornell University Press, 1980), pp. 239–43.

12. For the centrality of "national economics" to nineteenth-century nationalism, see J. Talmon, "The National Brotherhood and the International Confraternity:

Nationalism and Socialism," in *The Unique and the Universal: Some Historical Reflections* (London: Secker and Warburg, 1965), p. 45.

13. The Chamber of Commerce of Lorient, cited in S. Elwitt, *The Making of the Third Republic: Class and Politics in France, 1868–1884* (Baton Rouge: Louisiana State University Press, 1975), p. 246.

14. J. Laffey, "Racism and Imperialism: French Views of the 'Yellow Peril,' 1894–1914," *Third Republic*, no. 1 (1976): 8.

15. H. Lebovics, "Protection against Labour Troubles: The Campaign of the Association de l'Industrie Française for Economic Stability and Social Peace during the Great Depression, 1880–1896," *International Review of Social History* 31 (1986): 147. But for the residual strength of free trade among the more confident French industrialists, see D. Gordon, *Liberalism and Social Reform: Industrial Growth and Progressiste Politics in France, 1880–1914* (Westport, Conn.: Greenwood Press, 1996), pp. 4–5.

16. Statutes of the Ligue Antisémitique, cited in Z. Sternhell, *La Droite révolutionnaire, 1885–1914: Les Origines françaises du fascisme* (Paris: Seuil, 1978), p. 221.

17. For the Christian Democrats, see M. Montuclard, *Conscience religieuse et démocratie: La Deuxième Démocratie Chrétienne en France, 1891–1902* (Paris: Seuil, 1968), chap. 3. For the liberals and Radicals, see Lebovics, *Alliance of Iron and Wheat*, chap. 2.

18. *Le Travail National*, 10 February 1895, cited in H. Lebovics, "La Grande Dépression: Aux Origines d'un nouveau conservatisme français, 1880–1896," *Francia* 13 (1985): 443. But for the difficulties of this attempt at social protectionism, see K. Passmore, "The French Third Republic: Stalemate Society or Cradle of Fascism?" *French History* 7 (1993): 422–25.

19. For a summation, see R. Schor, "Racisme et xénophobie dans le mouvement ouvrier français avant 1939," *Nouvelle Revue Socialiste*, January–February 1984, p. 85. The similar international trend is described in C. Weill, "Le Débat sur les migrations ouvrières dans la IIe Internationale," *Pluriel-Débat*, no. 13 (1978): 55–73.

20. M. Perrot, "Comment les ouvriers parisiens voyaient la crise d'après l'enquête parlementaire de 1884," in *Conjoncture économique/structures sociales: Hommage à Ernest Labrousse* (Paris: Mouton, 1974), pp. 194–95.

21. On this protectionist and antiprotectionist dynamic of class collaboration, see R. Girault, "Place et rôle des échanges extérieures," in *Histoire économique et sociale de la France*, vol. 4, *L'Ere industrielle et la société d'aujourd'hui (siècle 1880–1980)*, book 1, *Ambiguïtés des débuts et croissance effective (années 1880–1914)* (Paris: Presses Universitaires de France, 1979), p. 219. For the Guesdists' violent hatred of these dynamics, see L. Greffier, *Petites conférences éducatives sur le socialisme* (Grenoble: 1904), esp. p. 16.

22. Paul Lafargue, "Le Lendemain de la révolution," *Le Socialiste*, 31 December 1887.

23. B., "Patriotisme et emprunt," *Le Socialiste*, 10 October 1891.

24. For Marx's views, see I. Cummins, *Marx, Engels, and National Movements* (London: Croom Helm, 1980), p. 178.

25. "Une Découverte économique," *Le Socialiste*, 26 February 1887.

26. "Appel au prolétariat anglais," *Le Socialiste*, 22 January 1899.

27. As brilliantly expressed in K. Marx and F. Engels, *Manifesto of the Communist Party* [1848], in *Collected Works* (London: Lawrence and Wishart, 1976), 6: 486–89—a position discussed in E. Gellner, "Nationalism and Marxism," in *Encounters with Nationalism* (Oxford: Blackwell, 1994), pp. 13–14. For an instance of the Guesdists' explicit agreement with Marx's support for capitalist globalization, see Paul Lafargue, "La Production capitaliste," *L'Egalité*, 30 July 1882.

28. "Protection et libre échange," *Le Socialiste*, 10 July 1886. The Guesdists systematically ignored the possibility that proletarians in the more developed capitalist world might prosper despite, or even *because* of, misery inflicted by global capitalism in its newer and more primitive domains—a typical blindness that, Ernest Gellner has argued, accounts for Marxism's systematic underestimation of national divisions within a putatively international proletariat. E. Gellner, *Thought and Change* (London: Weidenfeld and Nicolson, 1965), p. 172.

29. "Impôt sur le pain," *Le Socialiste*, 31 December 1887.

30. For a discussion of the Guesdists' peasant constituency, see G. Landauer, "The Guesdists and the Small Farmer: Early Erosion of French Marxism," *International Review of Social History* 6 (1961): 211–34.

31. Paul Lafargue, "Notes économiques," *L'Egalité*, 19 February 1882.

32. C. Bonnier, "Parti Ouvrier et patriotisme," *La Jeunesse Socialiste*, no. 9 (1895): 456.

33. Paul Lafargue, "La Finance," *Le Socialiste*, 10 November 1887.

34. For these dreams, see P. Nord, "Social Defense and Conservative Regeneration," in *Nationhood and Nationalism in France, from Boulangism to the Great War, 1889–1919*, ed. R. Tombs (London: HarperCollins Academic, 1991), p. 214.

35. O.D., "L'Invasion chinoise," *Le Socialiste*, 30 April 1893.

36. "La Concurrence des Indes," *Le Socialiste*, 11 September 1886.

37. E. F., "La Dernière marche funèbre," *Le Socialiste*, 10 April 1886. Nonetheless, Fortin concluded that international solidarity alone offered long-term abatement of labor's torments.

38. The polemical metaphor of "invasion" was a commonplace of the time, according to Y. Lequin, "L'Invasion pacifique," in *Histoire des Etrangers et de l'Immigration en France*, ed. Y. Lequin (Paris: Larousse, 1992), p. 325. Guesde himself used the image. J. Guesde, "L'Invasion!" *Le Cri du Peuple*, 18 February 1886. For the ugly nationalist implications of such rhetoric, see the insightful musing in I. Ousby, *The Road to Verdun: World War I's Most Momentous Battle and the Folly of Nationalism* (New York: Jonathan Cape, 2002), p. 184.

39. P. Sorlin, *La Société française, 1840–1914* (Paris: Arthaud, 1969), p. 167. For the 1880s figure, see M. Perrot, "Les Classes populaires urbaines," in *Histoire économique et sociale de la France,* bk. 4, *L'Ere industrielle et la société d'aujourd'hui (siècle 1880–1980),* vol. 1, *Ambiguïtés des débuts et croissance effective (années 1880–1914)* (Paris: Presses Universitaires de France, 1979), p. 459; and for that of the 1890s, M. Perrot, "La Classe ouvrière au temps de Jaurès," in *Jaurès et la classe ouvrière* (Paris: Editions Ouvrières, 1981), p. 69.

40. P.-A. Taguieff, *Le Couleur et le sang* (Paris: Editions Mille et Une Nuits, 1998), pp. 76–77.

41. M. Barrès, *Scènes et doctrines du nationalisme* (Paris, 1902), 2: 161, cited in *On Human Diversity: Nationalism, Racism, and Exoticism in French Thought,* by T. Todorov (Cambridge, Mass.: Harvard University Press, 1993), p. 247.

42. D. Landes, "Religion and Enterprise: The Case of the French Textile Industry," in *Enterprise and Entrepreneurs in Nineteenth and Twentieth-Century France,* ed. E. Carter, R. Forster, and J. Moody (Baltimore: Johns Hopkins University Press, 1976), p. 48. See also J. Reardon, "Belgian and French Workers in Nineteenth-Century Roubaix," in *Class Conflict and Collective Action,* ed. L. and C. Tilly (London: Sage, 1981), pp. 167–83; and L. Marty, *Chanter pour survivre: Culture ouvrière, travail et techniques dans le textile—Roubaix, 1850–1914* (Lille: Fédération Léo Larange, 1982), pp. 75–80.

43. A. Dantoing, "Une Manifestation de défense ouvrière contre le travail étranger dans les mines du Pas-de-Calais en 1892," *Revue Belge d'Histoire Contemporaine* 5 (1974): 427.

44. J. Singer-Kérel, "Foreign Workers in France, 1891–1936," *Ethnic and Racial Studies* 14 (1991): 279–92. Immigrant labor "was a means of displacing the tensions inherent in a society which was unwilling to fully bear the burden of capitalism." G. Cross, *Immigrant Workers in Industrial France: The Making of a New Laboring Class* (Philadelphia: Temple University Press, 1983), p. 12.

45. Contemporary saying cited in Y. Lequin, *Les Ouvriers de la région lyonnaise: La Formation de la classe ouvrière régionale* (Lyon: Presses Universitaires de France, 1977), p. 153. For France's experience of such divisiveness, see M. Perrot, "Les Rapports entre ouvriers français et ouvriers étrangers (1871–1893)," *Bulletin de la Société d'Histoire Moderne* 58 (1960): 5–9. For ethnic differentiation in labor markets as a disorganizing force generally, see E. Hobsbawm, "What is the Workers' Country?" in *Worlds of Labour: Further Studies in the History of Labour* (London: Weidenfeld and Nicolson, 1984), pp. 55, 64.

46. M. Hanagan, "Organisation du travail et action revendicative: Verriers et métalurgistes de Rive-de-Gier à la fin du XIXe siècle," *Cahiers d'Histoire* 26 (1981): 19–20.

47. N. Green, "Eléments pour une étude du mouvement ouvrier juif à Paris au début du siècle," *Mouvement Social,* no. 110 (1980): 51–73.

48. Lequin, *Les Ouvriers de la région lyonnaise,* p. 519.

49. Evidence in J. Kergoat, "France," in *The Formation of Labour Movements, 1870–1914: An International Perspective*, ed. M. van der Linden and J. Rojahn (Leiden: Brill, 1990), 1: 170 suggests that such conflict increased during the founding years of the POF. And violence against foreign workers was concentrated in areas of Guesdist strength, particularly in the Nord and Pas-de-Calais (D. Gordon, "Liberalism and Socialism in the Nord: Eugène Motte and Republican Politics in Roubaix," *French History* 3 [1989]: 319; and J.-P. Courtheoux, "Naissance d'une conscience de classe dans le prolétariat textile du Nord," *Revue Economique* 8 [1957]: 130–31), in Nantes (Y. Guin, *Le Mouvement ouvrier nantais* [Paris: Maspero, 1976], p. 252), in Languedoc (J. Sagnes, *Le Mouvement ouvrier en Languedoc: Syndicalistes et socialistes de l'Hérault de la fondation des Bourses du Travail à la naissance du Parti Communiste* [Toulouse: Privat, 1980], p. 32), and in the Southeast (Y. Lequin, *Les Ouvriers de la région lyonnaise: Les Intérêts de classe et la république* [Lyon: Presses Universitaires de France, 1977], p. 91; and P. Barral, *Le Département de l'Isère sous la IIIe République: Histoire sociale et politique* [Paris: Fondation Nationale des Sciences Politiques, 1962], pp. 211–12).

50. B., "Rivalités internationales," *Le Socialiste*, 2 September 1893. See the striking instance of antiimmigrant and antisocialist symbiosis investigated in C. Collot, "Le Socialisme en Meuse avant 1914," *Bulletin des Sociétés d'Histoire et d'Archéologie de la Meuse*, no. 5 (1968): 104–5. For Aigues-Mortes, see P. Milza, "Le Racisme anti-italien en France: La 'Tuerie d'Aigues-Mortes' (1893)," *L'Histoire*, no. 10 (1979); and L. D'Angelo, "L'Eccidio d'Aigues-Mortes (1893) e la sue ripercussione in Italia e in Francia," *Critica Storica* 13 (1976): 78–123 (with thanks to Professor Lorenzo Polizzotto for aid in translation).

51. Translated in S. Wilson, *Ideology and Experience: Anti-Semitism in France at the Time of the Dreyfus Affair* (London: Associated University Presses, 1982), p. 295. For discussion, see M. Crapez, *La Gauche réactionnaire: Mythes de la plèbe et de la race* (Paris: Berg International, 1997), pp. 221–24.

52. G. Mosse, "The French Right and the Working Classes: Les Jaunes," *Journal of Contemporary History* 7 (1972): 185–208; and E. Arnold, "The Right Wing and the Working Classes: The Case of the 'Syndicats Jaunes' (1899–1912)," in *The Development of the Radical Right in France: From Boulanger to Le Pen*, ed. E. Arnold (London: Macmillan, 2000), pp. 46–47. For Barrès' xenophobic labor program, see C. Doty, *From Cultural Rebellion to Counterrevolution: The Politics of Maurice Barrès* (Athens: Ohio University Press, 1976), pp. 107–9; Z. Sternhell, *Maurice Barrès et le nationalisme français* (Brussels: Fayard, 1985), p. 159; and R. Soucy, *Fascism in France: The Case of Maurice Barrès* (Berkeley: University of California Press, 1972), pp. 234–35, 240, 251. For the anti-Semites' similar militancy, see S. Wilson, *Ideology and Experience*, pp. 290–97. And, for the Ligue des Patriotes, see P. Rutkoff, *Revanche and Revision: The Ligue des Patriotes and the Origins of the Radical Right in France, 1882–1900* (Athens: Ohio University Press, 1981), p. 37. There is thus absolutely nothing new about Le Pen's anti-immigrant rhetoric, as pointed out in P. Hainsworth, "The Extreme Right in Post-War France: The Emergence and Success of the Front National," in *The Extreme Right in Europe and the USA*, ed. P. Hainsworth (New York: St. Martin's Press, 1992), p. 31.

53. M. Barrès, *Contre les étrangers: Etude pour la protection des ouvriers français* (Paris, 1893), p. 18, cited in Z. Sternhell, "National Socialism and Anti-Semitism: The Case of Maurice Barrès," *Journal of Contemporary History* 8 (1973): 53–54.

54. J. Guesde, "Duperie et réaction," *Le Socialiste*, 31 July 1898.

55. G. Noiriel, "Français et étrangers," in *Les Lieux de mémoire*, vol. 3, *Les France*, book 1, *Conflits et partages*, ed. P. Nora (Paris: Gallimard, 1992), p. 286; and C. Prochasson, "Les Années 1880: Au Temps du Boulangisme," in *Histoire de l'extrême droite en France*, ed. M. Winock (Paris: Seuil, 1993), p. 80.

56. Lequin, *Les Intérêts de classe et la république*, p. 91. On Liévin, see Dantoing, "Une Manifestation de défense ouvrière," pp. 430 and 437. For the Guesdists' dismayed response to the Liévin incidents, see Le Conseil National du Parti Ouvrier Français, "Aux Mineurs du Pas-de-Calais et du Borinage," *Le Socialiste*, 19 September 1892.

57. A. Delon, *La Revue philosophique et le socialisme intégral* (Paris, n.d.), p. 729. Pierre Birnbaum gives the impression that the Guesdists were systematically hostile to foreign workers. P. Birnbaum, *Jewish Destinies: Citizenship, State, and Community in Modern France* (New York: Hill and Wang, 2000), p. 179.

58. "Quarante-quatre farceurs," *Le Socialiste*, 26 December 1885.

59. Speech on the law "sur le séjour des étrangers en France et la protection du travail national," *Journal Officiel: Chambre des Députés*, 3 May 1893. Jourde was never given space in his Party's official press for such nationalist excess.

60. A charge that Guesde favored anti-immigrant regulation is made, without serious evidence, in Crapez, *La Gauche réactionnaire*, p. 221.

61. Untitled (column 3, page 1), *Le Socialiste*, 2 July 1887.

62. For the dependency of working-class ethnic identities upon a late nineteenth-century process of "nationalization" through "la carte et le code," and the novelty and instability of such identities during the Guesdists' period, see G. Noiriel, *Le Creuset français: Histoire de l'immigration XIXe–XXe siècles* (Paris: Seuil, 1988), pp. 73–98.

63. Paul Lafargue, "Les Ouvriers étrangers," *Le Socialiste*, 9 July 1887.

64. See, for instance, Geva, "Les Ouvriers étrangers," *Le Socialiste*, 20 November 1886.

65. J. Guesde, "Misérables et imbéciles," *Le Cri du Peuple*, 21 February 1885. An alternative strategy was to "naturalize" the foreign worker, pointing out that he had often been actually born in France, or at least had lived there for many years—a strategy that implicitly conceded considerable ground to nationalist prejudice. See, for instance, H.G., "Encore les ouvriers étrangers," *Le Socialiste*, 4 February 1888.

66. Geva, "L'Internationalisme," *Le Socialiste*, 19 February 1887.

67. See, for instance, Geva, "Les Ouvriers étrangers," *Le Socialiste*, 20 November 1886.

68. Ibid. An interesting variation on this theme stressed the beneficent effects of labor migration upon the *originating* society, the development of a world market in labor supposedly ensuring that "the more the population of a capitalist country will be varied as a consequence of national differences," the more influential the class war would be in the immigrants' home societies. "Variété: Les Chemins de fer chinois et le prolétariat européen," *Le Socialiste*, 15 January 1887.

69. "Organisation corporative ou de métiers," *L'Egalité*, 21 May 1882.

70. J. Guesde, "Patriotisme patronal," *Le Cri du Peuple*, 21 February 1884.

71. Geva, "Emigration et immigration," *Le Socialiste*, 27 January 1894—written shortly *after* the Aigues-Mortes atrocity!

72. "L'Assassinat politique," *Le Socialiste*, 30 June 1894. For further development of this antichauvinist response to the crisis, see "Le Parti Ouvrier en France—Lyon," *Le Socialiste*, 30 June 1894; and "La Semaine," *Le Socialiste*, 7 July 1894.

73. G. Haupt, "La Classe ouvrière française au temps de Jaurès—annexes," in *Jaurès et la Classe Ouvrière* (Paris: Editions Ouvrières, 1981), pp. 204–5.

74. Noiriel, *Le Creuset français*, chap. 4, on the processes of "réenracinement" among immigrants, including the importance of intermarriage. For the number of naturalizations, Perrot, "Les Classes populaires urbaines," p. 460.

75. Noiriel, *Le Creuset français*, pp. 270–1.

76. Geva, "Les Ouvriers étrangers," *Le Socialiste*, 20 November 1886.

77. Ibid., for an earlier killing. For the POF's embarrassed analysis of Aigues-Mortes itself, see B., "Rivalités internationales," *Le Socialiste*, 2 September 1893.

78. "B.," "Les Vêpres d'Aigues-Mortes," *Le Socialiste*, 6 January 1894. For Marxism's dubious theses on the lumpenproletariat, see H. Draper, "The Concept of the 'Lumpenproletariat' in Marx and Engels," *Economies et Sociétés*, no. 15 (1972): 2285–302; and, for the Guesdists' exploitation of this tradition, R. Stuart, *Marxism at Work: Ideology, Class and French Socialism during the Third Republic* (Cambridge: Cambridge University Press, 1992), pp. 147–54.

79. B., "Rivalités internationales," *Le Socialiste*, 2 September 1893.

80. J. Guesde and P. Lafargue, *Programme du Parti Ouvrier: Son Histoire, ses considérants, ses articles* (Paris, n.d.), pp. 90–91.

81. A well-founded allegation. For official hopes that such conflicts would disrupt working-class organization, see Reardon, "Belgian and French Workers in Nineteenth-Century Roubaix," p. 167.

82. B., "Rivalités internationales," *Le Socialiste*, 2 September 1893.

83. See, for instance, the bitter response to an article in *Le Temps*. B. (Charles Bonnier), "Internationalisme," *Le Socialiste*, 4 September 1892. There are acute discussions of this challenge to Marxism in Giddens, *Contemporary Critique of Historical Materialism*, esp. pp. 242–43; and in F. Parkin, *Marxism and Class Theory: A Bourgeois Critique* (London: Tavistock, 1979), pp. 29–43. For the alternative argument that eth-

nic conflict between workers actually *confirms* the Marxist analysis of capitalism, see J. McMurtry, *The Structure of Marx's World View* (Princeton, N.J.: Princeton University Press, 1978), pp. 87–88; and E. Bonacich, "Class Approaches to Ethnicity and Race," *Insurgent Sociologist* 10 (1980): 18–32.

84. On social security, see, for instance, "Patriotisme bourgeois," *Le Socialiste*, 26 February 1887, and on union membership, Gabriel Deville, "Les Syndicats professionnels," *L'Egalité*, 9 July 1882. On one occasion, French Marxists accused Tourcoing's bourgeois administration of planning a tramway across the border so that Belgian workers could reside in their own country, with its lower cost of living, while working in the French city for consequently lower wages! Report of a speech by Paul Lafargue, "Une Triple manifestation," *Le Socialiste*, 1 July 1893.

85. Jules Guesde, "Les Responsables," *Le Socialiste*, 19 September 1892.

86. J. Guesde, "L'Enseignement secondaire des filles et la morale," *L'Egalité*, 29 January 1882. Note the acceptance of the category "nationals."

87. Jules Guesde, "Les Responsables," *Le Socialiste*, 19 September 1892.

88. Gordon, *Liberalism and Social Reform*, p. 41.

89. For Marx's views, see K. Marx and F. Engels, *On Britain* (Moscow: Foreign Language Publishing House, 1962), p. 357; and, for a discussion of the implications of the Australian and South African experiences, Hobsbawm, "What Is the Workers' Country?" p. 55.

90. Guesde and Lafargue, *Le Programme du Parti Ouvrier*, p. 93.

91. "La Semaine," *Le Socialiste*, 20 May 1893.

92. See, for instance, Geva, "La Réduction de la journée de travail," *Le Socialiste*, 28 January 1888.

93. Paul Lafargue, "Les Ouvriers étrangers," *Le Socialiste*, 9 July 1887.

94. Carrette, Desobry, Lepers, "Le Parti Ouvrier au conseil général du Nord," *Le Socialiste*, 28 August 1892. An astonishing travesty of Marxist value-theory.

95. Geva, "L'Impôt sur les étrangers," *Le Socialiste*, 13 February 1886. Note this contradiction of the Guesdists' usual belief that depressed wages resulted from capitalism, not immigration.

96. For the general problem, see Dr. Z. [Pierre Bonnier], "Difficultés," *Le Socialiste*, 10 January 1897. On accident insurance in particular, see "Les Ouvriers étrangers," *Bulletin Mensuel des Elus Socialistes*, no. 23 (1 October 1901): 6. And, for the law of 1848 banning strikes and unionization among immigrants, see A.Z., "Ultra-protectionnisme," *Le Socialiste*, 6 January 1894.

97. Speech by Jourde on the law "sur le séjour des étrangers en France et la protection du travail national," *Journal Officiel: Chambre des Députés*, 3 May 1893. Again, Jourde was never able to make such points in his Party's official journals.

98. Joseph Sarraute, "Réformes!" *Le Socialiste*, 29 November 1896. See the Guesdists' similar dogmatism vis-à-vis the welfare state, as discussed in chapter 2 above.

99. For an explicit statement of this point—whereby a proposal for a universal minimum wage applied to nationals and foreigners alike was juxtaposed to the absolute impossibility of such a proposal ever being accepted by the ruling class—see "Patriotisme patronal," *Le Socialiste*, 23 January 1886.

100. Geva, "L'Internationalisme," *Le Socialiste*, 19 February 1887.

101. For Guesdist utopianism, see Stuart, *Marxism at Work*, pp. 479–91.

102. The Guesdists seriously argued, against massive evidence, that conflicts such as that at Aigues-Mortes only occurred where the POF had not yet spread its message. B., "Rivalités internationales," *Le Socialiste*, 2 September 1893.

103. Message from the Italian socialist Oddino Morgari to the POF of Marseille, upon being expelled from France, in *Le Socialiste*, 9 September 1900 (columns 3 and 4, page 1).

104. C. Bonnier and P. Bonnier, "La Crise du nationalisme," *Le Devenir Social* nos. 11–12 (1897): 914.

105. J.G. [Guesde], "Le Congrès de Reims," *L'Egalité*, 11 December 1881. Guesdists were obviously uneasily aware of this slippage, so that they sometimes pointed out that property would be appropriated for "the nation today, the international tomorrow" ("Mines et mineurs," *Le Socialiste*, 13 March 1886), although they never specified the modalities of such "inter-nationalization." There is a retrospective defense of the POF's "socialization equals nationalization" program in A. Zévaès, *Les Guesdistes* (Paris: Rivière, 1911), pp. 92–94—a defense no doubt influenced by the Hervétist antinationalism of the publication's period. For critique of such equation, see B. Anderson, introduction to *Mapping the Nation*, ed. G. Balakrishnan and B. Anderson (London: Verso, 1996), p. 7; and M. Freeden, "Is Nationalism a Distinct Ideology?" *Political Studies* 46 (1998): 756–57.

106. D.Z. [Pierre Bonnier], "La Patrie," *Le Socialiste*, 25 August 1895 (stress again in the original).

107. P. Bonnier, "Nationisme" [*sic*], *Le Socialiste*, 3–10 February 1901.

108. Bonnier and Bonnier, "La Crise du nationalisme," p. 913.

109. B., "Nationalisme politique et nationalisme économique," *Le Socialiste*, 11–18 September 1904.

110. For the dangers of socialist appropriation of organicism, see S. Quinlan, "The Racial Imagery of Degeneration and Depopulation: Georges Vacher de Lapouge and 'Anthroposociology' in Fin-de-Siècle France," *History of European Ideas* 24 (1999): 399.

111. B., "La Politique coloniale," *Le Socialiste*, 26 May 1895.

112. J. Dunn, "Unimagined Communities: The Deceptions of Socialist Internationalism," in *Rethinking Modern Political Theory* (Cambridge: Cambridge University Press, 1985), p. 105.

113. "Appel au prolétariat anglais," *Le Socialiste*, 22 January 1899.

114. Paul Lafargue, "La Campagne pariotarde—les sans patrie," *Le Socialiste*, 17 June 1893.

115. Dr. Z. [Pierre Bonnier], "Difficultés," *Le Socialiste*, 10 January 1897.

116. For the nation-state telos inherent in Second International socialism, see the extended critique in S. Yeo, "Socialism, the State, and Some Oppositional Englishness," in *Englishness: Politics and Culture, 1880–1920*, ed. R. Colls and P. Dodd (London: Croom Helm, 1986), pp. 308–69. A. James Gregor has been one of the most categorical of the many "totalitarianists" who have equated socialist nationalism with national socialism, most recently in *The Faces of Janus: Marxism and Fascism in the Twentieth Century* (New Haven, Conn.: Yale University Press, 2000). For critical discussion of this thesis, see J. Schwarzmantel, "Class and Nation: Problems of Socialist Nationalism," *Political Studies* 35 (1987): 239–55.

117. For the relationship between the material realities of capitalist economic geography and the dilemmas of socialist theory and practice, see D. Harvey, *Spaces of Hope* (Edinburgh: Edinburgh University Press, 2000), chap. 3.

118. For gloating capitalist triumphalism based on this reality ("the political base of any party of the Left remains an essentially national one, while the problems of economic inequality that the Left seeks to remedy can today be addressed only at an international level, and require governance mechanisms that are extremely unlikely ever to be created."), see F. Fukuyama, "Second Thoughts," *National Interest*, 1999, accessed at http://www.britannica.com/bcom/magazine/article/0,5744,250415,00.html.

4. "Proletarian Patriotism": The Guesdists and the Nationalist Temptation

1. M. Canovan, *Nationhood and Political Theory* (Cheltenham: Edward Elgar, 1996), pp. 86–92.

2. For a powerful expression of the argument that universalism must always be embodied in the particular, see M. Walzer, *Spheres of Justice: A Defense of Pluralism and Equality* (Oxford: Robertson, 1983), esp. pp. 28–31. It has been pointed out that even today's "social constructionist" and "deconstructionist" critics of nationalist essentialism—the Gellners and Hobsbawms of recent theory—deconstruct nationalism within taken-for-granted national contexts, thereby tacitly affirming what they overtly delegitimize. N. Stargardt, "Beyond the Liberal Idea of the Nation," in *Imagining Nations*, ed. G. Cubitt (Manchester: Manchester University Press, 1998), p. 23.

3. Z. Sternhell, *The Birth of Fascist Ideology: From Cultural Rebellion to Political Revolution* (Princeton, N.J.: Princeton University Press, 1994), pp. 12–27. The "revision" identified by Sternhell consisted of repudiating materialism, political economy, class analysis, and internationalism. One wonders what was left of Marxism, after such "revisionism"!

4. For a comparison of these contradictory positions at their most sophisticated, see the discussion of the Hobsbawm (cosmopolitanism) versus Nairn (socialist national-

ism) debate in R. Beiner, "1989: Nationalism, Internationalism, and the Nairn-Hobsbawm Debate," *Archives Européennes de Sociologie* 40 (1999): 171–84. Ephraim Nimni is wrong when he argues that "nationalism was unanimously defined by classical Marxists as a bourgeois phenomenon alien to Marxism." E. Nimni, "Great Historical Failure: Marxist Theories of Nationalism," *Capital and Class* 9 (1985): 59. He is certainly wrong about the Guesdists, who do not figure in his survey of Second International Marxists.

5. C. Vogler, *The Nation-State: The Neglected Dimension of Class* (Aldershot: Gower, 1985), pp. 27–30.

6. Anthony Smith has repeatedly demonstrated the implausibility of any "lived" cosmopolitan identity. See, in particular, A. Smith, *Nations and Nationalism in a Global Era* (Oxford: Polity, 1995), pp. 23–24.

7. P. James, "The Janus Faces of History: Cleaving Marxist Theories of Nation and Nationalism," *Canadian Review of Studies in Nationalism* 18 (1991): 13–24; and M. Freitag, "Théorie Marxiste et question nationale: Autopsie d'un malentendu," *Pluriel-Débat*, no. 26 (1981): 5–6, 31.

8. M. Guibernau, "Marx and Durkheim on Nationalism," in *Rethinking Nationalism and Ethnicity: The Struggle for Meaning and Order in Europe*, ed. H.-R. Wicker (Oxford: Berg, 1997), p. 79. For Marx and Engels's unthinking usage of the term and concept "nation," see P. James, "Marx and the Abstract Nation," *Arena*, no. 1 (1993): 179; and J. Cocks, *Passion and Paradox: Intellectuals Confront the National Question* (Princeton, N.J.: Princeton University Press, 2002), pp. 40–41.

9. See, for instance, Renaldo Munck's telling elision: "concrete social formations (countries)." R. Munck, *The Difficult Dialogue: Marxism and Nationalism* (London: Zed, 1986), p. 146.

10. M. Forman, *Nationalism and the International Labor Movement: The Idea of the Nation in Socialist and Anarchist Theory* (University Park: Pennsylvania State University Press, 1998), p. 1. Forman's study challenges this facile conclusion.

11. Post-Marxists have so surrendered to the "politics of difference" as to subscribe to virtually any nationalist nonsense. For an instance of this post-Marxist flaccidity, see the chapter on nationhood in R. Munck, *Marx@2000: Late Marxist Perspectives* (London: Macmillan, 2000). (chap. 7) But even Eric Hobsbawm, the insightful Marxist and unequalled historian of the nexus between nationalism and socialism, has sadly concluded that, while nationalism is unlikely to extinguish the fundamental working-class interest embodied in an irreducible trade-unionist solidarity, it must almost always prevail against the more fragile and ephemeral socialist consciousness. E. Hobsbawm, "What Is the Workers' Country?" in *Worlds of Labour: Further Studies in the History of Labour* (London: Weidenfeld and Nicolson, 1984), pp. 49–65.

12. For this understanding of what has come to be known as the "hegemonic articulation" of socialism and nationalism, see T. Purvis, "Marxism and Nationalism," in *Marxism and Social Science*, ed. A. Gamble, D. Marsh, and T. Tant (London: Macmillan, 1999), p. 233. See also Pierre Vilar's typically insightful analysis along these lines in his "On Nations and Nationalism," *Marxist Perspectives* 1 (1979): 8–30; and R. Berki, *State, Class, Nation* (Hull: Hull University Press, 1986), esp. pp. 12–13.

13. M. Löwy, "Fatherland or Mother Earth? Nationalism or Internationalism from a Socialist Perspective," *Socialist Register*, 1989, pp. 213–14. For the polyvalence of nationalism, so "thin-centered" as to be "adaptable to *any* ideology" (p. 749), see M. Freeden, "Is Nationalism a Distinct Ideology?" *Political Studies* 46 (1998): 748–65 (emphasis in original). There is discussion of the resultant valance between nationalism and socialism in P. Lekas, "The Supra-Class Rhetoric of Nationalism," *East European Quarterly* 30 (1996): 275; and K. Verdery, "Whither 'Nation' and 'Nationalism,'" in *Mapping the Nation*, ed. G. Balakrishnan and B. Anderson (London: Verso, 1996), p. 230.

14. A. Finlayson, "Ideology, Discourse, and Nationalism," *Journal of Political Ideology* 3 (1998): 103.

15. For nationalism as an "empty signifier," see B. Jenkins, "Socialism, National Identity and Nationalism: Contribution to the Theoretical Discussion," *Journal of Area Studies* 5 (1982): 14–15. The most impressive study of such articulation of ideology and nationhood is E. Laclau, *Politics and Ideology in Marxist Theory: Capitalism, Fascism, Populism* (London: New Left Books, 1979). For a focused instance of such analysis, see S. Hall, *The Hard Road to Renewal: Thatcherism and the Crisis of the Left* (London: Verso, 1988), with its influential interpretation of Thatcherism as just such a hegemonic project. For the ways in which *all* of France's competing ideologies appropriated nationalism to their cause, see C. Charle, "Sentiment national et nationalisme en France au XIXe siècle," *Bulletin de la Société d'Histoire Moderne et Contemporaine*, nos. 1–2 (1996): 22.

16. S. Hall, "Ethnicity: Identity and Difference," in *Becoming National: A Reader*, ed. G. Eley and R. Suny (Oxford: Oxford University Press, 1996), p. 347 (emphasis in original). That even cosmopolitans must be grounded in the particular in order to be cosmopolitan is argued in B. Robbins, "Actually Existing Cosmopolitanism," in *Cosmopolitics: Thinking and Feeling beyond the Nation*, ed. P. Cheah and B. Robbins (London: University of Minnesota Press, 1998), pp. 1–19.

17. J. Dunn, *Western Political Theory in the Face of the Future* (Cambridge: Cambridge University Press, 1979), p. 56. The suggestion that "nationalism was unanimously defined by classical Marxism as a bourgeois phenomenon alien to Marxism" (E. Nimni, "Marxism and Nationalism," in *Marxist Sociology Revisited: Critical Assessments*, ed. M. Shaw [London: Macmillan, 1985], p. 102) is astonishingly perverse.

18. E. Carr, *Nationalism and After* (London: Macmillan, 1968), p. 19. For discussion of the socialist co-option of nationalism, and the consequent nationalist co-option of socialism, in the French case, see M. Winock, "Socialisme et Patriotisme en France, 1891–1894," *Revue d'Histoire Moderne et Contemporaine* 20 (1973): 411–12.

19. That there is an ambient "*habitus* national" that renders consistent antinationalism or even anationality virtually impossible has been argued by Norbert Elias in his *La Société des individus* (Paris, 1991), as presented in G. Noiriel, "La Question nationale comme objet de l'histoire sociale," *Genèses*, no. 4 (1991): 92. For Jourde's nationalism, P. Hutton, "The Impact of the Boulangist Crisis upon the Guesdist Party at Bordeaux," *French Historical Studies* 7 (1971): 230.

20. For discussion of Marxism's opportunism in appropriating nationalism for its own socialist purposes, see J. Schwarzmantel, *Socialism and the Idea of the Nation* (New York: Harvester, 1991), esp. chap. 8; E. Hobsbawm, "Some Reflections on *The Break-up of Britain,*" *New Left Review*, no. 105 (1977): 9; and E. Benner, *Really Existing Nationalism: A Post-Communist View from Marx and Engels* (Oxford: Clarendon, 1995), esp. chap. 2. For this dimension of Marx and Engels's thought, and its problematic legacy to Marxism, see the discussions in R. Berki, "On Marxian Thought and the Problem of International Relations," *World Politics* 24 (1971): 86; Löwy, "Fatherland or Mother Earth?" p. 222; and J. Blaut, *The National Question: Decolonising the Theory of Nationalism* (London: Zed, 1987), pp. 134–35.

21. Paul Lafargue, "La Campagne patriotarde—La France une et indivisible," *Le Socialiste*, 10 June 1893. For French socialists and their faith in French destiny, see the insightful argument in K. Steven Vincent, "Nationalism and Patriotism in Nineteenth Century French Socialist Thought," *History of European Ideas* 15 (1992): 217–19; and K. Steven Vincent, "National Consciousness, Nationalism and Exclusion: Reflections on the French Case," *Historical Reflections* 19 (1993): 440. On Marx's intimate connections to this tradition, see I. Cummins, *Marx, Engels and National Movements* (London: Croom Helm, 1980), pp. 16–17.

22. Report of a speech by Guesde, "Le Parti Ouvrier en France—Paris," *Le Socialiste*, 9 December 1893. For the theme of France as the embodiment of progress and reason, particularly in its republican and revolutionary moments, see T. Zeldin, *France, 1848–1945: Intellect and Pride* (Oxford: Oxford University Press, 1977), pp. 6–9; and for the resonance of this theme among socialists of the Guesdists' period, see K. Steven Vincent, *Between Marxism and Anarchism: Benoît Malon and French Reformist Socialism* (Berkeley: University of California Press, 1992), pp. 114–15. There is a dated and unsatisfactory study in J. Puech, *La Tradition socialiste en France et la société des nations* (Paris: Garnier, 1921), chap. 1.

23. "Une Interview de Lafargue," *Le Socialiste*, 14 November 1892. For the world-historical significance of this French moment of transnational nationalism, see M. Cohen, "Rooted Cosmopolitanism: Thoughts on the Left, Nationalism, and Multiculturalism," *Dissent*, Fall 1992, p. 480.

24. For the importance of affirmation or negation of the Revolution in distinguishing nationalists of the Right from nationalists of the Left, see E. Cahm, *Péguy et le Nationalisme français: De l'Affaire Dreyfus à la Grande Guerre* (Paris: Cahiers de l'Amitié Charles Péguy, 1972), pp. 10–18; and R. Girardet, *Le Nationalisme français, 1871–1914* (Paris: A. Colin, 1966), pp. 20–21.

25. On Soloviev's devastating critique of the nationalist teleology toward anti-universalism, see Royal Institute of International Affairs, *Nationalism* (London: Cass, 1963), p. 71. Ernst Nolte emphasizes the antitranscendent dimension of fascism and protofascism, with particular reference to Maurras, and makes a sharp contrast with Marxism, in E. Nolte, *Three Faces of Fascism: Action Française, Italian Fascism, National Socialism* (New York: Mentor, 1965), pp. 537–43.

26. J. Guesde, "Une Triple manifestation," *Le Socialiste*, 24 June 1893.

27. Paul Lafargue, "La Campagne patriotarde—La France une et indivisible," *Le Socialiste*, 10 June 1893.

28. "Une Prophétie de M. Bismarck," *Le Socialiste*, 3 April 1886.

29. Paul Lafargue, "Socialisme et patriotisme," *Le Socialiste*, 20 August 1887. Engels was dismayed by this socialist chauvinism. L. Derfler, *Paul Lafargue and the Flowering of French Socialism, 1882–1911* (Cambridge, Mass.: Harvard University Press, 1996), p. 137.

30. Jules Guesde, *Journal Officiel: Chambre des Députés*, 20 February 1897.

31. Report of a speech by Dormoy, "Mouvement social—Montluçon," *Le Socialiste*, 26 November 1887.

32. C. Bonnier, "Parti Ouvrier et patriotisme," *La Jeunesse Socialiste*, no. 9 (1895): 458. There is an analysis of the fin de siècle canonization of Joan, by both Left and Right, in M. Winock, "Jeanne d'Arc," in *Les Lieux de Mémoire*, vol. 3, *Les France*, book 3, *De L'Archive à l'emblème*, ed. P. Nora (Paris: Gallimard, 1992), pp. 674–75. See also G. Krumeich, "Joan of Arc between Right and Left," in *Nationhood and Nationalism in France from Boulangism to the Great War*, ed. R. Tombs (London: HarperCollins Academic, 1991), pp. 63–73.

33. "Le Parti Ouvrier en France—Montpellier," *Le Socialiste*, 7 April 1895. For the tendency of universalism—whether in the hands of French Jacobins, Russian Bolsheviks, or American Wilsonians—to degenerate into nationalist imperialism, see Canovan, *Nationalism and Political Theory*, chap. 8.

34. Paul Lafargue, "La Campagne patriotarde—La France une et indivisible," *Le Socialiste*, 10 June 1893. For an authoritative statement of the Guesdists' readiness for "national" defense," see Guesde's passionate speech to the Chamber of Deputies, *Journal Officiel: Chambre des Deputés*, 20 February 1897.

35. *Onzième congrès national du Parti Ouvrier tenu à Paris du 7 au 9 octobre 1893* (Lille, 1893), p. 20.

36. On this much-studied catastrophe, see the classic studies of M. Drachkovitch, *Les Socialismes français et allemand et le problème de la guerre (1870–1914)* (Geneva: Droz, 1953); and G. Haupt, *Socialism and the Great War: The Collapse of the Second International* (Oxford: Clarendon, 1972). Both make much of the collapse of Marxist cosmopolitanism.

37. An otherwise sympathetic reader of this study suggested that synchronic analysis of the Guesdist mentality fails to explain how Guesde could have signed up with the "bourgeois republic," once it was fighting the German invaders of 1914—a suggestion that supposes a historical trajectory from early Guesdist cosmopolitanism to later nationalism. There was no such trajectory. This book demonstrates how the choice of 1914 could have been made at *any* point in the Parti Ouvrier's history. Just as Guesde rallied to national defense in 1914, so he would have done in 1882, if France had been invaded by Bismarck's armies. He said as much, many times. The Guesde of 1882 was, after all, as much a socialist nationalist as the Guesde of 1914, while both the Guesde of 1882 and the Guesde of 1914 held fast to cosmopolitan convictions.

The ultimate tragedy lay in the contradictions inherent in these passionate convictions, in the Marxist failure to synthesize them within modernity's brutal "world of nations." These contradictions, this failure of synthesis, constitute the real historical problem, the subject of this book.

38. For the actual similarities between the Marxist and anarchist views on nationalism, see J. Maitron, *Le Mouvement anarchiste en France*, vol. 2, *Des Origines à 1914* (Paris: F. Maspero, 1975), pp. 368–70.

39. "Autre méthode," *Le Socialiste*, 10 June 1893. See, for a general attack on anarchist antinationalism, J. Vingtras, *Socialisme et patriotisme* (Lille, 1900), p. 21.

40. Paul Brousse, cited in Derfler, *Paul Lafargue and the Flowering of French Socialism*, p. 25. Even otherwise acute historical studies have seconded this libel, arguing that the POF was a sickly German graft upon the spreading tree of French socialism—its "new imported Marxism" (R. Magraw, "Socialism, Syndicalism and French Labour before 1914," in *Labour and Socialist Movements in Europe before 1914*, ed. D. Geary [Oxford: Berg, 1989], p. 71) having to be "learnt like a foreign language" (M. Perrot, "Controverses sur l'introduction du marxisme en France," *Annales: Economies, Sociétés, Civilisations* 22 [1967]: 707). For striking instances of this perversion of historical understanding by less sensible historians, see L. Laurat, "La Pénétration du Marxisme en France," *La Nef* 7 (1950): 55–63; and the pathetic D. Lindenberg, "Marx et les 'Mystères de Paris,'" in *Marx en perspective*, B. Chavance (Paris: Editions de l'Ecole des Hautes Etudes en Sciences Sociales, 1985), pp. 571–83. Tony Judt is surely correct in arguing that Marxism is no less "French" than any other general system of thought. T. Judt, *Marxism and the French Left: Studies in Labour and Politics in France, 1830–1981* (Oxford: Clarendon, 1986), pp. 17–18. For discussion of this issue in general, see J. Schwarzmantel, "Class and Nation: Problems of Socialist Nationalism," *Political Studies* 35 (1987): 252; and, for the French case, M. Rebérioux, "Le Socialisme français de 1871 à 1914," in *Histoire générale du socialisme*, vol. 2, *De 1875 à 1918*, ed. J. Droz (Paris: Presses Universitaires de France, 1974), p. 148.

41. Pamphlet entitled "Le Collectivisme, voilà l'ennemi!" Archives Nationales F[7] 12.872, cited in S. Wilson, *Ideology and Experience: Anti-Semitism in France at the Time of the Dreyfus Affair* (London: Associated University Presses, 1982), p. 342. For the period's identification of Marxist "collectivism" as "German," see B. Blick, "What Is Socialism? French Liberal Views in the 1890s," in *Crucible of Socialism*, ed. L. Patsouras (Atlantic Highlands, N.J.: Humanities Press International, 1987), pp. 388, 392. Ironically, in Britain, with its long tradition of seeing France as the "national enemy," conservatives indicted socialism as "French." P. Ward, *Red Flag and Union Jack: Englishness, Patriotism and the British Left, 1881–1924* (Woodbridge: Boydell Press, 1998), p. 37.

42. M. Barrès, "Socialisme et nationalisme," *La Patrie*, 27 February 1903, cited in Z. Sternhell, "National Socialism and Anti-Semitism: The Case of Maurice Barrès," *Journal of Contemporary History* 8 (1973): 54. For Barrès's systematic identification of Marxism as Jewish and German, M. Barrès, *L'Ennemi des lois*, pp. 174, 177–78, cited in Z. Sternhell, *Maurice Barrès et le nationalisme français* (Paris: Fayard, 1972), p. 203. There is discussion of this aspect of Barrèsian national socialism in Z. Sternhell, "Bar-

rès et la gauche: Du Boulangisme à *La Cocarde* (1889–1895)," *Mouvement Social*, no. 75 (1971): 121, 123. For Déroulède's conversion experience, see R. Soucy, *French Fascism: The First Wave, 1924–1933* (New Haven, Conn.: Yale University Press, 1986), p. 2; and M. Winock, "Le Nationalisme français," *Histoire*, no. 73 (1984): 14–15; and for his campaign against the red flag, Z. Sternhell, "Paul Déroulède and the Origins of Modern French Nationalism," *Journal of Contemporary History* 6 (1971): 56.

43. C. Maurras, *Enquête sur la monarchie*, cited in W. Buthman, *The Rise of Integral Nationalism in France* (New York: Columbia University Press, 1939), p. 286. For Maurras's anti-Marxist anticosmopolitanism, see Nolte, *Three Faces of Fascism*, p. 92; and for his perception of the POF as a German invasion, J. McClelland, "The Reactionary Right: The French Revolution, Charles Maurras and the Action Français," in *The Nature of the Right*, ed. R. Eatwell and N. O'Sullivan (London: Pinter, 1989), p. 83.

44. G. Rouanet, "Le Matéralisme économique de Marx et le socialisme français," *La Revue Socialiste*, no. 29 (1887): 395, cited in Z. Sternhell, *Neither Right nor Left: Fascist Ideology in France* (Berkeley: University of California Press, 1986), p. 40. There is a stinging refutation of Rouanet's indictment in Gabriel Deville, "Un Critique de Marx," *Le Socialiste*, 11 June 1887. For Malon's seconding of Rouanet, see P. Pierrard, "Antisémitisme de droite et de gauche au 19ème siècle et au début du 20ème siècle," in *L'Antisémitisme, hier et aujourd'hui* (Paris: Université de Paris–Sorbonne, 1983), p. 44; and G. Lichtheim, "Socialism and the Jews," *Dissent*, July–August 1968, p. 324. For the Blanquists' anti-Marxist nationalism, see P. Hutton, *The Cult of the Revolutionary Tradition: The Blanquists in French Politics, 1864–1893* (Berkeley: University of California Press, 1981), pp. 157–58.

45. For the liberals, see D. Gordon, "Liberalism and Socialism in the Nord: Eugène Motte and Republican Politics in Roubaix, 1898–1912," *French History* 3 (1989): 324–25.

46. The Guesdists bitterly pointed out that their enemies systematically exaggerated the SPD's German nationalism. See, for instance, Bernard, "Le Cas Volmar," *Le Socialiste*, 8 July 1891. For discussion of this anti-Marxist tactic, see J. Howorth, "French Workers and German Workers: The Impossibility of Internationalism, 1900–1914," *European History Quarterly* 15 (1985): 82–83; and Derfler, *Paul Lafargue and the Flowering of French Socialism*, p. 24.

47. Election poster in the Archives Départementales du Nord, M. 37/33, pièce 521, cited in C. Willard, "Engels et le mouvement socialiste en France (1891–1895) à travers la correspondance Engels-Lafargue, t. III," *Annali dell'Istituto Giangiacomo Feltrinelli* 3 (1960): 757. The poster is discussed and repudiated in *Le Socialiste* of 9 September 1893 (Anon., "Pour servir à l'histoire d'une élection"). For the widespread acceptance of the charge that the Guesdists accepted German money, see S. Wilson, *Ideology and Experience*, p. 341.

48. R. Baker, "A Regional Study of Working-Class Organization in France: Socialism in the Nord, 1870–1924" (Ph.D. thesis, Stanford University, 1967), p. 84. On Delory's travails, see B. Simler, "Gustave Delory et les débuts du mouvement

socialiste à Lille et dans la région du Nord sous la Troisième République," *Les Pays-Bas Français*, 1982, p. 126; for Roubaix and Guesde, D. Gordon, *Liberalism and Social Reform: Industrial Growth and Progressiste Politics in France* (Westport, Conn.: Greenwood Press, 1996), pp. 58–59; and L. Marty, *Chanter pour survivre: Culture ouvrière, travail et technique dans le textile à Roubaix (1850–1914)* (Lille: Fédération Léo Lagrange, 1882), pp. 183–88; and, for Parisian nationalism and the Guesdists, C. Willard, *Le Mouvement socialiste en France (1893–1905): Les Guesdistes* (Paris: Editions Sociales, 1965), p. 251.

49. "Le Conseil National du Parti Ouvrier aux Travailleurs de France," *Le Socialiste*, 17 June 1893 (stress in original).

50. B., "Importation allemande et produits indigènes," *Le Socialiste*, 2 January 1892.

51. Gabriel Deville, "Un Critique de Marx," *Le Socialiste*, 11 June 1887.

52. "A Travers la semaine," *Le Socialiste*, 18–25 September 1904.

53. Derfler, *Paul Lafargue and the Flowering of French Socialism*, p. 243.

54. H. Ghesquière, "L'Unité dans la solidarité," *Le Socialiste*, 7–14 April 1901.

55. Gabriel Deville, "Un Critique de Marx," *Le Socialiste*, 11 June 1887.

56. "Fleur de patriotisme," *Le Socialiste*, 27 October 1894. For the dangers of such socialist nationalism evolving into national socialism, see Schwarzmantel, "Class and Nation," p. 253.

57. Eric Hobsbawm has written wisely of socialist and proletarian ability to hold these contradictory identities simultaneously, with only self-aware ideologists conscious of the resultant aporias. E. Hobsbawm, "Working-Class Internationalism," in *Internationalism in the Labour Movement, 1830–1940*, ed. F. van Holthoon and M. van der Linden (Leiden: Brill, 1988), 1: 13–14.

58. For this tradition, see J.-M. Donegani and M. Sadoun, "Les Droites au miroir des gauches," in *Histoire des droites en France*, vol. 3, *Sensibilités*, ed. J.-F. Sirinelli (Paris: Gallimard, 1992), pp. 765–66; and K. Steven Vincent, "National Consciousness, Nationalism and Exclusion," pp. 444–48. For the tradition's resonance among the working class, see M. Perrot, "Le Regard de l'autre: Les Patrons français vus par les ouvriers (1880–1914)," in *Le Patronat de la seconde industrialisation*, ed. M. Lévy-Leboyer (Paris: Editions Ouvrières, 1979), p. 297. On this strategy of nationalist "othering" more generally, see A. Finlayson, "Ideology, Discourse, and Nationalism," *Journal of Political Ideology* 3 (1998): 109–11.

59. J. Guesde, "L'Enseignement secondaire des filles et la morale," *L'Egalité*, 29 January 1882.

60. G. Crépin, "Leur patriotisme," *Le Socialiste*, 14 August 1886.

61. E. Beau de Loménie, *Les Responsabilités des dynasties bourgeoises*, 5 vols. (Paris: Librairie Française, 1977)—a perverted masterpiece of national-socialist historiography.

62. "Le Patriotisme des Périer [*sic*]," *Le Socialiste*, 1 September 1894.

63. "Industrie et patriotisme," *Le Socialiste*, 30 October 1886.

64. See, for instance, J.G., "Les 'Avec patrie,'" *Le Socialiste*, 8 February 1894.

65. "Le Parti de l'étranger," *Le Socialiste*, 4 November 1893.

66. Report of a speech by J. Guesde. "Une Triple manifestation," *Le Socialiste*, 24 June 1893.

67. Ed. Fortin, "Concurrence et salariat," *Le Socialiste*, 6 October 1895.

68. "Patriotisme bourgeois," *Le Socialiste*, 19 February 1887.

69. Louis Marle, "Patriotisme patronal," *Le Socialiste*, 4 December 1898.

70. Bonnier, "Traîtres," *Le Socialiste*, 23 October 1898.

71. "La Trahison," *Le Socialiste*, 13 January 1895. Dreyfus's German investments were largely a nationalist invention.

72. Paul Lafargue, "Encore les financiers," *Le Socialiste*, 7 November 1891.

73. "Un Bagne capitaliste," *Le Socialiste*, 28 November 1885.

74. See, for instance, Jules Guesde, "La France se meurt . . . ," *Le Socialiste*, 10 September 1887. There is a study of this aspect of Guesdist thought in L. Grani, "Jules Guesde, Paul Lafargue et les problèmes de population," *Population* 34 (1979): 1024–44.

75. "Les Anti-patriotes" (citing a speech by Lafargue in the Chamber of Deputies), *Le Socialiste*, 14 November 1892. This "biological" critique of capitalism could lead militants from Marxist socialism to nationalist racism, as with the emblematic case of Vacher de Lapouge. See S. Quinlan, "The Racial Imagery of Degeneration and Depopulation: Georges Vacher de Lapouge and 'Anthroposociology' in Fin-de-Siècle France," *History of European Ideas* 24 (1999): 393–413.

76. Untitled (columns 4–5, page 1), *Le Socialiste*, 8 October 1887.

77. Paul Lafargue, "La Campagne patriotarde—Les Sans patrie," *Le Socialiste*, 17 June 1893.

78. Ibid.

79. "L'Internationalisme de la science," *Le Socialiste*, 26 June 1886. For the ways in which the experience of the Commune underpinned a working-class nationalism opposed to the traitorous bourgeoisie, see T. van Tijn, "Nationalism and the Socialist Workers' Movement, 1830–1940," in *Internationalism in the Labour Movement, 1830–1940*, ed. F. van Holthoon and M. van der Linden (Leiden: Brill, 1988), 2: 614–15. For more general discussion of the Left seizing a national cause let fall by a defeated ruling elite, see Jenkins, "Socialism, National Identity and Nationalism," p. 17.

80. Geva, "Les Ouvriers étrangers," *Le Socialiste*, 20 November 1886.

81. "La Semaine," *Le Socialiste*, 22 July 1893.

82. P. Lafargue, "Patriotes bourgeois," *Le Socialiste*, 14 December 1890.

83. "Patriotisme gouvernemental," *Le Socialiste*, 31 March 1894.

84. Report of a speech by Guesde, "A Calais," *Le Socialiste*, 14 February 1892. Leslie Derfler suggests that the Guesdists moderated their hostility to the Russian alliance. Derfler, *Paul Lafargue and the Flowering of French Socialism*, pp. 135–36. Such moderation does not appear in the party press, which continued to lambaste the alliance unremittingly.

85. B., "Patriotisme et emprunt," *Le Socialiste*, 10 October 1891.

86. Untitled (column 4, page 1), *Le Socialiste*, 30 July 1887.

87. "La Semaine," *Le Socialiste*, 13 October 1894.

88. K. Marx and F. Engels, *Manifesto of the Communist Party* [1848], in *Collected Works* (London: Lawrence and Wishart, 1976), 6: 502–3. Neo-Marxists often attribute the concept of proletarians as the nation's leading class to Gramsci. In fact, it has been an aspect of the Marxist project from its inception. For a representative attribution to Gramsci, see Nimni, "Great Historical Failure," p. 78.

89. R. Gallissot, "La Patrie des prolétaires," *Mouvement Social*, no. 147 (1989): 11–25.

90. M. Rodinson, "Le Marxisme et la nation," *L'Homme et la Société*, 1968, p. 132. See also the discussion in S. Bloom, *The World of Nations: A Study of the National Implications in the Work of Karl Marx* (New York: Columbia University Press, 1967), pp. 58–61. For the crucial distinction between class collaboration in "bourgeois" nationalism and class hegemony in socialist nationalism, see B. Jenkins, *Nationalism in France: Class and Nation since 1789* (London: Routledge, 1990), p. 118.

91. A case made in Munck, *Difficult Dialogue*, p. 156. For the structural necessity of national identity for hegemonic socialism, see G. Balakrishnan, "The National Imagination," in *Mapping the Nation*, ed. G. Balakrishnan and B. Anderson (London: Verso, 1996), p. 199. There is elucidation of the logic behind the empirical evidence for this point in N. Lazarus, "The Necessity of Universalism," *Differences: A Journal of Feminist Cultural Studies* 7 (1995): 75–145, esp. pp. 91–93; and Berki, *State, Class, Nation*, pp. 13–14.

92. C. Morazé, *Les Bourgeois conquérants* (Paris: A. Colin, 1957).

93. René Chauvin, "Coalisons-nous," *Le Socialiste*, 28 April 1895.

94. For this dynamic during the period of the Second International, see Hobsbawm, "Working-Class Internationalism," p. 14.

95. *La Démocratie-Socialiste Allemande devant l'histoire* (Paris: 1893), p. 2.

96. Paul Lafargue, "L'Armée et les gouvernants bourgeois," *Le Socialiste*, 17 June 1900. For an analysis of the ways in which different classes construct alternative "national" interests, see P. Vilar, "Nationalism," *Marxist Perspectives* 2 (1979): 10. For critique of Marxists' usage (or nonusage) of this perception, see R. Okey, "Working Class Movements and Nations: Towards a Typology," *Journal of Area Studies* 5 (1982): 21.

97. C. Bonnier, "Parti Ouvrier et patriotisme," *La Jeunesse socialiste*, no. 9 (1895): 456 (stress in original).

98. Paul Lafargue, "L'Expédition de Madagascar," *Le Socialiste*, 8 December 1894.

99. Paul Lafargue, "La Campagne patriotarde," *Le Socialiste*, 27 May 1893. There is discussion of this socialist-nationalist strategy in J. Schwarzmantel, "Nation versus Class: Nationalism and Socialism in Theory and Practice," in *The Social Origin of Nationalist Movements: The Contemporary West European Experience*, ed. J. Coakley (London: Sage, 1992), pp. 45–61. For the argument that all class ideologies, including Marxism, must articulate themselves with "national popular" discourse, see Laclau, *Politics and Ideology in Marxist Theory*, esp. pp. 108–9.

100. C. Bonnier, "Parti Ouvrier et patriotisme," p. 455.

101. Charles Bonnier, "Internationale," *Le Socialiste*, 5 August 1900.

102. Guesde's speech to the Chamber of Deputies, *Journal Officiel: Chambre des Deputés*, 20 February 1897.

103. Charles Bonnier, "Internationale," *Le Socialiste*, 5 August 1900.

104. Ibid. On such articulation, see K. Appiah, "Against National Culture," in *Text and Nation: Cross-Disciplinary Essays on Cultural and National Identities*, ed. P. Pfeiffer and L. Garcia-Moreno (Columbia, S.C.: Camden House, 1996), pp. 175–90. For Engels's urging of this point on the POF, see Engels to Lafargue, 20 June 1893, in *Friedrich Engels et Paul et Laura Lafargue: Correspondance*, vol. 3 (Paris: Editions Sociales, 1956).

105. Report of speech by Guesde, "Une Triple manifestation," *Le Socialiste*, 24 June 1893 (stress in the original). An exactly equivalent argument was adduced by the POF to prove that Guesdists, often ferocious critics of "the bourgeois family," in fact offered the only salvation for endangered family life—with socialism creating the broader solidarity within which the lesser solidarity of the domestic realm could survive the otherwise corrosive effects of capitalism. R. Stuart, "Whores and Angels: Women and the Family in the Discourse of French Marxism, 1882–1905," *European History Quarterly* 27 (1997): 351–56.

106. Guesde, preface to *Socialisme et patriotisme*, by J. Vingtras (Lille, 1900), p. 3.

107. Alexandre Zévaès, "Nationalisme et internationalisme," *Le Socialiste*, 31 January 1897.

108. F. Fanon, "On National Culture," in *The Wretched of the Earth* (New York: McGibbon and Kee, 1963), p. 247.

109. For this demoralizing dynamic, see J. Howorth, "The Left in France and Germany, Internationalism and War: A Dialogue of the Deaf, 1900–1914," in *Socialism and Nationalism in Contemporary Europe (1848–1945)*, ed. E. Cahm and V. Fisera (Nottingham: Spokesman, 1979), 2: 85. That this maneuver contradicted the common anti-Marxist charge that the POF was a subsidiary of the SPD bothered conservative polemicists not at all, of course.

110. For this critique, see A. Colás, "Putting Cosmopolitanism into Practice: The Case of Socialist Internationalism," *Millennium: Journal of International Studies* 23 (1994): 513–34. On the disillusioning wars between socialist states, see G. Evans and K. Rowley, *Red Brotherhood at War* (London: Verso, 1984).

111. B., "Le Frisson," *Le Socialiste*, 6 January 1895. For the Guesdists' characteristic refusal to recognize "contradictions" within the working class, see R. Stuart, *Marxism at Work: Ideology, Class and French Socialism during the Third Republic* (Cambridge: Cambridge University Press, 1992), pp. 134–73.

112. Guesde, preface to *Socialisme et patriotisme*, by J. Vingtras (Lille, 1900), p. 4.

5. "Savage, Brutal, and Bestial Mentalities": The Guesdists and Racism

1. C. Digeon, *La Crise allemande de la pensée française, 1870–1914* (Paris: Presses Universitaires de France, 1959), pp. 75–76; and I. Ousby, *The Road to Verdun: World War I's Most Momentous Battle and the Folly of Nationalism* (New York: Jonathan Cape, 2002), pp. 203–4, 219–20. On the racist metahistories of the time, see Z. Sternhell, "Les Origines intellectuelles du racisme en France," *Histoire*, no. 17 (1979): 106–14.

2. For the centrality of racism to Barrèsian national socialism, see P. Guiral, "Idée de race et pensée politique en France (gauche et droite) au XIXeme siècle," in *L'Idée de race dans la pensée politique française contemporaine*, ed. P. Guiral and E. Témime (Paris: Editions du Centre National de la Recherche Scientifique, 1977), pp. 34–47; and M. Rebérioux, "Le Mot race au tournant du siècle," *Mots: Les Langages du Politique*, no. 33 (1992): 53–58. For Le Bon's strategy of interpreting class differences as racial distinctions, see R. Nye, *The Origins of Crowd Psychology: Gustave Le Bon and the Crisis of Mass Democracy in the Third Republic* (London: Sage, 1975), pp. 49–54; and T. Todorov, *On Human Diversity: Nationalism, Racism, and Exoticism in French Thought* (Cambridge, Mass.: Harvard University Press, 1993), pp. 113–14. On Vacher de Lapouge's racism, see S. Quinlan, "The Racial Imagery of Degeneration and Depopulation: Georges Vacher de Lapouge and 'Anthroposociology' in Fin-de-Siècle France," *History of European Ideas* 24 (1999): 393–413; and for Soury's, T. Gelfand, "From Religious to Bio-Medical Anti-Semitism: The Career of Jules Soury," in *French Medical Culture in the Nineteenth Century*, ed. A. LaBerge and M. Feingold (Amsterdam: Rodopi, 1994), pp. 248–79.

3. Useful theoretical, if completely unhistorical, analyses of the conflict between Marxist class ideology and racism may be found in J. Gabriel and G. Ben-Tovim, "Marxism and the Concept of Racism," *Economy and Society* 7 (1978): 118–54; E. Bonacich, "Class Approaches to Ethnicity and Race," *Insurgent Sociologist* 10 (1980): 9–23; and M. Rodinson, "Marxisme et racisme," *La Nef* 21 (1964): 18–37.

4. For discussion of the ambiguity of the term "race" in France, see C. Guillaumin, "'Race' and Discourse," in *Race, Discourse and Power in France*, ed. M. Silverman (Aldershot: Avebury, 1991), pp. 5–13. The conflation of "nationhood" and "race"

seems particularly characteristic of France, according to M. Silverman, *Deconstructing the Nation: Immigration, Racism and Citizenship in Modern France* (London: Routledge, 1992), pp. 7–8.

5. There is analysis of "Gobinism" as an alternative to socialism in P.-A. Taguieff, *Le Couleur et le Sang* (Paris: Editions Mille et Une Nuits, 1998), pp. 21–58. For Marxist hostility within the POF to such Gobinism, see the discussion in L. Derfler, *Paul Lafargue and the Founding of French Marxism, 1842–1882* (Cambridge, Mass.: Harvard University Press, 1991), p. 77. On Marxism's universalistic incompatibility with racism, see R. Berki, "On Marxian Thought and the Problem of International Relations," *World Politics* 24 (1971): 80–105.

6. For comment on Marx's occasional racist rhetoric and his actual impermeability to racism, see J. Talmon, *The Myth of the Nation and the Vision of Revolution: The Origins of Ideological Polarization in the Twentieth Century* (London: Secker and Warburg, 1981), p. 227; and H. Davis, *Nationalism and Socialism: Marxist and Labor Theories of Nationalism to 1917* (New York: Monthly Review Press, 1967), pp. 71–73. There is a refreshing celebration of even Marx's "obnoxious" denigrations of ethnicity in J. Cocks, *Passion and Paradox: Intellectuals Confront the National Question* (Princeton, N.J.: Princeton University Press, 2002), p. 22.

7. "A l'Etranger—Allemagne," *Le Socialiste*, 16 June 1894.

8. J.M. [Massard], "La Théorie des races," *L'Egalité*, 14 May 1882. The Guesdists' common polemical strategy of disaggregating supposed "races," however, very occasionally lapsed into a certain "microracism," as with Massard's attempt to discredit the idea of a unified Italian racial identity—an attempt that demonstrated that "Italy" was really composed of "different races: Lombards, Greeks, Ostrogoths, etc."!

9. Ibid.

10. Joseph Sarraute, "Vienne aux antisémites," *Le Socialiste*, 13 October 1895.

11. C.B., "Question de race," *Le Socialiste*, 18 June 1899.

12. "Contre le lynchage des nègres," *Le Socialiste*, 6–13 December 1903.

13. Jules Guesde, "Antisémitisme et socialisme," *Le Socialiste*, 12 May 1895.

14. C.B., "Question de race," *Le Socialiste*, 18 June 1899.

15. J. Guesde and P. Lafargue, *Le Programme du Parti ouvrier, son histoire, ses considérants, ses articles* (Paris, 1883), p. 121. A program easily implemented, unfortunately, only so long as the red blacks of the Antilles and the red whites of Roubaix were separated by the deep blue Atlantic Ocean.

16. The Guesdists were, nonetheless, intensely aware of racial conflict in the United States, and frequently expressed their support for black victims of racist violence there. For today's post-Marxist preoccupation with race, see, for instance, E. Balibar, "Racism and Crisis," in *Race, Nation, Class: Ambiguous Identities*, by E. Balibar and I. Wallerstein (London: Verso, 1991), pp. 217–27.

17. Theoretically, it would be preferable to consider the "Jewish question" and anti-Semitism under the rubric of nationalism, rather than of racism, given race's usual

identification with transcontinental rather than intra-European "difference." Both scholarly analysis and fin de siècle mentalities, however, have treated "Jewry" and "Semitism" as racial issues, and this book perforce follows suit. At the other extreme of the argument, anti-Semitism articulates a radically different form of racism from that which distinguishes, for instance, "blacks" from "whites." The latter distinction is based upon a "discriminatory" racism that measures the two races against a universal standard, finds one race inferior, and thereby justifies its subordination. Anti-Semitism usually involves a "differential" racism that refuses any common measure, defining the Jews as radically other—and thereby as fit only for exclusion . . . or extermination. For the (literally) vital distinction between "discriminatory" and "differential" racisms, see P.-A. Taguieff, "Le Néo-racisme différentialiste," *Langage et Société*, no. 34 (1985): 69–98. This book thus discusses anti-Semitism separately from other racisms.

18. On the difficulties of the RSDLP in dealing with an independent Jewish socialism, see J. Frankel, *Prophecy and Politics: Socialism, Nationalism and the Russian Jews, 1862–1917* (Cambridge: Cambridge University Press, 1981), pp. 171–257. Despite the Guesdists' prolonged and intense interest in the East European Jewish proletariat, the Bund was never once mentioned in their press.

19. P. Lafargue, "Le Parti Ouvrier: La Base philosophique du parti," *L'Egalité*, 19 March 1882. Lafargue uses the distinction to demonstrate that it is in the "economic realm alone where one must search for the causes of social ills and human vices"—a clear refutation of the anthropological foundations of racism.

20. Indeed, they made the valid point that racism contradicted nationalism by subsuming nations into broader races (France into the "Latin" race, for instance—J.M., "Pan-Latins, Pan-Germains, et Pan-Compagnie," *L'Egalité*, 7 May 1882), or by disaggregating them into racial subgroups (for France, a Germanic North, a Celtic West, and a Latin South—J.M., "La Théorie des races," *L'Egalité*, 14 May 1882). For elaboration of this contradiction between racism and nationalism, see B. Anderson, *Imagined Communities* (London: Verso, 1983), chap. 8.

21. B., "La Politique coloniale," *Le Socialiste*, 26 May 1895.

22. The mixture is described in Leslie Derfler's invaluable *Paul Lafargue and the Flowering of French Socialism, 1882–1911* (Cambridge, Mass.: Harvard University Press, 1998), p. 1. For Lafargue's pride in his hybridity, see L. Derfler, "Paul Lafargue: The First Marxist Literary Critic," *Nineteenth-Century French Studies* 17 (1989): 382n.1.

23. C.B. [Charles Bonnier], "Question de Race," *Le Socialiste*, 18 June 1899.

24. The Gobineau quotation cited in Quinlan, "Racial Imagery of Degeneration and Depopulation," p. 397.

25. P. Lafargue, "Au Comité des Associations Populaires Milanaises," *Le Socialiste*, 15 April 1891.

26. Paul Lafargue, "Juifs et socialistes," *Le Cri du Peuple*, 2 October 1886.

27. "La Semaine," *Le Socialiste*, 7 November 1892. Note the assumptions that all "Western" workers were adult heterosexual males.

28. J. Guesde, “La Vraie solidarité,” *Le Citoyen,* 7 May 1882.

29. “L’Idéal capitaliste,” *Le Socialiste*, 17 July 1886—allegedly a characterization of the French proletariat by the haut-bourgeois Société d’Economie Politique. For these labor migration plans in actuality, see Y. Lequin, “L’Invasion pacifique,” in *Histoire des Etrangers et de l’Immigration en France*, ed. Y. Lequin (Paris: Larousse, 1992), p. 333.

30. J. Guesde, “L’Enseignement secondaire des filles et la morale,” *L’Egalité*, 29 January 1882 (stress in original).

31. Cl., “Les Singes ouvriers,” *Le Socialiste*, 26 March 1887.

32. B., “La Conquête jaune,” *Le Socialiste*, 6 October 1895.

33. “L’Invasion jaune,” *Le Socialiste*, 10 November 1895.

34. B., “La Politique coloniale,” *Le Socialiste*, 26 May 1895.

35. B., “La Conquête jaune,” *Le Socialiste*, 6 October 1895.

36. See Bernard-Henri Lévy, for instance, citing Michelle Perrot (Lévy has not consulted original Guesdist texts) on Guesde’s (highly atypical) praise of working-class antagonism to coolie labor in California. B.-H. Lévy, *L’Idéologie française* (Paris: Grasset, 1981), p. 129.

37. “L’Invasion jaune,” *Le Socialiste*, 10 November 1895. For this argument in Marxism, see Talmon, *Myth of the Nation and the Vision of Revolution*, p. 49.

38. O.D., “L’Invasion chinois,” *Le Socialiste*, 30 April 1893.

39. “L’Invasion jaune,” *Le Socialiste*, 10 November 1895.

40. Charles Bonnier, “Le Drapeau de l’Europe,” *Le Socialiste*, 15 July 1900.

41. Report of responses to a speech by Legitimus in “Le Congrès de la Gironde,” *Le Socialiste*, 28 May 1899.

42. “Responsables,” *Le Socialiste*, 18 February 1900.

43. “Le Parti Ouvrier en France—Romilly-sur-Seine,” *Le Socialiste*, 7 August 1898.

44. “Victoire!” *Le Socialiste*, 14 January 1900. Guesdist willingness to occasionally exploit anti-Asian prejudice may well have reflected the fact that the POF had no Asian constituency, in contrast to the importance of its black supporters in the Caribbean, who effectively immunized French Marxists against anti-Negro racism.

45. C.B., “Question de race,” *Le Socialiste*, 18 June 1899.

46. Derfler, *Paul Lafargue and the Founding of French Marxism*, p. 15. Translation by Derfler.

47. P.G., “Cri du cœur,” *Le Socialiste*, 1–8 June 1902.

48. See, for instance, H. Legitimus, “A la Guadeloupe,” *Le Socialiste*, 7 August 1898.

49. This equation seems to be implied in, for instance, “Aux Camarades de France,” *Le Socialiste*, 28 May 1899.

50. "Parti Ouvrier Français," *Le Socialiste*, 26 March 1899.

51. A. Zévaès, speech to the Chamber of Deputies, *Journal Officiel: Chambre des Deputés*, 26 March 1900.

52. For an account of this incident, see "Le Parti Ouvrier en France—Nantes," *Le Socialiste*, 12 February 1899.

53. S. Wilson, *Ideology and Experience: Anti-Semitism in France at the Time of the Dreyfus Affair* (London: Associated University Presses, 1982), pp. 334–35. Wilson seeks to amend Silberner's exculpation of Guesdism, which, although now dated, is essentially correct in its assessment. E. Silberner, "French Socialism and the Jewish Question, 1865–1914," *Historia Judaica* 16 (1954): 3–38. For the most widely diffused but least sustainable allegation of Guesdist anti-Semitism, see Lévy, *L'Idéologie français*, pp. 127–32. For a study that attempts to make virtually all France anti-Semitic during the Dreyfus affair, see P. Birnbaum, *Le Moment antisémite: Un Tour de la France en 1898* (Paris: Fayard, 1998), with pp. 125–26 as an indictment of the socialists.

54. Indeed, it has become all too common to attribute popular anti-Semitism first of all to this socialist tradition, thereby devaluing the much more pervasive Catholic and Conservative hostility to Jews that undoubtedly contributed far more to fin de siècle racism. For this priority, see, for instance, D. Schnapper, "Le Juif Errant," in *Histoire des Etrangers et de l'Immigration en France*, ed. Y. Lequin (Paris: Larousse, 1992), pp. 365–68; and M. Marrus, "Popular Anti-Semitism," in *The Dreyfus Affair: Art, Truth, and Justice*, ed. N. Kleeblatt (Berkeley: University of California Press, 1987), pp. 50–52, with Catholic anti-Semitism relegated to an afterthought, p. 57. On the Fourierist and Proudhonian traditions of anti-Semitism, see L. Poliakov, *The History of Anti-Semitism* (London: Routledge, 1975), 3: 364–79.

55. On Bernard Lazare, see N. Wilson, *Bernard-Lazare: Anti-Semitism and the Problem of Jewish Identity in Late Nineteenth-Century France* (Cambridge: Cambridge University Press, 1978), chap. 4; and J. Verdès-Leroux, *Scandale financier et anti-sémitisme catholique: Le Krach de l'Union Générale* (Paris: Editions du Centurion, 1969), p. 104. For Clemenceau at Carlsbad, see L. Poliakov, *The History of Anti-Semitism* (London: Routledge, 1975), 4: 64. For anti-Semitic stereotypes in Zola, see ibid., pp. 69–70. On Jaurès, see M. Marrus, *The Politics of Assimilation: A Study of the French Jewish Community at the Time of the Dreyfus Affair* (Oxford: Clarendon, 1971), pp. 133–34n.3; and Verdès-Leroux, *Scandale financier et antisémitisme catholique*, pp. 159–60. For the universality of a casual anti-Semitism, even among such good liberals as Paul Leroy-Beaulieu, see P. Birnbaum, "Accepter la pluralité: Haines et préjugés," in *Histoire des droites en France*, vol. 3, *Sensibilités*, ed. J.-F. Sirinelli (Paris: Gallimard, 1992), p. 429.

56. S. Wilson, "The Ligue antisémitique française," *Wiener Library Bulletin* 25 (1972): 33. On the Blanquist origins of French anti-Semitic national socialism, see P. Hutton, *The Cult of the Revolutionary Tradition: The Blanquists in French Politics, 1864–1893* (Berkeley: University of California Press, 1981), pp. 158–59; and, on the Monument Henry, S. Wilson, "Le Monument Henry: La Structure de l'antisémitisme en France, 1898–1899," *Annales: Economies, Sociétés, Civilisations* 32 (1977): 273.

57. For this argument, see A. Leca, "Les Thèmes idéologiques de l'antisémitisme chez les socialistes français (1845–1890)," *Revue de la Recherche Juridique*, no. 3 (1995): 984–85; and M. Winock, "Edouard Drumont et Cie," in *Edouard Drumont et Cie: Antisémitisme et Fascisme en France* (Paris: Seuil, 1982), p. 47. For the most scholarly indictment of Marx, see J. Carlebach, *Karl Marx and the Radical Critique of Judaism* (London: Routledge, 1978), which contains an invaluable annotated bibliography assessing the literature on Marx's alleged anti-Semitism. For a comprehensive and convincing dismissal of this charge, see E. Traverso, *The Marxists and the Jewish Question: The History of a Debate (1843–1943)* (Atlantic Highlands, N.J.: Humanities, 1994), chap. 1. Traverso's very useful study, unfortunately, follows the universal pattern of general studies of "Marxism and Nationalism"—moving from an initial chapter on the "founding fathers" to discussions of Eastern and Central Europeans, thereby ignoring the vital instance of the POF. Traverso mentions the Guesdists' engagement with the Jewish question in only a few sentences (pp. 1–2).

58. R. Byrnes, *Anti-Semitism in Modern France* (New York: Fertig, 1969), p. 117. There is discussion of the use of Marx's pamphlet on the Jewish question by the French anti-Semites in Z. Sternhell, *La Droite révolutionnaire, 1885–1914: Les Origines françaises du fascisme* (Paris: Seuil, 1984), p. 188. Guesdists repeatedly and furiously repudiated the charge that their master had been anti-Semitic—which may say little about Marx, but says a great deal about the Parti Ouvrier. See, for instance, C. Bonnier, "La Question juive," *Le Socialiste*, 12 February 1899.

59. C. Willard, *Le Mouvement socialiste en France (1893–1905): Les Guesdistes* (Paris: Editions Sociales, 1965), pp. 410–11. His citation (in the original carefully nuanced by reference to simultaneous denunciations of anti-Semitism) has been appropriated by subsequent scholarship. See, for instance, Sternhell, *La Droite révolutionnaire*, p. 239; R. Wistrich, "French Socialism and the Dreyfus Affair," *Wiener Library Bulletin*, no. 28 (1975): 11; P. Pierrard, "Antisémitisme de droite et de gauche au 19ème siècle et au début du 20ème siècle," in *L'Antisémitisme, hier et aujourd'hui* (Paris: Université de Paris—Sorbonne, 1983), p. 45; and H. Bulakow, "Les Socialistes et l'Affaire," *Nouveaux Cahiers* 27 (1971–72): 27. Most of the Guesdists' provincial press simply reproduced Parisian material, so that the national organs' anti-anti-Semitism was in fact very widely diffused—making Narbonne even less representative.

60. For the eccentricity of Narbonnais Guesdism, see R. Pech, "Les Thèmes économiques et sociaux du socialisme férrouliste à Narbonne (1880–1914)," in *Droite et gauche en Languedoc-Roussillon: Actes du colloque de Montpellier, 9–10 juin 1973* (Montpellier: Centre d'Histoire Contemporaine du Languedoc Méditerranéan et du Roussillon, Université Paul Valéry, 1975), pp. 256–69; and P. Guidoni, *La Cité Rouge: Le Socialisme à Narbonne, 1871–1921* (Toulouse: Privat, 1979).

61. Willard, *Le Mouvement socialiste en France*, pp. 410–11; and for the same peculiar point, Z. Sternhell, *Maurice Barrès et le nationalisme français* (Paris: Fayard, 1972), p. 244. Instances of Willard's strange argument being appropriated by subsequent studies may be found in Leca, "Les Thèmes idéologiques," p. 987n.36; S. Wilson, *Ideology and Experience*, p. 338; and M. Winock, *Nationalisme, antisémitisme et fascisme en France* (Paris: Seuil, 1982), p. 195. Jeannine Verdès-Leroux, however, has

pointed out the absurdity of Willard's point. Verdès-Leroux, *Scandale financier et antisémitisme catholique*, p. 155. For proof of how ferociously hostile to anti-Semitism these Guesdist interventions really were, see, for instance, the transcript of Guesde's debate with Drumont and Guérin in J. Guesde, "Duperie et réaction," *Le Socialiste*, 31 July 1898.

62. S. Wilson, *Ideology and Experience*, p. 69; P. Birnbaum, *La France aux français: Histoire des haines nationalistes* (Paris: Seuil, 1993), p. 24; and Birnbaum, "Accepter la pluralité," p. 431. Guesde was essentially indifferent to the "Jewish question," and hostile to its intrusion, pro or con, into debate about "the social question"—a blameworthy attitude, no doubt, during a period of rabid anti-Semitism, but *not* itself anti-Semitic. For quotation of your enemies as complicity with their politics, see Winock, *Nationalisme, antisémitisme et fascism en France*, pp. 194–95.

63. For Lévy's point, *L'Idéologie française*, pp. 127–28. See also Y. Lequin, "La Classe ouvrière," in *Histoire des droites en France*, vol. 3, *Sensibilités*, ed. J.-F. Sirinelli (Paris: Gallimard, 1992), p. 503; and P. Birnbaum, *Jewish Destinies: Citizenship, State, and Community in Modern France* (New York: Hill and Wang, 2000), p. 54. Robert Byrnes actually suggests that Lafargue *cooperated* with Drumont in attacking the perpetrators of the Fourmies massacre. The solidity of Byrnes's research on the Guesdists is somewhat undermined, however, by his accompanying claim that the notoriously anti-Semitic Auguste Chirac contributed to Guesde's *Egalité* in 1890 and 1891, although the paper ceased publication in 1883 (apart from a single number in 1886), and Chirac never contributed to the Guesdist press at any time. Byrnes, *Anti-Semitism in Modern France*, pp. 168–69.

64. B., "La Maison Nucingen," *Le Socialiste*, 22 January 1893.

65. "Juifs et monarchistes," *Le Socialiste*, 5 February 1893. It has been pointed out that nineteenth-century socialist hostility to "Jewish finance" derived to a considerable extent from financiers' close associations with the repressive regimes so hated by socialists—both the Orleanist July Monarchy and the Second Empire having corruptly favored finance while repressing the Left. Pierrard, "Antisémitisme de droite et de gauche," p. 38. And note the identification of "Jewish" as a religious rather than racial identity—the dominant mode in Guesdist discourse, and further evidence of largely nonracial paradigm within which the Parti Ouvrier operated.

66. Report of a speech by Lafargue, "Les Juifs dans l'histoire européenne," *Le Socialiste*, 2 October 1898. It was widely believed at the time that Drumont had Jewish ancestry, according to F. Busi, *The Pope of Anti-Semitism: The Career and Legacy of Edouard-Adolphe Drumont* (Lanham, Md.: University Press of America, 1986), p. 11, and the Guesdists often referred to him as, for instance, "a Jew, traitor to his race, that Judas Drumont." "Resolution on Anti-Semitism," *XVIe Congrès National du Parti Ouvrier Français tenu à Montluçon du 17 au 20 septembre 1898* (Paris, 1898), p. 32. In fact, one of the Guesdists' favorite anti-anti-Semitic tropes was to accuse the anti-Semites of being hand-in-glove with the Jewish financiers they allegedly hated, as with Lafargue's charge that "the salons and the countinghouses of the Rothschilds, Ephrussis, Camondos and others of the Jewish royalty of gold are encumbered with these ferocious anti-Semites. . . . The duchess who pretends to faint at the mere odor of Jew,

kisses their hands in public and other things in private in order to gain stock market tips." Paul Lafargue, "L'Antisémitisme," *Le Socialiste*, 24 July 1898.

67. Report of a speech by Lafargue, "Les Juifs dans l'histoire européenne," *Le Socialiste*, 2 October 1898.

68. For the importance in ideology-study of "pragmatics" (an ideology's "usage" in context, as opposed to its internal "semantics and syntactics"), see J. Dunn, "The Identity of the History of Ideas," in *Political Obligation in Its Historical Context: Essays in Political Theory* (Cambridge: Cambridge University Press, 1980), pp. 13–58.

69. P.M. André, "Ni Lutaud, ni Régis," *Le Socialiste*, 9–16 June 1901. For the Guesdists' very similar hostility to the "identity politics" of feminism and (anti)clericalism, see R. Stuart, "'Calm, with a Grave and Serious Temperament, Rather Male': French Marxism, Gender and Feminism, 1882–1905," *International Review of Social History* 41 (1996): 57–82; and R. Stuart, "Marxism and Anticlericalism: The Parti Ouvrier Français and the War Against Religion, 1882–1905," *Journal of Religious History* 22 (1998): 287–303.

70. B, "Le Procès Ahlwardt," *Le Socialiste*, 18 December 1892.

71. "L'Antisémitisme en Allemagne," *Le Socialiste*, 11 November 1893. For a study of the ways in which Marxist understanding of anti-Semitism has been transformed by the Holocaust, see E. Traverso, *Understanding the Nazi Genocide: Marxism after Auschwitz* (London: Pluto, 1999).

72. Joseph Sarraute, "Vienne aux antisémites," *Le Socialiste*, 13 October 1895. The Guesdists followed Austrian politics attentively, but always with the confident, and not entirely misplaced, expectation that Vienna's future belonged to Social Democracy, not to Lueger's momentarily victorious anti-Semites.

73. Paul Dramas, "Antisémites," *Le Socialiste*, 14 July 1895. But note the implied acceptance of the anti-Semites' point that the Jews did, indeed, belong to a race other than "our own," although Dramas seems to be, at this point, paraphrasing the anti-Semites he is attacking.

74. Ibid.

75. J. Sarraute, "Vienne aux antisémites," *Le Socialiste*, 13 October 1895. The article leaves it in no doubt that the Guesdist writer saw the anti-Semites' program as proposing mass murder.

76. Bonnier, "Manque d'estomac," *Le Socialiste*, 7 January 1899.

77. Ibid.

78. J.M., "La Théorie des races," *L'Egalité*, 14 May 1882.

79. "Juifs et catholiques," *Le Socialiste*, 7 August 1886.

80. Untitled (column 4, page 1), *Le Socialiste*, 5 June 1892.

81. S. Wilson, *Ideology and Experience*, p. 273. For the traditional linkage between the reactionary royalists and wealthy Jews, see W. Irvine, *The Boulanger Affair Reconsidered* (Oxford: Oxford University Press, 1989), p. 169.

82. P.-M. André, "Ni Lutaud, ni Régis," *Le Socialiste,* 2–9 June 1901.

83. S. Wilson, *Ideology and Experience,* p. 188.

84. Charles Brunellière, letter to Cedet, 27 January 1898, in *La Correspondance de Charles Brunellière: Socialiste Nantais, 1880–1917,* ed. C. Willard (Paris: Editions Sociales, 1968), p. 155.

85. "Un 'Lowe' chrétien," *Le Socialiste,* 1 January 1893.

86. The Baron Alphonse de Rothschild in *Le Figaro,* 14 September 1892, cited in Leca, "Les Thèmes idéologiques," p. 984. For such equations with reference to the Panama affair, see Poliakov, *History of Anti-Semitism,* 4: 48.

87. See the Guesdists' angry response to this conflation in Paul Grados, "L'Autre presse," *Le Socialiste,* 1 July 1900. On police suspicions, see S. Wilson, *Ideology and Experience,* p. 332. For the liberal amalgamation of socialists and anti-Semites, see A. Leroy-Beaulieu, *L'Antisémitisme* (Paris, 1897), esp. p. 5. On the belief that socialism and anti-Semitism were one and the same, as held even among the more conservative of the "establishment" who might otherwise have been sympathetic to the anti-Semites, see Irvine, *Boulanger Affair Reconsidered,* pp. 169–70; and J.-P. Rioux, *Nationalisme et conservatisme: La Ligue de la Patrie Française* (Paris: Editions Beauchesne, 1977), p. 40.

88. E. Drumont, *La Fin du monde* (Paris, 1889), pp. 155, 159, cited in S. Wilson, *Ideology and Experience,* p. 332; and see Wilson's discussion of anti-Semitic sympathy for socialism, pp. 325–26. On Hughes, see M. Crapez, *La Gauche réactionnaire: Mythes de la plèbe et de la race* (Paris: Berg International, 1997), pp. 217–18. For the cooperation between Left and Right embodied in *La Cocarde,* see V. Nguyen, "Un Essai de pouvoir intellectuel au début de la Troisième République: *La Cocarde* de Maurice Barrès (5 septembre 1894–7 mars 1895)," *Etudes Maurrassiennes* 1 (1972): 145–55; and on *Le Cri du Peuple,* see Sternhell, *Maurice Barrès,* p. 244.

89. E. Drumont, *La Fin d'un monde* (Paris, 1889), pp. 165–66, cited in S. Wilson, *Ideology and Experience,* p. 326. Drumont was even willing to cite Marx, according to Busi, *Pope of Anti-Semitism,* p. 136; and for Drumont favorably citing Guesde, T. Anderson, "Edouard Drumont and the Origins of Modern Anti-Semitism," *Catholic Historical Review* 53 (1967): 36. However, Drumont made it very clear that the nationalist wing of the disintegrating Blanquists, "alone among the revolutionaries," had "the courage to lay claim to membership of the Aryan race and to affirm the superiority of that race." E. Drumont, *La Fin d'un monde* (Paris, 1889), p. 85, cited in S. Wilson, *Ideology and Experience,* p. 477. For a useful discussion, from a nostalgic and approving "national-socialist" perspective, of the cooperation between socialists and national socialists against bourgeois establishment figures such as Ferry, see E. Beau de Loménie, *Edouard Drumont ou l'anticapitalisme national* (Paris: Pauvert, 1968), pp. 106–9.

90. "Juifs et Catholiques," *Le Socialiste,* 7 August 1886. For socialists' alleged intimidation by or admiration for Drumont, see Sternhell, *La Droite révolutionnaire,* p. 193; and Leca, "Les Thèmes idéologiques," p. 985. Michelle Perrot and Annie Kriegel have accused the Guesdists of "keeping company" with Drumond [*sic*]. *Le Socialisme français et le pouvoir* (Paris: Etudes et Documentation Internationale, 1966), p. 66n.61.

91. "Frayeur bourgeois," *Le Socialiste,* 17 July 1886.

92. "Le Secret de Fourmies," *Le Socialiste,* 6 March 1892. The article nonetheless scathingly dismisses Drumont's "anti-Semitism of the sacristy," and denounces his fixation on Fourmies's Jewish subprefect as the author of the tragedy.

93. For the equation between the turn-of-the-century anti-Semites and the Boulangists, see Charles Bonnier, "Opposition," *Le Socialiste,* 3 June 1900. For Morès's alleged concession, see the report on a *conférence contradictoire* pitting Morès against Alexandre Zévaès, "Le Parti Ouvrier en France—Paris," *Le Socialiste,* 17 June 1893. On the time's socialist hopes for the anti-Semites' conversion to their cause, see S. Wilson, *Ideology and Experience,* p. 333; and V. Glasberg, "Intent and Consequences: The Jewish Question in the French Socialist Movement of the Late Nineteenth Century," *Jewish Social Studies* 36 (1974): 61–71.

94. B., "Anti Semites," *Le Socialiste,* 7 May 1892. The Guesdists closely followed the rise and fall of German anti-Semitism during the 1880s and 1890s. For the reality of the distinction between "Left" and "Right" anti-Semites in fin de siècle France, see Verdès-Leroux, *Scandale financier et antisémitisme catholique,* pp. 143–44.

95. "L'Antisémitisme en Allemagne," *Le Socialiste,* 11 November 1893.

96. J. Guesde, *Le Socialisme au jour le jour* (Paris, 1899), p. 170.

97. The Guesdists knew, appreciated, and appropriated Bebel's famous quip. See, for instance, B., "Le Procès Ahlwardt," *Le Socialiste,* 18 December 1892.

98. M. Barrès, "La Formule antijuive," *Le Figaro,* 22 February 1890, cited in Z. Sternhell, "National Socialism and Anti-Semitism: The Case of Maurice Barrès," *Journal of Contemporary History* 8 (1973): 61.

99. M. Barrès, quoted (without attribution) in J. Dietz, "Les Débuts de Maurice Barrès dans la vie politique," *La Revue Hebdomadaire,* 13 August 1931, p. 280.

100. Editorial in *Le Figaro,* 23 November 1892, cited in S. Wilson, *Ideology and Experience,* p. 326. For discussion of this hostility toward the anti-Semites on the part of the French haute bourgeoisie, see Winock, *Nationalisme, antisémitisme, et fascisme en France,* pp. 195–96.

101. This wrongheaded conclusion is reached in Silberner, "French Socialism and the Jewish Question," p. 14. For the victimization of Barrès's supporters by the Nancy bourgeoisie, see R. Soucy, *Fascism in France: The Case of Maurice Barrès* (Berkeley: University of California Press, 1972), p. 228.

102. Rebérioux, "Le Mot race au tournant du siècle," p. 53; and Wistrich, "French Socialism and the Dreyfus Affair," p. 18. Michael Burns, in his *Rural Society and French Politics: Boulangism and the Dreyfus Affair, 1886–1900* (Princeton, N.J.: Princeton University Press, 1984), p. 161, uses Alexandre Zévaès to exemplify this transition, when the Guesdist had actually been anti-anti-Semitic all along. In fact, the affair was much more of a turning point for the anti-Semites, who almost without exception moved dramatically toward the antisocialist Right, abandoning any residual commitment to a genuinely socialist national socialism. Beau de Loménie, *Edouard Drumont ou l'anticapitalisme national,* pp. 120–23.

103. P. Birnbaum, *Anti-Semitism in France: A Political History from Léon Blum to the Present* (Oxford: Blackwell, 1992), p. 35. See also Marrus, *Politics of Assimilation*, p. 210.

104. P. Birnbaum, *Le Peuple et les gros: Histoire d'un mythe* (Paris: Grasset, 1979), p. 25. Birnbaum, like so many French intellectuals, is much given to using rhetorical questions as assertions. Is not Birnbaum here manipulating us with sneaky rhetoric?

105. "Le Traître Dreyfus," *Le Reveil du Nord,* 11 November 1896, cited in Willard, *Le Mouvement socialiste en France,* p. 410.

106. J.-D. Bredin, *The Affair: The Case of Alfred Dreyfus* (New York: G. Braziller, 1986), pp. 295–96. Even Jaurès attributed Dreyfus's escape from the death penalty to the corrupt influence of "Jewry" on the judges. Poliakov, *History of Anti-Semitism,* 4: 54.

107. As he had been tempted by Boulangist vitality, so Lafargue was reluctant to abstain from the Dreyfus affair, arguing that the POF would suffer if it did not fully commit against the reactionary anti-Dreyfusards. Derfler, *Paul Lafargue and the Flowering of French Marxism,* chap. 13.

108. One of the few studies of the politics of anti-Semitism to make this point in favor of the Guesdists is Talmon, *Myth of the Nation and the Vision of Revolution,* p. 231.

109. C. Bonnier, "A Propos des massacres de Kichineff," *Le Socialiste,* 5–12 July 1903. For the general Marxist revulsion from this event, see Talmon, *Myth of the Nation and the Vision of Revolution,* p. 219.

110. See, for instance, Byrnes, *Anti-Semitism in Modern France,* p. 158; and Winock, "Edouard Drumont et Cie," p. 63. For a serious discussion of Lafargue and Rothschild, including Laura Lafargue's point that the issue was really "Rothschilds, Jewish or Christian," see Derfler, *Paul Lafargue and the Flowering of French Marxism,* pp. 50–52.

111. S. Wilson, *Ideology and Experience,* p. 335.

112. Paul Lafargue, "Encore les financiers," *Le Socialiste,* 7 November 1891.

113. Untitled (column 2, p. 3), *Le Socialiste,* 17 October 1891.

114. Paul Lafargue, "L'Affaire Dreyfus et la justice militaire," *Le Socialiste,* 9 October 1898. For melding of the Jews and capitalism by "Left" anti-Semitism, see P. Birnbaum, "Anti-Semitism and Anticapitalism in Modern France," in *The Jews in Modern France,* ed. F. Malino and B. Wasserstein (Hanover, N.H.: University Press of New England, 1985), pp. 214–23.

115. "Manifeste de Conseil National," *Le Socialiste,* 29 July 1893. Hirsch and Herz are here not identified as Jews, however, as would have been done by the anti-Semites.

116. Jules Guesde, "Duperie et réaction," *Le Socialiste,* 31 July 1898.

117. Paul Lafargue, "La Finance," *Le Socialiste,* 10 November 1887.

118. B. Jenkins, *Nationalism in France: Class and Nation since 1789* (London: Routledge, 1990), pp. 109–10; and Glasberg, "Intent and Consequence," pp. 66–69. Noncapitalized "jew" indicates social usage, the capitalized "Jew" indicates ethnicity. This discursive tactic resembled the similar distinction between "Jews," a contaminated term to be avoided as referring to the people, and "Israelites," the preferred term for the ethnie. For the often reiterated distinction between "Israelites" and "Jews" in French discourse, see Glasberg, "Intent and Consequence," pp. 68–69.

119. A. Toussenel, *Les Juifs, rois de l'époque: Histoire de la féodalité financière* (Paris, 1847), p. i. This preface is explicitly in response to those who would challenge his equation of ethnicity and usury, and he admits that some individual Jews are admirable—without resiling, however, from his racist equations.

120. Glasberg, "Intent and Consequence," p. 66.

121. Winock, "La Gauche et les Juifs," *L'Histoire*, no. 34 (1981): 14. Winock is elsewhere aware of the conflation of "Jew" and usurer. See Winock, "Edouard Drumont et Cie," pp. 45–46. For critique of this semantic issue, particularly as deployed against the Left by Winock, see M. Angenot, *Ce que l'on dit des Juifs en 1889: Antisémitisme et discours social* (Saint-Denis: Presses Universitaires de Vincennes, 1989), pp. 113–26.

122. Silberner, "French Socialism and the Jewish Question, 1865–1914," p. 30.

123. C. Bonnier and P. Bonnier, "La Crise du nationalisme," *Le Devenir Social*, nos. 11–12 (1897): 909 (italics inserted). The Bonniers had evidently actually read the introduction to Toussenel's book, and understood its (failed) attempt to use "Jew" as a nonracist synonym for usurer.

124. Untitled (column 3, p. 1), *Le Socialiste*, 31 July 1886 (italics inserted).

125. "L'Antisémitisme en Allemagne," *Le Socialiste*, 11 November 1893.

126. J. Guesde, "Duperie et réaction," *Le Socialiste*, 31 July 1898.

127. Carlebach's *Karl Marx and the Radical Critique of Judaism* gives an overview of the long debate over Marx's pamphlet

128. S. Veyrec, "Karl Marx et l'antisémitisme," *Le Socialiste*, 5 May 1894 (capitalization as in the original). "The Jews have emancipated themselves insofar as the Christians have become Jews." K. Marx, "On the Jewish Question" [1844], in *Collected Works*, by K. Marx and F. Engels (London: Lawrence and Wishart, 1975), 3: 170 (capitalization as in the original)

129. Paul Lafargue, "Juifs et socialistes," *Le Cri du Peuple*, 2 October 1886. On socialists' identification of Rothschild with capitalism, see Byrnes, *Anti-Semitism in Modern France*, p. 115; and for the broader French tendency to do the same, see Angenot, *Ce Que l'on dit des Juifs en 1889*, p. 119.

130. Bonnier, "Les Deux anarchies," *Le Socialiste*, 4 December 1898. Bonnier, however, also carefully stressed that he was attacking "les rois d'argent" in general, and that these lords of lucre included many non-Jews.

131. J. Guesde, "L'Epargne et ses caisses," *Le Salariat,* 25 May 1890, cited in Y. Marec, "Le Socialisme et l'épargne: Réactions de Jules Guesde," *Revue d'Economie Sociale,* no. 5 (1985): 48. I have not been able to check the original reference.

132. "L'Internationalisme de la science," *Le Socialiste,* 26 June 1886. This instance, it is worth noting, was actually deployed to show how stupid nationalism was under conditions of modernity, so that the Rothschilds were presented as unwitting agents of an internationalism cheered on by the POF—a very different position from the reactionary nationalism of the anti-Semites.

133. Marrus, *Politics of Assimilation,* p. 248.

134. Report of a speech by Guesde, "Antisémites et socialistes," *Le Socialiste,* 17 July 1892.

135. A. Zévaès, "M. Drumont et le socialisme," *Le Socialiste,* 11 October 1893.

136. See, for instance, P. Dramas, "Antisémites," *Le Socialiste,* 14 July 1895.

137. "A Travers la semaine," *Le Socialiste,* 10–17 July 1904. Guesde's comment had been made almost two decades previously in 1886.

138. A. Schlesinger, Jr., cited in M. Curtis, *Three Against the Third Republic: Sorel, Barrès, and Maurras* (Princeton, N.J.: Princeton University Press, 1959), p. 211.

139. Report of a speech by Guesde, "Antisémites et socialistes," *Le Socialiste,* 17 July 1892. For this aspect of Guesdist political economy, see R. Stuart, *Marxism at Work: Ideology, Class and French Socialism during the Third Republic* (Cambridge: Cambridge University Press, 1992), pp. 316–19.

140. See, for instance, "La Question juive," *Le Socialiste,* 26 June 1892.

141. Ibid.

142. Report of a speech by Guesde, "Antisémites et socialistes," *Le Socialiste,* 17 July 1892.

143. Jules Guesde, "Antisémitisme et socialisme," *Le Socialiste,* 12 May 1895.

144. Ibid. Pierre Birnbaum is correct in believing that the Guesdists thought that "les gros" controlled the French economy, an analysis that he himself strangely sees as a misleading myth. He is absolutely wrong, however, in believing that the Guesdists indulged in the "*gros* versus *petits*" rhetoric characteristic of the anti-Semites. Birnbaum, *Le Peuple et les gros,* p. 18.

145. "L'Antisémitisme démasqué," *Le Socialiste,* 3 July 1892 (stress in original). The piece largely consists of a letter from Engels making this classic diagnostic point.

146. Ibid.

147. Jules Guesde, "Antisémitisme et socialisme," *Le Socialiste,* 12 May 1895.

148. Bonnier, "Une Interpellation," *Le Socialiste,* 1 January 1899. For the role of anti-Semitism in transforming popular nationalism from its still vaguely leftist ideological orientation of the Boulanger affair to its overtly rightist manifestation before the First World War, see W. Serman, "The Nationalists of Meurthe-et-Moselle,

1888–1912," in *Nationhood and Nationalism in France from Boulangism to the Great War, 1889–1918*, ed. R. Tombs (London: HarperCollins Academic, 1991), pp. 127–28.

149. Anon., "Le Secret de Fourmies," *Le Socialiste*, 6 March 1892.

150. On Guesdism's enthusiasm for technological progress, see Stuart, *Marxism at Work*, pp. 110–18. For Drumont on lighting, see Byrnes, *Anti-Semitism in Modern France*, p. 165. Drumont's violent antimodernism is emphasized in R. Girardet, *Mythes et mythologies politiques* (Paris: Seuil, 1986), p. 55. For the Parisian antimodernist culture that sustained Drumontist racism, see P. Nord, *Paris Shopkeepers and the Politics of Resentment* (Princeton, N.J.: Princeton University Press, 1986), pp. 329–35.

151. E. Drumont, *La Fin d'un monde* (Paris, 1889), p. 81, cited in S. Wilson, *Ideology and Experience*, p. 255.

152. "La Question juive," *Le Socialiste*, 26 June 1892.

153. B., "Anti Sémites," *Le Socialiste*, 7 May 1892.

154. A. Zévaès, "M. Drumont et le socialisme," *Le Socialiste*, 11 October 1893.

155. Joseph Sarraute, "Vienne aux antisémites," *Le Socialiste*, 13 October 1895.

156. For the importance of absences in any assessment of ideological discourse, see H. White, "The Context in the Text: Method and Ideology in Intellectual History," in *The Content of the Form: Narrative Discourse and Historical Representation* (Baltimore: Johns Hopkins University Press, 1987), p. 192.

157. Leca, "Les Thèmes idéologiques," p. 987.

158. N. Green, "Socialist Anti-Semitism, Defence of a Bourgeois Jew and Discovery of the Jewish Proletariat: Changing Attitudes of French Socialists before 1914," *International Review of Social History* 30 (1985): 378–80; and Agenot, *Ce que l'on dit des Juifs en 1889*, p. 115.

159. P. Guiral, "Vue d'ensemble sur l'idée de race et la gauche française," in *L'Idée de race dans la pensée politique française contemporaine*, ed. P. Guiral and E. Temime (Paris: Editions du Centre National de la Recherche Scientifique, 1977), pp. 34–47. For the ways in which an anti-Guesdist such as Malon could identify Marxism as "Jewish," see G. Lichtheim, "Socialism and the Jews," *Dissent*, July–August 1968, p. 324. On Aryanism, see L. Poliakov, *The Aryan Myth: A History of Racist and Nationalist Ideas in Europe* (London: Chatto and Windus, 1974), where chapter 11 contains scattered but substantial discussion of French fin de siècle Aryanism.

160. For the Guesdists' own distinctive critique of Christianity, viewed exclusively in class rather than in racial or even religious terms, see Stuart, "'Jesus the *Sans-Culotte*,'" pp. 705–27. On the very different paradigm of anti-Christian anti-Semitism, see Crapez, *La Gauche réactionnaire*, pp. 120–75.

161. P. Grados, "L'Art falsifié," *Le Socialiste*, 27 September–4 October 1903. For the powerful aesthetic anti-Semitism of fin de siècle France, see N. Wilson, *Bernard-Lazare*, pp. 71–72.

162. "Signes de gâtisme-social," *Le Socialiste*, 21 November 1885.

163. Busi, *Pope of Anti-Semitism,* p. 117 discusses this sensationalism.

164. The Guesdists certainly highlighted the white slave trade, but as an abomination of capitalist commodification, never as a racial issue. See, for instance, P. Grados, "Plaies sociales," *Le Socialiste,* 20–27 November 1904.

165. It has been suggested that the Guesdists were afraid to challenge the formidable Rochefort, with his vast Parisian popularity. E. Cahm, "Le Mouvement socialiste face au nationalisme au temps de l'Affaire Dreyfus," *Bulletin de la Société des Etudes Jaurèsiennes,* no. 79 (1980): 11–12. In fact, the Guesdists repeatedly mocked the great gutter journalist, typically referring to him as "that old clown Rochefort." "Le Parti Ouvrier en France—Marseille," *Le Socialiste,* 12 February 1899.

166. "Le Parti Ouvrier en France—Lille: Conférence de Marquis de Morès," *Le Socialiste,* 26 December 1891. For the Guesdists' routing of Morès in subsequent anti-Semitic attempts to penetrate their bastions, see R. Byrnes, "Morès: The First National Socialist," *Review of Politics* 12 (1950): 358.

167. "Le Parti Ouvrier en France—Marseille," *Le Socialiste,* 12 February 1899.

168. E. Drumont, *La France juive* (Paris, 1886), 2: 3, cited in S. Wilson, *Ideology and Experience,* p. 351.

169. Georges Thiébaud, cited in S. Wilson, *Ideology and Experience,* p. 341. On the anti-Semites' anti-Marxist crusading, see S. Berstein, "La Ligue," in *Histoire des droites en France,* vol. 2, *Cultures,* ed. J.-F. Sirinelli (Paris: Gallimard, 1992), pp. 68, 78; and Sternhell, *La Droite révolutionnaire,* pp. 227–28.

170. E. Drumont, *Le Testament d'un antisémite* (Paris, 1891), p. 143, cited in S. Wilson, *Ideology and Experience,* p. 351. If such invective appears to contradict Drumont's occasional favorable references to Guesde, this merely demonstrates his characteristic inconsistency.

171. M. Barrès, "Socialisme et nationalisme," *La Patrie,* 27 February 1903, cited in Sternhell, "National Socialism and Anti-Semitism," p. 54. Sternhell elaborates on the incompatibility between Barrèsian "socialism" and "Jewish" Marxism in Z. Sternhell, "Barrès et la gauche: Du Boulangisme à *La Cocarde* (1889–1895)," *Mouvement Social,* no. 75 (1971): 121.

172. On Garnier's anti-Semitic anti-Marxism, see S. Wilson, *Ideology and Experience,* pp. 529 and 532. For the protofascist dimension of early Christian Democracy, see P. Nord, "Three Views of Christian Democracy in Fin de Siècle France," *Journal of Contemporary History* 19 (1984): 713–24; and A. Dansette, "The Rejuvenation of French Catholicism: Marc Sagnier's Sillon," *Review of Politics* 15 (1953): 34–52.

173. P. Biétry, "Les Propos du Jaune," *Le Jaune,* 5 October 1907, cited in Sternhell, *La Droite révolutionnaire,* p. 276, and see p. 287. There is an excellent discussion of the Jaunes's anti-Marxist anti-Semitism in E. Arnold, "Counter-Revolutionary Themes and the Working Class of France of the Belle Epoque: The Case of the Syndicats Jaunes, 1899–1912," *French History* 13 (1999): 117–19.

174. The Action Française's later flirtation with revolutionary syndicalism succumbed to the same logic. See E. Weber, *Action Française: Royalism and Reaction in Twentieth-Century France* (Stanford, Calif.: Stanford University Press, 1962), p. 76.

175. Joseph Sarraute, "Vienne aux antisémites," *Le Socialiste,* 13 October 1895. For a study that largely exonerates the POF of the common charge that they were implicitly or even explicitly anti-Semitic, see Cahm, "Le Mouvement socialiste face au nationalisme au temps de l'Affaire Dreyfus," p. 4.

176. B., "Nationalisme politique et nationalisme économique," *Le Socialiste,* 11–18 September 1904.

177. P. Lafargue, "Juifs et socialistes," *Le Cri du Peuple,* 2 October 1886.

178. Ibid.

179. See, for instance, Lafargue, "Les Juifs dans l'histoire européenne," *Le Socialiste,* 2 October 1898. For the Guesdists' appropriation of Jesus for socialism, see Stuart, "'Jesus the *Sans-Culotte*,'" pp. 713–14.

180. Paul Dramas, "Antisémites," *Le Socialiste,* 14 July 1895.

181. Dr. Z. (Pierre Bonnier), "Le Juif et la femme," *Le Socialiste,* 10 July 1892.

182. Ibid.

183. Paul Dramas, "Antisémites," *Le Socialiste,* 14 July 1895. "Wicked Jew" is explicitly a mocking of the anti-Semites. In fact, Dramas values these "bad" Jewish qualities exactly for creating the modernity so valued by Marxist socialists.

184. Dr. Z. (Pierre Bonnier), "Le Juif et la femme," *Le Socialiste,* 10 July 1892. Bonnier, with his scientific and medical pretensions, actually argues in this piece that Jews, through a process of "natural selection" founded upon their exclusion from manual labor and their specialization in "frontal brain" activities, were actually biologically superior to non-Jews—a weird (and potentially racist) inversion of anti-Semitic prejudice.

185. "L'Antisémitisme démasqué," *Le Socialiste,* 3 July 1892.

186. Paul Lafargue, "Juifs et socialistes," *Le Cri du Peuple,* 2 October 1886. For the reticence of French Jews toward socialism, see Marrus, *Politics of Assimilation,* pp. 132–33.

187. Silberner, "French Socialism and the Jewish Question," p. 37; and Lichtheim, "Socialism and the Jews," p. 331. It is not clear whether this "discovery" depended upon growing sociological awareness among French socialists—so that they finally noticed that many of France's Jews were not bankers, but instead worked as artisans in the Parisian garment and textile trades—or whether the mass migration from the Pale in the later nineteenth century created a highly evident Jewish proletariat, no less among Parisian garment workers than in London's East End. For the Jewish proletariat in France, see N. Green, "Eléments pour une étude du mouvement ouvrier juif à Paris au début du siècle," *Mouvement Social,* no. 110 (1980): 52; and N. Green, *Les Travailleurs immigrés juifs à la Belle Epoque: Le "Pletzl" de Paris* (Paris: Fayard, 1985).

188. The Guesdists attempted to backdate the Marxist discovery of the Jewish proletariat to Marx's vexing pamphlet "The Jewish Question," arguing that the seemingly anti-Semitic phrases in that work actually referred only to Jewish bankers, and that Marx knew full well that there was also a large and exploited Jewish proletariat. C. Bonnier, "La Question Juive," *Le Socialiste,* 12 February 1899. The pamphlet actually contains no such insight, Marx's own youthful experience and knowledge being confined to the bourgeois Jewish communities of the Rhineland and Netherlands.

189. Paul Lafargue, "Juifs et socialistes," *Le Cri du Peuple,* 2 October 1886.

190. J.M., "La Théorie des races," *L'Egalité,* 14 May 1882.

191. Ibid. For the very real conflicts between the largely assimilated French Jewish bourgeoisie and the largely Yiddish-speaking and immigrant Parisian Jewish working class, see Green, "Eléments pour une étude du mouvement ouvrier juif à Paris au début du siècle," p. 52.

192. Interpellation by Guesde, *Journal Officiel: Chambre des Députés,* 27 May 1895.

193. See, for instance, "Aux Antisémites," *Le Socialiste,* 2 September 1893.

194. Jules Guesde, "Antisémitisme et socialisme," *Le Socialiste,* 12 May 1895. It is worth stressing that anti-Semites were as hostile, if not more hostile, toward poor Jews as they were toward Jewish bankers. Verdès-Leroux, *Scandale financier et antisémitisme catholique*, p. 135.

195. For the most substantial instance of this illumination, see H. Phalippou, "Juifs de Russie," *Revue Socialiste* 24 (1899): 188–97.

196. "Appel aux hommes libres—Le Massacre de Kischineff," *Le Socialiste,* 10–17 May 1903.

197. See, in particular, the extended series "Les Juifs en Russie" presented in *Le Socialiste* on 31 December 1890, 7 January 1891, 4 February 1891, and 18 February 1891.

198. "Mouvement international—Russie," *Le Socialiste*, 17–24 May 1903.

199. Dr. Z. (Pierre Bonnier), "Le Juif et la femme," *Le Socialiste,* 10 July 1892. The French Right explicitly made the same connection between Jews, Marxism, and feminism, although with a very different valuation of the conjunction! R. Soucy, "Functional Hating: French Fascist Demonology between the Wars," *Contemporary French Civilization* 23 (1999): 170. For the Guesdists' sometimes radically feminist idea of revolution, see Stuart, "'Calm, with a Grave and Serious Temperament, Rather Male,'" p. 66.

200. "Aux Antisémites," *Le Socialiste,* 2 September 1893. In fact, the usual equations were "Israelites" for ethnic Jews, and "Jews" (or, rather, "jews") for financiers of whatever race or religion. The anonymous journalist here appears to have confused the categories.

201. C.B., "Question de race," *Le Socialiste*, 18 June 1899. It is worth noting that elements of the extreme Right made the same ideological distinction between good

and bad Jews, except in the opposite direction: defending bourgeois "French" Jews and attacking the "alien" Jewish working class. Soucy, "Functional Hating," p. 164.

202. S. Wilson, *Ideology and Experience*, p. 231. On the anti-Semites' "socialism," see S. Wilson, "The Anti-Semitic Riots of 1898 in France," *Historical Journal* 16 (1973): 804.

203. "La Semaine," *Le Socialiste*, 1 January 1899.

204. "Le Parti Ouvrier en France—Bordeaux," *Le Socialiste*, 25 December 1898.

205. J. Phalippou, "En Algérie," *Le Socialiste*, 20 November 1898.

206. Ibid.

207. "Le Parti Ouvrier en France—Mustapha," *Le Socialiste*, 7 July 1895.

208. "Le Parti Ouvrier en France—Nancy," *Le Socialiste*, 4 December 1898.

209. H. Ghesquière, "Le Socialisme en Algérie," *Le Socialiste*, 5–12 May 1901.

210. "La Semaine," *Le Socialiste*, 1 January 1899.

211. Given the insignificance of Zionism in France, there is little reference in the Guesdists' canon to Jewish nationalism. One of the Party's few references to "Sionism," however, identified it dismissively as "that faction favored by certain categories of Jews that tends to isolate them in a narrowly nationalist politics." Le docteur Cherechewski (identified as a member of the Parti Socialiste de France, the alliance of the POF and the Left Blanquists that preceded the founding of the SFIO), "Contre la Tsarisme, aux Mille Colonnes," *Le Socialiste*, 31 May–7 June 1903. On Guesdist opposition to particularistic Jewish organization within the labor movement itself, see the police report of 8 January 1900 in the file on the POF, AN F7 12.886. In welcoming Jewish workers who identified themselves primarily as socialists but rejecting Jews who identified themselves primarily in religious or nationalist terms, the Guesdists, as socialists, mirrored the French liberals who had established the "Rights of Man and the Citizen," and who had welcomed Jews into the French nation as individual citizens, but threatened their expulsion if they insisted on retaining their traditional exclusive identity. See G. Noiriel, "Français et étrangers," in *Les Lieux de Mémoire:* vol. 3, *Les France,* book 1, *Conflits et partages*, ed. P. Nora (Paris: Gallimard, 1992), p. 278.

212. For an exploration of the difference principle in the "politics of recognition," by an ostentatiously "former" Marxist, see C. Taylor, "The Politics of Recognition," in *Multiculturalism: Examining the Politics of Recognition*, ed. A. Gutman (Princeton, N.J.: Princeton University Press, 1994), pp. 25–73. Nancy Fraser has illuminated the clash between Marxism's commitment to universality and this post-Marxist commitment to "difference," including ethnic (and class?) difference. See N. Fraser, "From Redistribution to Recognition? Dilemmas of Justice in a 'Post-Socialist' Age," *New Left Review*, no. 212 (1995): 68–93; and N. Fraser, "Rethinking Recognition," *New Left Review*, n.s., no. 3 (2000): 107–20. Her debate with Iris Young further clarifies the issue. I. Young, "Unruly Categories: A Critique of Nancy Fraser's Dual Systems Theory," *New Left Review*, no. 222 (1997): 147–60; and N. Fraser, "A Rejoinder to Iris Young," *New Left Review*, no. 223 (1997): 126–29.

213. *Congrès international ouvrier socialiste, tenu à Bruxelles du 16 au 23 août 1891* (Brussels, 1893), p. 248. See, for an instance of condemnation, Winock, "La Gauche et les juifs," p. 19.

214. Birnbaum, *Anti-Semitism in France,* pp. 34–35.

215. B., "Le Procès Ahlwardt," *Le Socialiste,* 18 December 1892. The passage goes on to affirm that the POF "recognizes only two elements in society: capitalists and the proletariat."

216. For a defense of "positive racism," see P. Gilbert, *Peoples, Cultures and Nations in Political Philosophy* (Edinburgh: Edinburgh University Press, 2000), pp. 18–19.

217. There is a wise discussion along these lines in George Mosse's *Toward the Final Solution: A History of European Racism* (London: J. M. Dent, 1978), pp. 154–55. For the perverse possibility of an "anti-Semitic Zionism," a possibility actually embodied in Drumont, see Poliakov, *History of Anti-Semitism,* 4: 65. On the ways in which seemingly benign recognition of "difference" can be mobilized behind an exclusionary racism, see P.-A. Taguieff, "The New Cultural Racism in France," *Telos,* no. 83 (1990): 116–22.

6. "A Class of Madmen": Marxists Confront National Socialism

1. For the LdP as protofascist, see R. Soucy, *French Fascism: The First Wave, 1924–1933* (New Haven, Conn.: Yale University Press, 1986), pp. 1–4; and S. Payne, "Fascism in Western Europe," in *Fascism: A Reader's Guide,* ed. W. Laqueur (London: Penguin, 1979), p. 301.

2. On Barrès as protofascist, see R. Soucy, *Fascism in France: The Case of Maurice Barrès* (Berkeley: University of California Press, 1972); and also Z. Sternhell, "Strands of French Fascism," in *Who Were the Fascists? Social Roots of European Fascism,* ed. S. Larsen, B. Hagtvet, and J. Myklebust (Bergen: Universitetsforlaget, 1980), p. 479. For Drumont as a precursor of Nazism, see M. Winock, "Edouard Drumont et Cie," in *Edouard Drumont et Cie: Antisémitisme et Fascisme en France* (Paris: Seuil, 1982), pp. 35–36. The characterization of Morès as a protofascist may be found in P. Milza, *Fascisme français: Passé et présent* (Paris: Flammarion, 1987), pp. 82–83, and for his "doctrine du faisceau," A. Kaplan, *Reproductions of Banality: Fascism, Literature, and French Intellectual Life* (Minneapolis: University of Minnesota Press, 1986), p. xxviii. For an early, profound, and still influential statement of the French origins of fascism, see E. Nolte, *The Three Faces of Fascism: Action Française, Italian Fascism, National Socialism* (New York: Mentor, 1969), pt. 2, chap. 1. There is now a massive literature on the French origins of fascism, in contrast to the pre-1980 situation, when it was still possible to bemoan the gap in the literature, as does Steven Wilson in his "L'Action Française et le mouvement nationaliste français entre les années 1890 et 1900," *Etudes Maurassiennes* 4 (1980): 309. Since then, the distinguished work of Zeev Sternhell, in particular, has cast an intense light on the protofascist politics of fin de siècle France,

and has provoked both emulators and critics whose own works have further advanced our understanding. For a few of the critical discussions of Sternhell's contribution, see J. Bingham, "Defining French Fascism, Finding Fascists in France," *Canadian Journal of History* 24 (1994): 525–43; A. Costa Pinto, "Fascist Ideology Revisited: Zeev Sternhell and His Critics," *European History Quarterly* 16 (1986): 465–83; R. Soucy, *French Fascism: The Second Wave, 1933–1939* (New Haven, Conn.: Yale University Press, 1995), pp. 8–12; R. Wohl, "French Fascism, Both Right and Left: Reflections on the Sternhell Controversy," *Journal of Modern History* 63 (1991): 91–98; and, for a particularly insightful critique, albeit from an Italian perspective, D. Roberts, "How Not to Think about Fascism and Ideology, Intellectual Antecedents and Historical Meaning," *Journal of Contemporary History* 35 (2000): 185–211. The "birth of fascist ideology" was, of course, a pan-European phenomenon, but Sternhell is surely correct in arguing that France contributed to it, if not necessarily in suggesting that France initiated it.

3. S. Berstein, "La Ligue," in *Histoire des droites en France*, vol. 2, *Cultures*, ed. J.-F. Sirinelli (Paris: Gallimard, 1992), p. 68.

4. On "dialogical" method in ideology study, see K. Baker, "On the Problem of the Ideological Origins of the French Revolution," in *Modern European Intellectual History: Reappraisals and New Perspectives*, ed. D. LaCapra and S. Kaplan (Ithaca, N.Y.: Cornell University Press, 1982), pp. 200–203. For such a dialogical conceptualization of fascism, see C. Dandeker, "Fascism and Ideology," *Ethnic and Racial Studies* 8 (1985): 349–67. For its relevance to Left and Right in the French case, see J.-M. Donegani and M. Sadoun, "Les Droites au miroir des Gauches," in *Histoire des droites en France*, vol. 3, *Sociabilités*, ed. J.-F. Sirinelli (Paris: Gallimard, 1992), p. 759; and J. Julliard, "De l'Extrémisme à droite," *1900: Revue d'Histoire Intellectuelle* 9 (1991): 8.

5. A dynamic far more evident in the Marxist discourse of their period than in Marx and Engels's own work, given the rise of the "new nationalism" at the fin de siècle, according to E. Benner, *Really Existing Nationalisms: A Post-Communist View from Marx and Engels* (Oxford: Clarendon, 1995), p. 16. Dave Renton has argued that the Marxist theory of fascism indeed developed before the formal inauguration of fascism in 1919, but focuses upon Marx rather than upon the Marxists who actually engaged with the protofascists of the fin de siècle. D. Renton, *Fascism: Theory and Practice* (London: Pluto, 1999), p. 47. For Second International Marxism's self-defining engagement with the new ultranationalist Right, see G. Haupt, "Les Marxistes et la question nationale: L'Histoire du problème," in *Les Marxistes et la question nationale, 1848–1914*, by G. Haupt, M. Löwy, and C. Weill (Paris: François Maspero, 1974), p. 33; and M. Winock, "Socialisme et patriotisme en France (1891–1894)," *Revue d'Histoire Moderne et Contemporaine* 20 (1973): 377. For this dialectic from the opposite side, see R. Szporluk, *Communism and Nationalism: Karl Marx versus Friedrich List* (Oxford: Oxford University Press, 1988), chap. 12—which nonetheless completely ignores the relationship between the Guesdists and the French ultranationalists, while discussing Germany, Austria, Italy, and even Bulgaria!

6. Dr. Z. (P. Bonnier), "La Patrie," *Le Socialiste*, 25 August 1895.

7. "Dzim-Boum-Boum!" *Le Socialiste*, [21 August 1898].

8. Dr Z. (P. Bonnier), "Les Dégénérés," *Le Socialiste*, 26 September 1891.

9. J. Dunn, "Nationalism," in *Western Political Theory in the Face of the Future* (Cambridge: Cambridge University Press, 1979), p. 61.

10. J. Phalippou, "Au Cabinet," *Le Socialiste*, 5 March 1899.

11. "Patriotisme," *Le Socialiste*, 24 July 1886. More seriously, the Guesdists never ceased to remind the French of Déroulède's bloody role in the suppression of the Commune. For Déroulède and the Commune, see P. Rutkoff, *Revanche and Revision: The Ligue des Patriotes and the Origins of the Radical Right in France, 1882–1900* (Athens: Ohio State University Press, 1981), p. 23.

12. The spoof was lifted from *Le Journal*, and appears in "Les Patriotards," *Le Socialiste*, 25 March 1894. For the rather general tendency to laugh at Déroulède's posturing, see J.-C. Petitfils, *L'Extrème Droite en France* (Paris: Presses Universitaires de France, 1983), p. 13.

13. "Qui fait peur?" *Le Socialiste*, 30 July 1887.

14. Brunellière, "Le Héros de Fashoda," *Le Socialiste*, 11 June 1899. The article contains harrowing material on the Sudanese slave trade, and manifests indignant sympathy for "the unfortunate and inoffensive natives" supposedly being harvested by Marchand's commercial protégés.

15. Pierre Bonnier, "Nationisme [*sic*]," *Le Socialiste*, 3–10 February 1901. This insouciant attitude is strikingly paralleled by the initial Marxist attitude toward fascism during the early 1920s, when Mussolini could be portrayed as comic and Hitler as a fool. See, for instance, the material in R. Wistrich, "Leon Trotsky's Theory of Fascism," *Journal of Contemporary History* 11 (1976): 158.

16. See, for instance, PL, "La Défaite des patriotes," *Le Socialiste*, 3 October 1891. For the protofascists' pathetic attacks on the "intrusion" of German culture (not to mention German beer) into France, see J. Ziolkowski, "Le Nationalisme en France, 1890–1914," *Cahiers d'Histoire et de Politique International*, no. 7 (1987): 91–93.

17. For the "volkish" or even racist dimension of supposedly "civic" Republican nationalism, see Z. Sternhell, "The Political Culture of Nationalism," in *Nationhood and Nationalism in France from Boulangism to the Great War, 1889–1918*, ed. R. Tombs (London: HarperCollins Academic, 1991), pp. 30–32; and I. Ousby, *The Road to Verdun: World War I's Most Momentous Battle and the Folly of Nationalism* (New York: Jonathan Cape, 2002), pp. 230–40. On the Bonapartist "socialism" that survived into the Guesdists' period, see J. Rothney, *Bonapartism after Sedan* (Ithaca, N.Y.: Cornell University Press, 1969), pp. 92–101. Marx's musing are in *The Eighteenth Brumaire of Louis Bonaparte* [1851], in *Collected Works of Marx and Engels* (London: Lawrence and Wishart, 1979), 11: 148–50. The filiation between Bonapartism and the protofascism of the fin de siècle is affirmed (contre Rémond), in P. Burrin, "Le Fascisme," in *Histoire des droites en France*, vol. 1, *Politique*, ed. J.-F. Sirinelli (Paris: Gallimard, 1992), p. 625.

18. Petitfils, *L'Extrème droite en France*, pp. 41–42; and Z. Sternhell, *La Droite révolutionnaire 1885–1914: Les Origines françaises du fascisme* (Paris: Seuil, 1978), pp.

127–28. For the enormous impact of Rochefort, in particular, see R. Williams, *Henri Rochefort: Prince of the Gutter Press* (New York: Scribner, 1966). For the Blanquists and the Ligue des Patriotes, P. Rutkoff, "The Ligue des Patriotes: The Nature of the Radical Right and the Dreyfus Affair," *French Historical Studies* 8 (1974): 591. And, for the Blanquist evolution toward national socialism more generally, P. Hutton, *The Cult of the Revolutionary Tradition: The Blanquists in French Politics, 1864–1893* (Berkeley: University of California Press, 1981), pp. 157–59. For the national-socialist and anti-Marxist tendencies of some Independent Socialists, see M. Crapez, *La Gauche réactionnaire: Mythes de la plèbe et de la race* (Paris: Berg International, 1997), pp. 217–20.

19. For this indictment, see B.-H. Lévy, *L'Idéologie française* (Paris: Grasset, 1981), p. 126 (this tirade of a book is, throughout, a smear of the French Left as complicit with anti-Semitic nationalism). For a more defensible and more nuanced suggestion to the same end, see E. Cahm, "Le Mouvement socialiste face au nationalisme au temps de l'Affaire Dreyfus," *Bulletin de la Société des Etudes Jaurésiennes*, no. 79 (1980): 4.

20. See chapter 4. For the pervasiveness of this rhetoric of "blood and belonging" in France, on both Left and Right, see P. Sorlin, "Words and Images of Nationhood," in *Nationhood and Nationalism in France from Boulangism to the Great War, 1889–1918*, ed. R. Tombs (London: HarperCollins Academic, 1991), p. 78. Philippe Burrin's exhaustive study of the slippage from leftism toward the fascist Right between the wars further suggests the national-socialist potential in French "socialist nationalism." P. Burrin, *La Dérive fasciste: Doriot, Déat, Bergery, 1933–1945* (Paris: Seuil, 1986), p. 23. On this troubling phenomenon in general, see J. Schwarzmantel, "Class and Nation: Problems of Socialist Nationalism," *Political Studies* 35 (1987): 253; and E. Hobsbawm, *Nations and Nationalism since 1780: Programme, Myth, Reality* (Cambridge: Cambridge University Press, 1990), pp. 123–24, 145–46.

21. For the "totalitarianist" thesis in fin de siècle embryo by one of the most authorized spokesmen of French liberalism, see A. Leroy-Beaulieu, *L'Antisémitisme* (Paris, 1897), esp. p. 5. This contemporaneous perspective is illuminated in W. Irvine, *The Boulanger Affair Reconsidered: Royalism, Boulangism and the Origins of the Radical Right in France* (Oxford: Oxford University Press, 1989), pp. 169–70; and J.-P. Rioux, *Nationalisme et conservatisme: La Ligue de la Patrie Française* (Paris: Editions Beauchesne, 1977), p. 40. For scholarly studies written from the same perspective, see N. O'Sullivan, *Fascism* (London: J. M. Dent and Sons, 1983); and E. Weber, "Revolution, Counterrevolution, What Revolution?" in *Fascism: A Reader's Guide*, ed. W. Laqueur (London: Penguin, 1979), pp. 415–34. Commentary on such argument may be found in A. Gregor, *Interpretations of Fascism* (Morristown, N.J.: General Learning Press, 1974), chap. 7.

22. See, for instance, Paul Grados, "L'Autre presse," *Le Socialiste*, 1 July 1900.

23. *XVIe Congrès national du Parti Ouvrier Français tenu à Montluçon du 17 au 20 septembre 1898* (Paris, 1898), p. 48. For a particularly sophisticated instance of this Marxist conflation of liberalism and fascism, and one well-aware of the broader game being played by all sides (p. 8), see H. Marcuse, "The Struggle against Liberalism in the Totalitarian View of the State," in *Negations: Essays in Critical Theory* (London: Allen Lane, 1968), pp. 3–42.

24. For analysis of this fin de siècle confusion of Marxist socialism and liberal capitalism by the French Right, see J. Verdès-Leroux, *Scandale financier et antisémitisme catholique: Le Krach de l'Union Générale* (Paris: Editions du Centurion, 1969), p. 123.

25. The fin de siècle throughout Europe, in one analysis, was dominated by exactly such a tripartite competition between liberal democracy, Marxist socialism, and ultranationalism, with national patterns of alliances and enmities structured by the local state of play. In France, where the liberal democrats ruled, conjunctions between their socialist and nationalist enemies were to be expected. See the startling insights in R. Wiebe, *Who We Are: A History of Popular Nationalism* (Princeton, N.J.: Princeton University Press, 2002), chap. 3. That the polymorphous nature of the extreme Right empowered the liberals and Marxists' conflation of their other enemies with fascism and protofascism is argued in A. Wolfe, "Waiting for Righty: A Critique of the 'Fascism Hypothesis,'" *Review of Radical Political Economics* 5 (1973): 47–48.

26. See Lafargue to Engels, 27 May 1888, *Correspondence: Friedrich Engels and Paul and Laura Lafargue*, vol. 2 (Moscow: Foreign Language Publishing House, 1960), pp. 129–30. For discussion of the Lafargue/Engels disagreement, see G. Bottigelli, introduction to ibid., 1: xxvii; and R. Girault, introduction to *Paul Lafargue: Textes choisis* (Paris: Editions Sociales, 1970), pp. 64–68. There is an indictment of Lafargue for his supposed complicity with the Boulangists in M. Winock, *Nationalisme, antisémitisme et fascisme en France* (Paris: Seuil, 1990), p. 307. For a more nuanced analysis, see L. Derfler, *Paul Lafargue and the Flowering of French Socialism, 1882–1911* (Cambridge, Mass.: Harvard University Press, 1998), pp. 57–68.

27. For Boulangism as the seedbed of working-class socialism, see Z. Sternhell, *Maurice Barrès et le nationalisme français* (Paris: Fayard, 1972), p. 165. On Hugues, see Y. Lequin, "La Classe ouvrière," in *Histoire des droites en France*, vol. 3, *Sensibilités*, ed. J.-F. Sirinelli (Paris: Gallimard, 1992), p. 500. On Bordeaux, see P. Hutton, "The Impact of the Boulangist Crisis upon the Guesdist Party of Bordeaux," *French Historical Studies* 7 (1971): 226–44.

28. Cahm, "Le Mouvement socialiste face au nationalisme au temps de l'Affaire Dreyfus," p. 5. For Barrès' transient enthusiasm for the Guesdist leaders, see C. Doty, *From Cultural Rebellion to Counterrevolution: The Politics of Maurice Barrès* (Athens: Ohio State University Press, 1976), p. 94. On parliamentary alliances between the socialist Left and the national-socialist Right, see C. Doty, "Parliamentary Boulangism after 1889," *Historian* 21 (1970): 269; and Z. Sternhell, "Barrès et la gauche: Du Boulangisme à *La Cocarde* (1889–1895)," *Mouvement Social*, no. 75 (1971): 107.

29. *Le Socialiste*, 9 September 1900 (column 3, p. 1). See Biétry's letter of thanks, "Une Lettre," *Le Socialiste*, 21 October 1900, and the subscription opened in support of the arrested militant in *Le Socialiste*, 21 October 1900 (column 3, page 6). For Biétry's militant origins in the POF, see E. Arnold, "The Right Wing and the Working Classes: The Case of the 'Syndicats Jaunes' (1899–1912)," in *The Development of the Radical Right in France: From Boulanger to Le Pen*, ed. E. Arnold (London: Macmillan, 2000), p. 38.

30. On Zévaès, see Z. Sternhell, *Neither Right nor Left: Fascist Ideology in France* (Berkeley: University of California Press, 1986), p. 18. Hervé himself seems to have

been influenced by French Marxism during his early career, according to M. Loughlin, "Gustave Hervé's Transition from Socialism to National Socialism: Another Example of French Fascism?" *Journal of Contemporary History* 36 (2001): 10. On Vaugeois, see W. Buthman, *The Rise of Integral Nationalism in France* (New York: Columbia University Press, 1939), p. 257. For Vacher de Lapouge's early career in the POF, see G. Thuillier, "Un Anarchiste positiviste: Georges Vacher de Lapouge," in *L'Idée de race dans la pensée politique française contemporaine*, ed. P. Guiral and E. Témime (Paris: Editions du Centre National de la Recherche Scientifique, 1977), pp. 53–54. Jacques Julliard is surely correct, however, in arguing that national-socialist figures who repudiated the Left can hardly then implicate the Left in their national socialism. Julliard, "De l'Extrémisme à droite," p. 10.

31. E. Drumont, *Le Testament d'un antisémite* (Paris, 1891), p. 49, cited in S. Wilson, *Ideology and Experience: Anti-Semitism in France at the Time of the Dreyfus Affair* (London: Associated University Presses, 1982), p. 619. For discussion of this dimension of Drumont's thought, see Z. Sternhell, "The Roots of Popular Anti-Semitism in the Third Republic," in *The Jews of Modern France*, ed. F. Malino and B. Wasserstein (Hanover, N.H.: University Press of New England, 1985), p. 109; and R. Byrnes, *Anti-Semitism in Modern France: A Prologue to the Dreyfus Affair* (New York: Fertig, 1969), chap. 4. On the more general interpenetration of leftist and rightist anticapitalism, see R. Griffiths, "Anticapitalism and the French Anti-Parliamentary Right, 1870–1940," *Journal of Contemporary History* 15 (1978): 721–40; A. Rowley, "L'Economie et le marché," in *Histoire des droites en France*, vol. 3, *Sensibilités*, ed. J.-F. Sirinelli (Paris: Gallimard, 1992), pp. 381–419; and M. Flynn, "Royalist and Fascist Nationalism and National Socialism in France," *History of European Ideas* 15 (1992): 804–5.

32. P. Grados, "Plaies sociales," *Le Socialiste*, 20–27 November 1904.

33. E. Weber, *Action Française: Royalism and Reaction in Twentieth-Century France* (Stanford, Calif.: Stanford University Press, 1962), pp. 68–76; and M. Sutton, *Nationalism, Positivism and Catholicism: The Politics of Charles Maurras and French Catholics, 1890–1914* (Cambridge: Cambridge University Press, 1982), pp. 249–50. For the most sustained study of the AF's flirtation with anticapitalism, see P. Mazgaj, *The Action Française and Revolutionary Syndicalism* (Chapel Hill, N.C.: University of North Carolina Press, 1979), esp. chap. 2. On Bracconnier's movement, see G. Le Béguec and J. Prévotat, "L'Eveil à la modernité politique," in *Les Droites françaises: De la Révolution à nos jours*, ed. J.-F. Sirinelli (Paris: Gallimard, 1992), pp. 483–84. For Legitimist hostility to "Orleanist money-grubbers" and consequent proletarian enthusiasms, see Lequin, "La Classe ouvrière," p. 477.

34. E. Drumont, *La France juive* (Paris, 1886), cited in S. Wilson, *Ideology and Experience*, p. 251. There is an analysis of Drumont's quasi-Marxist distinction between producer and parasite in T. Anderson, "Edouard Drumont and the Origins of Modern Anti-Semitism," *Catholic Historical Review* 53 (1967): 39. An alignment between the POF and such anti-Semitic anticapitalism is asserted in S. Wilson, *Ideology and Experience*, pp. 252, 255; Sternhell, "Roots of Popular Anti-Semitism in the Third Republic," p. 109; and Byrnes, *Anti-Semitism in Modern France*, chap. 4; while the more gen-

eral congruence between socialist Left and reactionary Right in the critique of "alienation" is highlighted in P. Birnbaum, "Catholic Identity, Universal Suffrage and 'Doctrines of Hatred,'" in *The Intellectual Revolt against Liberal Democracy, 1870–1945*, ed. Z. Sternhell (Jerusalem: Israel Academy of Sciences and Humanities, 1996), p. 238.

35. J.-M. Mayeur, "Les Congrès nationaux de la Démocratie Chrétienne à Lyon (1896–1897–1898)," *Revue d'Histoire Moderne et Contemporaine* 9 (1962): 202.

36. *La Croix*, 27 January 1886, cited in P. Sorlin, *"La Croix" et les Juifs (1880–1899): Contribution à l'histoire de l'antisémitisme contemporain* (Paris: Grasset, 1967), p. 61.

37. M. Barrès, "Opprimés et humiliés," *La Cocarde*, 14 September 1894, cited in Sternhell, *Maurice Barrès*, p. 184.

38. M. Barrès, in *Le Courier de l'Est*, 22 January 1889, cited in M. Curtis, *Three against the Third Republic: Sorel, Barrès, and Maurras* (Princeton, N.J.: Princeton University Press, 1959), p. 187.

39. Barrès's Nancy Program, as cited in S. Wilson, *Ideology and Experience*, p. 436. For further discussion of this anticapitalist dimension of Barrès's thought, see V. Nguyen, "Un Essai de pouvoir intellectuel au début de la Troisième République: *La Cocarde* de Maurice Barrès (5 septembre 1894–7 mars 1895)," *Etudes Maurrassiennes* 1 (1972): 149.

40. C. Maurras, in the *Action Française* of 23 March 1908, cited in E. Weber, "Nationalism, Socialism, and National-Socialism in France," *French Historical Studies* 2 (1962): 277.

41. T. Maulnier, "Charles Maurras et le socialism," *Revue Universelle*, 1 January 1937, paraphrased in Weber, "Nationalism, Socialism, and National-Socialism in France," p. 277.

42. E. Drumont, *La France juive* (Paris, 1886), 1: 287, cited in S. Wilson, *Ideology and Experience*, p. 622.

43. E. Drumont, *De l'or, de la boue, du sang: Du Panama à l'anarchie* (Paris, 1896), p. 40, cited in S. Wilson, *Ideology and Experience*, p. 319. There is a startling presentation of Drumont as a quasi-Marxist socialist by a "Left-Drumontist" in E. Beau de Lomenie, *Edouard Drumont ou l'anticapitalisme national* (Paris: Pauvert, 1968).

44. M. Barrès, "Socialisme et nationalisme," *La Patrie*, 27 February 1903, cited in Z. Sternhell, "National Socialism and Anti-Semitism: The Case of Maurice Barrès," *Journal of Contemporary History* 8 (1973): 52. See the discussion of this social dimension of Barrèsian doctrine in Z. Sternhell, *The Birth of Fascist Ideology: From Cultural Rebellion to Political Revolution* (Princeton, N.J.: Princeton University Press, 1994), p. 11.

45. M. Barrès, "Le Flot qui monte," *Le Courier de l'Est*, 26 May 1889, cited in Sternhell, *Maurice Barrès*, p. 154. Sternhell explicitly links this rhetoric to the influence of France's Marxists on Barrès and his movement. Ibid., pp. 154–55.

46. Rioux, *Nationalisme et Conservatisme*, p. 33.

47. For such conjunction between national-socialist "ouvrierisme" and Marxist socialism, see Dandeker, "Fascism and Ideology," pp. 359–60. On the French national socialists' occasional priority to socialism over nationalism, see R. Griffiths, "From Nostalgia to Pragmatism: French Royalism and the Dreyfus Watershed," in *The Right in France, 1789–1997*, ed. N. Atkin and F. Tallett (London: Tauris, 1998), p. 121—an observation made with particular reference to the Ligue Antisémitique de France. National socialists, however, always sympathized with workers as victims, never, like the Marxists, as the heroic embodiment of a messianic future.

48. E. Drumont, *La Fin d'un monde* (Paris, 1889), pp. 25–26, cited in S. Wilson, *Ideology and Experience*, p. 366. There is a discussion of the conjuncture of Left and Right antiparliamentarianisms in K. Offen, *Paul de Cassagnac and the Authoritarian Tradition in Nineteenth-Century France* (New York: Garland, 1991), pp. 140–41, 178–79. For "democratic" antiliberalism, see P. Mazgaj, "The Origins of the French Radical Right: A Historiographical Essay," *French Historical Studies* 15 (1987): 295; and for this tradition dating to the early counterrevolutionaries, see Griffiths, "From Nostalgia to Pragmatism," pp. 119–21; and A. Hirschman, *Deux siècles de rhétorique réactionnaire* (Paris: Fayard, 1991), pp. 28–50.

49. J. Bainville, "Antidémocrates d'extrème gauche," *L'Action Française*, 15 July 1902, cited in Sternhell, *La Droite révolutionnaire*, p. 364. For scholarly attacks on this tacit alliance of socialists and national socialists against liberal democracy, see P. Birnbaum, *La France aux français: Histoire des haines nationalistes* (Paris: Seuil, 1993), pp. 90–91. Birnbaum also emphasizes the explicit similarity of this democratic antidemocracy as practiced by Guesdists and the Right in Birnbaum, "Catholic Identity, Universal Suffrage and 'Doctrines of Hatred,'" p. 240.

50. Paul Lafargue, "Nationalisme et socialisme," *Le Socialiste*, 27 May 1900. For Leroy-Beaulieu's unhappy expectations, see Winock, *Nationalisme, antisémitisme et fascisme*, pp. 195–96.

51. P. Bonnier and C. Bonnier, "La Crise du nationalisme," *Le Devenir Social*, nos. 11–12 (1897): 912.

52. M. Barrès, *Scènes et doctrines du nationalisme* (Paris, 1902), 1: 96, cited in T. Todorov, *On Human Diversity: Nationalism, Racism, and Exoticism in French Thought* (Cambridge, Mass.: Harvard University Press, 1993), p. 57. For the fundamental opposition between the universalist internationalism, if not cosmopolitanism, of the Left, and the exclusionary particularism of the Right's nationalism, see E. Cahm, *Péguy et le Nationalisme Français: De l'Affaire Dreyfus à la Grande Guerre* (Paris: Cahiers de l'Amitié Charles Péguy, 1972), pp. 10–18.

53. P. Levillain, "Les Droites en République," in *Les Droites françaises: De la Révolution à nos jours*, ed. J.-F. Sirinelli (Paris: Gallimard, 1992), p. 377.

54. A. Smith, *The Ethnic Origins of Nations* (Oxford: Blackwell, 1986). For the comparison of classes and nations *an sich* and *für sich*, see M. Canovan, *Nationhood and Political Theory* (Cheltenham: Edward Elgar, 1996), p. 8; and R. Suny, *The Revenge of the Past: Nationalism, Revolution and the Collapse of the Soviet Union* (Stanford, Calif.: Stanford University Press, 1993), chap. 1.

55. For an excellent analysis of the difference between an exclusive or hierarchical view of the nation and a pluralist and even "cosmopolitan" nationalism, see C. Calhoun, "Nationalism and Civil Society: Democracy, Diversity and Self-Determination," in *Social Theory and the Politics of Identity*, ed. C. Calhoun (Oxford: Blackwell, 1994), pp. 325–29. One suspects that any nationalist willing to accept Calhoun's irenic pluralism would be a postnationalist, in the same way that "Marxists" who have abandoned the primacy of class are best conceived as "post-Marxists."

56. This two-front war sustained by the "bourgeois republic" is illuminated in J. McClelland, *The French Right (From De Maistre to Maurras)* (London: Jonathan Cape, 1970), pp. 13–36; and P. Davies, *The Extreme Right in France, 1789 to the Present* (London: Routledge, 2002), p. 15. For the ways in which the Legitimist tradition foreshadowed protofascism and fascism, see I. Berlin, "Joseph de Maistre and the Origins of Fascism," in *The Crooked Timber of Humanity: Chapters in the History of Ideas* (New York: Knopf, 1991), pp. 91–174. Arguing that the national socialists repudiated the French Revolution may seem to be contradicted by Barrès's willingness to incorporate the First Republic into his historical mythology. It was the nationalism and militarism of the First Republic that he recuperated, however, not its ideological values. See Curtis, *Three Against the Third Republic*, pp. 82–83; and, for the ultra-Right and its appropriation of the First Republic's militarism and nationalism more generally, C. Amalvi, "Nationalist Responses to the Revolution," in *Nationhood and Nationalism in France: From Boulangism to the Great War, 1889–1918*, ed. R. Tombs (London: HarperCollins Academic, 1991), pp. 39–49.

57. There are hundreds of accounts of such embattled encounters in *Le Socialiste*. For a striking instance, see "Le Parti Ouvrier en France—Marne," *Le Socialiste*, 25 February 1900. Lafargue actually boasted, unfortunately falsely, that his party had driven the ultranationalists from the public arena! Lafargue to Engels, 26 January 1893, in *Correspondance: Friedrich Engels et Paul et Laura Lafargue* (Paris: Editions Sociales, 1956), 3: 248.

58. B. "Nationalisme politique et nationalisme économique," *Le Socialiste*, 11–18 September 1904. It has been claimed, wrongly in the case of the Guesdists, that it was not until the Dreyfus affair that socialism and national socialism became distinct and antagonistic movements. R. Wistrich, "French Socialism and the Dreyfus Affair," *Wiener Library Bulletin*, no. 28 (1975): 18.

59. See, for instance, Gabriel Bertrand, "Le Complot militaire," *Le Socialiste*, 16 October 1898.

60. P. Biétry, *Le Socialisme et les Jaunes* (Paris, 1906), p. 3, quoted in Arnold, "Right Wing and the Working Classes," p. 47.

61. J. Phalippou, "En Algérie," *Le Socialiste*, 20 November 1898.

62. A. Chebel d'Appollonia, *L'Extrème-Droite en France: De Maurras à Le Pen* (Brussels, Edition Complexe, 1988), p. 53.

63. For these alternatives in the French context, see P. Barral, "La Patrie," in *Histoire des droites en France*, vol. 3, *Sensibilités*, ed. J.-F. Sirinelli (Paris: Gallimard, 1992), pp. 109–15. They are developed as the fundamental distinction between Marxist

socialism and national socialism in M. Löwy, "Fatherland or Mother Earth? Nationalism and Internationalism from a Socialist Perspective," *Socialist Register*, 1989, pp. 213–14; and M. Neocleous, *Fascism* (Buckingham: Open University Press, 1997), chap. 2.

64. B. Joly, "The Jeunesse Antisémite et Nationaliste, 1894–1904," in *Nationhood and Nationalism in France: From Boulangism to the Great War, 1889–1918*, ed. R. Tombs (London: HarperCollins Academic, 1991), p. 148.

65. M. Barrès, *Contre les étrangers: Etude pour la protection des ouvriers français* (Paris, 1893), p. 13, cited in Sternhell, "National Socialism and Anti-Semitism," p. 53.

66. Jules Lemaître in the *Echo de Paris*, 8 May 1900, cited in D. Watson, "The Nationalist Movement in Paris, 1900–1906," in *The Right in France, 1890–1919*, ed. D. Schapiro (London: Chatto and Windus, 1962), p. 66. On Drumont, McClelland, *French Right*, p. 85.

67. "La Semaine," *Le Socialiste*, 9 October 1898.

68. This indiscriminate use of "socialist" to designate anyone opposed to absolute laissez-faire is still used by some historians to assert the "socialism" of the French ultranationalist Right. See Mazgaj, "Origins of the French Radical Right," pp. 300–301; and Weber, "Nationalism, Socialism, and National-Socialism in France," pp. 273–307, where difficulties in the usage are eventually dismissed with the comment that "socialism, in any case, has become a practically meaningless term" (p. 294).

69. S. Wilson, *Ideology and Experience*, pp. 329–30.

70. For Barrès's contrasting campaigns, see Sternhell, "National Socialism and Anti-Semitism," p. 55. On the Ligue's evolution, see P. Rutkoff, "Rémond, Nationalism and the Right," *Proceedings of the Fifth Annual Meeting of the Western Society for French History* 5 (1978): 295. For the Parisian comparison, see Watson, "Nationalist Movement in Paris," pp. 49–84.

71. J. Talmon, "The National Brotherhood and the International Confraternity: Nationalism and Socialism," in *The Unique and the Universal: Some Historical Reflections* (London: Secker and Warburg, 1965), p. 44.

72. A recent study of nationalist ideology as a "discourse of the sacred" (p. 97) uses Barrès as its exemplary case. P. Taminiaux, "Sacred Text, Sacred Nation," in *Text and Nation: Cross-Disciplinary Essays on Cultural and National Identities*, ed. P. Pfeiffer and L. Garcia-Moreno (Columbia, S.C.: Camden House, 1996), pp. 91–104. For the systematic idealism of nationalist thought, and the consequent difficulties Marxists have experienced in understanding its ramifications, see T. Nairn, "Scotland and Europe," in *Becoming National*, ed. G. Eley and R. Suny (New York: Oxford University Press, 1996), p. 86. There is an analysis of the ways in which a "spiritual revision" ("repudiation" would be a better characterization than "revision") of Marxist materialism, not least in fin de siècle France, led toward fascism in Z. Sternhell, "The 'Anti-materialist' Revision of Marxism as an Aspect of the Rise of Fascist Ideology," *Journal of Contemporary History* 22 (1987): 379–400.

73. On the primacy of politics as characteristic of "reactionary modernism," see J. Herf, *Reactionary Modernism: Technology, Culture, and Politics in Weimar and the Third*

Reich (Cambridge: Cambridge University Press, 1984), p. 2; and for its centrality to French fascism and protofascism, see Burrin, "Le Fascisme," p. 624. On the advocacy of this ideal by the Ligue des Patriotes, see Sternhell, "Paul Déroulède and the Origins of Modern French Nationalism," p. 63; for the Boulangists, see P. Seager, *The Boulanger Affair: Political Crossroads of France, 1886–1889* (Ithaca, N.Y.: Cornell University Press, 1969), p. 74; and for the 1890s national socialists and Bismarckian "state socialism," see Sternhell, *Maurice Barrès*, p. 169.

74. Paul Lafargue, "Le Socialisme chrétien et les sociétés anonymes," *Le Socialiste*, 26 March 1899. For Barrès's characterization of Marxism, see Sternhell, "Barrès et la Gauche," p. 121; and for Barrès' own "emotive" politics, see G. Putnam, "The Meaning of Barrèsisme," *Western Political Quarterly* 7 (1954): 165–71.

75. Paul Grados, "L'Autre presse," *Le Socialiste*, 1 July 1900. For the Barrèsians as "Conservative revolutionaries," see J.-M. Domenach, "Barrésisme et révolution conservatrice," in *Barrès: Une Tradition dans la modernité*, ed. A. Guyaux, J. Jurt, and R. Kopp (Paris: Champion, 1991), pp. 139–43. On the "Conservative revolution" in general and its relation to fascism and protofascism, see the discussion in M. Blinkhorn, "Allies, Rivals, or Antagonists: Fascists and Conservatives in Modern Europe," in *Fascists and Conservatives: The Radical Right and the Establishment in Twentieth-Century Europe*, ed. M. Blinkhorn (London: Unwin Hyman, 1990), pp. 1–13. For the intimate connections between the fin de siècle's ultranationalism and the traditional Right, see the classic, if now much-questioned, analysis in R. Rémond, *Les Droites en France* (Paris: Aubier-Montaigne, 1982), p. 167.

76. For this contrast in France between leftist historical optimism and the national socialists' pessimism and antimodernism, see Winock, *Nationalisme, antisémitisme et fascisme*, pp. 43–44. On the more general antipathy between nationalism and Marxism centered upon the saliency of past and future, see M. Guibernau, "Marx and Durkheim on Nationalism," in *Rethinking Nationalism and Ethnicity: The Struggle for Meaning and Order in Europe*, ed. H.-R. Wicker (Oxford: Berg, 1997), p. 79; and J. Rée, "Cosmopolitanism and the Experience of Nationality," in *Cosmopolitics: Thinking and Feeling Beyond the Nation*, ed. P. Cheah and B. Robbins (London: University of Minnesota Press, 1998), pp. 84–85. There is an explicit contrast between forward-looking Marxism and the nostalgia of most other French political traditions in R. Girardet, *Mythes et mythologies politiques* (Paris: Seuil, 1986), pp. 103, 117. Pierre Birnbaum suggests that the Guesdists joined the Right in this obsession with decadence, but is simply wrong. P. Birnbaum, *Jewish Destinies: Citizenship, State, and Community in Modern France* (New York: Hill and Wang, 2000), pp. 102–3.

77. M. Barrès, *Mes Cahiers*, 14: 74, cited in Sternhell, *Maurice Barrès*, p. 156. There are few hints in the vast Guesdist textual legacy of any romantic nostalgia for a medieval "Merrie France" equivalent to the Merrie England so popular with the British Left of the period. For a nostalgic medievalism among even British Marxists, see P. Ward, *Red Flag and Union Jack: Englishness, Patriotism and the British Left, 1881–1924* (Woodbridge: Boydell Press, 1998), pp. 5, 22–36.

78. M. Barrès, "Coup d'oeil sur la session parlementaire qui vient de finir," *Le Courier de l'Est*, 30 March 1890, cited in Sternhell, *Maurice Barrès*, p. 229. On the

Jaunes's anti-modernism, see Sternhell, *La Droite révolutionnaire*, pp. 296–99. For Marx on "reactionary socialism," see K. Marx and F. Engels, *Manifesto of the Communist Party* [1848], in Karl Marx and Frederick Engels, *Collected Works* (London: Lawrence and Wishart, 1976), 6: 507–8. The Guesdists followed this trope, quoting Engels to the effect that the new anti-Semitic Right was "a variety of feudal socialism that we must have nothing to do with." "L'Antisémitisme démasqué," *Le Socialiste*, 3 July 1892.

79. R. Girardet, *Le Nationalisme français, 1871–1914* (Paris: A. Colin, 1966), pp. 26–28; and P. Hutton, "Popular Boulangism and the Advent of Mass Politics in France, 1886–90," *Journal of Contemporary History* 11 (1976): 87.

80. For analysis of this uneasy synthesis between ultra-Conservative ideology and ultramodern technique in France, see Davies, *Extreme Right in France*, pp. 12–13; and, more generally, G. Eley, "What Produces Fascism: Preindustrial Traditions or a Crisis of the Capitalist State?" *Politics and Society* 12(1983): 53–82; and Herf, *Reactionary Modernism*, pp. 1–17. Herf is simply wrong, however, when he argues that "reactionary modernism" is one of the peculiarities of *German* history. Ibid., p. 10. For the contrary argument, see Kaplan, *Reproductions of Banality*, esp. pp. 25–28.

81. For the Proudhonian tradition in French national socialism, see J. Schapiro, "Pierre Joseph Proudhon: Harbinger of Fascism," *American Historical Review* 50 (1945): 714–37. For the ways in which anti-Semitic antimodernism distinguished Marx from Proudhon, see J. Talmon, *The Myth of the Nation and the Vision of Revolution: The Origins of Ideological Polarisation in the Twentieth Century* (London: Secker and Warburg, 1981), pp. 227–28. For Barrès on Proudhon, see E. Weber, "Inheritance, Dilettantism, and the Politics of Maurice Barrès," in *My France: Politics, Culture, Myth* (London: Belknap Press, 1991), p. 233n.33. For Drumont, see S. Wilson, *Ideology and Experience*, p. 332. For the Jaunes, see Sternhell, *La Droite révolutionnaire*, p. 286; and Arnold, "Right Wing and the Working Classes," p. 45. And for Sorel, see Sternhell, *Birth of Fascist Ideology*, p. 44.

82. J. Sarraute, "Vienne aux Antisémites," *Le Socialiste*, 13 October 1895.

83. Dr. Z., "Les Dégénérés," *Le Socialiste*, 26 September 1891.

84. The Guesdists, unfortunately, never seem to have attained genuine insight into nationalism's ability to combine archaism and ultramodernity; instead, they relentlessly indicted "integral nationalism" as *only* a residue of premodernity. For the ways in which nationalist "antimodernism" is nonetheless an integral part of modernity, see C. Taylor, "Nationalism and Modernity," in *Theorizing Nationalism*, ed. R. Beiner (Albany: SUNY Press, 1999), pp. 219–46. For a caustic deconstruction of Marxist blindness to this dialectic, see E. Traverso, "Auschwitz, Marx, and the Twentieth Century," in *Understanding the Nazi Genocide: Marxism after Auschwitz* (London: Pluto Press, 1999), p. 20.

85. J. Guesde, "L'Emeute de la Rue Cadet," *Le Socialiste*, 19 December 1891. Even Eugen Weber, seeking to equate Marxist socialism with national socialism, had to concede that class collaboration was "indeed a fundamental difference between the two systems." E. Weber, *Varieties of Fascism: Doctrines of Revolution in the Twentieth Century* (New York: Van Nostrand, 1964), p. 45.

86. For the fundamental distinction between class-conflictual Marxism and class-collaborationist nationalism in France, see B. Jenkins, *Nationalism in France: Class and Nation since 1789* (London: Routledge, 1990), p. 118. For the decisive separation during the 1880s between populists who viewed social conflict in terms of class and those who viewed it in terms of race, see the comments in E. Weber, "Gauls versus Franks: Conflict and Nationalism," in *Nationhood and Nationalism in France: From Boulangism to the Great War, 1889–1918*, ed. R. Tombs (London: HarperCollins Academic, 1991), p. 16. On the fundamental hostility of all nationalist ideology to any internal divisions of the "nation," see E. Gellner, *Culture, Identity and Politics* (Cambridge: Cambridge University Press, 1987), p. 10; P. Lekas, "The Supra-Class Rhetoric of Nationalism," *East European Quarterly* 30 (1996): 271–82; Talmon, "National Brotherhood and the International Confraternity," pp. 44–45; L. Greenfeld, *Nationalism: Five Roads to Modernity* (London: Harvard University Press, 1992), pp. 3–4; and J. Coakley, "The Social Origins of Nationalist Movements and Explanations of Nationalism: A Review," in *The Social Origins of Nationalist Movements: The Contemporary West European Experience*, ed. J. Coakley (London: Sage, 1992), p. 1.

87. There was an alternative position on the racist Right in which class divisions were real enough, but were manifest in the racial superiority of the ruling class and the racial inferiority of the poor—a position best theorized by Gustave Le Bon. This essentially "aristocratic" racism, however, was a poor instrument for a national-socialist politics aimed at seducing the working class—and thus became very rare at the fin de siècle. For Le Bon's racial class theory, see P.-A. Taguieff, *Le Couleur et le sang* (Paris: Editions Mille et Une Nuits, 1998), pp. 73–79.

88. Prochasson, "Les Années 1880," p. 70. For Morès and class collaboration, see S. Schwarzchild, "The Marquis de Morès: The Story of a Failure (1898–1896)," *Jewish Social Studies* 22 (1960): 17; on Biétry, see Mosse, "French Right and the Working Classes," pp. 199–200; on Sorel, see Sternhell, *Neither Right nor Left*, p. 17; and on Barrès, see Sternhell, "Barrès et la gauche," p. 84.

89. E. Drumont, *La Dernière Bataille* (Paris, 1890), p. 38, cited in S. Wilson, *Ideology and Experience*, p. 364.

90. Watson, "Nationalist Movement in Paris," p. 64.

91. For this useful distinction, see Todorov, *On Human Diversity*, pp. 231–32.

92. C. Maurras, "Sur le nom de socialiste," *L'Action Française*, 15 November 1900, p. 865, cited in Sternhell, *La Droite révolutionnaire*, p. 72. For the new Right's "revolution in favor of hierarchy," see S. Wilson, *Ideology and Experience*, p. 364; and for the violent antiegalitarianism of the new Right's "social science," see Taguieff, *Le Couleur et le sang*, p. 81.

93. Byrnes, "Morès," p. 341. For the aristocratic dimension of fin de siècle elitism, see M. Anderson, *Conservative Politics in France* (London: Allen and Unwin, 1974), pp. 136–37.

94. C. Maurras, *Dictionnaire politique et critique*, cited in Weber, "Nationalism, Socialism, and National-Socialism in France," p. 277.

95. E. Picard, *Synthèse de l'antisémitisme* (Paris, 1892), p. 43, cited in S. Wilson, *Ideology and Experience*, p. 266. Even such a convinced "totalitarianist" as A. James Gregor has recognized the radical difference between Marxism's sincere commitment to democracy and fascism and protofascism's antidemocratic ferocity. A. Gregor, *The Ideology of Fascism: The Rationale of Totalitarianism* (New York: Free Press, 1969), pp. 7–10.

96. Mermeix, *Les Antisémites en France: Notice sur un fait contemporain* (Paris, 1892), p. 42, cited in Sternhell, *La Droite révolutionnaire*, p. 203. The Parti Ouvrier detested the national socialists' conviction that they could solve the social question overnight simply by confiscating Jewish wealth. See, for an instance of Guesdist outrage, Alexandre Zévaès, "Antisémitisme et collectivisme," *Le Socialiste*, 23 September 1893. For a critique of attempts to present French national-socialist "socialism" as in any way anticapitalist, see J. Julliard, "Le Peuple," in *Les Lieux de mémoire*, vol. 3, *Les France*, bk. 1, *Conflits et partages*, ed. P. Nora (Paris: Gallimard, 1992), pp. 220–21; and Soucy, *French Fascism: The Second Wave*, pp. xiii–xix.

97. E. Drumont, *Le Testament d'un antisémite* (Paris, 1891), pp. x–xi, cited in S. Wilson, *Ideology and Experience*, p. 356.

98. "Déclaration," *Cahiers du Cercle Proudhon*, January–February 1912, cited in Sternhell, *Neither Right nor Left*, p. 25.

99. L. Greffier, *Petits conférences éducatives sur le socialisme* (Grenoble, 1904), p. 16. For Guesdism's self-definition through class conflict and through hostility to class collaboration, see R. Stuart, *Marxism at Work: Ideology, Class and French Socialism during the Third Republic* (Cambridge: Cambridge University Press, 1992), chap. 3.

100. J. Guesde, "Un Candidat Ouvrier," *Le Cri du Peuple*, 29 August 1885.

101. Biétry in *Le Jaune*, cited in S. Wilson, *Ideology and Experience*, p. 345.

102. "Mines et mineurs," *Le Socialiste*, 13 March 1886. For Laur's campaign, see Hutton, "Popular Boulangism," pp. 88, 101–2; and Sternhell, *Droite révolutionnaire*, pp. 67–68.

103. A. Gabriel, "La Participation aux bénéfices," *Le Courrier de l'Est*, 21 March 1891, cited in Sternhell, *Maurice Barrès*, p. 171. On profit sharing as a national-socialist class-collaborationist panacea, see Sternhell, *La Droite révolutionnaire*, pp. 289–90.

104. Sternhell, *Barrès*, p. 200n.3. On the "social fascist" theme in Marxist theory and polemic, see L. Ceplair, *Under the Shadow of War: Fascism, Anti-Fascism and Marxists, 1918–1939* (New York: Columbia University Press, 1987), chap. 4.

105. Resolution of the Congress of Montluçon, 1898. *XVIe Congrès national du Parti Ouvrier Français tenu à Montluçon du 17 au 20 Septembre 1898* (Paris, 1898), p. 36.

106. P. Lafargue, "Le Problème social," *Le Socialiste*, 2 September 1900. For the Guesdists' vision of utopia in more detail, see Stuart, *Marxism at Work*, pp. 479–89.

107. On the national-socialist repudiation of any challenge to private-property rights, see Sternhell, "Barrès et la gauche," pp. 85–87.

108. For critique of historians who have taken the national socialists' attacks on laissez-faire as proof of their "socialism," see Costa-Pinto, "Fascist Ideology Revisited," p. 479.

109. Massard, "Le Socialisme Bismarkien [*sic*]," *L'Egalité*, 15 January 1882.

110. Sternhell, *Maurice Barrès*, pp. 158; 161. For the national socialists' very infrequent questioning of large-scale industrial enterprise, see Rowley, "L'Economie et le marché," pp. 381–419.

111. P. Biétry, cited without attribution in S. Wilson, *Ideology and Experience*, p. 343.

112. M. Barrès, "Les Pères de 89," *Le Courrier de l'Est*, 10 August 1890, cited in Sternhell, "The Roots of Popular Anti-Semitism in the Third Republic," p. 109.

113. Michel Winock even suggests that what he describes as this "'anticapitalisme' de propriétaires" *necessitated* anti-Semitism as its corollary. Winock, "Edouard Drumont et Cie," p. 37. For this dichotomy between productive and unproductive capital as fundamental to fascist and protofascist "economic theory," see C. Maier, "The Economics of Fascism and Nazism," in *In Search of Stability: Explorations in Historical Political Economy* (Cambridge: Cambridge University Press, 1987), pp. 76–79. There is an analysis of this paradigm in France in P. Birnbaum, *Le Peuple et les gros: Histoire d'un mythe* (Paris: Grasset, 1979), pp. 15–26.

114. S. Wilson, *Ideology and Experience*, p. 269. For the increasing conflict between "national industry" and "cosmopolitan finance," see S. Elwitt, *The Making of the Third Republic: Class and Politics in France, 1868–1884* (Baton Rouge: Louisiana State University Press, 1975), p. 234. On industrialists' qualms about "international" finance, see P. Nord, "Social Defence and Conservative Regeneration: The National Revival, 1900–1914," in *Nationhood and Nationalism in France from Boulangism to the Great War, 1889–1918*, ed. R. Tombs (London: HarperCollins Academic, 1991), p. 214. For "free silver" and the ultra-Right, see Schwarzchild, "Marquis de Morès," p. 22.

115. E. Drumont, *La Fin d'un monde* (Paris, 1889), p. 39, cited in S. Wilson, *Ideology and Experience*, p. 623.

116. P. Biétry, *Le Socialisme et les Jaunes* (Paris, 1906), p. 14, cited in Sternhell, *Neither Right nor Left*, p. 50.

117. J. Morin, "Socialistes," *L'Antijuif*, 21 May 1899, cited in Sternhell, "Roots of Popular Anti-Semitism in the Third Republic," p. 113.

118. *La Croix*, 22 November 1894, cited in Sorlin, *"La Croix" et les juifs*, pp. 109–10.

119. Jacques de Biez of the National Anti-Semitic League, cited in F. Busi, *The Pope of Anti-Semitism: The Career and Legacy of Edouard-Adolphe Drumont* (Lanham, Md.: University Press of America, 1986), p. 92. See also V. Glasberg, "Intent and Consequence: The 'Jewish Question' in the French Socialist Movement of the Late Nineteenth Century," *Jewish Social Studies* 36 (1974): 64–65, who points out that one of the distinguishing features of anti-Semitic socialists such as Auguste Chirac was a focus upon "la féodalité financière" as the locus of exploitation, rather than upon capital as such.

120. Paul Lafargue, "Socialisme et patriotisme," *Le Socialiste*, 20 August 1887.

121. "La Bonne foi des antisémites," *Le Socialiste*, 15 January 1893.

122. Paul Lafargue, "La Finance," *Le Socialiste*, 5 February 1893.

123. B., "Anti Sémites," *Le Socialiste*, 7 May 1892.

124. A. Zévaès, "M. Drumont et le socialisme," *Le Socialiste*, 11 October 1893.

125. Recycling of a speech by Guesde made in 1892, "Duperie et réaction," *Le Socialiste*, 31 July 1898.

126. Jules Guesde, "Antisémitisme et socialisme," *Le Socialiste*, 12 May 1895.

127. See, for instance, the report of a speech by Guesde, "Antisémites et socialistes," *Le Socialiste*, 17 July 1892.

128. J. Guesde, "Duperie et réaction," *Le Socialiste*, 31 July 1898.

129. J. Guesde, "La Fin de la crise," *Le Citoyen*, 25 January 1882.

130. J. Guesde, "Duperie et réaction," *Le Socialiste*, 31 July 1898.

131. For the all-pervasiveness of conspiracy theories in the French political culture, see Girardet, *Mythes et mythologies politiques*, pp. 25–62; R. Tombs, *France, 1814–1914* (London: Longman, 1996), chap. 4; and D. Parry, "Articulating the Third Republic by Conspiracy Theory," *European History Quarterly* 28 (1998): 163–88. In fact, the Guesdists seem to have been much less liable to this affliction of the political imaginary than most of fin de siècle Paris's other political clans.

132. Jules Guesde, "Antisémitisme et socialisme," *Le Socialiste*, 12 May 1895 (italics in the original).

133. "La Question juive," *Le Socialiste*, 26 June 1892 (the text prefigures, sometimes in exactly the same words, the preceding reference).

134. See, for instance, Jules Guesde, "Pas d'illusion," *Le Socialiste*, 30 July 1887. It is a commonplace in the literature on French fascism and protofascism to dismiss both movements as representing "merely" traditional Bonapartism. See, for instance, P. Machefer, *Ligues et fascismes en France* (Paris: Presses Universitaires de France, 1974), pp. 7, 32. Such analysis underestimates the formidable protofascist force of the Bonapartist tradition.

135. Jules Guesde, "Pas d'illusion," *Le Socialiste*, 30 July 1887.

136. *Le Socialiste* serialized Edouard Fortin's translation of Marx's *Eighteenth Brumaire of Louis Bonaparte* during 1891. For Marxism's "Bonapartist" theory of fascism and protofascism, see J. Düffler, "Bonapartism, Fascism and National-Socialism," *Journal of Contemporary History* 11 (1976): 109–28; F. Adler, "Thalheimer, Bonapartism, and Fascism," *Telos*, no. 40 (1979): 95–108; and M. Kitchen, "August Thalheimer's Theory of Fascism," *Journal of the History of Ideas* 34 (1973): 67–78.

137. Paul Lafargue, "Nationalisme et socialisme," *Le Socialiste*, 27 May 1900.

138. Winock, *Nationalisme, antisémitisme et fascisme*, pp. 215–16. For critique of an exclusively "heteronomic" interpretation of fascism and protofascism, see M. Kitchen, *Fascism* (London: Macmillan, 1976), pp. x, 3, 81–82.

139. "L'Internationale jaune," *Le Socialiste*, 27 May 1900. On Leroy-Beaulieu's compromising association with the national socialists, see Sternhell, *La Droite révolu-*

tionnaire, p. 313. For the purchasing of nationalism by capital for the bourgeois politics of social defense, see the analysis in Nord, "Social Defence and Conservative Regeneration," pp. 210–28. On Biétry, see Lequin, "La Classe ouvrière," pp. 491–92; and Sternhell, *La Droite révolutionnaire*, pp. 249, 257. The financing of the Ligue des Patriotes is discussed in Sternhell, *La Droite révolutionnaire*, pp. 113–14.

140. Sternhell highlights this dilemma in his *Maurice Barrès*, pp. 160–61.

141. See, for instance, Bonnier, "Manque d'estomac," *Le Socialiste*, 7 January 1899, where Bonnier explicitly links the new Right to the old Right of Bonald and de Maistre. For Marxists identifying fascism not only as an instrument of reaction, but also of *antibourgeois* reaction, see J. Cammett, "Communist Theories of Fascism," *Science and Society* 21 (1967): 150.

142. Ch. Brunellière, "L'Antisémitisme à Nantes," *Le Socialiste*, 1 January 1899—an article that explicitly associates Nantes' ultranationalists with Brittany's Chouan tradition. There were, indeed, subterranean connections between national-socialist militancy and the court in exile. See Soucy, *French Fascism: The First Wave*, p. 5.

143. *XVIe Congrès national du Parti Ouvrier Français tenu à Montluçon du 17 au 20 septembre 1898* (Paris, 1898), p. 31. For the very real prominence of the traditional aristocracy among the supporters of the anti-Semites, see S. Wilson, "Le Monument Henry: Le Structure de l'antisémitisme en France, 1898–1899," *Annales: Economies, Sociétés, Civilisations* 32 (1977): 275.

144. Joseph Sarraute, "Vienne aux antisémites," *Le Socialiste*, 13 October 1895.

145. See for instance, Paul Lafargue, "L'Antisémitisme," *Le Socialiste*, 24 July 1898.

146. On Catholic ultranationalism, see E. Weber, "The Nationalist Revival before 1914," in *My France: Politics, Culture, Myth* (London: Belknap Press, 1991), p. 190.

147. M. Winock, "Edouard Drumont et l'antisémitisme en France avant l'Affaire Dreyfus," *Esprit* 39 (1971): 1098. For the linkage between Christian Democracy and anti-Semitic national socialism, see P. Birnbaum, "Affaire Dreyfus, Culture catholique et antisémitisme," in *Histoire de l'extrème droite en France*, ed. M. Winock (Paris: Seuil, 1993), p. 87. For the close links between the anti-Semites and French Catholic politics, see Wilson, "Ligue antisémitique française," p. 35; S. Wilson, *Ideology and Experience*, pp. 520, 524–32; P. Pierrard, *Juifs et catholiques français: De Drumont à Jules Isaac (1886–1945)* (Paris: Fayard, 1970); and P. Pierrard, "Antisémitisme de droite et de gauche au 19ème siècle et au début du 20ème siècle," in *Antisémitisme, hier et aujourd'hui* (Paris: Université de Paris–Sorbonne, 1983), p. 42.

148. Pierre Bonnier, "Nationisme [*sic*]," *Le Socialiste*, 3–10 February 1901. For the Left's paranoia about "clerical conspiracy," see B. Jenkins, "Religion and Nationalism in Late Nineteenth-Century France," in *Problems in French History*, ed. M. Cornick and C. Crossley (London: Palgrave, 2000), pp. 104–24. This study also illuminates the very real connections between French Catholicism and the new ultranationalism of the fin de siècle.

149. B. "Nationalisme," *Le Socialiste*, 28 August 1898.

150. For analysis of protofascism as a continuation of traditional Conservatism in a modern context, see B. Moore, *The Social Origins of Dictatorship and Democracy* (Boston: Beacon Press, 1967), pp. 446–54; J. Weiss, *The Fascist Tradition: Radical Right-Wing Extremism in Modern Europe* (New York: Harper and Row, 1967), pp. 9–30; and A. Mayer, *The Persistence of the Old Regime: Europe to the Great War* (London: Croom Helm, 1981), pp. 299–305. For this transition from the traditionalist Right to ultranationalism in the French context, see W. Irvine, "Royalists and the Politics of Nationalism," in *Nationhood and Nationalism in France from Boulangism to the Great War, 1889–1918*, ed. R. Tombs (London: HarperCollins Academic, 1991), p. 117; and Le Béguec and Prévotat, "L'Eveil à la modernité politique," esp. pp. 384–85.

151. See, for instance, C., "Dictature," *Le Socialiste*, 3 March 1899 for bourgeois bankruptcy in favor of reaction; and "Arche-Sainte," *Le Socialiste*, 30 December 1893, for the reactionaries' rapprochement with the bourgeoisie. For the bourgeoisie's "conversion" of the time, see E. Tannenbaum, "The Myth of Counterrevolution in France, 1870–1914," in *Ideas in History*, ed. R. Herr and H. Parker (Durham, N.C.: Duke University Press, 1965), p. 272.

152. See, for instance, "M. Déroulède, agent russe," *Le Socialiste*, 23 October 1886.

153. "La Semaine," *Le Socialiste*, 11 September 1892.

154. "La Question juive," *Le Socialiste*, 26 June 1892.

155. For the membership of the League, see Sternhell, *Droite révolutionnaire*, p. 96. For that of the POF, see C. Willard, *Le Mouvement socialiste en France (1893–1905): Les Guesdistes* (Paris: Editions Sociales, 1965), p. 91. Impressed by the same figures, historians have increasingly agreed that the anti-Semitic protofascism of the fin de siècle deserves a nonreductive etiology that might explain its popular appeal. Some suggest that it was a "natural" response to the disorientation and anomie of the new society created by the "second industrial revolution"; others that it was an equally natural response to the economic distress of the "Great Depression" that devastated France during the 1880s and well into the 1890s. For the "anomic" interpretation, see, in particular, the suggestions of Steven Wilson in his "The Anti-Semitic Riots of 1898 in France," *Historical Journal* 16 (1973): 801. For the attribution to the Great Depression, see J.-G. Duroselle, "L'Antisémitisme en France de 1886 à 1914," *Cahiers Paul Claudel* 7 (1968): 54–55.

156. B., "Nationalisme," *Le Socialiste*, 28 August 1898.

157. Ibid.

158. "L'Internationalisme de la science," *Le Socialiste*, 26 June 1886.

159. B., "Les Etudiants," *Le Socialiste*, 9 April 1892.

160. M. Barrès, "La Glorification de l'énergie," *La Cocarde*, 19 December 1894, cited in Sternhell, *La Droite révolutionnaire*, p. 64.

161. R. Soucy, "Barrès and Fascism," *French Historical Studies* 5 (1967): 68.

162. "Honneur à Grenoble!" *Le Socialiste*, 28 May 1899. For Marx's attribution of popular Bonapartism to the lumpenproletariat, see K. Marx, *The Eighteenth Brumaire of Louis Bonaparte* [1851], in *Collected Works*, by Karl Marx and Frederick Engels (London: Lawrence and Wishart, 1979), 11: 148–49. For the usefulness of the lumpenproletariat to Marxist apologetics, see F. Bovenkerk, "The Rehabilitation of the Rabble: How and Why Marx and Engels Wrongly Depicted the Lumpenproletariat as a Reactionary Force," *Netherlands Journal of Sociology* 20 (1984): 13–41.

163. B., "Noël anarchiste," *Le Socialiste*, 30 December 1893—a scathing commentary on a newspaper article by Barrès praising the criminal culture of Montmartre. For workers' hatred of the underclass, see M. Perrot, *Les Ouvriers en grève: France, 1871–1890* (Paris: Mouton, 1974), 2: 546. For the nationalist proclivities of Montmartre's demimonde, see P. Nord, *Paris Shopkeepers and the Politics of Resentment* (Princeton, N.J.: Princeton University Press, 1986), p. 334.

164. For this derogatory usage (with servants characterized as "parasites of parasites"), see, for instance, P. Lafargue, "Caractère fatidique des misères prolétariennes," *Le Socialiste*, 18–25 September 1898. On servants and anti-Semitism, see S. Wilson, "Le Monument Henry," p. 272; on Yellow unions, see Sternhell, *La Droite révolutionnaire*, p. 312; and on servants' social significance, see P. Codaccioni, *De l'Inégalité sociale dans une grande ville industrielle: Le Drame de Lille de 1850 à 1914* (Lille: Université de Lille, 1976), pp. 205–6.

165. M. Perrot, "On the Formation of the French Working Class," in *Working Class Formation: Nineteenth-Century Patterns in Western Europe and the United States*, ed. I. Katznelson and A. Zolberg (Princeton, N.J.: Princeton University Press, 1986), pp. 98–99.

166. Bonnier, "Une Interpellation," *Le Socialiste*, 1 January 1899. For a similar attribution of today's "ethnic nationalism" to "peasant backwardness," see T. Nairn, "The Curse of Rurality: Limits of Modernisation Theory," in *The State of the Nation: Ernest Gellner and the Theory of Nationalism*, ed. J. Hall (Cambridge: Cambridge University Press, 1998), pp. 107–34.

167. "L'Antisémitisme en Allemagne," *Le Socialiste*, 11 November 1893.

168. For the Marxist tradition of viewing rural life in terms of "idiocy," see H. Mayer, "Marx, Engels and the Politics of the Peasantry," *Cahiers de l'Institut de Science Economique Appliquée*, no. 102 (1960): 91–152. For a Marxist who was fully aware of the authenticity of the "nonsynchronous" rural mentality, and of Marxism's failure to engage with and appropriate its force, consider Ernst Bloch as discussed in A. Rabinbach, "Unclaimed Heritage: Ernst Bloch's *Heritage of Our Times* and the Theory of Fascism," *New German Critique*, no. 11 (1977): esp. pp. 6 and 13. On the Yellow unions and farm laborers, see Sternhell, *La Droite révolutionnaire*, pp. 250–51. The "grounding" of nationalist ideology in general within the peasantry is discussed in Lekas, "The Supra-Class Rhetoric of Nationalism," p. 274; while, for the French case, see H. Lebovics, "Creating the Authentic France: Struggles over French Identity in the First Half of the Twentieth Century," in *Commemorations: The Politics of National Identity*, ed. J. Gillis (Princeton, N.J.: Princeton University Press, 1994), p. 241. Fortunately, the French anti-Semitic Right ultimately failed to mobilize peasant society. M. Burns,

Rural Society and French Politics: Boulangism and the Dreyfus Affair, 1886–1900 (Princeton, N.J.: Princeton University Press, 1984), pp. 160–65.

169. Petit-bourgeois xenophobia is highlighted in G. Noiriel, *Le Creuset français: Histoire de l'immigration, XIXe–XXe siècles* (Paris: Seuil, 1988), p. 272; and Nord, *Paris Shopkeepers and the Politics of Resentment*, pp. 325–28.

170. "Le Parti Ouvrier à l'étranger—Autriche," *Le Socialiste*, 15 April 1891. There is an analysis of this Marxist relegation of anti-Semitism to national backwardness in E. Traverso, *The Marxists and the Jewish Question: The History of a Debate (1843–1943)* (Atlantic Highlands, N.J.: Humanities, 1990), esp. pp. 232–33. For the French petite bourgeoisie and its growing attraction to anti-Semitism during the 1890s, see Nord, *Paris Shopkeepers and the Politics of Resentment*, pp. 372–92.

171. Paul Dramas, "Antisémites," *Le Socialiste*, 14 July 1895. The article explicitly contrasts France with Germany, where there were "still vestiges of feudalism," and which had "failed its bourgeois revolution." Guesdists seemed to believe in the German *Sonderweg*.

172. Charles Bonnier, "L'Exposition," *Le Socialiste*, 26 February 1899.

173. For this argument, see Jenkins, *Nationalism in France*, p. 91. The divergent trajectories of these two components of "the people" may be traced to the rupture point constituted by the Boulanger affair. See the argument in Nord, *Paris Shopkeepers and the Politics of Resentment*, chap. 7, and for the move by the petite bourgeoisie toward the extreme Right during the decisive 1890s, chaps. 8–9. It has been suggested that ultranationalism has come to serve the petite bourgeoisie as socialism has served the proletariat: as an indispensable basis for class solidarity. V. Kiernan, "Nationalist Movements and Social Classes," in *Nationalist Movements*, ed. A. Smith (New York: Macmillan, 1976), p. 112; and Talmon, *Myth of the Nation and the Vision of Revolution*, pp. 12–13.

174. Wilson, *Ideology and Experience*, p. 288. Guesdists occasionally attributed the anti-Semitic campaign against Jewish commerce to exactly such wealthy Catholic retailers, whose motives supposedly "were to hike their own dividends" with a "crusade against Jewish stores." Report of a speech by Charles Brunellière, "Le Parti Ouvrier en France," *Le Socialiste*, 26 March 1899.

175. M. Barrès, *L'Appel au Soldat*, cited in Sternhell, *Maurice Barrès*, p. 239.

176. Adrien Poccaron, police report APP B/a 1107, 31 March 1898, cited in Nord, *Paris Shopkeepers and the Politics of Resentment*, pp. 382–83.

177. On Guérin as exemplifying the national-socialist petit bourgeois, see Sternhell, *La Droite révolutionnaire*, p. 220; and on the LAF and the petite bourgeoisie, see Wilson, "Ligue antisémitique française," p. 34. For the LdP, see Y.-M. Hilaire, "1900–1945: L'Ancrage des idéologies," in *Histoire des droites en France*, vol. 1, *Politique*, ed. J.-F. Sirinelli (Paris: Gallimard, 1992), p. 523.

178. S. Wilson, *Ideology and Experience*, p. 282.

179. "A l'Etranger—Allemagne," *Le Socialiste*, 16 June 1894.

180. Ibid.

181. For socialist consumer cooperatives as impelling petit-bourgeois Rightism, see M. Rebérioux, "Les Socialistes français et le petit commerce au tournant du siècle," *Mouvement Social*, no. 114 (1981): 67–69; P. Nord, "Le Mouvement des petits commerçants et la politique en France de 1888 à 1914," *Mouvement Social*, no. 114 (1981): 45; and D. Gordon, "Liberalism and Socialism in the Nord: Eugène Motte and Republican Politics in Roubaix, 1898–1912," *French History* 3 (1989): 316, 320, 324. For the more generalized antisocialism of this stratum, H.-G. Haupt, "The Petite Bourgeoisie in France, 1850–1914: In Search of the *Juste Milieu*," in *Shopkeepers and Master Artisans in Nineteenth-Century Europe*, ed. G. Crossick and H.-G. Haupt (London: Methuen, 1984), pp. 98–101; and Nord, *Paris Shopkeepers and the Politics of Resentment*, pp. 81–82, 268, 363.

182. Ch. Brunellière, "L'Antisémitisme à Nantes," *Le Socialiste*, 1 January 1899. Note the assumption that workers were male.

183. J. Guesde, *Le Collectivisme* (Lille, 1891), p. 13.

184. "La Petite bourgeoisie," *Le Socialiste*, 9 October 1886. This Marxist hostility to small business certainly helped turn the petite bourgeoisie toward the Right. Nord, *Paris Shopkeepers and the Politics of Resentment*, pp. 361–64.

185. Charles Bonnier, "L'Exposition," *Le Socialiste*, 26 February 1899.

186. Charles Bonnier, "Opposition," *Le Socialiste*, 3 June 1900. There are startling parallels at times, as in this case, between Guesdist interpretation and that of Trotsky when he was confronted by petit-bourgeois fascism. See M. Kitchen, "Trotsky and Fascism," *Social Praxis* 2 (1975): 120–21.

187. On Marx's forebodings, see Benner, *Really Existing Nationalism*, p. 215. For a late instance of Marxist denial of any potential for working-class fascism, see T. Eagleton, "What is Fascism?" *New Blackfriars* 57 (1976): 106; and for that of the Third International, see A. Mayer, *Dynamics of Counterrevolution in Europe, 1870–1956: An Analytic Framework* (New York: Harper and Row, 1971), p. 17. Only the Austro-Marxists, with characteristic theoretical acuity, seem to have seriously analyzed working-class ultranationalism. See G. Botz, "Austro-Marxist Interpretations of Fascism," *Journal of Contemporary History* 11 (1976): 136–37. There are critiques of Marxism for diverting attention from "authentic" working-class racism in E. Balibar, "Class Racism," in *Race, Nation, Class: Ambiguous Identities*, by E. Balibar and I. Wallerstein (London: Verso, 1991), p. 207; and from ultranationalism in G. Kitching, "Nationalism: The Instrumental Passion," *Capital and Class* 29 (1985): 99.

188. M. Barrès, *Mes Cahiers*, cited in Sternhell, "National Socialism and Anti-Semitism," p. 52.

189. Placarded in Le Mans, February 1898, in S. Wilson, *Ideology and Experience*, p. 682. There seems to have been a national campaign. Michael Burns reports much the same kind of placard in the Marne. Burns, *Rural Society and French Politics*, p. 138.

190. For the genuinely proletarian dimension of prewar protofascism, see Milza, *Fascisme français*, pp. 83–87; and Arnold, "Right Wing and the Working Classes," pp.

34–35. Winock argues that the radical Right has only been able to gain momentum if it makes inroads into the working-class clientele of the Left. M. Winock, "Socialism and Boulangism, 1887–89," in *The Development of the Radical Right in France: From Boulanger to Le Pen*, ed. E. Arnold (London: Macmillan, 2000), p. 14.

191. Lequin, "La Classe ouvrière," pp. 505, 479–80; for the best statement of the importance of the Jaunes within working-class politics, see E. Arnold, "Counter-Revolutionary Themes and the Working Class in France of the Belle Epoque: The Case of the Syndicats Jaunes, 1899–1912," *French History* 13 (1999): 110–11. On the class relations of La Villette, see Nord, *Paris Shopkeepers and the Politics of Resentment*, pp. 388–90. For deference and aspiration among French workers as empowering the ultranationalists, see Berstein, "La Ligue," p. 84. There is a discussion of the theoretical logic leading to such working-class anti-Marxist nationalism in J. Ehrenreich, "Socialism, Nationalism and Capitalist Development," *Review of Radical Political Economics* 15 (1983): 1–42. For reactionary corporatist nostalgia among French workers, see Sternhell, *Droite révolutionnaire*, pp. 298–99; and Milza, *Fascisme français*, pp. 83–87. On the ultras' challenge to the Guesdists in working-class Lille, see Byrnes, *Anti-Semitism in Modern France*, p. 254; and for Méry's Ligue, see Mosse, "French Right and the Working Classes," p. 190. On the geography of working-class national socialism in Paris, see Watson, "Nationalist Movement in Paris," pp. 74–76.

192. L. Berlanstein, "Parisian White-Collar Employees and Nationalism in the Belle Epoque," in *Nationhood and Nationalism in France from Boulangism to the Great War, 1889–1918*, ed. R. Tombs (London: HarperCollins Academic, 1991), pp. 159–67.

193. Joseph Sarraute, "Vienne aux antisémites," *Le Socialiste*, 13 October 1895.

194. Jules Guesde, "Antisémitisme et socialisme," *Le Socialiste*, 12 May 1895.

195. This question has obsessed scholars working on fascism and protofascism. There is an impressive series of answers collected in *Who Were the Fascists? Social Roots of European Fascism*, ed. S. Larsen, B. Hagtvet, and J. Myklebust (Bergen: Universitetsforlaget, 1980).

196. For the class polyvalence of nationalism as a challenge to Marxism, see Lekas, "Supra-Class Rhetoric of Nationalism," p. 271; and for this point in a French context, S. Hoffmann, "The Nation: What For? Vicissitudes of French Nationalism, 1871–1973," in *Decline or Renewal? France since the 1930s* (New York: Viking Press, 1974), p. 409. William Sheridan Allen repudiates class analysis on exactly these grounds in "Farewell to Class Analysis in the Rise of Nazism," *Central European History* 17 (1984): 54–62.

197. There have been a number of recent arguments in favor of such a complex class analysis of nationalism and ultranationalism. For theoretical discussion, see N. Poulantzas, *State, Power, Socialism* (London: New Left Books, 1978), p. 115; N. Poulantzas, "A Propos de l'impact populaire du fascisme," in *Eléments pour une analyse du fascisme*, ed. M. Macciocchi (Paris: Union Générale des Editions, 1976), pp. 18–24; M. Dunn, "Marxism and the National Question," *Arena*, no. 40 (1975): 31–32; and B. Berberoglu, "Nationalism, Class Conflict and Social Transformation in the Twentieth Century," *International Review of Modern Sociology* 29 (1999): 80. And, as applied in

the French case, see G. Noiriel, "La Question nationale comme objet de l'histoire sociale," *Genèses*, no. 4 (1991): 93.

198. D. Beetham, ed., *Marxists in the Face of Fascism: Writings by Marxists on Fascism from the Inter-War Period* (Totowa, N.J.: Barnes and Noble, 1984).

Conclusion

1. M. Freitag, "Théorie Marxiste et question nationale: Autopsie d'un malentendu," *Pluriel-Débat*, no. 26 (1981): 3.

2. Karl Marx and Frederick Engels, *Manifesto of the Communist Party* [1848], in *Collected Works* (London: Lawrence and Wishart, 1976), 6: 487–88.

3. For three alternative practices vis-à-vis ethnicity available to socialism (namely, socialist cosmopolitanism, socialist nationalism, and managing national labor for international capital), see C. Vogler, *The Nation State: The Neglected Dimension of Class* (Aldershot: Gower, 1985), pp. 24–36 (Vogler misses the national-socialist option of managing national labor for *national* capital). Guesdists, of course, never imagined Vogler's third alternative, that is, managing national labor for international capital—and would have been utterly dismayed if they had foreseen Tony Blair and his fellow "Third Way" management specialists.

4. There is a good depiction of Communist vacillations over the "national question" in D. Caute, *Communism and the French Intellectuals, 1914–1960* (London: Deutsch, 1964), pp. 197–201.

5. For the possibility of such a "national cosmopolitanism," see C. Calhoun, "Nationalism and Civil Society: Democracy, Diversity and Self-Determination," in *Social Theory and the Politics of Identity*, ed. C. Calhoun (Oxford: Blackwell, 1994), pp. 325–29.

6. Meghnad Desai's *Marx's Revenge: The Resurgence of Capitalism and the Death of Statist Socialism* (London: Verso, 2002) is an extended "thought experiment" along these lines.

Appendix A

1. For a forceful statement of the continuing utility of the Left-Right differential, and of its historical foundation in the ongoing war between egalitarians and anti-egalitarians, see N. Bobbio, *Left and Right: The Significance of a Political Distinction* (Cambridge: Polity, 1996). There is a similar argument applied to France in G. Rossi-Landi, *Le Chassé croisé: La Droite et la gauche en France de 1789 à nos jours* (Paris: Lattès, 1978), esp. pp. 191–201.

2. There is a impassioned defense of terminological clarity in ideological discourse, with particular reference to the meaning of "liberal," in The Editors, "There's a

word for that, and we want it back," *Economist*, 6 November 2004. This urging by today's foremost journal of global liberalism parallels the usages advocated in this appendix.

3. Thereby making it extraordinarily difficult to "think" the great post-1789 distinction between Left and Right (a distinction either denied altogether in these lands of liberal monoculture) or (given the absence of a surviving Conservative tradition) limited to an impoverished dichotomy between a liberal "Right" (a nonsense denomination for long-term and comparative historical understanding) and a residual socialist Left.

4. S. Holmes, *The Anatomy of Antiliberalism* (Cambridge, Mass.: Harvard University Press, 1993).

5. Alternatively, Conservatives might be conceived of as "counterrevolutionaries," but only if "revolution" is assumed to be always on the Left—a comforting assumption, no doubt, for the more radical among liberals and socialists, but one that is not very useful for comparative historical understanding. "Revolution" is best understood simply as the overthrow of an established political order, even if that established political order is liberal (Weimar in 1933, with its "Nazi revolution") or socialist (Czechoslovakia in 1989, with its "Velvet Revolution").

6. A characterization urged by George Mosse in his "Toward a General Theory of Fascism," in *Masses and Man: Nationalist and Fascist Perceptions of Reality* (New York: H. Fertig, 1980), p. 164; and Eugen Weber in his *Varieties of Fascism: Doctrines of Revolution in the Twentieth Century* (New York: Van Nostrand, 1964), p. 25. The term is both premonitory, linking "la terre et les morts" to "blood and soil," and substantive, indicating the movement's nationalist populism.

7. This study rejects the silly idea that there could be no fascism before Mussolini used the term in 1919. As if there was no liberalism before the Spanish civil wars of the early nineteenth century first popularized the word! Or as if no one could have died of AIDS before virologists designated the disease.

8. As suggested, albeit without reference to the traumas of 1871, in E. Nolte, *The Three Faces of Fascism: Action Française, Italian Fascism, National Socialism* (New York: Mentor, 1969), pt. 2, chap. 1. The conceptual and terminological clarifications above should make it clear why this study accepts the "Sternhell thesis" on France's protofascist precocity, albeit without accepting other aspects of Sternhell's work (Germanic Central Europe, pace Sternhell, had its protofascists, for instance).

Bibliography

Adler, F. "Thalheimer, Bonapartism, and Fascism." *Telos*, no. 40 (1979).

Allardyce, G. "What Fascism Is Not: Thoughts on the Deflation of a Concept." *American Historical Review* 84 (1979).

Allen, W. "Farewell to Class Analysis in the Rise of Nazism." *Central European History* 17 (1984).

Althusser, L. "Ideology and Ideological State Apparatuses." In *Lenin and Philosophy and Other Essays*. London: New Left Books, 1971.

Amalvi, C. "Nationalist Responses to the Revolution." In *Nationhood and Nationalism in France: From Boulangism to the Great War, 1889–1918*, ed. R. Tombs. London: HarperCollins Academic, 1991.

Amin, S. *Imperialism and Unequal Development*. London: Monthly Review Press, 1977.

Anderson, B. *Imagined Communities: Reflections on the Origins and Spread of Nationalism*. London: Verso, 1983.

———. Introduction to *Mapping the Nation*, ed. G. Balakrishnan and B. Anderson. London: Verso, 1996.

Anderson, M. *Conservative Politics in France*. London: Allen and Unwin, 1974.

Anderson, P. "Internationalism: Metamorphoses of a Meaning," Sanford S. Elberg Lecture in International Studies, University of California, April 2001, available at http://globetrotter.berkele.edu/Elberg/Anderson.

Anderson, T. "Edouard Drumont and the Origins of Modern Anti-Semitism." *Catholic Historical Review* 53 (1967).

Angenot, M. *Ce que l'on dit des Juifs en 1889: Antisémitisme et discours social*. Saint-Denis: Presses Universitaires de Vincennes, 1989.

Appiah, K. "Against National Culture." In *Text and Nation: Cross-Disciplinary Essays on Cultural and National Identities*, ed. P. Pfeiffer and L. Garcia-Moreno. Columbia, S.C.: Camden House, 1996.

Arnold, E. "Counter-Revolutionary Themes and the Working Class in France of the Belle Epoque: The Case of the Syndicats Jaunes, 1899–1912." *French History* 13 (1999).

———. "The Right Wing and the Working Classes: The Case of the 'Syndicats Jaunes' (1899–1912)." In *The Development of the Radical Right in France: From Boulanger to Le Pen*, ed. E. Arnold. London: Macmillan, 2000.

Avineri, S. "Marxism and Nationalism." In *The Impact of Western Nationalism*, ed. J. Reinharz and G. Mosse. London: Sage, 1992.

———. "Toward a Socialist Theory of Nationalism." *Dissent*, Fall 1990.

Azéma, J.-P. and M. Winock. *La IIIe République (1870–1940)*. Paris: Hachette, 1976.

Baker, K. "On the Problem of the Ideological Origins of the French Revolution." In *Modern European Intellectual History: Reappraisals and New Perspectives*, ed. D. LaCapra and S. Kaplan. Ithaca, N.Y.: Cornell University Press, 1982.

Baker, R. "A Regional Study of Working-Class Organization in France: Socialism in the Nord, 1870–1924." Ph.D. thesis, Stanford University, 1967.

Balakrishnan, G. "The National Imagination." In *Mapping the Nation*, ed. G. Balakrishnan and B. Anderson. London: Verso, 1996.

Balibar, E. "Class Racism." In *Race, Nation, Class: Ambiguous Identities*, by E. Balibar and I. Wallerstein. London: Verso, 1991.

———. "Racism and Crisis." In *Race, Nation, Class: Ambiguous Identities*, by E. Balibar and I. Wallerstein. London: Verso, 1991.

Barral, P. *Le Département de l'Isère sous la IIIe République: Histoire sociale et politique*. Paris: Fondation Nationale des Sciences Politiques, 1962.

———. "La Patrie." In *Histoire des droites en France*, ed. J.-F. Sirinelli. Vol. 3, *Sensibilités*. Paris: Gallimard, 1992.

Bauman, Z. "Soil, Blood, and Identity." *Sociological Review* 47 (1992).

———. "Strangers: The Social Construction of Universality and Particularity." *Telos* no. 78 (1988–89).

Baycroft, T. "Changing Identities in the Franco-Belgian Borderland in the Nineteenth and Twentieth Centuries." *French History* 13 (1999).

Beau de Lomenie, E. *Edouard Drumont ou l'anticapitalisme national*. Paris: Pauvert, 1968.

———. *Les Responsabilités des dynasties bourgeoises*. Paris: Librarie Française, 1977.

Becker, J.-J. *1914: Comment les français sont entrés dans la guerre*. Paris: Presses de la Fondation Nationale des Sciences Politiques, 1977.

Beetham, D., ed. *Marxists in the Face of Fascism: Writings by Marxists on Fascism from the Inter-War Period*. Totowa, N.J.: Barnes and Noble, 1984.

Benner, E. *Really Existing Nationalism: A Post-Communist View from Marx and Engels*. Oxford: Clarendon, 1995.

Berberoglu, B. "Nationalism, Class Conflict and Social Transformation in the Twentieth Century." *International Review of Modern Sociology* 29 (1999).

Berki, R. "Marxism and European Unity." In *European Unity in Context*, ed. P. Stirk. London: Pinter, 1989.

———. "On Marxian Thought and the Problem of International Relations." *World Politics* 24 (1971).

———. *State, Class, Nation.* Hull: Hull University Press, 1986.

Berlanstein, L. "Parisian White-Collar Employees and Nationalism in the Belle Epoque." In *Nationhood and Nationalism in France from Boulangism to the Great War, 1889–1918,* ed. R. Tombs. London: HarperCollins Academic, 1991.

Berlin, I. "Joseph de Maistre and the Origins of Fascism." In *The Crooked Timber of Humanity: Chapters in the History of Ideas.* New York: Knopf, 1991.

Berstein, S. "La France des années trente allergique au fascisme: À propos d'un livre de Zeev Sternhell." *XXe Siècle,* no. 2 (1984).

———. "La Ligue." In *Histoire des droites en France.* Vol. 2, *Cultures,* ed. J.-F. Sirinelli. Paris: Gallimard, 1992.

Bingham, J. "Defining French Fascism, Finding Fascists in France." *Canadian Journal of History* 24 (1994).

Birnbaum, P. "Accepter la pluralité: Haines et préjugés." In *Histoire des droites en France,* ed. J.-F. Sirinelli. Vol. 3, *Sensibilités.* Paris: Gallimard, 1992.

———. "Affaire Dreyfus, Culture catholique et antisémitisme." In *Histoire de l'extrème droite en France,* ed. M. Winock. Paris: Seuil, 1993.

———. "Anti-Semitism and Anticapitalism in Modern France." In *The Jews in Modern France,* ed. F. Malino and B. Wasserstein. Hanover, N.H.: University Press of New England, 1985.

———. *Anti-Semitism in France: A Political History from Léon Blum to the Present.* Oxford: Blackwell, 1992.

———. "Catholic Identity, Universal Suffrage and 'Doctrines of Hatred.'" In *The Intellectual Revolt against Liberal Democracy, 1870–1945,* ed. Z. Sternhell. Jerusalem: Israel Academy of Sciences and Humanities, 1996.

———. *La France aux français: Histoire des haines nationalistes.* Paris: Seuil, 1993.

———. *Jewish Destinies: Citizenship, State, and Community in Modern France.* New York: Hill and Wang, 2000.

———. *Le Moment antisémite: Un Tour de la France en 1898.* Paris: Fayard, 1998.

———. *Le Peuple et les gros: Histoire d'un mythe.* Paris: Grasset, 1979.

Blaut, J. *The National Question: Decolonising the Theory of Nationalism.* London: Zed Press, 1987.

Blick, B. "What Is Socialism? French Liberal Views in the 1890s." In *Crucible of Socialism,* ed. L. Patsouras. Atlantic Highlands, N.J.: Humanities Press International, 1987.

Blinkhorn, M. "Allies, Rivals, or Antagonists: Fascists and Conservatives in Modern Europe." In *Fascists and Conservatives: The Radical Right and the Establishment in Twentieth Century Europe,* ed. M. Blinkhorn. London: Unwin Hyman, 1990.

Bloom, S. *The World of Nations: A Study of the National Implications in the Work of Karl Marx.* New York: Columbia University Press, 1967.

Bobbio, N. *Left and Right: The Significance of a Political Distinction.* Cambridge: Polity, 1996.

Bonacich, E. "Class Approaches to Ethnicity and Race." *Insurgent Sociologist* 10 (1980).

Bottigelli, G. Introduction to *Correspondence: Friedrich Engels and Paul and Laura Lafargue.* Moscow: Foreign Language Publishing House, 1960.

Botz, G. "Austro-Marxist Interpretations of Fascism." *Journal of Contemporary History* 11 (1976).

Bovenkerk, F. "The Rehabilitation of the Rabble: How and Why Marx and Engels Wrongly Depicted the Lumpenproletariat as a Reactionary Force," *Netherlands Journal of Sociology* 20 (1984).

Bredin, J.-D. *The Affair: The Case of Alfred Dreyfus.* New York: G. Braziller, 1986.

Breuilly, J. *Nationalism and the State.* Manchester: Manchester University Press, 1982.

Brubaker, R. *Citizenship and Nationhood in France and Germany.* Cambridge, Mass.: Harvard University Press, 1992.

———. "De l'immigré au citoyen: Comment le *jus soli* s'est imposé en France à la fin du XIXe siècle." *Actes de la Recherche en Sciences Sociales*, no. 99 (1993).

Brustein, W. "A Regional Mode-of-Production Analysis of Political Behavior: The Cases of Western and Mediterranean France." *Politics and Society* 10 (1981).

Bulakow, H. "Les Socialistes et l'Affaire." *Nouveaux Cahiers* 27 (1971–72).

Burns, M. *Rural Society and French Politics: Boulangism and the Dreyfus Affair, 1886–1900.* Princeton, N.J.: Princeton University Press, 1984.

Burrin, P. *La Dérive fasciste: Doriot, Déat, Bergery, 1933–1945.* Paris: Seuil, 1986.

———. "Le Fascisme." In *Histoire des droites en France*, ed. J.-F. Sirinelli. Vol. 1, *Politique.* Paris: Gallimard, 1992.

Busi, F. *The Pope of Anti-Semitism: The Career and Legacy of Edouard-Adolphe Drumont.* Lanham, Md.: University Press of America, 1986.

Buthman, W. *The Rise of Integral Nationalism in France.* New York: Columbia University Press, 1939.

Byrnes, R. *Anti-Semitism in Modern France: A Prologue to the Dreyfus Affair.* New York: Fertig, 1969.

———. "Morès: The First National Socialist." *Review of Politics* 12 (1950).

Cahm, E. "Le Mouvement socialiste face au nationalisme au temps de l'Affaire Dreyfus." *Bulletin de la Société des Etudes Jaurèsiennes*, no. 79 (1980).

———. *Péguy et le nationalisme français: De l'Affaire Dreyfus à la Grande Guerre.* Paris: Cahiers de l'Amitié Charles Péguy, 1972.

Calhoun, C. *Nationalism.* Buckingham: Open University Press, 1997.

———. "Nationalism and Civil Society: Democracy, Diversity and Self-Determination." In *Social Theory and the Politics of Identity*, ed. C. Calhoun. Oxford: Blackwell, 1994.

———. "Social Theory and the Politics of Identity." In *Social Theory and the Politics of Identity*, ed. C. Calhoun. Oxford: Blackwell, 1994.

Cammett, J. "Communist Theories of Fascism." *Science and Society* 21 (1967).

Canovan, M. *Nationhood and Political Theory.* Cheltenham: Edward Elgar, 1996.

Carlebach, J. *Karl Marx and the Radical Critique of Judaism.* London: Routledge, 1978.

Caron, F. "Essai d'analyse historique d'une psychologie du travail." *Mouvement Social*, no. 50 (1965).

Carr, E. *Nationalism and After.* London: Macmillan, 1968.

Caute, D. *Communism and the French Intellectuals.* London: A. Deutsch, 1964.

Ceplair, L. *Under the Shadow of War: Fascism, Anti-Fascism and Marxists, 1918–1939.* New York: Columbia University Press, 1987.

Charle, C. "Sentiment national et nationalisme en France au XIXe siècle." *Bulletin de la Société d'Histoire Moderne et Contemporaine*, nos. 1–2 (1996).

Cheah, P. "The Cosmopolitical—Today." In *Cosmopolitics: Thinking and Feeling beyond the Nation*, ed. P. Cheah and B. Robbins. London: University of Minnesota Press, 1998.

Chebel d'Appollonia, A. *L'Extrème-droite en France: De Maurras à Le Pen.* Brussels: Edition Complexe, 1988.

Citron, S. *Le Mythe national: L'Histoire de France en question.* Paris: Editions Ouvrières, 1987.

Coakley, J. "The Social Origins of Nationalist Movements and Explanations of Nationalism: A Review." In *The Social Origins of Nationalist Movements: The Contemporary West European Experience*, ed. J. Coakley. London: Sage, 1992.

Cocks, J. *Passion and Paradox: Intellectuals Confront the National Question.* Princeton, N.J.: Princeton University Press, 2002.

Codaccioni, P. *De l'Inégalité sociale dans une grande ville industrielle: Le Drame de Lille de 1850 à 1914.* Lille: Université de Lille, 1976.

Cohen, G. *History, Labour, and Freedom.* Oxford: Clarendon, 1988.

Cohen, M. "Rooted Cosmopolitanism: Thoughts on the Left, Nationalism, and Multiculturalism." *Dissent*, Fall 1992.

Colás, A. "Putting Cosmopolitanism into Practice: The Case of Socialist Internationalism." *Millennium: Journal of International Studies* 23 (1994).

Collot, C. "Le Socialisme en Meuse avant 1914." *Bulletin des Sociétés d'Histoire et d'Archéologie de la Meuse*, no. 5 (1968).

Connor, W. *The National Question in Marxist-Leninist Theory and Strategy.* Princeton, N.J.: Princeton University Press, 1984.

Costa Pinto, A. "Fascist Ideology Revisited: Zeev Sternhell and His Critics." *European History Quarterly* 16 (1986).

Courtheoux, J.-P. "Naissance d'une conscience de classe dans le prolétariat textile du Nord." *Revue Economique* 8 (1957).

Crapez, M. *La Gauche réactionnaire: Mythes de la plèbe et de la race*. Paris: Berg International, 1997.

Cross, G. *Immigrant Workers in Industrial France: The Making of a New Laboring Class*. Philadelphia: Temple University Press, 1983.

Cummins, I. *Marx, Engels, and National Movements*. London: Croom Helm, 1980.

Curtis, M. *Three Against the Third Republic: Sorel, Barrès, and Maurras*. Princeton, N.J.: Princeton University Press, 1959.

Dallmayr, F. "Polis and Cosmopolis." In *Margins of Political Discourse*. Albany: State University of New York Press, 1989.

Dandeker, C. "Fascism and Ideology." *Ethnic and Racial Studies* 8 (1985).

D'Angelo, L. "L'Eccidio d'Aigues-Mortes (1893) e la sue ripercussione in Italia e in Francia." *Critica Storica* 13 (1976).

Dansette, A. "The Rejuvenation of French Catholicism: Marc Sagnier's Sillon." *Review of Politics* 15 (1953).

Dantoing, A. "Une Manifestation de défense ouvrière contre le travail étranger dans les mines du Pas-de-Calais en 1892." *Revue Belge d'Histoire Contemporaine* 5 (1974).

Davies, P. *The Extreme Right in France, 1789 to the Present*. London: Routledge, 2002.

Davis, H. *Nationalism and Socialism: Marxist and Labor Theories of Nationalism to 1917*. New York: Monthly Review Press, 1967.

———. *Toward a Marxist Theory of Nationalism*. New York: Monthly Review Press, 1978.

Debray, R. "Marxism and the National Question." *New Left Review*, no. 105 (1977).

Derfler, L. *Alexandre Millerand: The Socialist Years*. The Hague: Mouton, 1977.

———. "Paul Lafargue: The First Marxist Literary Critic." *Nineteenth-Century French Studies* 17 (1989).

———. *Paul Lafargue and the Flowering of French Socialism*. Cambridge, Mass.: Harvard University Press, 1998.

———. *Paul Lafargue and the Founding of French Marxismm, 1842–1882*. Cambridge, Mass.: Harvard University Press, 1991.

Desai, M. *Marx's Revenge: The Resurgence of Capitalism and the Death of Statist Socialism*. London: Verso, 2002.

Deutscher, I. "On Internationals and Internationalism." In *Marxism in Our Time*, by I. Deutscher. Berkeley, Calif.: Ramparts Press, 1971.

Digeon, C. *La Crise allemande de la pensée française, 1870–1914.* Paris: Presses Universitaires de France, 1959.

Domenach, J.-M. "Barrésisme et révolution conservatrice." In *Barrès: Une Tradition dans la modernité,* ed. A. Guyaux, J. Jurt, and R. Kopp. Paris: Champion, 1991.

Donegani, J.-M. and M. Sadoun, "Les Droites au miroir des Gauches." In *Histoire des droites en France,* ed. J.-F. Sirinelli. Vol. 3, *Sociabilités.* Paris: Gallimard, 1992.

Doty, C. *From Cultural Rebellion to Counterrevolution: The Politics of Maurice Barrès.* Athens: Ohio State University Press, 1976.

———. "Parliamentary Boulangism after 1889." *Historian* 21 (1970).

Drachkovitch, M. *Les Socialismes français et allemand et le problème de la guerre (1870–1914).* Geneva: E. Droz, 1953.

Draper, H. "The Concept of the 'Lumpenproletariat' in Marx and Engels." *Economies et Sociétés,* no. 15 (1972).

Dray, W. "Narrative versus Analysis in History." In *Rationality, Relativism and the Human Sciences,* ed. J. Margolis, M. Krausz, and R. Burian. Dordrecht: Nijhoff, 1986.

Düffler, J. "Bonapartism, Fascism and National Socialism." *Journal of Contemporary History* 11 (1976).

Dunn, J. "The Identity of the History of Ideas." In *Political Obligation in its Historical Context: Essays in Political Theory,* by J. Dunn. Cambridge: Cambridge University Press, 1980.

———. "Nationalism." In *Western Political Theory in the Face of the Future.* Cambridge: Cambridge University Press, 1979.

———. "Unimagined Communities: The Deceptions of Socialist Internationalism." In *Rethinking Modern Political Theory.* Cambridge: Cambridge University Press, 1985.

Dunn, M. "Marxism and the National Question." *Arena,* no. 40 (1975).

Duroselle, J.-G. "L'Antisémitisme en France de 1886 à 1914." *Cahiers Paul Claudel* 7 (1968).

Eagleton, T. "Nationalism: Irony and Commitment." In *Nationalism, Colonialism, and Literature,* by T. Eagleton, F. Jameson, and E. Said. Minneapolis: University of Minnesota Press, 1990.

———. "What Is Fascism?" *New Blackfriars* 57 (1976).

Ehrenreich, J. "Socialism, Nationalism and Capitalist Development." *Review of Radical Political Economics* 15 (1983).

Eley, G. "Culture, Nation and Gender." In *Gendered Nations: Nationalisms and Gender Order in the Long Nineteenth Century,* ed. I. Blom, K. Hagemann, and C. Hall. Oxford: Berg, 2000.

———. "Defining Social Imperialism: Use and Abuse of an Idea." *Social History* 1 (1976).

———. "What Produces Fascism: Preindustrial Traditions or a Crisis of the Capitalist State?" *Politics and Society* 12 (1983).

Eley, G. and R. Suny. "Introduction: From the Moment of Social History to the Work of Cultural Representation." In *Becoming National*, ed. G. Eley and R. Suny. Oxford: Oxford University Press, 1996.

Elwitt, S. *The Making of the Third Republic: Class and Politics in France, 1868–1884.* Baton Rouge: Louisiana State University Press, 1975.

———. *The Third Republic Defended: Bourgeois Reform in France, 1880–1914.* Baton Rouge: Louisiana State University Press, 1986.

Evans, G. and K. Rowley. *Red Brotherhood at War.* London: Verso, 1984.

Fanon, F. "On National Culture." In *The Wretched of the Earth.* New York: McGibbon and Kee, 1963.

Figuerès, L. "Engels et le mouvement ouvrier français." *Cahiers du Communisme* 46 (1970).

Finlayson, A. "Ideology, Discourse, and Nationalism." *Journal of Political Ideology* 3 (1998).

Fisera, V. and G. Minnerup. "Marx, Engels and the National Question." In *Socialism and Nationalism*, ed. E. Cahm and V. Fisera. Nottingham: Spokesman, 1978.

Flynn, M. "Royalist and Fascist Nationalism and National Socialism in France." *History of European Ideas* 15 (1992).

Forman, M. *Nationalism and the International Labor Movement: The Idea of the Nation in Socialist and Anarchist Theory.* University Park: Pennsylvania State University Press, 1998.

Frankel, J. *Prophecy and Politics: Socialism, Nationalism and the Russian Jews, 1862–1917.* Cambridge: Cambridge University Press, 1981.

Fraser, N. "From Redistribution to Recognition? Dilemmas of Justice in a 'Post-Socialist' Age." *New Left Review*, no. 212 (1995).

———. "A Rejoinder to Iris Young." *New Left Review*, no. 223 (1997).

———. "Rethinking Recognition." *New Left Review*, n.s., no. 3 (2000).

Freeden, M. "Is Nationalism a Distinct Ideology?" *Political Studies* 46 (1998).

Freitag, M. "Théorie Marxiste et question nationale: Autopsie d'un malentendu." *Pluriel-Débat*, no. 26 (1981).

Friedman, G. "Capitalism, Republicanism, Socialism and the State: France, 1871–1914." *Social Science History* 14 (1990).

———. "The State and the Making of the Working Class: France and the United States, 1880–1914." *Theory and Society* 17 (1988).

Fukuyama, F. "Second Thoughts," *National Interest*, 1999. http://www.britannica.com/bcom/magazine/article/0,5744,250415,00.html.

Gabriel, J. and G. Ben-Tovim. "Marxism and the Concept of Racism." *Economy and Society* 7 (1978).

Gallie, W. *Philosophers of Peace and War: Kant, Clausewitz, Marx, Engels and Tolstoy.* Cambridge: Cambridge University Press, 1975.

Gallissot, R. "La Patrie des prolétaires." *Mouvement Social,* no. 147 (1989).

Gelfand, T. "From Religious to Bio-Medical Anti-Semitism: The Career of Jules Soury." In *French Medical Culture in the Nineteenth Century,* ed. A. LaBerge and M. Feingold. Amsterdam: Rodopi, 1994.

Gellner, E. *Culture, Identity and Politics.* Cambridge: Cambridge University Press, 1987.

———. "Nationalism and Marxism." In *Encounters with Nationalism.* Oxford: Blackwell, 1994.

———. *Nations and Nationalism.* Oxford: Blackwell, 1983.

———. *Thought and Change.* London: Weidenfeld and Nicolson, 1965.

Gibson, R. "The Intensification of National Consciousness in Modern Europe." In *Nations, Nationalism and Patriotism in the European Past,* ed. C. Bjørn, A. Grant, and K. Stringer. Copenhagen: Academic Press, 1994.

Giddens, A. *A Contemporary Critique of Historical Materialism.* London: Macmillan, 1981.

———. *The Nation-State and Violence: Volume Two of a Contemporary Critique of Historical Materialism.* Cambridge: Polity, 1985.

———. "Marx on Internationalism and War." *Philosophy and Public Affairs* 7 (1978).

Gilbert, P. *Peoples, Cultures and Nations in Political Philosophy.* Edinburgh: Edinburgh University Press, 2000.

Girardet, R. *Mythes et mythologies politiques.* Paris: Seuil, 1986.

———. *Le Nationalisme français, 1871–1914.* Paris: A. Colin, 1966.

Girault, R. Introduction to *Paul Lafargue: Textes choisis,* ed. R. Girault. Paris: Editions Sociales, 1970.

———. "Place et rôle des échanges extérieures." In *Histoire économique et sociale de la France.* Vol. 4, *L'Ere industrielle et la société d'aujourd'hui (siècle 1880–1980).* Book 1, *Ambiguïtés des débuts et croissance effective (années 1880–1914).* Paris: Presses Universitaires de France, 1979.

Glasberg, V. "Intent and Consequence: The 'Jewish Question' in the French Socialist Movement of the Late Nineteenth Century." *Jewish Social Studies* 36 (1974).

Gordon, D. "Liberalism and Socialism in the Nord: Eugène Motte and Republican Politics in Roubaix, 1898–1912." *French History* 3 (1989).

———. *Liberalism and Social Reform: Industrial Growth and Progressiste Politics in France, 1880–1914.* Westport, Conn.: Greenwood Press, 1996.

Gouldner, A. *The Two Marxisms: Contradictions and Anomalies in the Development of Theory.* New York: Macmillan, 1980.

Grani, L. "Jules Guesde, Paul Lafargue et les problèmes de population." *Population* 34 (1979).

Green, N. "Eléments pour une étude du mouvement ouvrier juif à Paris au début du siècle." *Mouvement Social,* no. 110 (1980).

———. "Socialist Anti-Semitism, Defence of a Bourgeois Jew and Discovery of the Jewish Proletariat: Changing Attitudes of French Socialists before 1914." *International Review of Social History* 30 (1985).

———. *Les Travailleurs immigrés juifs à la Belle Epoque: Le "Pletzl" de Paris.* Paris: Fayard, 1985.

Greenfeld, L. *Nationalism: Five Roads to Modernity.* London: Harvard University Press, 1992.

Gregor, A. *The Faces of Janus: Marxism and Fascism in the Twentieth Century.* New Haven, Conn.: Yale University Press, 2000.

———. *The Ideology of Fascism: The Rationale of Totalitarianism.* New York: Free Press, 1969.

———. *Interpretations of Fascism.* Morristown, N.J.: General Learning Press, 1974.

Griffiths, R. "Anticapitalism and the French Anti-Parliamentary Right, 1870–1940." *Journal of Contemporary History* 13 (1978).

———. "From Nostalgia to Pragmatism: French Royalism and the Dreyfus Watershed." In *The Right in France, 1789–1997,* ed. N. Atkin and F. Tallett. London: Tauris, 1998.

Guibernau, M. "Marx and Durkheim on Nationalism." In *Rethinking Nationalism and Ethnicity: The Struggle for Meaning and Order in Europe,* ed. H.-R. Wicker. Oxford: Berg, 1997.

Guidoni, P. *La Cité rouge: Le Socialisme à Narbonne, 1871–1921.* Toulouse: Privat, 1979.

Guillaumin, C. "'Race' and Discourse." In *Race, Discourse and Power in France,* ed. M. Silverman. Aldershot: Avebury, 1991.

Guin, Y. *Le Mouvement ouvrier nantais.* Paris: Maspero, 1976.

Guiral, P. "Idée de race et pensée politique en France (gauche et droite) au XIX siècle." In *L'Idée de race dans la pensée politique française contemporaine,* ed. P. Guiral and E. Témime. Paris: Editions du Centre National de la Recherche Scientifique, 1977.

———. "Vue d'ensemble sur l'idée de race et la gauche française." In *L'Idée de race dans la pensée politique française contemporaine,* ed. P. Guiral and E. Témime. Paris: Editions du Centre National de la Recherche Scientifique, 1977.

Hainsworth, P. "The Extreme Right in Post-War France: The Emergence and Success of the Front National." In *The Extreme Right in Europe and the USA,* ed. P. Hainsworth. New York: St. Martin's Press, 1992.

Hall, S. "Ethnicity: Identity and Difference." In *Becoming National: A Reader*, ed. G. Eley and R. Suny. Oxford: Oxford University Press, 1996.

———. *The Hard Road to Renewal: Thatcherism and the Crisis of the Left.* London: Verso, 1988.

Halliday, F. "Bringing the 'Economic' Back In: The Case of Nationalism." *Economy and Society* 21 (1992).

Hanagan, M. "Organisation du travail et action revendicative: Verriers et métalurgistes de Rive-de-Giers à la fin du XIXe siècle." *Cahiers d'Histoire* 26 (1981).

Harvey, D. *Spaces of Hope.* Edinburgh: Edinburgh University Press, 2000.

Haupt, G. "La Classe ouvrière française au temps de Jaurès—annexes." In *Jaurès et la Classe Ouvrière.* Paris: Editions Ouvrières, 1981.

———. "Les Marxistes face à la question nationale: L'Histoire du problème." In *Les Marxistes et la question nationale, 1848–1914,* by G. Haupt, M. Löwy, and C. Weill. Paris: Maspero, 1974.

———. *Socialism and the Great War: The Collapse of the Second International.* Oxford: Clarendon, 1972.

Haupt, H.-G. "The Petite Bourgeoisie in France, 1850–1914: In Search of the *Juste Milieu.*" In *Shopkeepers and Master Artisans in Nineteenth-Century Europe*, ed. G. Crossick and H.-G. Haupt. London: Methuen, 1984.

Hazareesingh, S. *Political Traditions in Modern France.* Oxford: Oxford University Press, 1994.

Herf, J. *Reactionary Modernism: Technology, Culture, and Politics in Weimar and the Third Reich.* Cambridge: Cambridge University Press, 1984.

Herod, C. *The Nation in the History of Marxian Thought: The Concept of Nations with History and Nations without History.* The Hague: Martinus Nijhoff, 1976.

Hilaire, Y.-M. "1900–1945: L'Ancrage des idéologies." In *Histoire des droites en France,* ed. J.-F. Sirinelli. Vol. 1, *Politique.* Paris: Gallimard, 1992.

Hirschman, A. *Deux siècles de rhétorique réactionnaire.* Paris: Fayard, 1991.

Hobsbawm, E. "Ethnicity and Nationalism in Europe Today." In *Mapping the Nation,* ed. G. Balakrishnan and B. Anderson. London: Verso, 1996.

———. *Nations and Nationalism since 1780: Programme, Myth, Reality.* Cambridge: Cambridge University Press, 1990.

———. "Reflections on Nationalism." In *Imagination and Precision in the Social Sciences,* ed. T. Nossiter, A. Hanson, and S. Rokkan. London: Faber and Faber, 1972.

———. "Some Reflections on *The Break-up of Britain.*" *New Left Review,* no. 105 (1977).

———. "What Is the Workers' Country?" In *Worlds of Labour: Further Studies in the History of Labour.* London: Weidenfeld and Nicolson, 1984.

———. "Working-Class Internationalism." In *Internationalism in the Labour Movement, 1830–1940*, ed. F. van Holthoon and M. van der Linden. Leiden: Brill, 1988.

Hoffmann, S. "The Nation: What For? Vicissitudes of French Nationalism, 1871–1973." In *Decline or Renewal? France since the 1930s*. New York: Viking Press, 1974.

Holmes, S. *The Anatomy of Antiliberalism*. Cambridge, Mass.: Harvard University Press, 1993.

Howorth, J. "French Workers and German Workers: The Impossibility of Internationalism, 1900–1914." *European History Quarterly* 15 (1985).

———. "The Left in France and Germany, Internationalism and War: A Dialogue of the Deaf, 1900–1914." In *Socialism and Nationalism in Contemporary Europe (1848–1945)*, ed. E. Cahm and V. Fisera. Nottingham: Spokesman, 1979.

———. "Migration, Class Formation and Radicalism in Nineteenth-Century France." *History Workshop Journal*, no. 24 (1987).

Hutton, P. *The Cult of the Revolutionary Tradition: The Blanquists in French Politics, 1864–1893*. Berkeley: University of California Press, 1981.

———. "The Impact of the Boulangist Crisis upon the Guesdist Party of Bordeaux." *French Historical Studies* 7 (1971).

———. "Popular Boulangism and the Advent of Mass Politics in France, 1886–90." *Journal of Contemporary History* 11 (1976).

Irvine, W. *The Boulanger Affair Reconsidered: Royalism, Boulangism and the Origins of the Radical Right in France*. Oxford: Oxford University Press, 1989.

———. "Royalists and the Politics of Nationalism." In *Nationhood and Nationalism in France from Boulangism to the Great War, 1889–1918*, ed. R. Tombs. London: HarperCollins Academic, 1991.

Ishay, M. *Internationalism and Its Betrayal*. London: University of Minnesota Press, 1995.

James, P. "The Janus Faces of History: Cleaving Marxist Theories of Nation and Nationalism." *Canadian Review of Studies in Nationalism* 18 (1991).

———. "Marx and the Abstract Nation." *Arena*, no. 1 (1993).

Jenkins, B. *Nationalism in France: Class and Nation since 1789*. London: Routledge, 1990.

———. "Religion and Nationalism in Late Nineteenth-Century France." In *Problems in French History*, ed. M. Cornick and C. Crossley. London: Palgrave, 2000.

———. "Socialism, National Identity and Nationalism: Contribution to the Theoretical Discussion." *Journal of Area Studies* 5 (1982).

Jenkins, B. and G. Minnerup. *Citizens and Comrades: Socialism in a World of Nation States*. London: Pluto Press, 1984.

Joly, B. "The Jeunesse Antisémite et Nationaliste, 1894–1904." In *Nationhood and Nationalism in France: From Boulangism to the Great War, 1889–1918*, ed. R. Tombs. London: HarperCollins Academic, 1991.

Judt, T. *Marxism and the French Left: Studies in Labour and Politics in France, 1830–1981.* Oxford: Clarendon, 1986.

Julliard, J. "De l'Extrémisme à droite." *1900: Revue d'Histoire Intellectuelle* 9 (1991).

———. "Les Ouvriers dans la société française: Intégration et autonomie." In *Histoire sociale, sensibilités collectives et mentalités: Mélanges Robert Mandrou.* Paris: Presses Universitaires de France, 1985.

———. "Le Peuple." In *Les Lieux de mémoire*, ed. P. Nora. Vol. 3, *Les France.* Book 1, *Conflits et partages.* Paris: Gallimard, 1992.

———. "Sur un fascisme imaginaire: A Propos d'un livre de Zeev Sternhell." *Annales: Economies, Sociétés, Civilisations* 39 (1984).

Kahan, A. "Nineteenth-Century European Experiences with Policies of Economic Nationalism." In *Economic Nationalism in Old and New States*, ed. H. Johnson. Chicago: University of Chicago Press, 1967.

Kaplan, A. *Reproductions of Banality: Fascism, Literature, and French Intellectual Life.* Minneapolis: University of Minnesota Press, 1986.

Keating, M. "Do the Workers Really Have No County? Peripheral Nationalism and Socialism in the United Kingdom, France, Italy and Spain." In *The Social Origins of National Movements: The Contemporary West European Experience*, ed. J. Coakley. London: Sage, 1992.

Kergoat, J. "France." In *The Formation of Labour Movements, 1870–1914: An International Perspective*, ed. M. van der Linden and J. Rojahn. Leiden: Brill, 1990.

Kiernan, V. "Conscription and Society in Europe before the War of 1914–1918." In *History, Classes and Nation-States: Selected Writings of V. G. Kiernan.* Cambridge: Polity, 1988.

———. *Marxism and Imperialism.* London: Edward Arnold, 1974.

———. "Nationalist Movements and Social Classes." In *Nationalist Movements*, ed. A. Smith. New York: Macmillan, 1976.

———. "On the Development of a Marxist Approach to Nationalism." *Science and Society* 34 (1970).

Kitchen, M. "August Thalheimer's Theory of Fascism." *Journal of the History of Ideas* 34 (1973).

———. *Fascism.* London: Macmillan, 1976.

———. "Trotsky and Fascism." *Social Praxis* 2 (1975).

Kitching, G. "Nationalism: The Instrumental Passion." *Capital and Class* 29 (1985).

Kriegel, A. "La IIe Internationale devant les questions nationales en Europe (1889–1914)." In *Le Pain et les roses: Jalons pour une histoire des socialismes.* Paris: Presses Universitaires de France, 1968.

Krumeich, G. "Joan of Arc between Right and Left." In *Nationhood and Nationalism in France from Boulangism to the Great War*, ed. R. Tombs. London: Harper-Collins Academic, 1991.

Laclau, E. "Fascism and Ideology." In *Politics and Ideology in Marxist Theory: Capitalism-Fascism-Populism.* London: New Left Books, 1977.

———. *Politics and Ideology in Marxist Theory: Capitalism-Fascism-Populism.* London: New Left Books, 1977.

———. "Universalism, Particularism, and the Question of Identity." In *The Politics of Difference: Ethnic Premises in a World of Power*, ed. E. Wilmsen and P. McAllister. Chicago: University of Chicago Press, 1996.

Laffey, J. "Racism and Imperialism: French Views of the 'Yellow Peril,' 1894–1914." *Third Republic*, no. 1 (1976).

Landauer, G. "The Guesdists and the Small Farmer: Early Erosion of French Marxism." *International Review of Social History* 6 (1961).

Landes, D. "Religion and Enterprise: The Case of the French Textile Industry." In *Enterprise and Entrepreneurs in Nineteenth and Twentieth-Century France*, ed. E. Carter, R. Forster, and J. Moody. Baltimore: Johns Hopkins University Press, 1976.

Laurat, L. "La Pénétration du marxisme en France." *La Nef* 7 (1950).

Lazarus, N. "The Necessity of Universalism." *Differences: A Journal of Feminist Cultural Studies* 7 (1995).

Le Béguec, G. and J. Prévotat. "L'Eveil à la modernité politique." In *Les Droites françaises: De la Révolution à nos jours*, ed. J.-F. Sirinelli. Paris: Gallimard, 1992.

Lebovics, H. "'Agrarians' versus 'Industrialisers': Social Conservative Resistance to Industrialism and Capitalism in late Nineteenth Century Germany." *International Review of Social History* 12 (1967).

———. *The Alliance of Iron and Wheat in the Third French Republic, 1860–1914: Origins of the New Conservatism.* Baton Rouge: Louisiana State University Press, 1988.

———. "Creating the Authentic France: Struggles over French Identity in the First Half of the Twentieth Century." In *Commemorations: The Politics of National Identity*, ed. J. Gillis. Princeton, N.J.: Princeton University Press, 1994.

———. "La Grande Dépression: Aux Origines d'un nouveau conservatisme français, 1880–1896." *Francia* 13 (1985).

———. "Protection against Labour Troubles: The Campaign of the Association de l'Industrie Française for Economic Stability and Social Peace during the Great Depression, 1880–1896." *International Review of Social History* 31 (1986).

Leca, A. "Les Thèmes idéologiques de l'antisémitisme chez les socialistes français (1845–1890)." *Revue de la Recherche Juridique*, no. 3 (1995).

Lefebvre, H. "Classe et nation depuis le *Manifeste* (1848)." *Cahiers Internationaux de Sociologie* 38 (1965).

Lekas, P. "The Supra-Class Rhetoric of Nationalism: An Introductory Comment." *East European Quarterly* 30 (1996).

Lequin, Y. "La Classe ouvrière." In *Histoire des droites en France*, ed. J.-F. Sirinelli. Vol. 3, *Sensibilités*. Paris: Gallimard, 1992.

———. "L'Invasion pacifique." In *Histoire des etrangers et de l'immigration en France*, ed. Y. Lequin. Paris: Larousse, 1992.

———. "'Métissages Imprudents.'" In *Histoire des Etrangers et de l'Immigration en France*, ed. Y. Lequin. Paris: Larousse, 1992.

———. *Les Ouvriers de la région lyonnaise: La Formation de la classe ouvrière régionale*. Lyon: Presses Universitaires de France, 1977.

———. *Les Ouvriers de la région lyonnaise: Les Intérêts de classe et la république*. Lyon: Presses Universitaires de France, 1977.

Levillain, P. "Les Droites en République." In *Les Droites françaises: De la Révolution à nos jours*, ed. J.-F. Sirinelli. Paris: Gallimard, 1992.

Lévy, B.-H. *L'Idéologie française*. Paris: Grasset, 1981.

Lichtheim, G. "Socialism and the Jews." *Dissent*, July–August 1968.

Linden, M. van der. "The National Integration of European Working Classes (1871–1914): Exploring the Causal Configuration." *International Review of Social History* 33 (1988).

Lindenberg, D. "Marx et les 'Mystères de Paris.'" In *Marx en perspective*, ed. B. Chavance. Paris: Editions de l'Ecole des Hautes Etudes en Sciences Sociales, 1985.

Linklater, A. *Beyond Realism and Marxism: Critical Theory and International Relations*. London: Macmillan, 1990.

Loughlin, M. "Gustave Hervé's Transition from Socialism to National Socialism: Another Example of French Fascism?" *Journal of Contemporary History* 36 (2001).

Löwy, M. *Fatherland or Mother Earth? Essays on the National Question*. London: Pluto Press, 1998.

———. "Fatherland or Mother Earth? Nationalism and Internationalism from a Socialist Perspective." *Socialist Register*, 1989.

———. "Marxism and the National Question." In *Revolution and Class Struggle: A Reader in Marxist Politics*, ed. R. Blackburn. London: Harvester, 1978.

———. "Marxists and the National Question." *New Left Review*, no. 96 (1976).

———. "Why Nationalism?" *Socialist Register*, 1993.

Ludz, P. "Socialism and the Nation." In *The Socialist Idea: A Reappraisal*, ed. L. Kolakowski and C. Hampshire. London: Quartet Books, 1974.

Machefer, P. *Ligues et fascismes en France*. Paris: Presses Universitaires de France, 1974.

Magraw, R. "Socialism, Syndicalism and French Labour before 1914." In *Labour and Socialist Movements in Europe before 1914*, ed. D. Geary. London: Berg, 1989.

Maier, C. "The Economics of Fascism and Nazism." In *In Search of Stability: Explorations in Historical Political Economy*, by C. Meier. Cambridge: Cambridge University Press, 1987.

Maitron, J. *Le Mouvement anarchiste en France.* Vol. 2, *Des Origines à 1914.* Paris: Maspero, 1975.

Mann, M. "Nation-States in Europe and Other Continents: Diversifying, Developing, not Dying." In *Mapping the Nation*, ed. G. Balakrishnan and B. Anderson. London: Verso, 1996.

Marcuse, H. "The Struggle against Liberalism in the Totalitarian View of the State." In *Negations: Essays in Critical Theory.* London: Allen Lane, 1968.

Marec, Y. "Le Socialisme et l'épargne: Réactions de Jules Guesde." *Revue d'Economie Sociale*, no. 5 (1985).

Marrus, M. *The Politics of Assimilation: A Study of the French Jewish Community at the Time of the Dreyfus Affair.* Oxford: Clarendon, 1971.

———. "Popular Anti-Semitism." In *The Dreyfus Affair: Art, Truth, and Justice*, ed. N. Kleeblatt. Berkeley: University of California Press, 1987.

Marty, L. *Chanter pour survivre: Culture ouvrière, travail et technique dans le textile à Roubaix (1850–1914).* Lille: Fédération Léo Lagrange, 1882.

Mayer, A. *Dynamics of Counterrevolution in Europe, 1870–1956: An Analytic Framework.* New York: Harper and Row, 1971.

———. "Internal Causes and Purposes of War in Europe, 1870–1956." *Journal of Modern History* 41 (1969).

———. *The Persistence of the Old Regime: Europe to the Great War.* London: Croom Helm, 1981.

Mayer, H. "Marx, Engels and the Politics of the Peasantry." *Cahiers de l'Institut de Science Economique Appliquée*, no. 102 (1960).

Mayeur, J.-M. "Les Congrès nationaux de la Démocratie Chrétienne à Lyon (1896–1897–1898)." *Revue d'Histoire Moderne et Contemporaine* 9 (1962).

Mazgaj, P. *The Action Française and Revolutionary Syndicalism.* Chapel Hill: University of North Carolina Press, 1979.

———. "The Origins of the French Radical Right: A Historiographical Essay." *French Historical Studies* 15 (1987).

McClelland, J. *The French Right (From De Maistre to Maurras).* London: Cape, 1970.

———. "The Reactionary Right: The French Revolution, Charles Maurras and the Action Française." In *The Nature of the Right*, ed. R. Eatwell and N. O'Sullivan. London: Pinter, 1989.

McLellan, D., ed. *Karl Marx: Interviews and Recollections.* London: Macmillan, 1981.

McMurtry, J. *The Structure of Marx's World View.* Princeton, N.J.: Princeton University Press, 1978.

Megill, A. "Recounting the Past: 'Description,' Explanation and Narrative in Historiography." *American Historical Review* 94 (1989).

Meznaric, S. "A Neo-Marxist Approach to the Sociology of Nationalism, Doomed Nations and Doomed Schemes." *Praxis International* 7 (1987).

Michel, J. "Syndicalisme minier et politique dans le Nord-Pas-de-Calais: Le Cas Basly (1880–1914)." *Mouvement Social*, no. 87 (1974).

Miliband, R. *Divided Societies: Class Struggle in Contemporary Capitalism.* Oxford: Clarendon, 1989.

———. "State Power and Class Interests." In *Class Power and State Power*, by R. Miliband. London: Verso, 1983.

Miller, D. "In What Sense Must Socialism Be Communitarian?" *Social Philosophy and Policy* 6 (1988/9).

———. "The Nation-State: A Modest Defence." In *Political Restructuring in Europe*, ed. C. Brown. London: Routledge, 1994.

———. *On Nationality.* Oxford: Clarendon, 1995.

Milner, S. *The Dilemmas of Internationalism: French Syndicalism and the International Labor Movement, 1900–1914.* New York: Berg, 1991.

Milza, O. *Les Français devant l'immigration.* Brussels: Edition Complexe, 1988.

Milza, P. *Fascisme français: Passé et présent.* Paris: Flammarion, 1987.

———. "Le Racisme anti-Italien en France: La Tuerie d'Aigues-Mortes (1893)." *L'Histoire*, no. 10 (1979).

Montuclard, M. *Conscience religieuse et démocratie: La Deuxième Démocratie Chrétienne en France, 1891–1902.* Paris: Seuil, 1968.

Moore, B. *The Social Origins of Dictatorship and Democracy.* Boston: Beacon Press, 1967.

Morazé, C. *Les Bourgeois conquérants.* Paris: A. Colin, 1957.

Moss, B. *The Origins of the French Labor Movement, 1830–1914: The Socialism of Skilled Workers.* Berkeley: University of California Press, 1976.

Mosse, G. "The French Right and the Working Classes: Les Jaunes." *Journal of Contemporary History* 7 (1972).

———. "Toward a General Theory of Fascism." In *Masses and Man: Nationalist and Fascist Perceptions of Reality*, by G. Mosse. New York: H. Fertig, 1980.

———. *Toward the Final Solution: A History of European Racism.* London: J. M. Dent, 1978.

Munck, R. *The Difficult Dialogue: Marxism and Nationalism.* London: Zed Press, 1986.

———. "Marxism and the Nation." In *Marx@2000: Late Marxist Perspectives*, by R. Munck. London: Macmillan, 2000.

Nairn, T. *The Breakup of Britain: Crisis and Neo-Nationalism.* London: New Left Books, 1981.

———. "The Curse of Rurality: Limits of Modernisation Theory." In *The State of the Nation: Ernest Gellner and the Theory of Nationalism*, ed. J. Hall. Cambridge: Cambridge University Press, 1998.

———. "Internationalism and the Second Coming." In *Mapping the Nation*, ed. G. Balakrishnan and B. Anderson. London: Verso, 1996.

———. "The Modern Janus." *New Left Review*, no. 94 (1975).

———. "Scotland and Europe." In *Becoming National*, ed. G. Eley and R. Suny. New York: Oxford University Press, 1996.

Neocleous, M. *Fascism*. Buckingham: Open University Press, 1997.

Nguyen, V. "Aperçus sur la conscience d'Oc autour des années 1900." In *Régions et régionalisme en France du XVIIIe siècle à nos jours*, ed. C. Gras and G. Livet. Paris: Presses Universitaires de France, 1977.

———. "Un Essai de pouvoir intellectuel au début de la Troisième République: *La Cocarde* de Maurice Barrès (5 septembre 1894–7 mars 1895)." *Etudes Maurrassiennes* 1 (1972).

Nielsen, K. "Socialism and Nationalism." *Imprints* 2 (1998).

Nimni, E. "Great Historical Failure: Marxist Theories of Nationalism." *Capital and Class* 9 (1985).

———. "Introduction for the English Language Audience." In O. Bauer, *The Question of Nationalities and Social Democracy*. Minneapolis: University of Minnesota Press, 2000.

———. "Marx, Engels, and the National Question." In *The Rights of Minority Cultures*, ed. W. Kymlicka. Oxford: Oxford University Press, 1995.

———. "Marxism and Nationalism." In *Marxist Sociology Revisited: Critical Assessments*, ed. M. Shaw. London: Macmillan, 1985.

———. *Marxism and Nationalism: Theoretical Origins of a Political Crisis*. London: Pluto Press, 1991.

Noiriel, G. *Le Creuset français: Histoire de l'immigration XIXe-XXe siècles*. Paris: Seuil, 1988.

———. "Français et étrangers." In *Les Lieux de mémoire*, ed. P. Nora. Vol. 3, *Les France*. Book 1, *Conflits et partages*. Paris: Gallimard, 1992.

———. "La Question nationale comme objet de l'histoire sociale." *Genèses*, no. 4 (1991).

Nolte, E. *Three Faces of Fascism: Action Française, Italian Fascism, National Socialism*. New York: Mentor, 1969.

Nord, P. "Le Mouvement des petits commerçants et la politique en France de 1888 à 1914." *Mouvement Social*, no. 114 (1981).

———. *Paris Shopkeepers and the Politics of Resentment*. Princeton, N.J.: Princeton University Press, 1986.

———. "Social Defence and Conservative Regeneration: The National Revival, 1900–1914." In *Nationhood and Nationalism in France from Boulangism to the Great War, 1889–1918*, ed. R. Tombs. London: HarperCollins Academic, 1991.

———. "Three Views of Christian Democracy in Fin de Siècle France." *Journal of Contemporary History* 19 (1984).

———. "The Welfare State in France, 1870–1914." *French Historical Studies* 18 (1994).

Nussbaum, M. "Patriotism and Cosmopolitanism." In *For Love of Country: Debating the Limits of Patriotism*, ed. J. Cohen. Boston: Beacon Press, 1996.

Nye, R. *The Origins of Crowd Psychology: Gustave Le Bon and the Crisis of Mass Democracy in the Third Republic.* London: Sage, 1975.

Offen, K. "Depopulation, Nationalism, and Feminism in Fin de Siècle France." *American Historical Review* 89 (1984).

———. *Paul de Cassagnac and the Authoritarian Tradition in Nineteenth-Century France.* New York: Garland, 1991.

Okey, R. "Working Class Movements and Nations: Towards a Typology." *Journal of Area Studies* 5 (1982).

O'Sullivan, N. *Fascism.* London: J. M. Dent, 1983.

Ousby, I. *The Road to Verdun: World War I's Most Momentous Battle and the Folly of Nationalism.* New York: Jonathan Cape, 2002.

Parekh, B. "Politics of Nationhood." In *Nationalism, Ethnicity and Cultural Identity in Europe*, ed. K. von Benda-Beckmann and M. Verkuyten. Utrecht: European Research Centre on Migration and Ethnic Relations, 1995.

Parkin, F. *Marxism and Class Theory: A Bourgeois Critique.* London: Tavistock, 1979.

Parry, D. "Articulating the Third Republic by Conspiracy Theory." *European History Quarterly* 28 (1998).

Passmore, K. "The French Third Republic: Stalemate Society or Cradle of Fascism?" *French History* 7 (1993).

Payne, S. "Fascism in Western Europe." In *Fascism: A Reader's Guide*, ed. W. Laqueur. London: Penguin, 1979.

Pech, R. "Les Thèmes économiques et sociaux du socialisme férrouliste à Narbonne (1880–1914)." In *Droite et gauche en Languedoc-Roussillon: Actes du colloque de Montpellier, 9–10 juin 1973.* Montpellier, Centre d'Histoire Contemporaine du Languedoc Méditerranéan et du Roussillon, Université Paul Valéry, 1975.

Pelczynski, Z. "Nation, Civil Society, State: Hegelian Sources of the Marxian Non-Theory of Nationality." In *The State and Civil Society: Studies in Hegel's Political Philosophy*, ed. Z. Pelczynski. Cambridge: Cambridge University Press, 1984.

Perrot, M. "La Classe ouvrière au temps de Jaurès." In *Jaurès et la classe ouvrière.* Paris: Editions Ouvrières, 1981.

———. "Les Classes populaires urbaines." In *Histoire économique et sociale de la France. Tome 4, L'Ere industrielle et la société d'aujourd'hui (siècle 1880–1980)*. Vol. 1, *Ambiguïtés des débuts et croissance effective (années 1880–1914)*. Paris: Presses Universitaires de France, 1979.

———. "Comment les ouvriers parisiens voyaient la crise d'après l'enquête parlementaire de 1884." In *Conjoncture économique/structures sociales: Hommage à Ernest Labrousse*. Paris: Mouton, 1974.

———. "Controverses sur l'introduction du marxisme en France." *Annales: Economies, Sociétés, Civilisations* 22 (1967).

———. "On the Formation of the French Working Class." In *Working Class Formation: Nineteenth-Century Patterns in Western Europe and the United States*, ed. I. Katznelson and A. Zolberg. Princeton, N.J.: Princeton University Press, 1986.

———. *Les Ouvriers en grève: France, 1871–1890*. Paris: Mouton, 1974.

———. "Les Rapports entre ouvriers français et ouvriers étrangers (1871–1893)." *Bulletin de la Société d'Histoire Moderne* 58 (1960).

———. "Le Regard de l'autre: Les Patrons français vus par les ouvriers (1880–1914)." In *Le Patronat de la seconde industrialisation*, ed. M. Lévy-Leboyer. Paris: Editions Ouvrières, 1979.

Perrot, M. and A. Kriegel. *Le Socialisme français et le pouvoir*. Paris: Etudes et Documentation Internationale, 1966.

Petitfils, J.-C. *L'Extrême droite en France*. Paris: Presses Universitaires de France, 1983.

Petras, J. "Marx and Engels on the National Question." *Journal of Politics* 33 (1971).

Pierrard, P. "Antisémitisme de droite et de gauche au 19ème siècle et au début du 20ème siècle." In *Antisémitisme, hier et aujourd'hui*. Paris: Université de Paris–Sorbonne, 1983.

———. *Juifs et catholiques français: De Drumont à Jules Isaac (1886–1945)*. Paris: Fayard, 1970.

Poliakov, L. *The Aryan Myth: A History of Racist and Nationalist Ideas in Europe*. London: Chatto and Windus, 1974.

———. *The History of Anti-Semitism*. London: Routledge, 1975.

Poole, R. "On National Identity: A Response to Jonathan Rée." *Radical Philosophy*, no. 62 (1992).

Poulantzas, N. "A Propos de l'impact populaire du fascisme." In *Eléments pour une analyse du fascisme*, ed. M. Macciocchi. Paris: Union Générale d'Editions, 1976.

———. *State, Power, Socialism*. London: New Left Books, 1978.

Prochasson, C. "Les Années 1880: Au Temps du Boulangisme." In *Histoire de l'extrême droite en France*, ed. M. Winock. Paris: Seuil, 1993.

Przeworski, A. "Class, Compromise, and the Transition to Socialism." *Politics and Society* 10 (1980).

Puech, J. *La Tradition socialiste en France et la société des nations.* Paris: Garnier, 1921.

Purvis, T. "Marxism and Nationalism." In *Marxism and Social Science*, ed. A. Gamble, D. Marsh, and T. Tant. London: Macmillan, 1999.

Putnam, G. "The Meaning of Barrèsisme." *Western Political Quarterly* 7 (1954).

Putnam, H. "Must We Choose between Patriotism and Universal Reason?" In *For Love of Country: Debating the Limits of Patriotism*, ed. J. Cohen. Boston: Beacon Press, 1996.

Quinlan, S. "The Racial Imagery of Degeneration and Depopulation: Georges Vacher de Lapouge and 'Anthroposociology' in Fin de Siècle France." *History of European Ideas* 24 (1999).

Rabinbach, A. "Unclaimed Heritage: Ernst Bloch's *Heritage of our Times* and the Theory of Fascism." *New German Critique*, no. 11 (1977).

Reardon, J. "Belgian and French Workers in Nineteenth-Century Roubaix." In *Class Conflict and Collective Action*, ed. L. and C. Tilly. London: Sage, 1981.

Rebérioux, M. "Le Mot race au tournant du siècle." *Mots: Les Langages du Politique*, no. 33 (1992).

———. "Le Socialisme français de 1871 à 1914." In *Histoire générale du socialisme*, ed. J. Droz. Vol. 2, *De 1875 à 1918*. Paris: Presses Universitaires de France, 1974.

———. "Les Socialistes français et le petit commerce au tournant du siècle." *Mouvement Social*, no. 114 (1981).

Rée, J. "Cosmopolitanism and the Experience of Nationality." In *Cosmopolitics: Thinking and Feeling Beyond the Nation*, ed. P. Cheah and B. Robbins. London: University of Minnesota Press, 1998.

———. "Internationality." *Radical Philosophy*, no. 60 (1992).

Rémond, R. *Les Droites en France.* Paris: Aubier-Montaigne, 1982.

Renton, D. *Fascism: Theory and Practice.* London: Pluto Press, 1999.

Rioux, J.-P. *Nationalisme et conservatisme: La Ligue de la Patrie Française.* Paris: Editions Beauchesne, 1977.

Robbins, B. "Actually Existing Cosmopolitanism." In *Cosmopolitics: Thinking and Feeling beyond the Nation*, ed. P. Cheah and B. Robbins. London: University of Minnesota Press, 1998.

Roberts, D. "How Not to Think about Fascism and Ideology, Intellectual Antecedents and Historical Meaning." *Journal of Contemporary History* 35 (2000).

Rodinson, M. "Le Marxisme et la nation." *L'Homme et la Société*, no. 38 (1968).

———. "Marxisme et racisme." *La Nef* 21 (1964).

Rosdolsky, R. *Engels and the "Nonhistoric" Peoples: The National Question in the Revolution of 1848.* Glasgow: Critique Books, 1986.

Rossi-Landi, G. *Le Chassé-Croisé: La Droite et la gauche en France de 1789 à nos jours.* Paris: Lattès, 1978.

Rothney, J. *Bonapartism after Sedan.* Ithaca, N.Y.: Cornell University Press, 1969.

Rowley, A. "L'Economie et le marché." In *Histoire des droites en France*, ed. J.-F. Sirinelli. Vol. 3, *Sensibilités.* Paris: Gallimard, 1992.

Royal Institute of International Affairs. *Nationalism.* London: Cass, 1963.

Rustin, M. "Place and Time in Socialist Theory." *Radical Philosophy*, no. 47 (1987).

Rutkoff, P. "The Ligue des Patriotes: The Nature of the Radical Right and the Dreyfus Affair." *French Historical Studies* 8 (1974).

———. "Rémond, Nationalism and the Right." *Proceedings of the Fifth Annual Meeting of the Western Society for French History* 5 (1978).

———. *Revanche and Revision: The Ligue des Patriotes and the Origins of the Radical Right in France, 1882–1900.* London: Ohio State University Press, 1981.

Sagnes, J. *Le Mouvement ouvrier en Languedoc: Syndicalistes et socialistes de l'Hérault de la fondation des Bourses du Travail à la naissance du Parti Communiste.* Toulouse: Privat, 1980.

Sahlins, P. *Boundaries: The Making of France and Spain in the Pyrenees.* Berkeley: University of California Press, 1989.

Schapiro, J. "Pierre Joseph Proudhon: Harbinger of Fascism." *American Historical Review* 50 (1945).

Schnapper, D. "Le Juif Errant." In *Histoire des etrangers et de l'immigration en France*, ed. Y. Lequin. Paris: Larousse, 1992.

Schor, R. "Racisme et xénophobie dans le mouvement ouvrier français avant 1939." *Nouvelle Revue Socialiste*, January-February 1984.

Schwarzchild, S. "The Marquis de Morès: The Story of a Failure (1898–1896)." *Jewish Social Studies* 22 (1960).

Schwarzmantel, J. *The Age of Ideology: Political Ideologies from the American Revolution to Postmodern Times.* New York: Macmillan, 1998.

———. "Class and Nation: Problems of Socialist Nationalism." *Political Studies* 35 (1987).

———. "Nation versus Class: Nationalism and Socialism in Theory and Practice." In *The Social Origin of Nationalist Movements: The Contemporary West European Experience*, ed. J. Coakley. London: Sage, 1992.

———. *Socialism and the Idea of the Nation.* New York: Harvester, 1991.

Seager, P. *The Boulanger Affair: Political Crossroads of France, 1886–1889.* Ithaca, N.Y.: Cornell University Press, 1969.

Serman, W. "The Nationalists of Meurthe-et-Moselle, 1888–1912." In *Nationhood and Nationalism in France from Boulangism to the Great War, 1889–1918*, ed. R. Tombs. London: HarperCollins Academic, 1991.

Shelton, A. "Rosa Luxemburg and the National Question." *East European Quarterly* 21 (1987).

Silberner, E. "French Socialism and the Jewish Question, 1865–1914." *Historia Judaica* 16 (1954).

Silverman, M. *Deconstructing the Nation: Immigration, Racism, and Citizenship in Modern France.* London: Routledge, 1992.

Simler, B. "Gustave Delory et les débuts du mouvement socialiste à Lille et dans la région du Nord sous la Troisième République." *Les Pays-Bas Français*, 1982.

Singer-Kérel, J. "Foreign Workers in France, 1891–1936." *Ethnic and Racial Studies* 14 (1991).

Smith, A. *The Ethnic Origins of Nations.* Oxford: Blackwell, 1986.

———. "National Identity and Myths of Ethnic Descent." *Research in Social Movements, Conflict and Change* 7 (1984).

———. "Nationalism and the Historians." In *Mapping the Nation*, ed. G. Balakrishnan and B. Anderson. London: Verso, 1996.

———. *Nations and Nationalism in a Global Era.* Cambridge: Polity, 1995.

Smith, M. *Tariff Reform in France, 1860–1900: The Politics of Economic Interest.* Ithaca, N.Y.: Cornell University Press, 1980.

Sorlin, P. *"La Croix" et les juifs (1880–1899): Contribution à l'histoire de l'antisémitisme contemporain.* Paris: Grasset, 1967.

———. *La Société française, 1840–1914.* Paris: Arthaud, 1969.

———. "Words and Images of Nationhood." In *Nationhood and Nationalism in France from Boulangism to the Great War, 1889–1918*, ed. R. Tombs. London: HarperCollins Academic, 1991.

Soucy, R. "Barrès and Fascism." *French Historical Studies* 5 (1967).

———. *Fascism in France: The Case of Maurice Barrès.* Berkeley: University of California Press, 1972.

———. *French Fascism: The First Wave, 1924–1933.* New Haven, Conn.: Yale University Press, 1986.

———. *French Fascism: The Second Wave, 1933–1939.* New Haven, Conn.: Yale University Press, 1995.

———. "Functional Hating: French Fascist Demonology between the Wars." *Contemporary French Civilisation* 23 (1999).

Stargardt, N. "Beyond the Liberal Idea of the Nation." In *Imagining Nations*, ed. G. Cubitt. Manchester: Manchester University Press, 1998.

Sternhell, Z. "The 'Anti-materialist' Revision of Marxism as an Aspect of the Rise of Fascist Ideology." *Journal of Contemporary History* 22 (1987).

———. "Barrès et la gauche: Du Boulangisme à *La Cocarde* (1889–1895)." *Mouvement Social*, no. 75 (1971).

———. *La Droite révolutionnaire, 1885–1914: Les Origines françaises du fascisme.* Paris: Seuil, 1978.

———. *Maurice Barrès et le nationalisme français.* Paris: Fayard, 1972.

———. *Naissance de l'idéologie fasciste.* Paris: Fayard, 1989. Translated as *The Birth of Fascist Ideology: From Cultural Rebellion to Political Revolution.* Princeton, N.J.: Princeton University Press, 1994.

———. "National Socialism and Anti-Semitism: The Case of Maurice Barrès." *Journal of Contemporary History* 8 (1973).

———. *Neither Right nor Left: Fascist Ideology in France.* Berkeley: University of California Press, 1986.

———. "Les Origines intellectuelles du racisme en France." *Histoire*, no. 17 (1979).

———. "Paul Déroulède and the Origins of Modern French Nationalism." *Journal of Contemporary History* 6 (1971).

———. "The Political Culture of Nationalism." In *Nationhood and Nationalism in France from Boulangism to the Great War, 1889–1918*, ed. R. Tombs. London: HarperCollins Academic, 1991.

———. "The Roots of Popular Anti-Semitism in the Third Republic." In *The Jews of Modern France*, ed. F. Malino and B. Wasserstein. Hanover, N.H.: University Press of New England, 1985.

———. "Strands of French Fascism." In *Who Were the Fascists? Social Roots of European Fascism*, ed. S. Larsen, B. Hagtvet, and J. Myklebust. Bergen: Universitetsforlaget, 1980.

Stone, J. *The Search for Social Peace: Reform Legislation in France, 1890–1914.* Albany: State University of New York Press, 1985.

Strikwerda, C. "Regionalism and Internationalism: The Working-Class Movement in the Nord and the Belgian Connection, 1871–1914." *Proceedings of the Western Society for French History* 12 (1984).

Stuart, R. "'Calm, with a Grave and Serious Temperament, Rather Male': French Marxism, Gender and Feminism, 1882–1905." *International Review of Social History* 41 (1996).

———. "A 'De Profundis' for Christian Socialism: French Marxists and the Critique of Political Catholicism, 1882–1905." *French Historical Studies* 22 (1999).

———. "Gendered Labor in the Ideological Discourse of French Marxism." *Gender and History* 9 (1997).

———. "Ideology, Theory and Mentality: Some Issues in the Historical Study of Ideology." *Labour History*, no. 50 (1986).

———. "'Jesus the *Sans-Culotte*': Marxism and Religion during the French *Fin de Siècle.*" *Historical Journal* 42 (1999).

———. "Marxism and Anticlericalism: The Parti Ouvrier Français and the War Against Religion, 1882–1905." *The Journal of Religious History* 22 (1998).

———. *Marxism at Work: Ideology, Class, and French Socialism during the Third Republic.* Cambridge: Cambridge University Press, 1992.

———. "Whores and Angels: Women and the Family in the Discourse of French Marxism, 1882–1905." *European History Quarterly* 27 (1997).

Suny, R. *The Revenge of the Past: Nationalism, Revolution and the Collapse of the Soviet Union.* Stanford, Calif.: Stanford University Press, 1993.

Sutton, M. *Nationalism, Positivism and Catholicism: The Politics of Charles Maurras and French Catholics, 1890–1914.* Cambridge: Cambridge University Press, 1982.

Szporluk, R. *Communism and Nationalism: Karl Marx versus Friedrich List.* New York: Oxford University Press, 1988.

Taguieff, P.-A. *Le Couleur et le sang.* Paris: Editions Mille et Une Nuits, 1998.

———. "Le Néo-racisme différentialiste." *Langage et Société,* no. 34 (1985).

———. "The New Cultural Racism in France." *Telos,* no. 83 (1990).

Talmon, J. *The Myth of the Nation and the Vision of Revolution: The Origins of Ideological Polarisation in the Twentieth Century.* London: Secker and Warburg, 1981.

———. "The National Brotherhood and the International Confraternity: Nationalism and Socialism." In *The Unique and the Universal: Some Historical Reflections.* London: Secker and Warburg, 1965.

Talmy, R. *Le Syndicalisme chrétien en France, 1871–1930: Difficultés et controverses.* Paris: Bloud et Gay, 1965.

Taminiaux, P. "Sacred Text, Sacred Nation." In *Text and Nation: Cross-Disciplinary Essays on Cultural and National Identities,* ed. P. Pfeiffer and L. Garcia-Moreno. Columbia, S.C.: Camden House, 1996.

Tannenbaum, E. "The Myth of Counterrevolution in France, 1870–1914." In *Ideas in History,* ed. R. Herr and H. Parker. Durham, N.C.: Duke University Press, 1965.

Tartakowski, D. "Le Mouvement ouvrier français et l'état de la Commune à la Première Guerre Mondiale." *Cahiers d'Histoire de l'Institut des Recherches Marxistes,* no. 11 (1972).

Taylor, C. "Nationalism and Modernity." In *Theorizing Nationalism,* ed. R. Beiner. Albany: State University Press of New York: 1999.

———. "The Politics of Recognition." In *Multiculturalism: Examining the Politics of Recognition,* ed. A. Gutman. Princeton: Princeton University Press, 1994.

Taylor, M. "Patriotism, History and the Left in Twentieth-Century Britain." *The Historical Journal* 33 (1990).

Thiesse, A.-M. "L'Invention du régionalisme à la Belle Epoque." *Le Mouvement Social,* no. 160 (1992).

Thuillier, G. "Un Anarchiste positiviste: Georges Vacher de Lapouge." In *L'Idée de race dans la pensée politique française contemporaine,* ed. P. Guiral and E. Témime. Paris: Editions du Centre National de la Recherche Scientifique, 1977.

Tijn, T. van. "Nationalism and the Socialist Workers' Movement, 1830–1940." In *Internationalism in the Labour Movement, 1830–1940*, ed. F. van Holthoon and M. van der Linden. Leiden: Brill, 1988.

Todorov, T. *On Human Diversity: Nationalism, Racism, and Exoticism in French Thought.* Cambridge, Mass.: Harvard University Press, 1993.

Tombs, R. *France, 1814–1914.* London: Longman, 1996.

Traverso, E. "Auschwitz, Marx, and the Twentieth Century." In *Understanding the Nazi Genocide: Marxism after Auschwitz.* London: Pluto Press, 1999.

———. *The Marxists and the Jewish Question: The History of a Debate (1843–1943).* Atlantic Highlands, N.J.: Humanities, 1994.

Verdery, K. "Whither 'Nation' and 'Nationalism.'" In *Mapping the Nation*, ed. G. Balakrishnan and B. Anderson. London: Verso, 1996.

Verdès-Leroux, J. *Scandale financier et antisémitisme catholique: Le Krach de l'Union Générale.* Paris: Editions du Centurion, 1969.

Vigier, P. "Régions et régionalisme en France au XIXe siècle." In *Régions et régionalisme en France du XVIIIe siècle à nos jours*, ed. C. Gras and G. Livet. Paris: Presses Universitaires de France, 1977.

Vilar, P. "On Nations and Nationalism." *Marxist Perspectives* 1 (1979).

Vincent, K. *Between Marxism and Anarchism: Benoît Malon and French Reformist Socialism.* Berkeley: University of California Press, 1992.

———. "National Consciousness, Nationalism and Exclusion: Reflections on the French Case." *Historical Reflections* 19 (1993).

———. "Nationalism and Patriotism in Nineteenth Century French Socialist Thought." *History of European Ideas* 15 (1992).

Viroli, M. *For Love of Country: An Essay on Patriotism and Nationalism.* Cambridge, Mass.: Clarendon, 1995.

Vogler, C. *The Nation State: The Neglected Dimension of Class.* Aldershot: Gower, 1985.

Wallerstein, I. "Class Formation in the Capitalist World-System." In *The Capitalist World-Economy.* Cambridge: Cambridge University Press, 1979.

———. "The Construction of Peoplehood: Racism, Nationalism, Ethnicity." *Sociological Forum* 2 (1987).

———. "The Ideological Tensions of Capitalism: Universalism versus Racism and Sexism." In *Race, Nation, Class: Ambiguous Identities*, by E. Balibar and I. Wallerstein. London: Verso, 1991.

———. Postscript to *Race, Nation, Class: Ambiguous Identities*, by E. Balibar and I. Wallerstein. London: Verso, 1991.

Walz, K. *Man, the State and War.* New York: Columbia University Press, 1959.

Walzer, M. "The New Tribalism: Notes on a Difficult Problem." In *Theorizing Nationalism*, ed. R. Beiner. Albany: State University of New York Press, 1999.

———. *Obligations: Essays on Disobedience, War and Citizenship.* Cambridge, Mass.: Harvard University Press, 1970.

———. *Spheres of Justice: A Defense of Pluralism and Equality.* New York: Robertson, 1983.

Ward, P. *Red Flag and Union Jack: Englishness, Patriotism and the British Left, 1881–1924.* Woodbridge: Boydell Press, 1998.

Warshaw, D. *Paul Leroy-Beaulieu and Established Liberalism in France.* De Kalb: Northern Illinois University Press, 1991.

Watson, D. "The Nationalist Movement in Paris, 1900–1906." In *The Right in France, 1890–1919*, ed. D. Schapiro. London: Chatto and Windus, 1962.

Weber, E. *Action Française: Royalism and Reaction in Twentieth-Century France.* Stanford, Calif.: Stanford University Press, 1962.

———. "Gauls versus Franks: Conflict and Nationalism." In *Nationhood and Nationalism in France: From Boulangism to the Great War, 1889–1918*, ed. R. Tombs. London: HarperCollins Academic, 1991.

———. "Inheritance, Dilettantism, and the Politics of Maurice Barrès." In *My France: Politics, Culture, Myth.* London: Belknap Press, 1991.

———. "Nationalism, Socialism, and National-Socialism in France." *French Historical Studies* 2 (1962).

———. "The Nationalist Revival before 1914." In *My France: Politics, Culture, Myth.* London: Belknap Press, 1991.

———. *The Nationalist Revival in France, 1905–1914.* Berkeley: University of California Press, 1959.

———. *Peasants into Frenchmen: The Modernization of Rural France, 1870–1914.* Stanford, Calif.: Stanford University Press, 1976.

———. "Revolution, Counterrevolution, What Revolution?" In *Fascism: A Reader's Guide*, ed. W. Laqueur. London: Penguin, 1979.

———. *Varieties of Fascism: Doctrines of Revolution in the Twentieth Century.* New York: Van Nostrand, 1964.

Weill, C. "Le Débat sur les migrations ouvrières dans la IIe Internationale." *Pluriel-Débat*, no. 13 (1978).

———. *L'Internationale et l'autre: Les Relations inter-ethniques dans la IIe Internationale (Discussions et débats).* Paris: Arcantère, 1987.

———. Introduction to *La Question des nationalités et la social-démocratie*, by O. Bauer. Montreal: Guérin, 1987.

Weiss, J. *The Fascist Tradition: Radical Right-Wing Extremism in Modern Europe.* New York: Harper and Row, 1967.

Weitz, M. "Varieties of Class-Collaborationist Ideology in the French Labor Movement before World War I." Ph.D. thesis, City University of New York: 1977.

White, H. "The Context in the Text: Method and Ideology in Intellectual History." In *The Content of the Form: Narrative Discourse and Historical Representation.* Baltimore: Johns Hopkins University Press, 1987.

———. "The Value of Narrativity in the Representation of Reality." *Critical Inquiry* 7 (1980).

Wiebe, R. *Who We Are: A History of Popular Nationalism.* Princeton, N.J.: Princeton University Press, 2002.

Willard, C. "Engels et le mouvement socialiste en France (1891–1895) à travers la correspondance Engels-Lafargue." *Annali dell'Istituto Giangiacomo Feltrinelli* 3 (1960).

———. *Jules Guesde: L'Apôtre et la loi.* Paris: Editions Ouvrières, 1991.

———. *Le Mouvement socialiste en France (1893–1905): Les Guesdistes.* Paris: Editions Sociales, 1965.

Williams, R. "The Culture of Nations." In *Towards 2000.* London: Penguin, 1983.

Williams, R. *Henri Rochefort: Prince of the Gutter Press.* New York: Scribner, 1966.

Wilson, N. *Bernard-Lazare: Anti-Semitism and the Problem of Jewish Identity in Late Nineteenth-Century France.* Cambridge: Cambridge University Press, 1978.

Wilson, S. "L'Action Française et le mouvement nationaliste français entre les années 1890 et 1900." *Etudes Maurassiennes* 4 (1980).

———. "The Anti-Semitic Riots of 1898 in France." *The Historical Journal* 16 (1973).

———. *Ideology and Experience: Anti-Semitism in France at the Time of the Dreyfus Affair.* London: Associated University Presses, 1982.

———. "The Ligue antisémitique française." *Wiener Library Bulletin* 25 (1972).

———. "Le Monument Henry: La Structure de l'antisémitisme en France, 1898–1899." *Annales: Economies, Sociétés, Civilisations* 32 (1977).

Winock, M. "Edouard Drumont et Cie." In *Edouard Drumont et Cie: Antisémitisme et fascisme en France.* Paris: Seuil, 1982.

———. "Edouard Drumont et l'antisémitisme en France avant l'Affaire Dreyfus." *Esprit* 39 (1971).

———. "Fascisme à la française ou fascisme introuvable." *Le Débat*, no. 25 (1983).

———. "La Gauche et les Juifs." *L'Histoire*, no. 31 (1981).

———. "Jeanne d'Arc." In *Les Lieux de mémoire*, ed. P. Nora. Vol. 3, *Les France.* Book 3, *De l'archive à l'emblème.* Paris: Gallimard, 1992.

———. *Nationalisme, antisémitisme et fascisme en France.* Paris: Seuil, 1990.

———. "Le Nationalisme français." *Histoire*, no. 73 (1984).

———. "Socialism and Boulangism, 1887–89." In *The Development of the Radical Right in France: From Boulanger to Le Pen*, ed. E. Arnold. London: Macmillan, 2000.

———. "Socialisme et patriotisme en France (1891–1894)." *Revue d'Histoire Moderne et Contemporaine* 20 (1973).

Wistrich, R. "French Socialism and the Dreyfus Affair." *Wiener Library Bulletin*, no. 28 (1975).

———. "Leon Trotsky's Theory of Fascism." *Journal of Contemporary History* 11 (1976).

Wohl, R. "French Fascism, Both Right and Left: Reflections on the Sternhell Controversy." *Journal of Modern History* 63 (1991).

Wolfe, A. "Waiting for Righty: A Critique of the 'Fascism Hypothesis.'" *Review of Radical Political Economics* 5 (1973).

Wood, E. "The Politics of Theory and the Concept of Class." *Studies in Political Economy* 9 (1982).

Wright, A. "Socialism and Nationalism." In *The Nation State*, ed. L. Tivey. Oxford: Robertson, 1981.

Yaari, A. *Le Défi national: Les Théories marxistes sur la question national à l'épreuve de l'histoire.* Paris: Editions Anthropos, 1978.

Yeo, S. "Socialism, the State, and Some Oppositional Englishness." In *Englishness: Politics and Culture, 1880–1920*, ed. R. Colls and P. Dodd. London: Croom Helm, 1986.

Young, I. "Unruly Categories: A Critique of Nancy Fraser's Dual Systems Theory." *New Left Review*, no. 222 (1997).

Zeldin, T. *France, 1848–1945: Intellect and Pride.* Oxford: Oxford University Press, 1977.

Ziolkowski, J. "Le Nationalisme en France, 1890–1914." *Cahiers d'Histoire et de Politique International*, no. 7 (1987).

Index